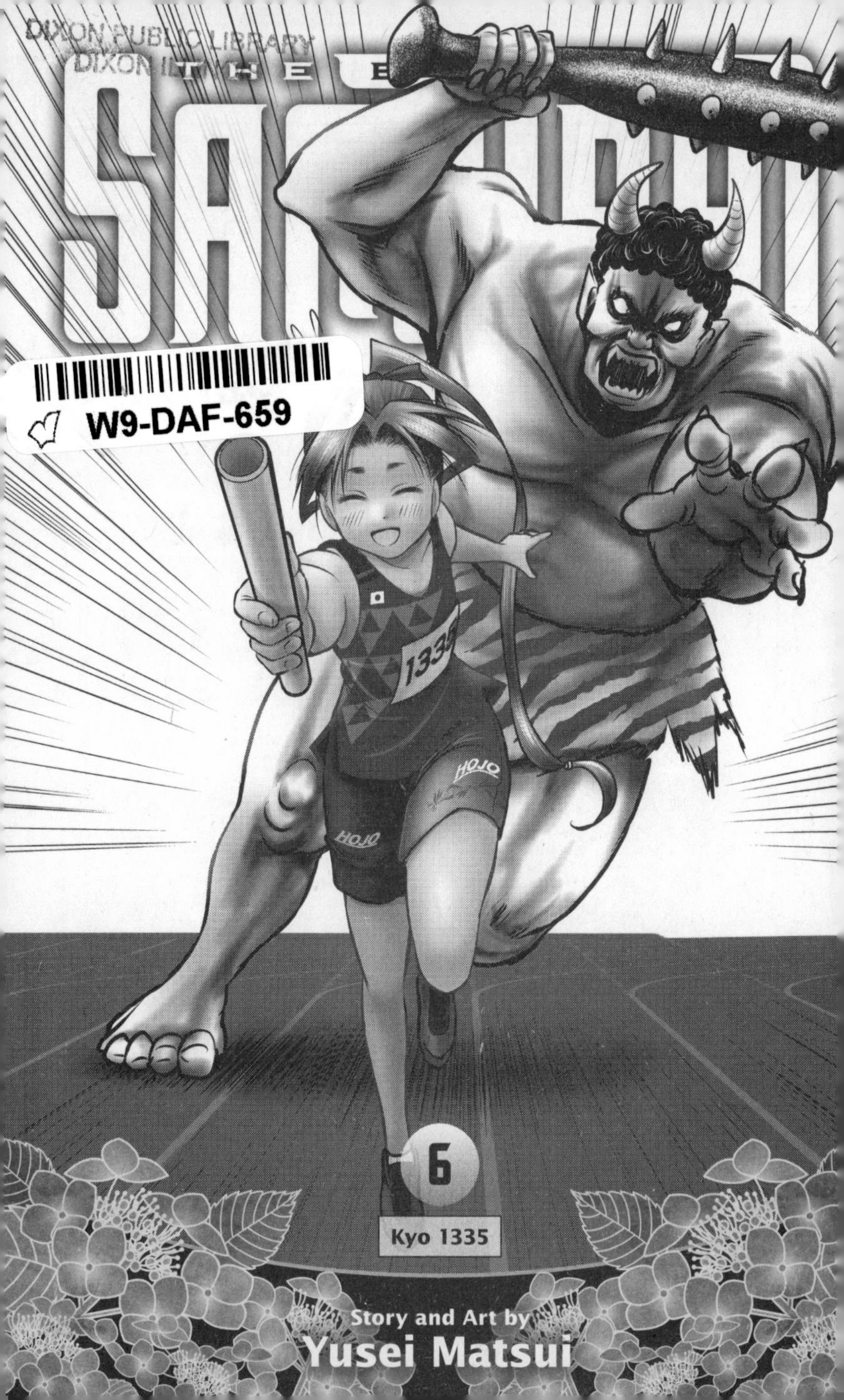
DIXON PUBLIC LIBRARY
DIXON IL
W9-DAF-659
6
Kyo 1335
Story and Art by
Yusei Matsui

CHARACTERS

SUWA FORCES

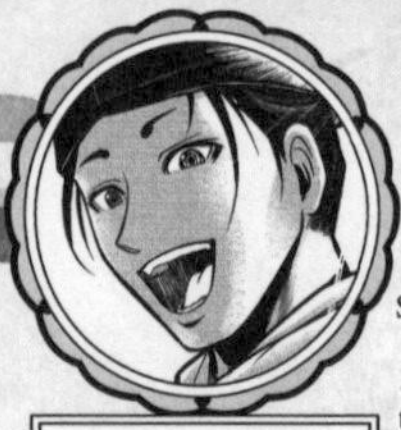

SUWA YORISHIGE

Head of Suwa Grand Shrine in Shinano Province. His divine power allows him to see the future, but it's not precise.

SUWA SECT

THE THREE GREAT GENERALS: YORISHIGE'S DIRECT RETAINERS

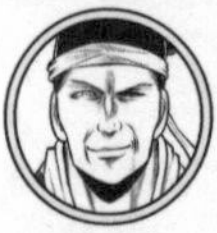

UNNO YUKIYASU

General of the Center

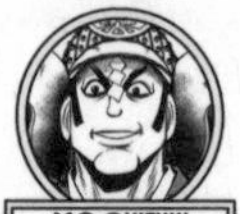

MOCHIZUKI SHIGENOBU

General of the Left

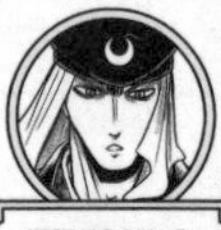

NEZU YORINAO

General of the Right

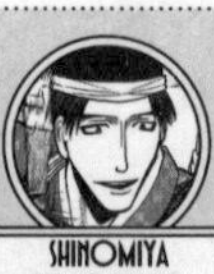

SHINOMIYA SAEMONTARO

Hoshina's comrade-in-arms.

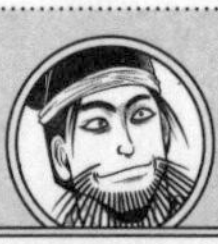

HOSHINA YASABURO

A minor lord in northern Shinano.

THE ELUSIVE WARRIORS

A group of friends with Tokiyuki as lord

HOJO TOKIYUKI

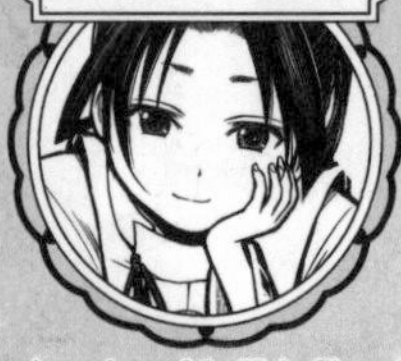

A survivor of the Hojo Clan who excels at fleeing. He is growing up in hiding at Suwa Grand Shrine.

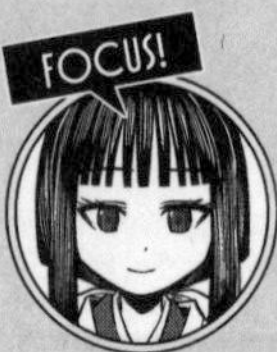
FOCUS!

SHIZUKU

A girl who uses divine power to commune with the mysteries of the universe. She admires Tokiyuki and calls him Nii-sama.

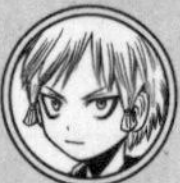

KOJIRO

A boy with outstanding swordsmanship.

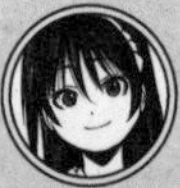

AYAKO

A girl with incredible physical strength.

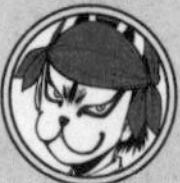

KAZAMA GENBA

A boy skilled at subterfuge.

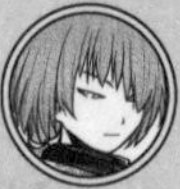

FUBUKI

A strategist who wields two blades.

THE STORY THUS FAR

Hojo Tokiyuki was heir to the Kamakura shogunate, but when Ashikaga Takauji suddenly rebelled, he lost everything, including his home and family. Suwa Yorishige is sheltering him in Shinano. When Suwa allies in northern Shinano rebel against the Ashikaga governor, Tokiyuki serves as a battlefield messenger in a preliminary skirmish. Suwa forces suffer casualties, but Tokiyuki's contribution to the battle raises morale and further unifies the Suwa sect!

IMPERIAL COURT (KENMU RESTORATION)

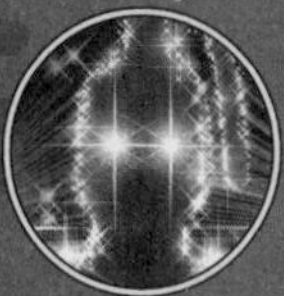

EMPEROR GO-DAIGO

He plotted with Ashikaga Takauji to overthrow the Kamakura shogunate and now holds the reins of government.

ASHIKAGA TAKAUJI

He overthrew the Kamakura shogunate and the Hojo clan. He possesses superhuman combat skills and charisma.

KONO MORONAO

An Ashikaga steward.

ASHIKAGA

They serve the emperor while secretly aiming to claim sole rulership.

SHINANO

KIYOHARA SHINANO-NO-KAMI

Kokushi of Shinano appointed by the emperor. He governs Shinano with a harsh hand.

SHINANO WARRIORS

OGASAWARA SADAMUNE

Shugo (governor) of Shinano. He's in league with Takauji and is obsessed with finding Hojo clan survivors.

ICHIKAWA SUKEFUSA

Sadamune's aide.

GUIDE TO STATS

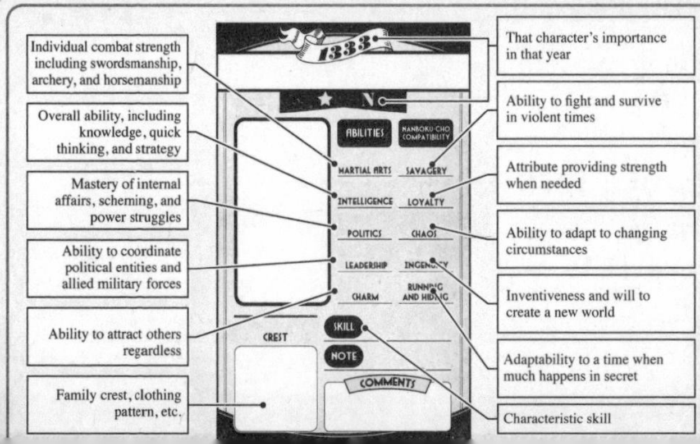

Individual combat strength including swordsmanship, archery, and horsemanship

Overall ability, including knowledge, quick thinking, and strategy

Mastery of internal affairs, scheming, and power struggles

Ability to coordinate political entities and allied military forces

Ability to attract others regardless

Family crest, clothing pattern, etc.

That character's importance in that year

Ability to fight and survive in violent times

Attribute providing strength when needed

Ability to adapt to changing circumstances

Inventiveness and will to create a new world

Adaptability to a time when much happens in secret

Characteristic skill

ABILITIES	NANBOKU-CHO COMPATIBILITY
MARTIAL ARTS	SAVAGERY
INTELLIGENCE	LOYALTY
POLITICS	CHAOS
LEADERSHIP	INGENUITY
CHARM	RUNNING AND HIDING

CREST

SKILL

NOTE

COMMENTS

THE ELUSIVE SAMURAI

6

CONTENTS

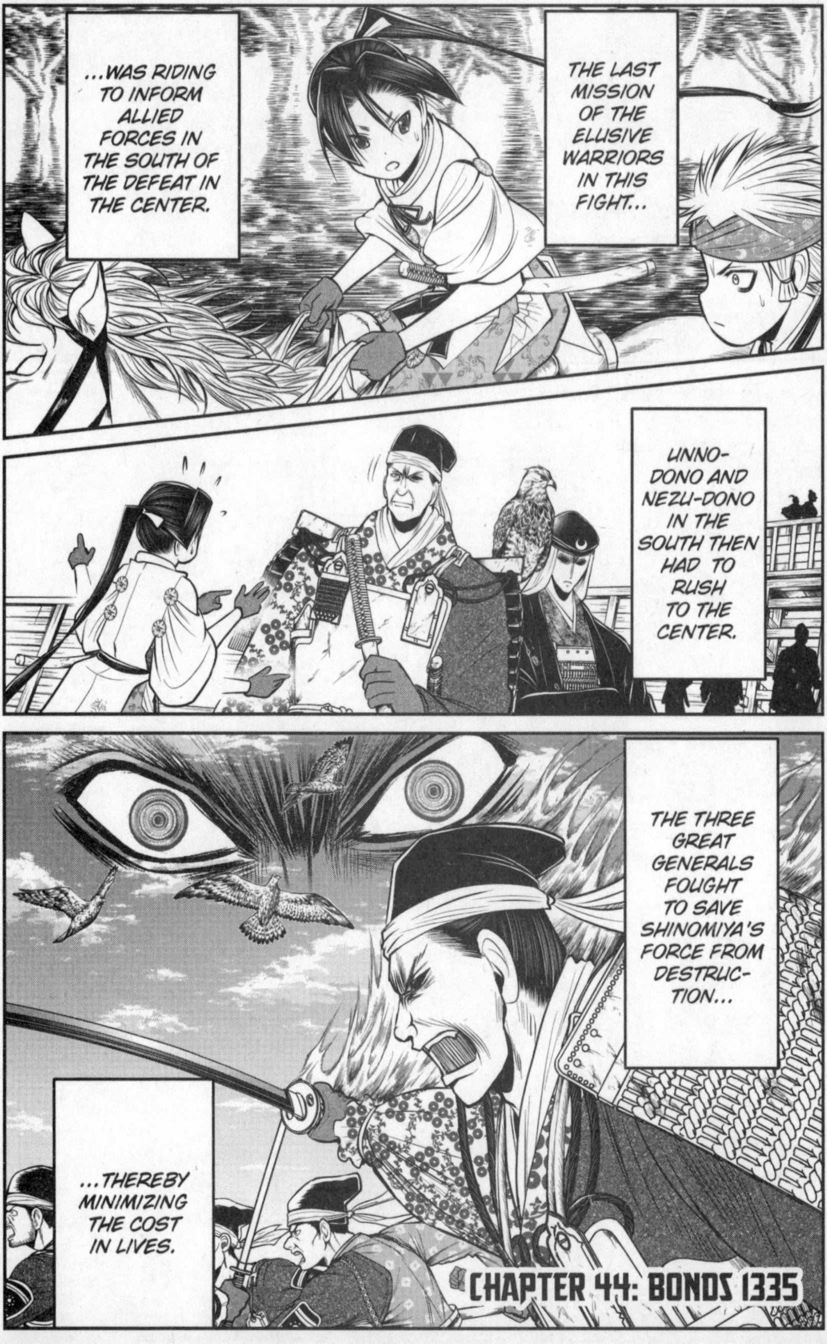
THE LAST MISSION OF THE ELUSIVE WARRIORS IN THIS FIGHT...
...WAS RIDING TO INFORM ALLIED FORCES IN THE SOUTH OF THE DEFEAT IN THE CENTER.
UNNO-DONO AND NEZU-DONO IN THE SOUTH THEN HAD TO RUSH TO THE CENTER.
THE THREE GREAT GENERALS FOUGHT TO SAVE SHINOMIYA'S FORCE FROM DESTRUCTION...
...THEREBY MINIMIZING THE COST IN LIVES.
CHAPTER 44: BONDS 1335

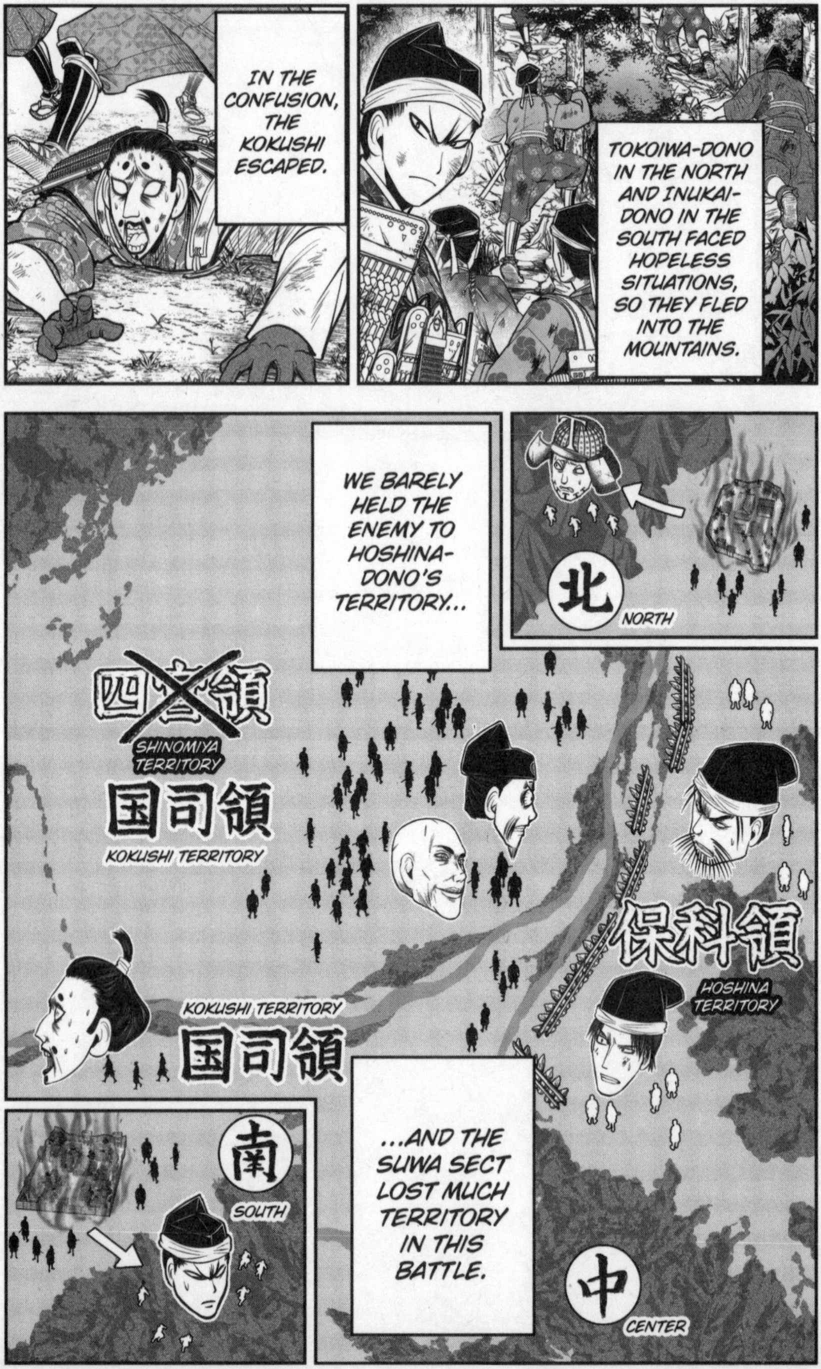
TOKOIWA-DONO IN THE NORTH AND INUKAI-DONO IN THE SOUTH FACED HOPELESS SITUATIONS, SO THEY FLED INTO THE MOUNTAINS.
IN THE CONFUSION, THE KOKUSHI ESCAPED.
北
NORTH
WE BARELY HELD THE ENEMY TO HOSHINA-DONO'S TERRITORY...
保科領
HOSHINA TERRITORY
四宮領
SHINOMIYA TERRITORY
国司領
KOKUSHI TERRITORY
KOKUSHI TERRITORY
国司領
...AND THE SUWA SECT LOST MUCH TERRITORY IN THIS BATTLE.
中
CENTER
南
SOUTH

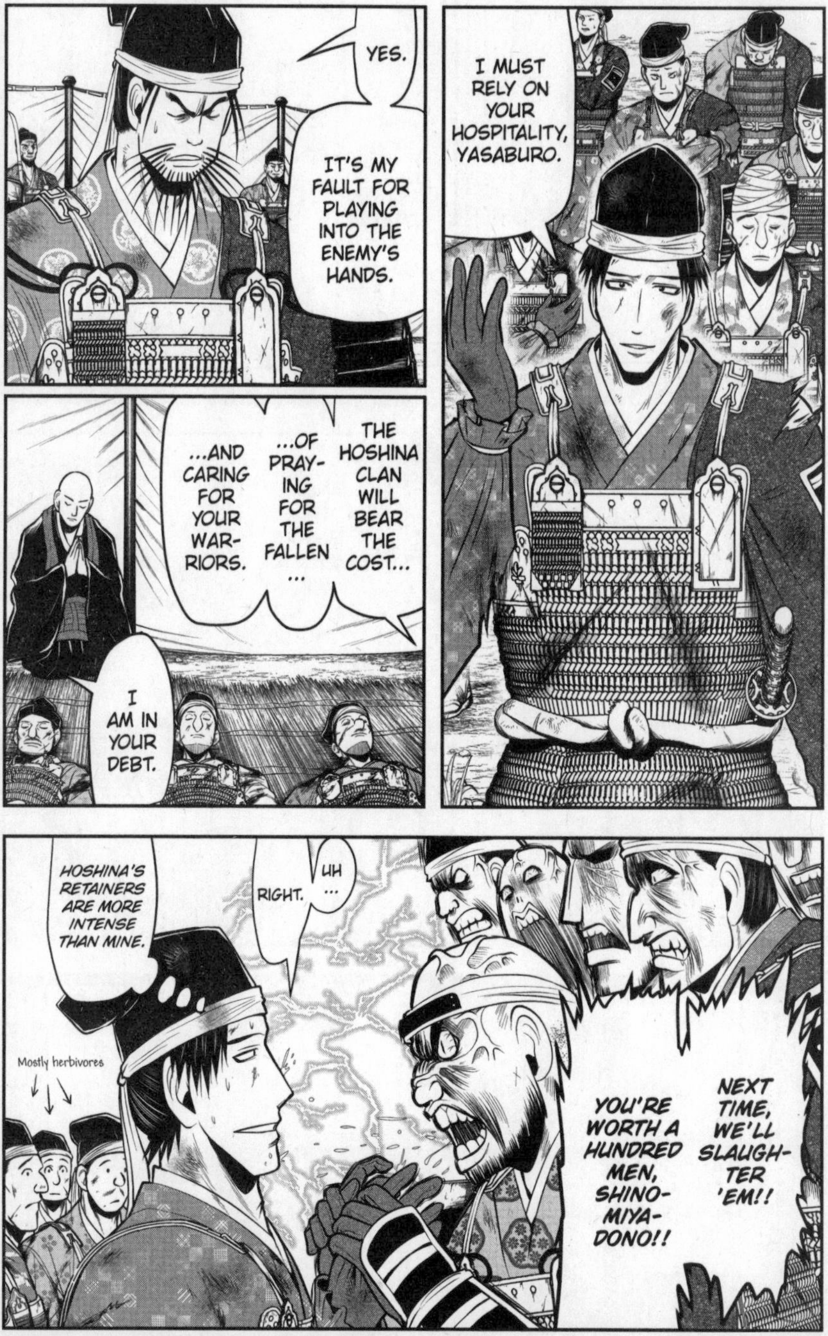
I MUST RELY ON YOUR HOSPITALITY, YASABURO.
YES.
IT'S MY FAULT FOR PLAYING INTO THE ENEMY'S HANDS.
THE HOSHINA CLAN WILL BEAR THE COST...
...OF PRAYING FOR THE FALLEN...
...AND CARING FOR YOUR WARRIORS.
I AM IN YOUR DEBT.
NEXT TIME, WE'LL SLAUGHTER 'EM!!
YOU'RE WORTH A HUNDRED MEN, SHINOMIYA-DONO!!
UH...
RIGHT.
HOSHINA'S RETAINERS ARE MORE INTENSE THAN MINE.
Mostly herbivores

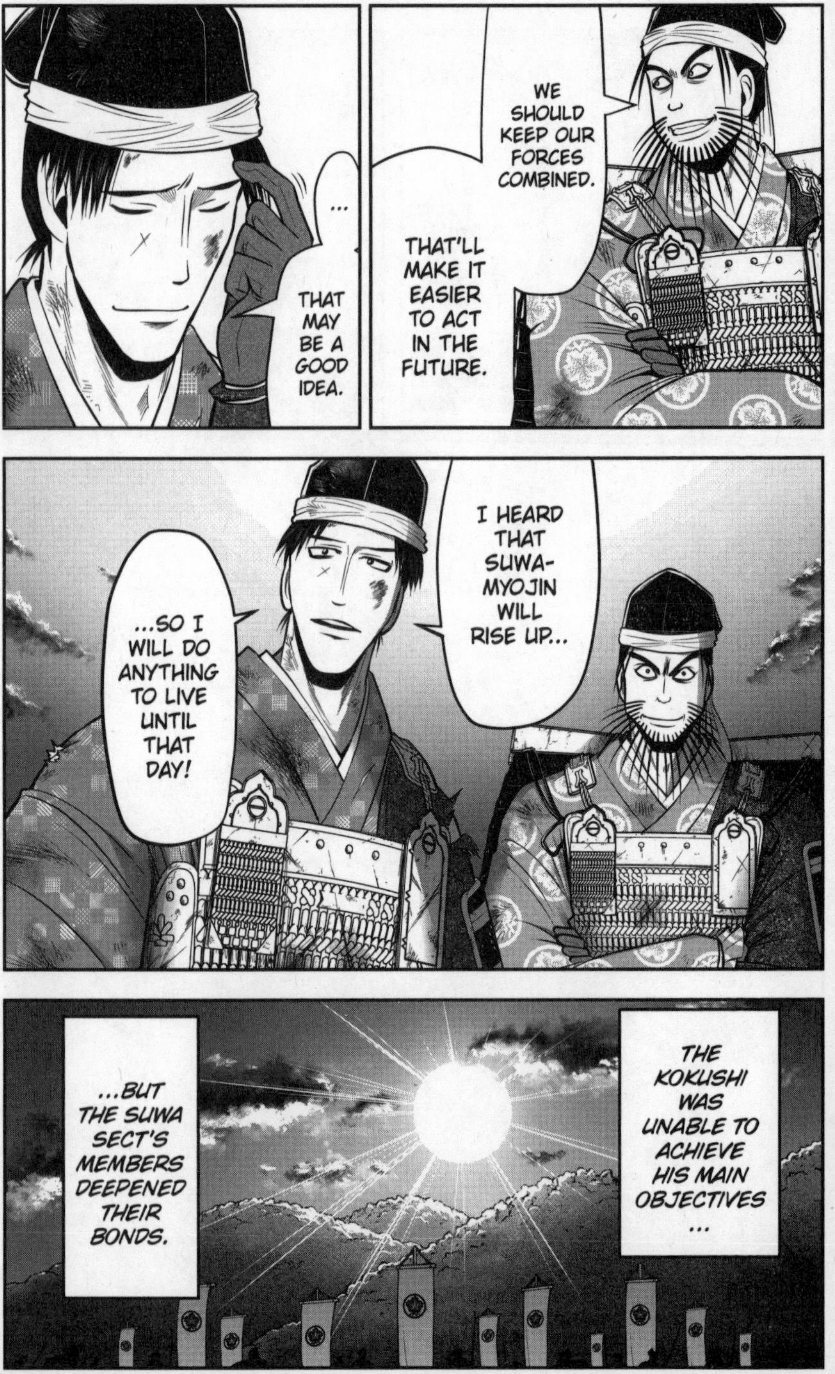
WE SHOULD KEEP OUR FORCES COMBINED.
THAT'LL MAKE IT EASIER TO ACT IN THE FUTURE.
...
THAT MAY BE A GOOD IDEA.
I HEARD THAT SUWA-MYOJIN WILL RISE UP...
...SO I WILL DO ANYTHING TO LIVE UNTIL THAT DAY!
THE KOKUSHI WAS UNABLE TO ACHIEVE HIS MAIN OBJECTIVES...
...BUT THE SUWA SECT'S MEMBERS DEEPENED THEIR BONDS.

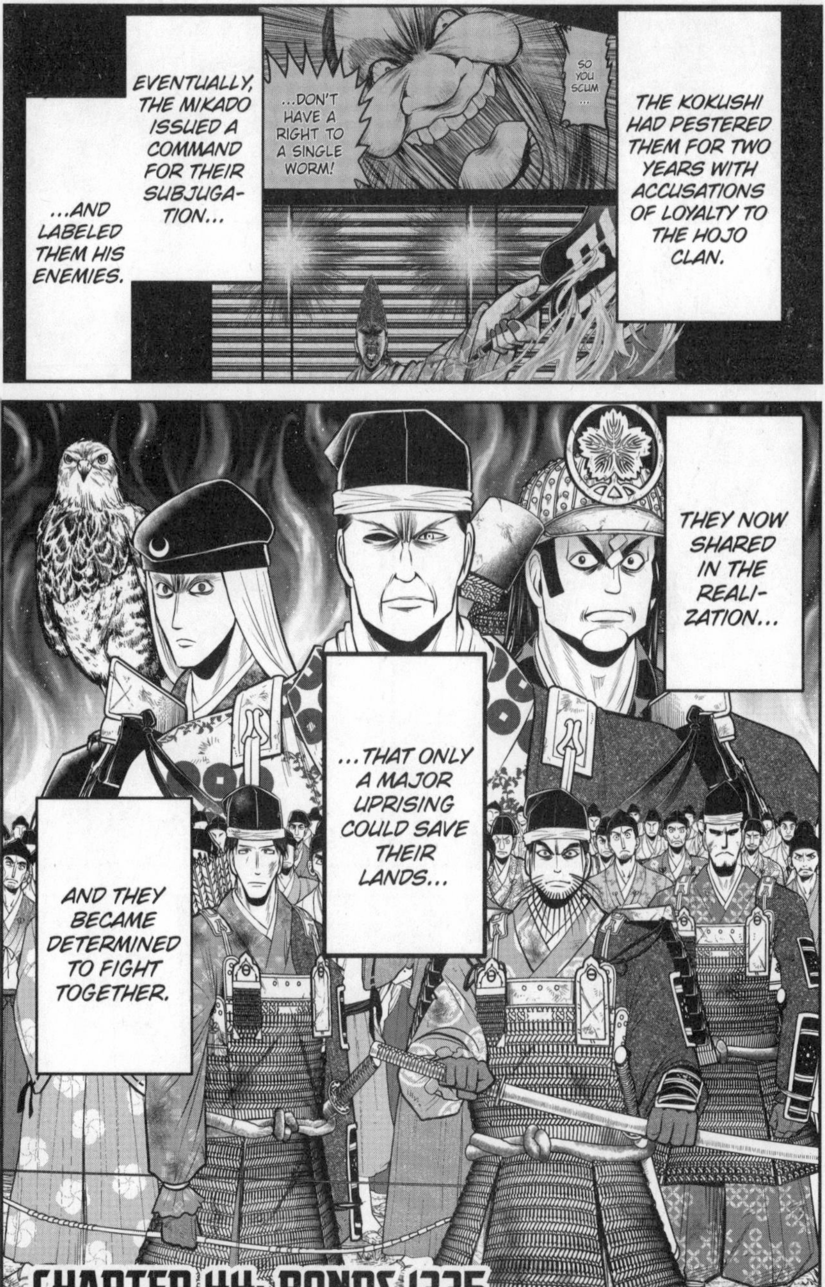
THE KOKUSHI HAD PESTERED THEM FOR TWO YEARS WITH ACCUSATIONS OF LOYALTY TO THE HOJO CLAN.
SO YOU SCUM...
...DON'T HAVE A RIGHT TO A SINGLE WORM!
EVENTUALLY, THE MIKADO ISSUED A COMMAND FOR THEIR SUBJUGATION...
...AND LABELED THEM HIS ENEMIES.
THEY NOW SHARED IN THE REALIZATION...
...THAT ONLY A MAJOR UPRISING COULD SAVE THEIR LANDS...
AND THEY BECAME DETERMINED TO FIGHT TOGETHER.
CHAPTER 44: BONDS 1335

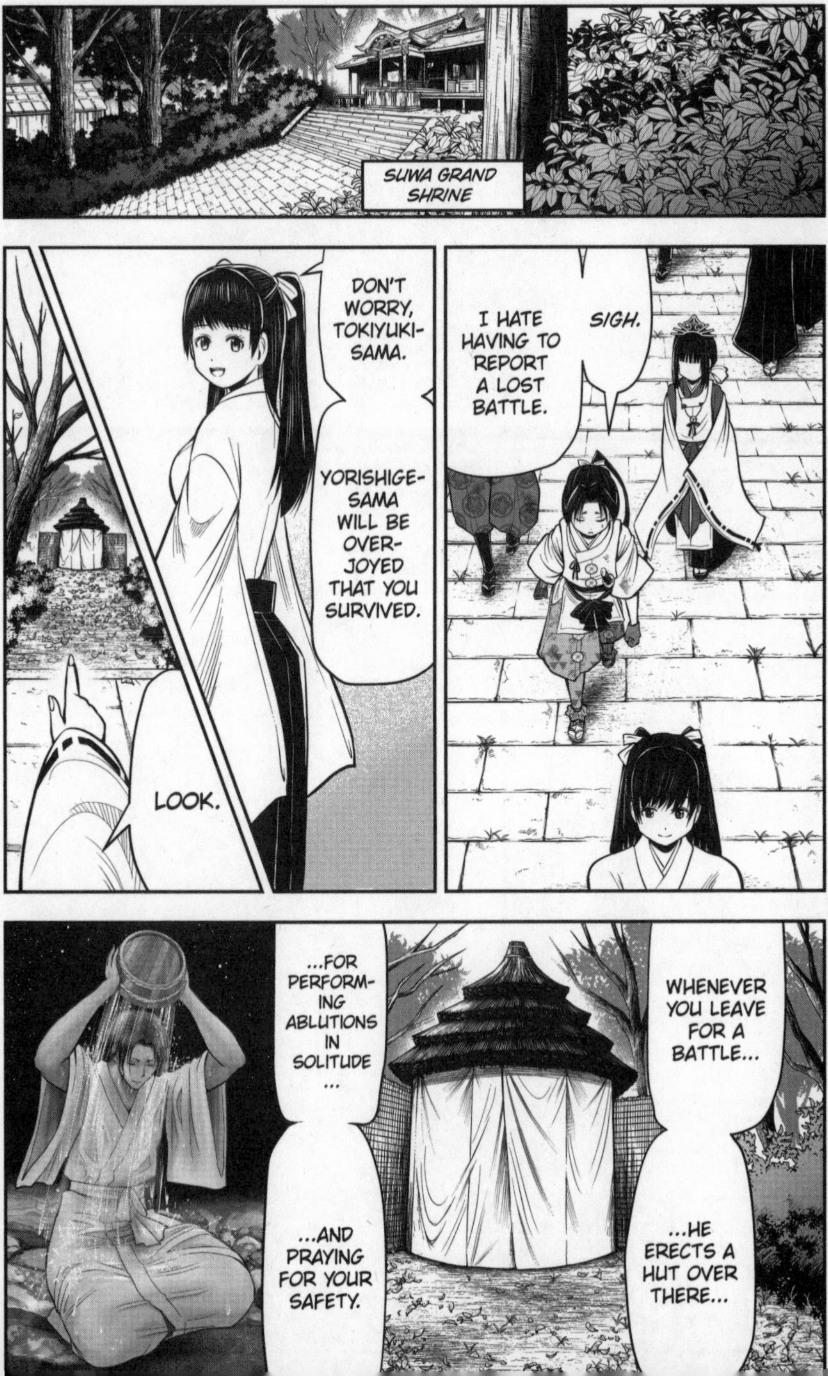
SUWA GRAND SHRINE
SIGH.
I HATE HAVING TO REPORT A LOST BATTLE.
DON'T WORRY, TOKIYUKI-SAMA.
YORISHIGE-SAMA WILL BE OVER-JOYED THAT YOU SURVIVED.
LOOK.
WHENEVER YOU LEAVE FOR A BATTLE...
...HE ERECTS A HUT OVER THERE...
...FOR PERFORM-ING ABLUTIONS IN SOLITUDE...
...AND PRAYING FOR YOUR SAFETY.

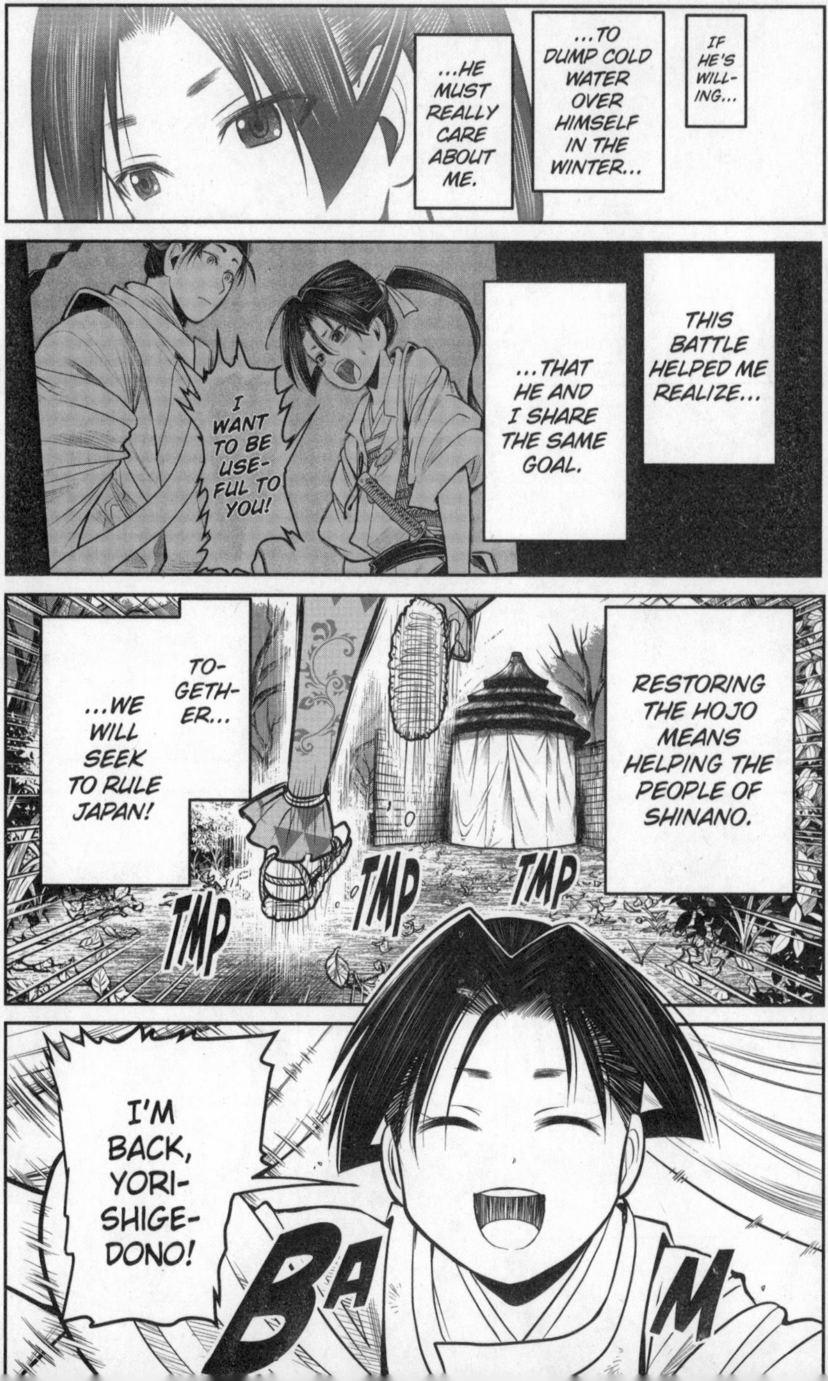
IF HE'S WILLING...
...TO DUMP COLD WATER OVER HIMSELF IN THE WINTER...
...HE MUST REALLY CARE ABOUT ME.
THIS BATTLE HELPED ME REALIZE...
...THAT HE AND I SHARE THE SAME GOAL.
I WANT TO BE USEFUL TO YOU!
RESTORING THE HOJO MEANS HELPING THE PEOPLE OF SHINANO.
TMP
TMP
TMP
TOGETHER...
...WE WILL SEEK TO RULE JAPAN!
I'M BACK, YORISHIGE-DONO!
BAM

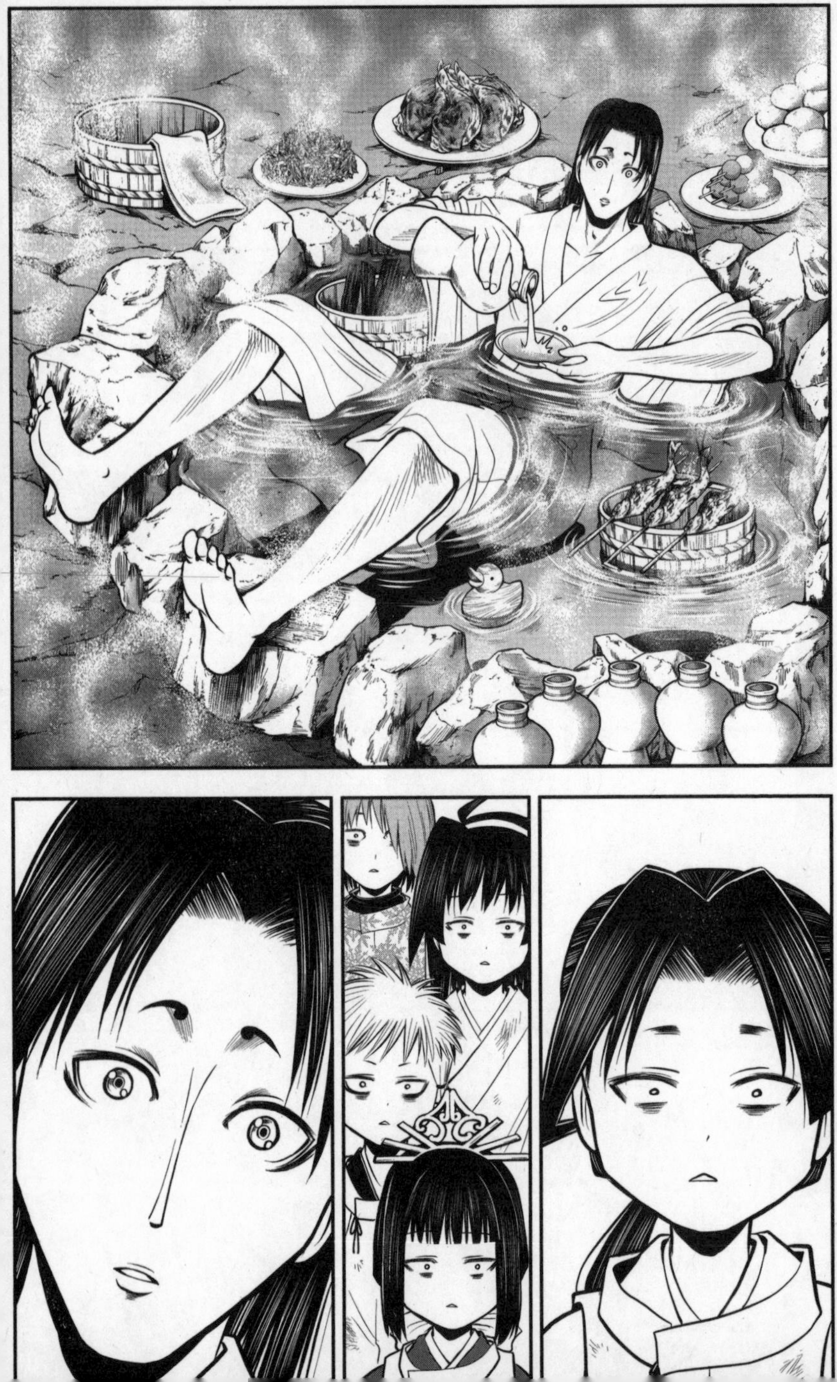

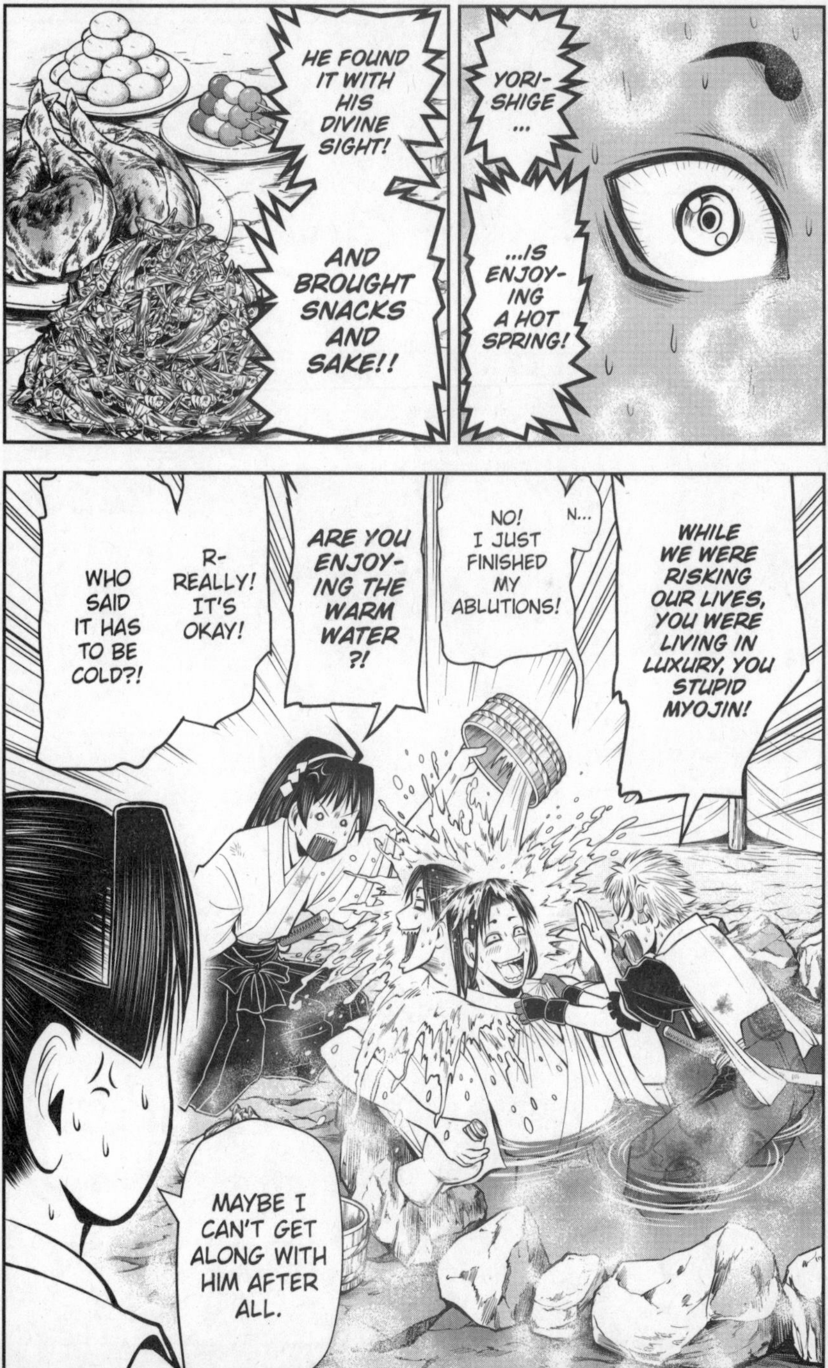
YORI-SHIGE...
...IS ENJOYING A HOT SPRING!
HE FOUND IT WITH HIS DIVINE SIGHT!
AND BROUGHT SNACKS AND SAKE!!
WHILE WE WERE RISKING OUR LIVES, YOU WERE LIVING IN LUXURY, YOU STUPID MYOJIN!
N...
NO! I JUST FINISHED MY ABLUTIONS!
ARE YOU ENJOYING THE WARM WATER?!
R-REALLY! IT'S OKAY!
WHO SAID IT HAS TO BE COLD?!
MAYBE I CAN'T GET ALONG WITH HIM AFTER ALL.

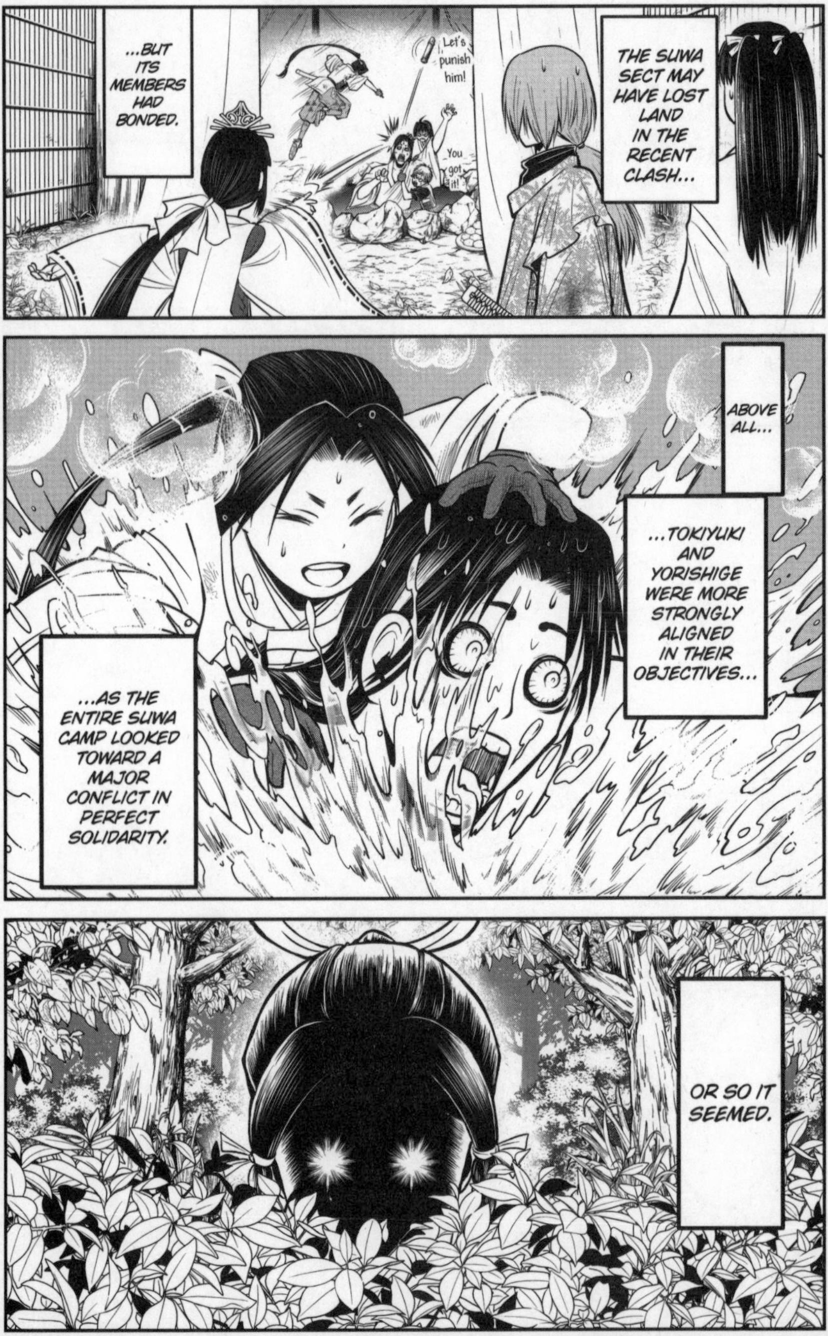
THE SUWA SECT MAY HAVE LOST LAND IN THE RECENT CLASH...
Let's punish him!
You got it!
...BUT ITS MEMBERS HAD BONDED.
ABOVE ALL...
...TOKIYUKI AND YORISHIGE WERE MORE STRONGLY ALIGNED IN THEIR OBJECTIVES...
...AS THE ENTIRE SUWA CAMP LOOKED TOWARD A MAJOR CONFLICT IN PERFECT SOLIDARITY.
OR SO IT SEEMED.

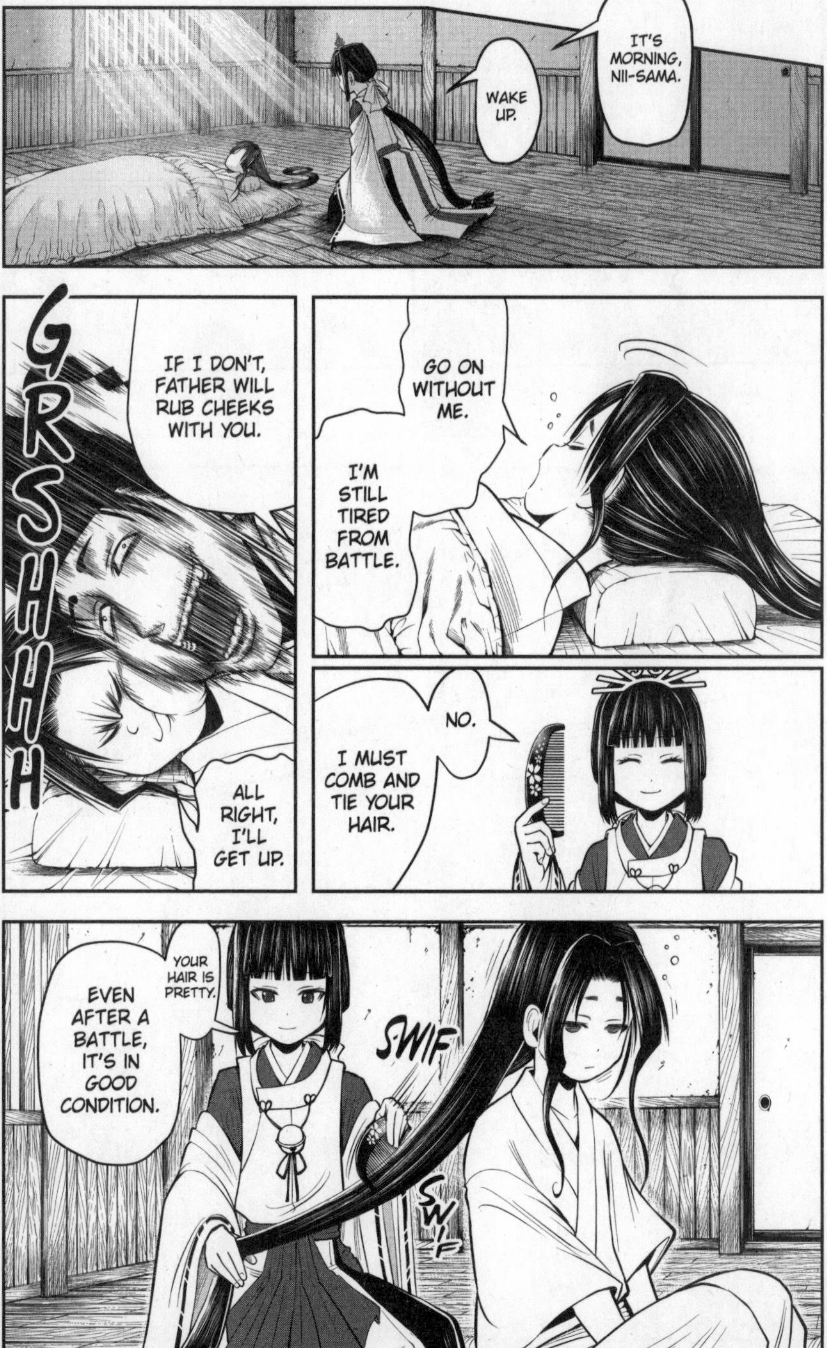
IT'S MORNING, NII-SAMA.
WAKE UP.
GO ON WITHOUT ME.
I'M STILL TIRED FROM BATTLE.
NO.
I MUST COMB AND TIE YOUR HAIR.
IF I DON'T, FATHER WILL RUB CHEEKS WITH YOU.
GRSHHHHH
ALL RIGHT, I'LL GET UP.
YOUR HAIR IS PRETTY.
EVEN AFTER A BATTLE, IT'S IN GOOD CONDITION.
S-WIF
SWIF

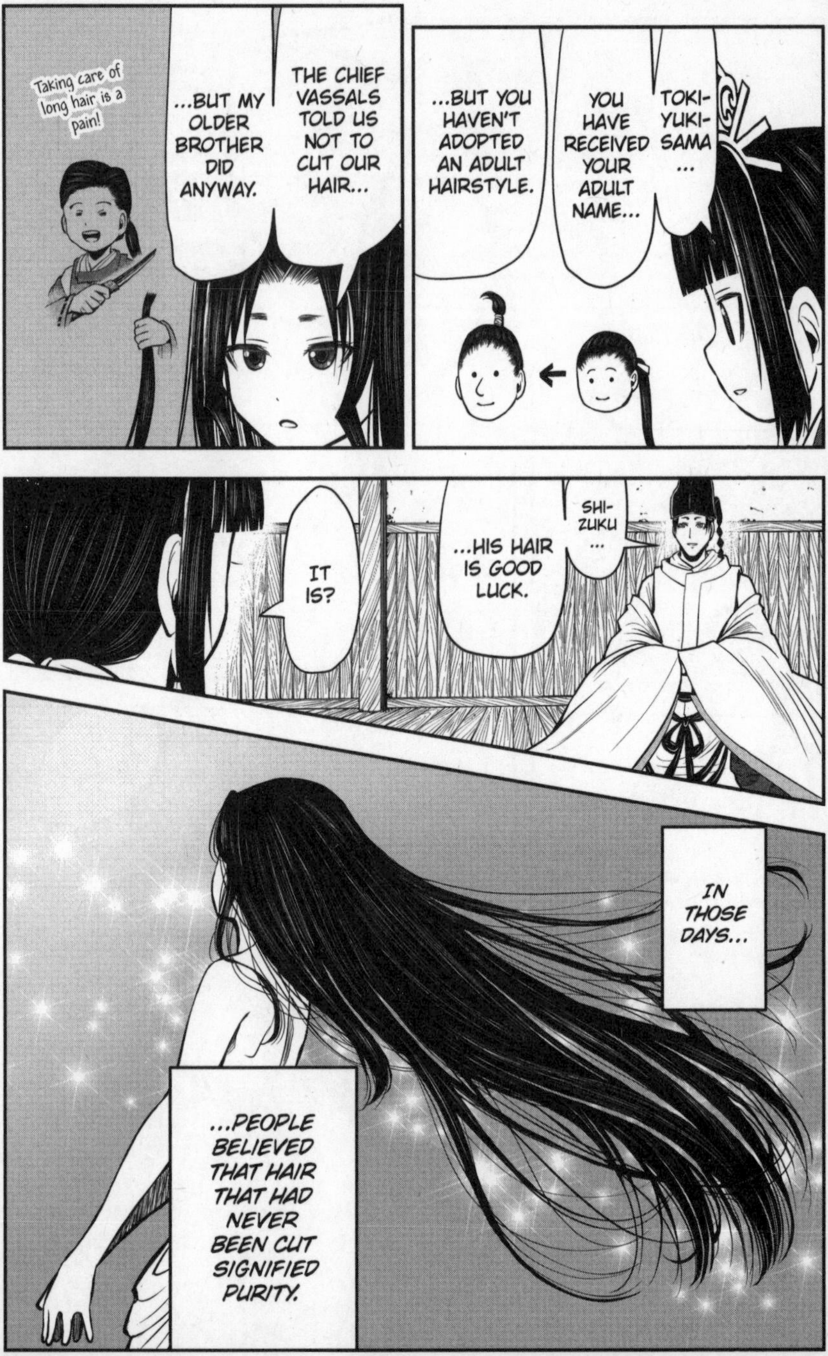

TOKI-YUKI-SAMA...
YOU HAVE RECEIVED YOUR ADULT NAME...
...BUT YOU HAVEN'T ADOPTED AN ADULT HAIRSTYLE.
THE CHIEF VASSALS TOLD US NOT TO CUT OUR HAIR...
...BUT MY OLDER BROTHER DID ANYWAY.
Taking care of long hair is a pain!
SHI-ZUKU...
...HIS HAIR IS GOOD LUCK.
IT IS?
IN THOSE DAYS...
...PEOPLE BELIEVED THAT HAIR THAT HAD NEVER BEEN CUT SIGNIFIED PURITY.

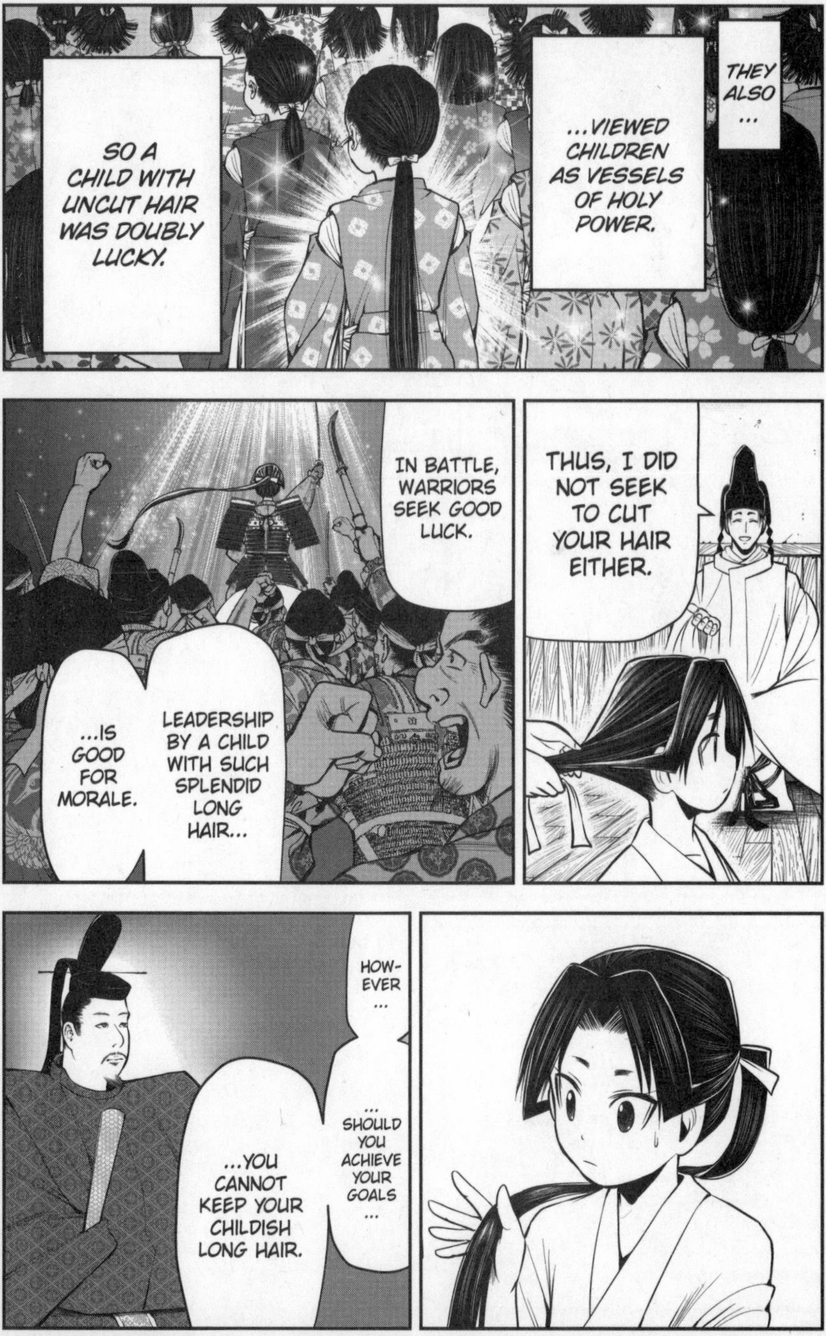
THEY ALSO ...
...VIEWED CHILDREN AS VESSELS OF HOLY POWER.
SO A CHILD WITH UNCUT HAIR WAS DOUBLY LUCKY.
THUS, I DID NOT SEEK TO CUT YOUR HAIR EITHER.
IN BATTLE, WARRIORS SEEK GOOD LUCK.
LEADERSHIP BY A CHILD WITH SUCH SPLENDID LONG HAIR...
...IS GOOD FOR MORALE.
HOW-EVER ...
... SHOULD YOU ACHIEVE YOUR GOALS ...
...YOU CANNOT KEEP YOUR CHILDISH LONG HAIR.

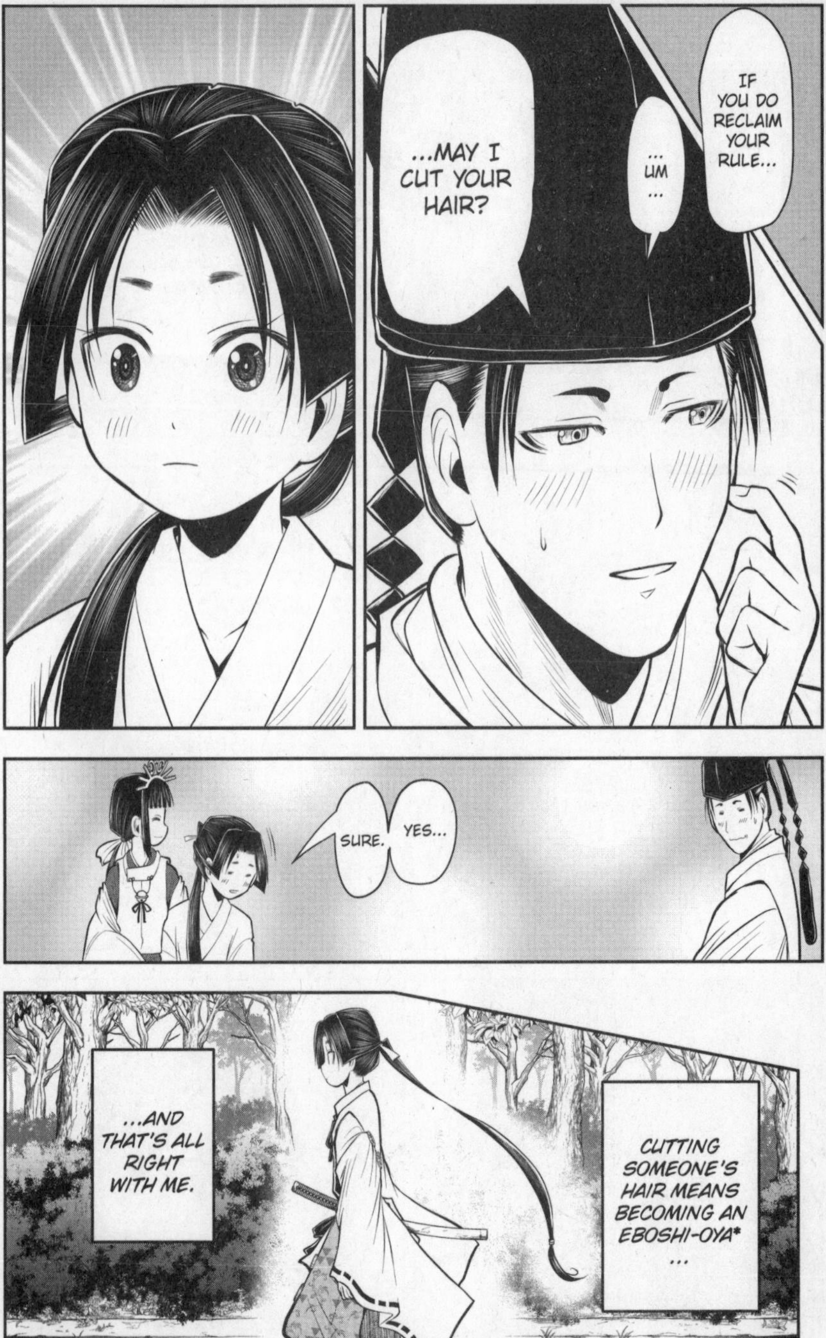
IF YOU DO RECLAIM YOUR RULE...
...UM...
...MAY I CUT YOUR HAIR?
YES...
SURE.
CUTTING SOMEONE'S HAIR MEANS BECOMING AN EBOSHI-OYA* ...
...AND THAT'S ALL RIGHT WITH ME.

*ONE WHO SERVES AS WITNESS AT A COMING-OF-AGE CEREMONY AND THEREFORE BECOMES LIKE A PARENT

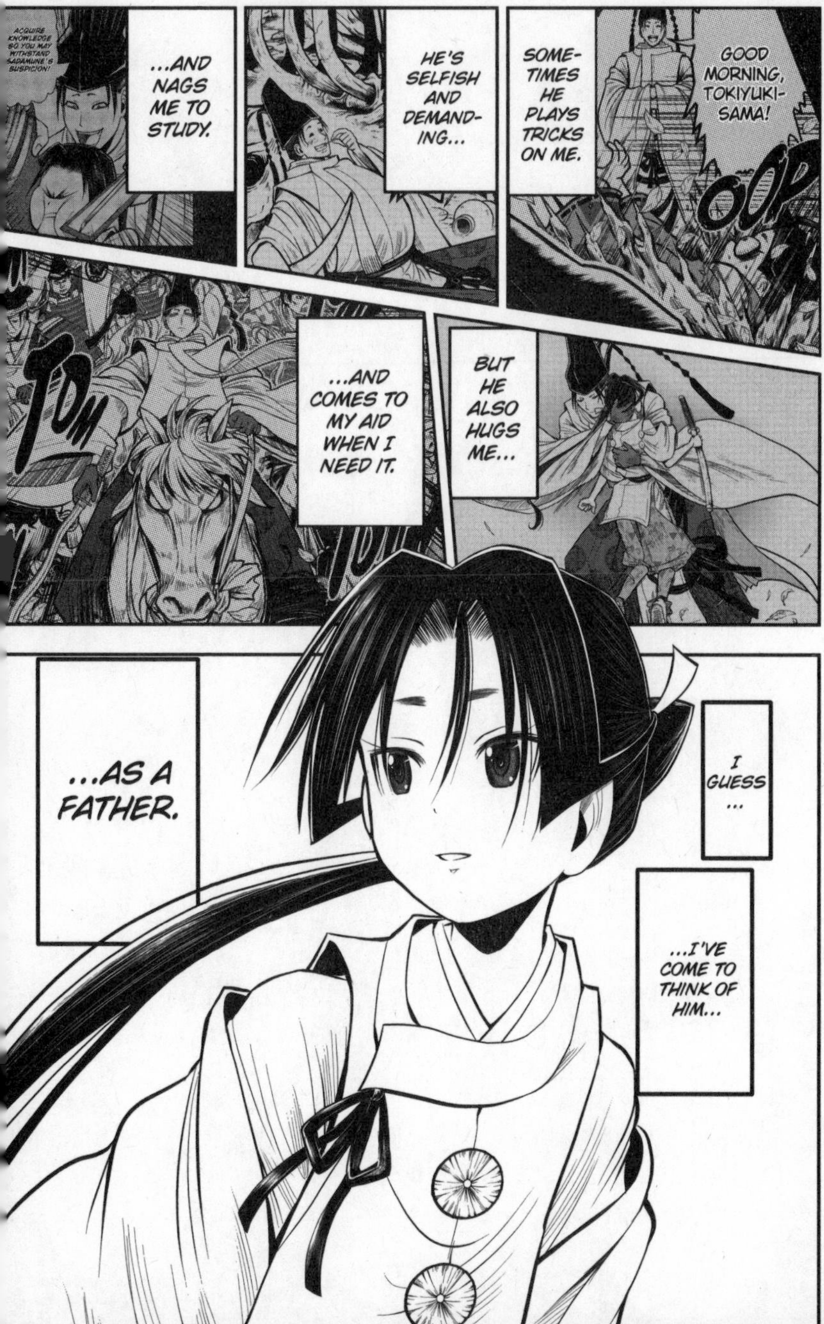
GOOD MORNING, TOKIYUKI-SAMA!
SOME-TIMES HE PLAYS TRICKS ON ME.
OOP
HE'S SELFISH AND DEMAND-ING...
...AND NAGS ME TO STUDY.
ACQUIRE KNOWLEDGE SO YOU MAY WITHSTAND SADAMUNE'S SUSPICION!
BUT HE ALSO HUGS ME...
...AND COMES TO MY AID WHEN I NEED IT.
TOM
I GUESS...
...I'VE COME TO THINK OF HIM...
...AS A FATHER.

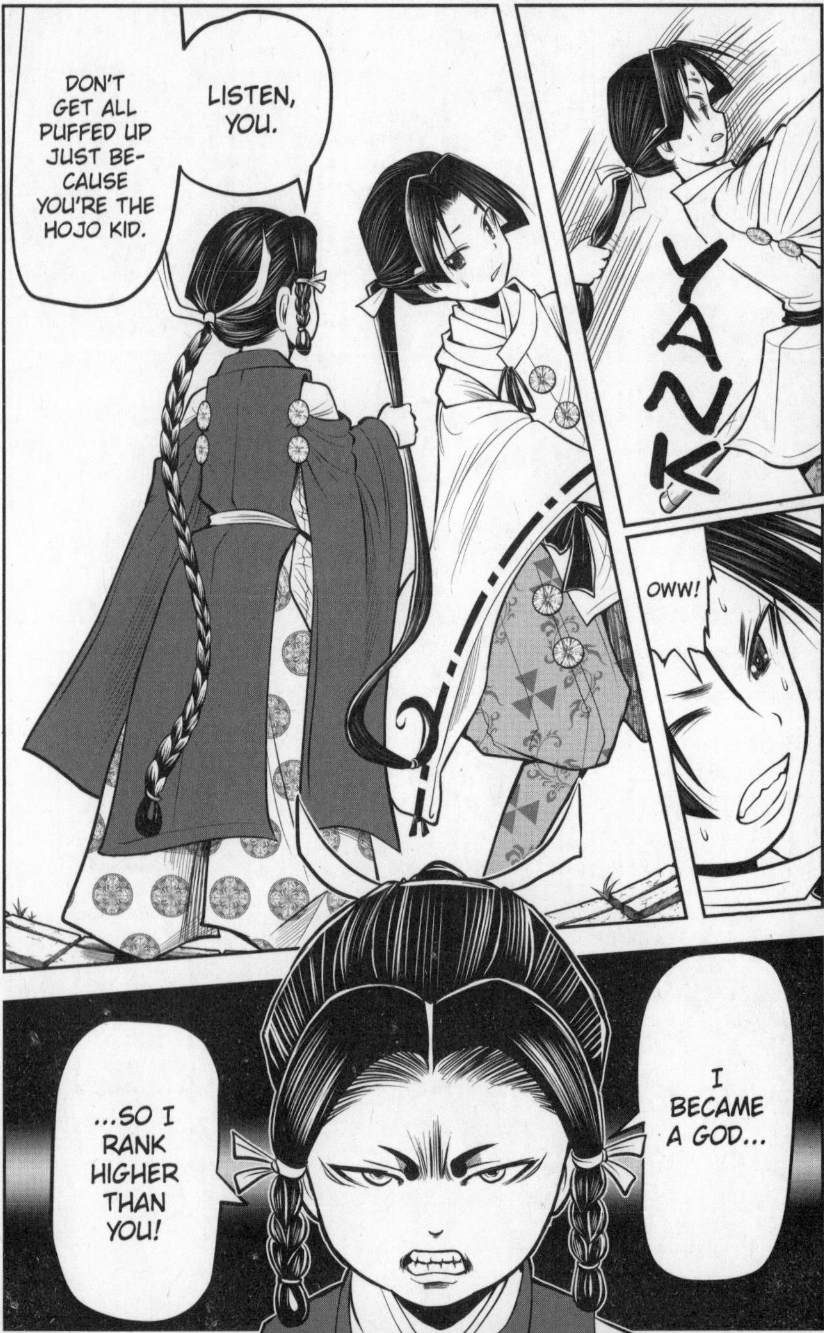
YANK
OWW!
LISTEN, YOU.
DON'T GET ALL PUFFED UP JUST BE-CAUSE YOU'RE THE HOJO KID.
I BECAME A GOD...
...SO I RANK HIGHER THAN YOU!

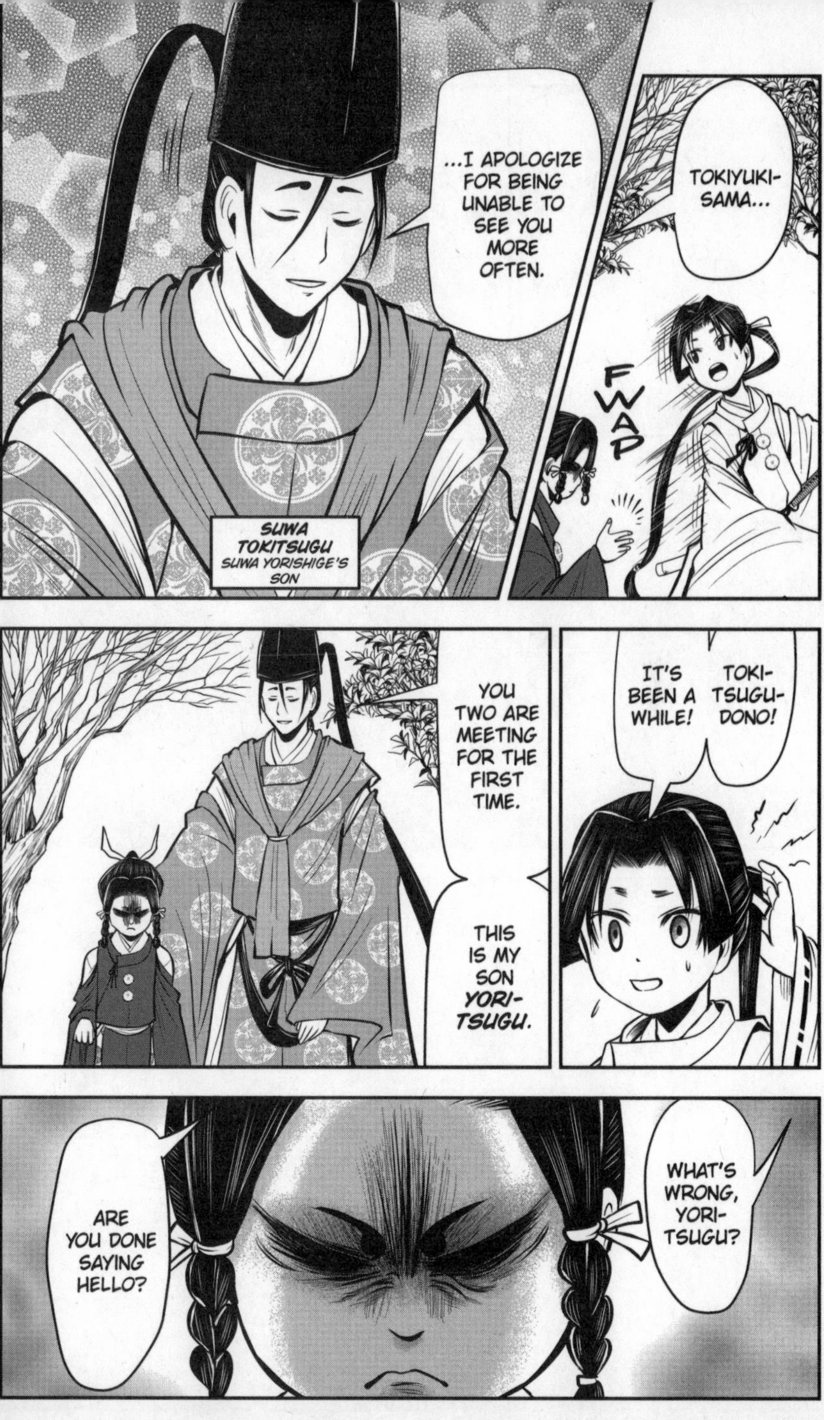
TOKIYUKI-SAMA...
FWAP
...I APOLOGIZE FOR BEING UNABLE TO SEE YOU MORE OFTEN.
SUWA TOKITSUGU
SUWA YORISHIGE'S SON
TOKI-TSUGU-DONO!
IT'S BEEN A WHILE!
YOU TWO ARE MEETING FOR THE FIRST TIME.
THIS IS MY SON YORI-TSUGU.
WHAT'S WRONG, YORI-TSUGU?
ARE YOU DONE SAYING HELLO?

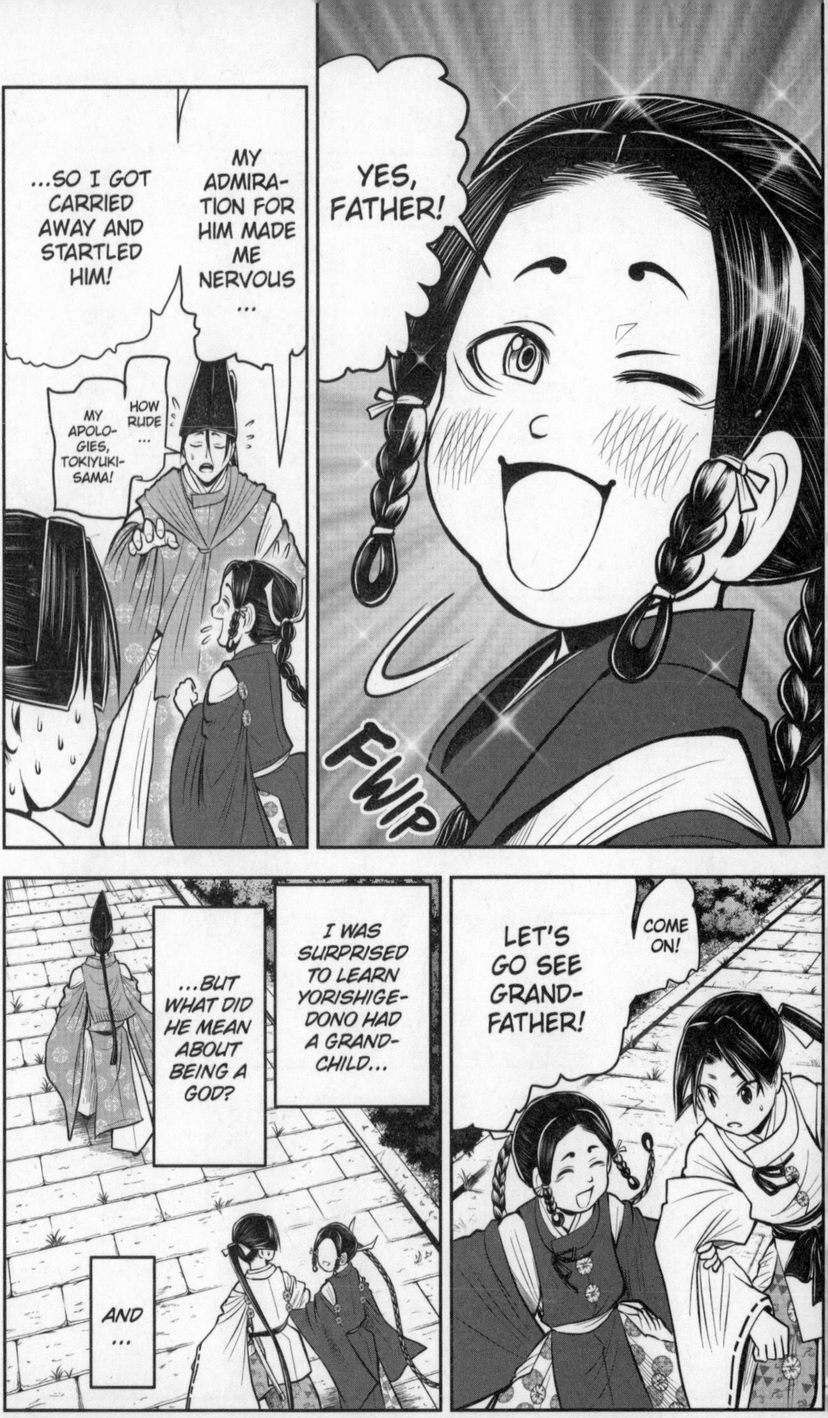
YES, FATHER!
FWIP
MY ADMIRATION FOR HIM MADE ME NERVOUS...
...SO I GOT CARRIED AWAY AND STARTLED HIM!
HOW RUDE...
MY APOLOGIES, TOKIYUKI-SAMA!
COME ON!
LET'S GO SEE GRANDFATHER!
I WAS SURPRISED TO LEARN YORISHIGE-DONO HAD A GRANDCHILD...
...BUT WHAT DID HE MEAN ABOUT BEING A GOD?
AND...

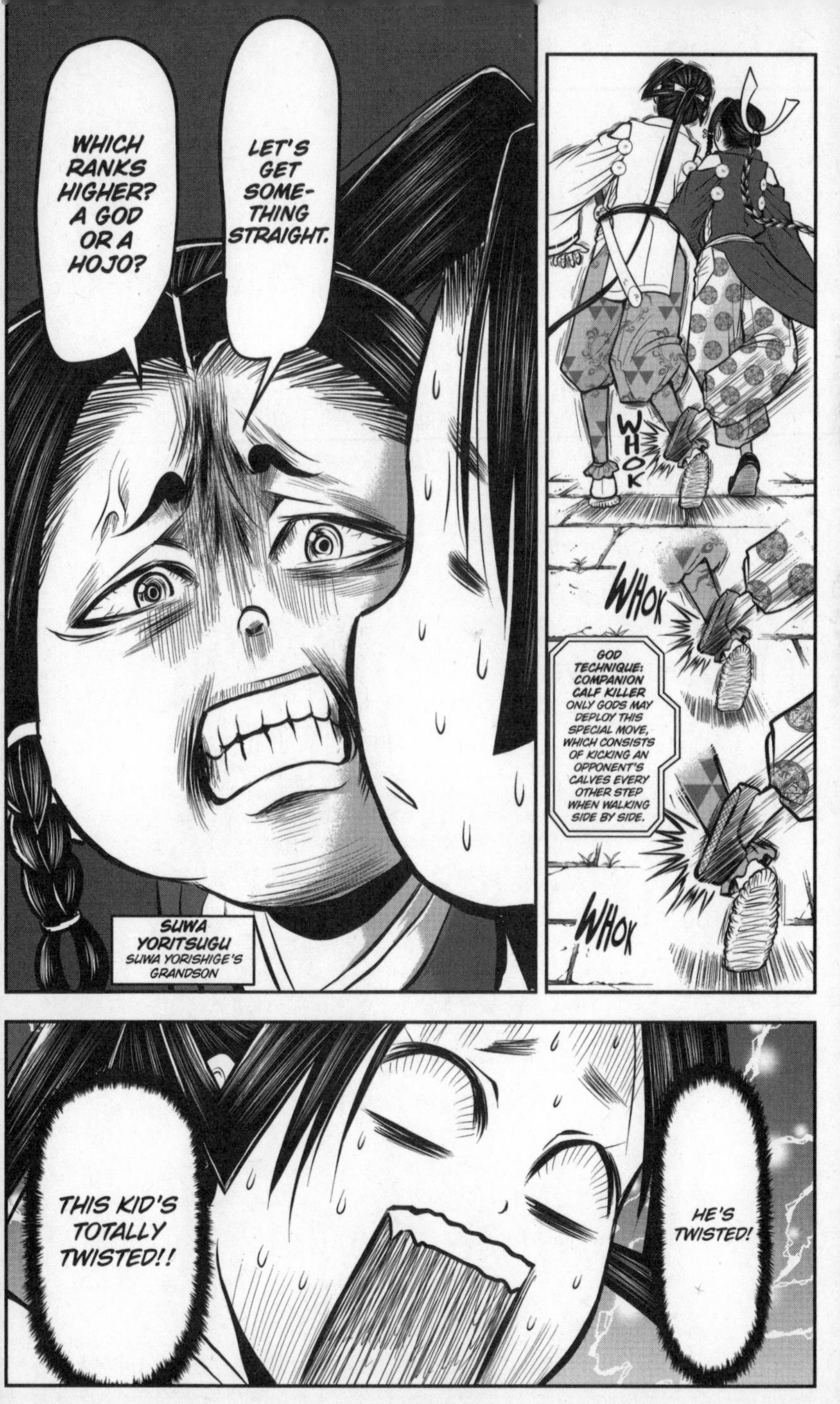
WHOK
WHOK
GOD TECHNIQUE: COMPANION CALF KILLER
ONLY GODS MAY DEPLOY THIS SPECIAL MOVE, WHICH CONSISTS OF KICKING AN OPPONENT'S CALVES EVERY OTHER STEP WHEN WALKING SIDE BY SIDE.
WHOK
LET'S GET SOME-THING STRAIGHT.
WHICH RANKS HIGHER? A GOD OR A HOJO?
SUWA YORITSUGU
SUWA YORISHIGE'S GRANDSON
HE'S TWISTED!
THIS KID'S TOTALLY TWISTED!!

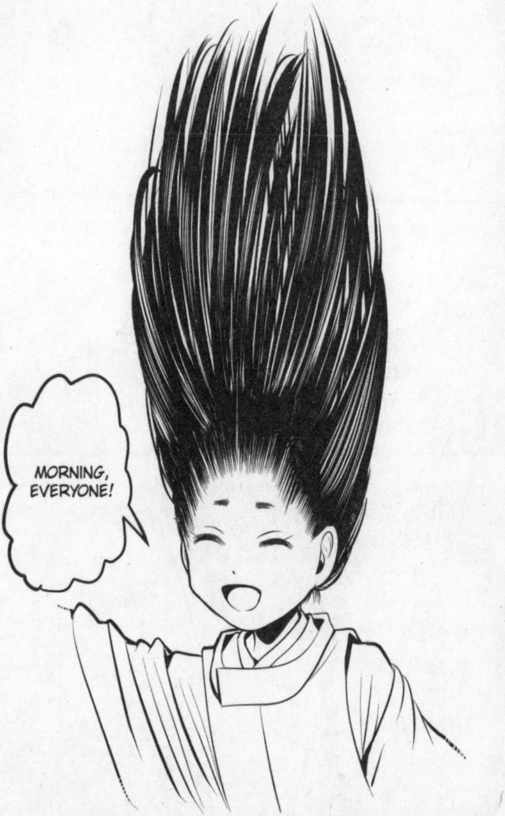
MORNING, EVERYONE!

IF HE OVERSLEEPS, SHIZUKU MESSES WITH HIS HAIR.

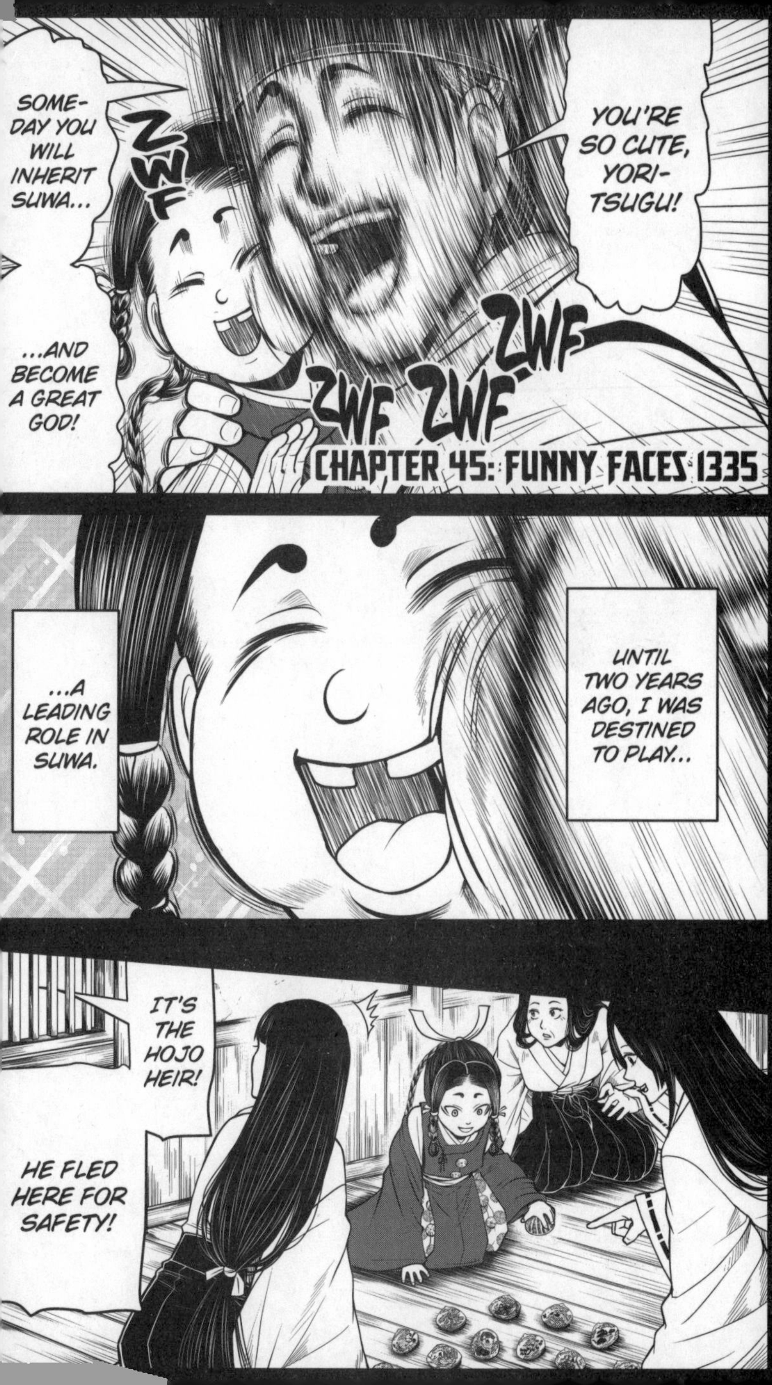
YOU'RE SO CUTE, YORI-TSUGU!
ZWF ZWF ZWF
SOME-DAY YOU WILL INHERIT SUWA...
ZWF
...AND BECOME A GREAT GOD!
CHAPTER 45: FUNNY FACES 1335
UNTIL TWO YEARS AGO, I WAS DESTINED TO PLAY...
...A LEADING ROLE IN SUWA.
IT'S THE HOJO HEIR!
HE FLED HERE FOR SAFETY!

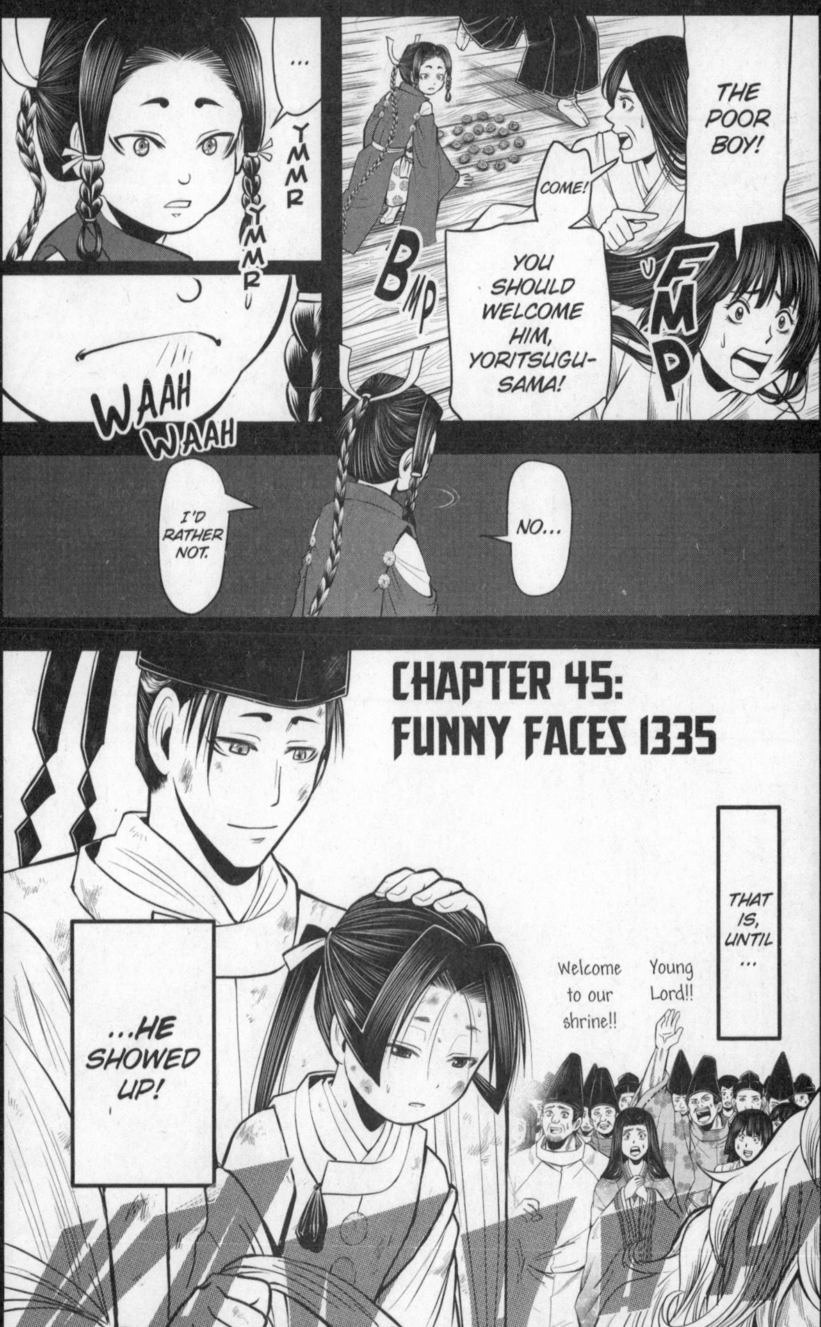
THE POOR BOY!
FMP
COME!
YOU SHOULD WELCOME HIM, YORITSUGU-SAMA!
BMP
...
YMMR
YMMR
WAAH
WAAH
NO...
I'D RATHER NOT.
CHAPTER 45: FUNNY FACES 1335
THAT IS, UNTIL...
Young Lord!!
Welcome to our shrine!!
...HE SHOWED UP!

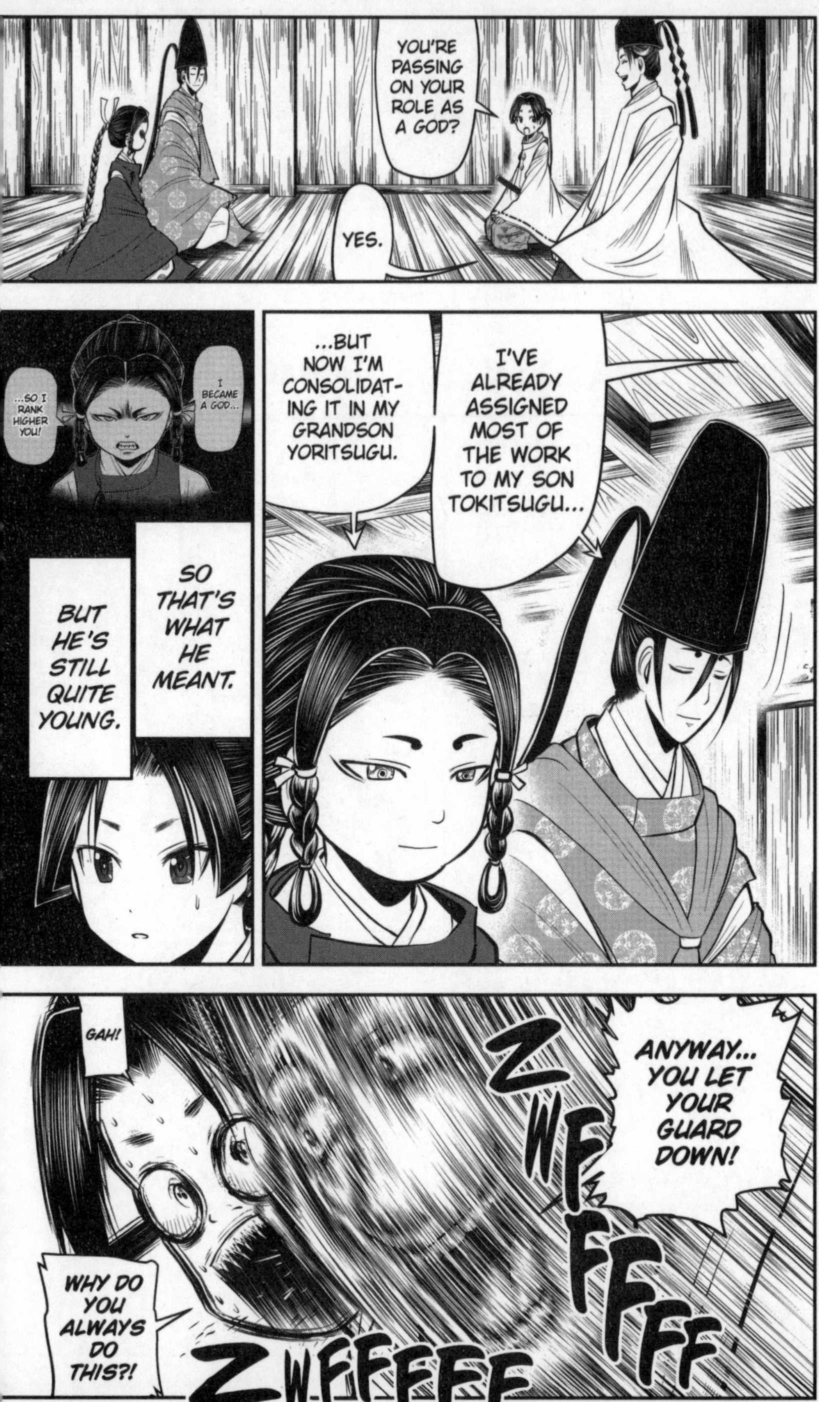
YOU'RE PASSING ON YOUR ROLE AS A GOD?
YES.
I'VE ALREADY ASSIGNED MOST OF THE WORK TO MY SON TOKITSUGU...
...BUT NOW I'M CONSOLIDATING IT IN MY GRANDSON YORITSUGU.
I BECAME A GOD...
...SO I RANK HIGHER YOU!
SO THAT'S WHAT HE MEANT.
BUT HE'S STILL QUITE YOUNG.
ANYWAY... YOU LET YOUR GUARD DOWN!
ZWFFFFF
GAH!
WHY DO YOU ALWAYS DO THIS?!
ZWFFFFFF

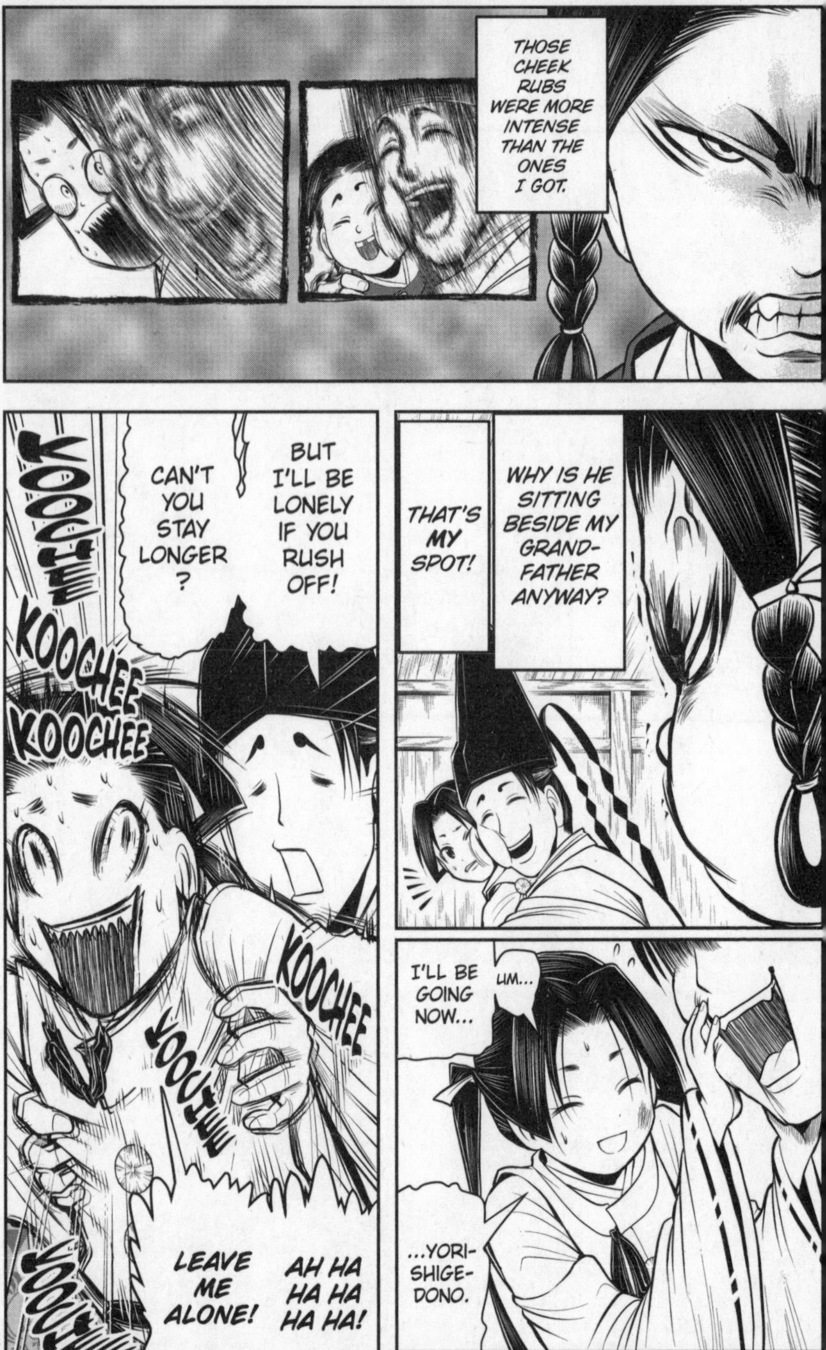
THOSE CHEEK RUBS WERE MORE INTENSE THAN THE ONES I GOT.
WHY IS HE SITTING BESIDE MY GRANDFATHER ANYWAY?
THAT'S MY SPOT!
UM...
I'LL BE GOING NOW...
...YORISHIGE-DONO.
BUT I'LL BE LONELY IF YOU RUSH OFF!
CAN'T YOU STAY LONGER?
KOOCHEE
KOOCHEE
KOOCHEE
KOOCHEE
AH HA HA HA HA HA!
LEAVE ME ALONE!

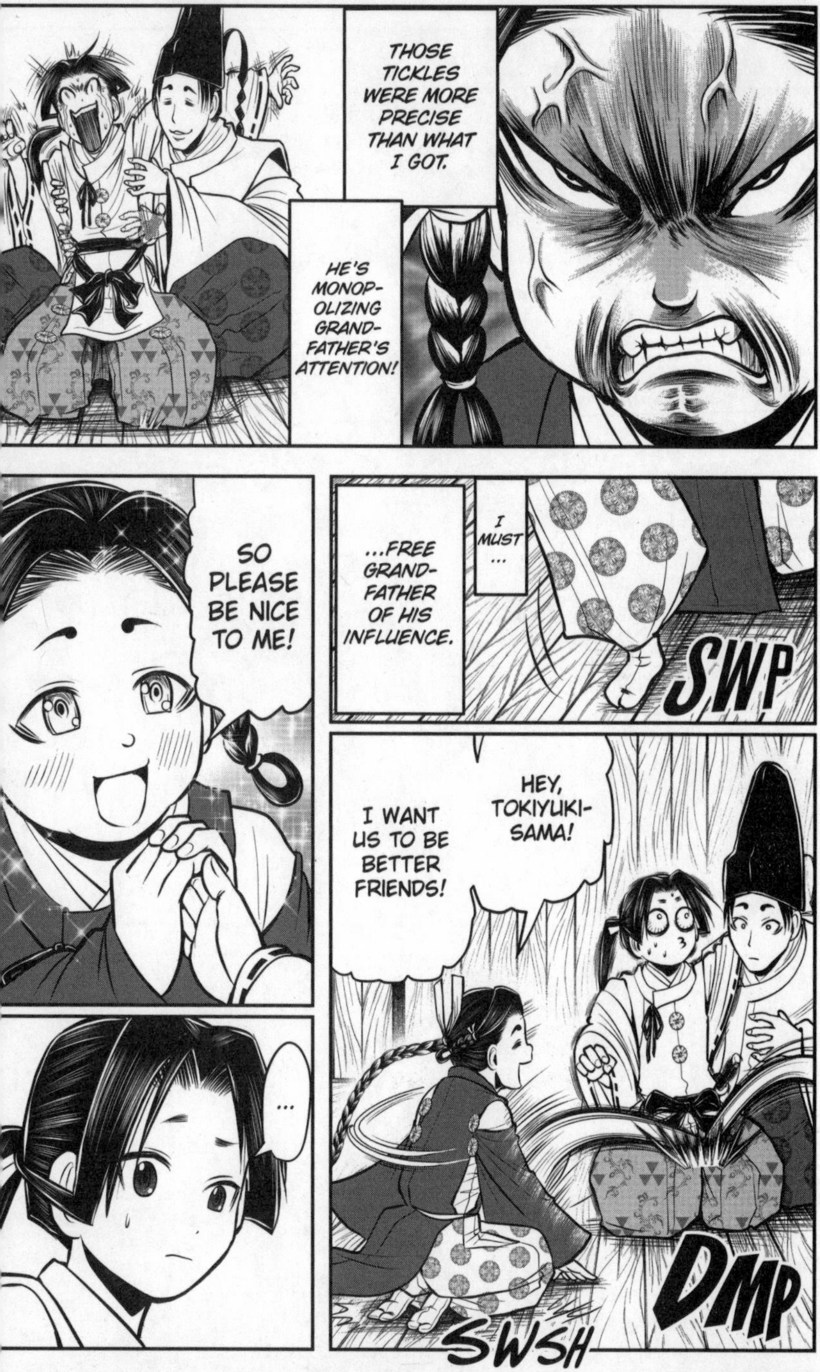

THOSE TICKLES WERE MORE PRECISE THAN WHAT I GOT.
HE'S MONOP-OLIZING GRAND-FATHER'S ATTENTION!
I MUST ...
...FREE GRAND-FATHER OF HIS INFLUENCE.
SWP
HEY, TOKIYUKI-SAMA!
I WANT US TO BE BETTER FRIENDS!
DMP
SWSH
SO PLEASE BE NICE TO ME!
...

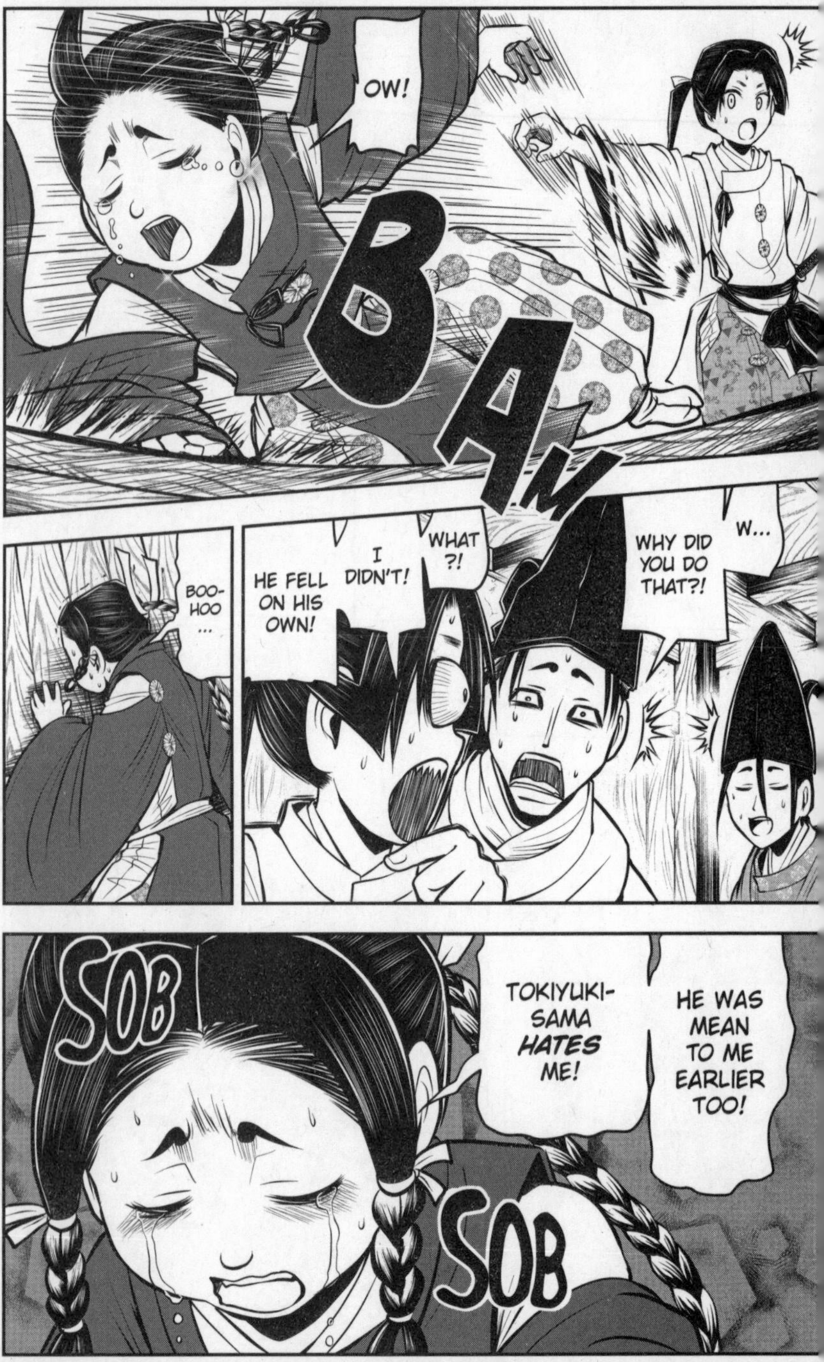

OW!
BAM
W...
WHY DID YOU DO THAT?!
WHAT?!
I DIDN'T!
HE FELL ON HIS OWN!
BOO-HOO ...
HE WAS MEAN TO ME EARLIER TOO!
TOKIYUKI-SAMA *HATES* ME!
SOB
SOB

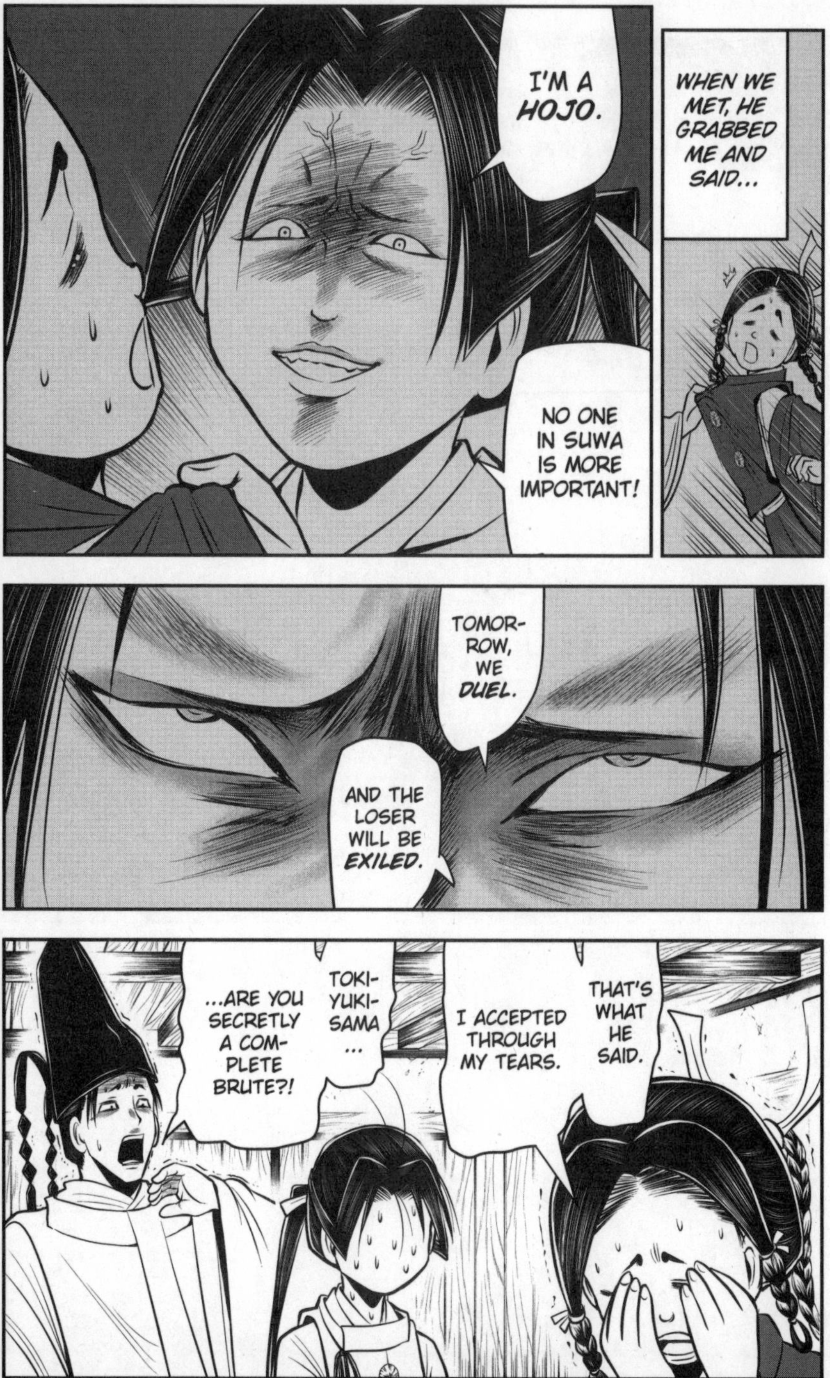
WHEN WE MET, HE GRABBED ME AND SAID...
I'M A HOJO.
NO ONE IN SUWA IS MORE IMPORTANT!
TOMORROW, WE DUEL.
AND THE LOSER WILL BE EXILED.
THAT'S WHAT HE SAID.
I ACCEPTED THROUGH MY TEARS.
TOKIYUKI-SAMA...
...ARE YOU SECRETLY A COMPLETE BRUTE?!

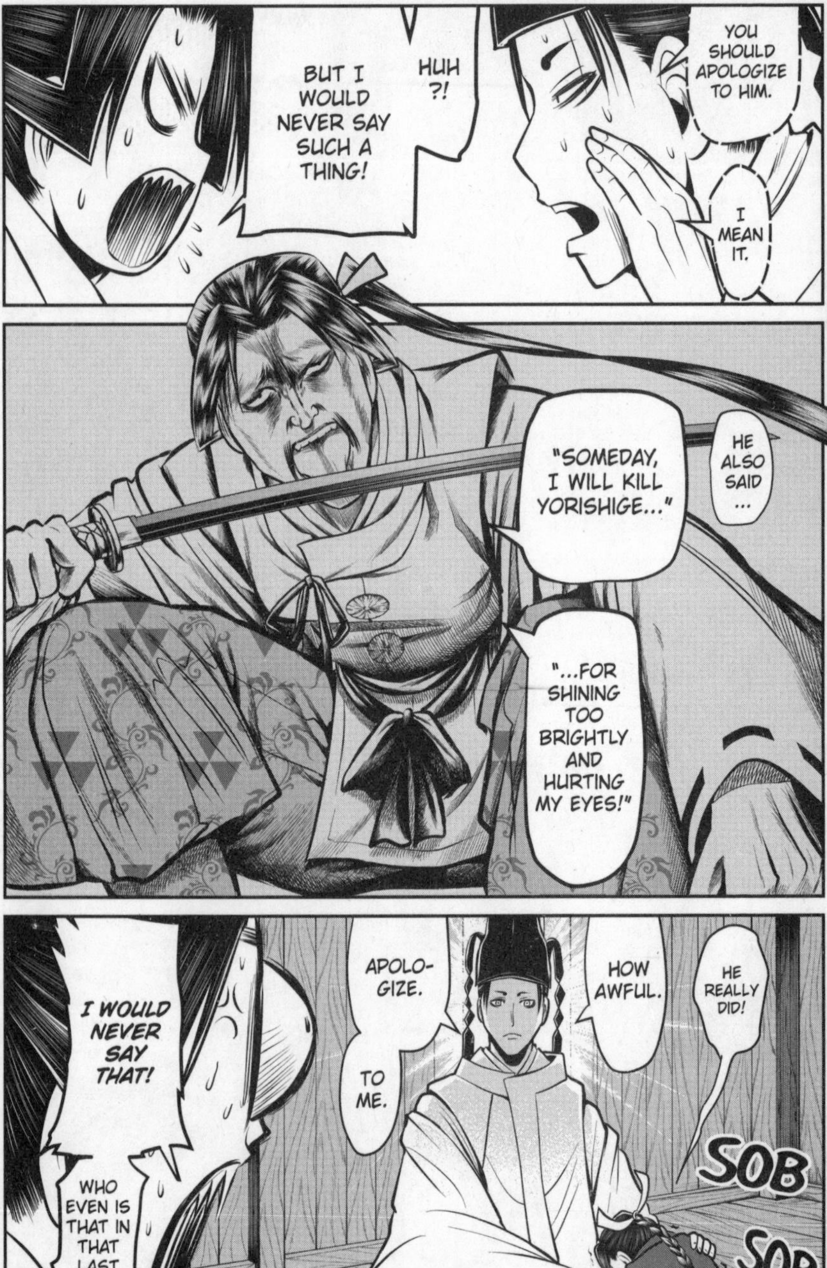
YOU SHOULD APOLOGIZE TO HIM.
I MEAN IT.
HUH?!
BUT I WOULD NEVER SAY SUCH A THING!
HE ALSO SAID ...
"SOMEDAY, I WILL KILL YORISHIGE..."
"...FOR SHINING TOO BRIGHTLY AND HURTING MY EYES!"
HE REALLY DID!
SOB
SOB
HOW AWFUL.
APOLOGIZE.
TO ME.
I WOULD NEVER SAY THAT!
WHO EVEN IS THAT IN THAT LAST PANEL?!

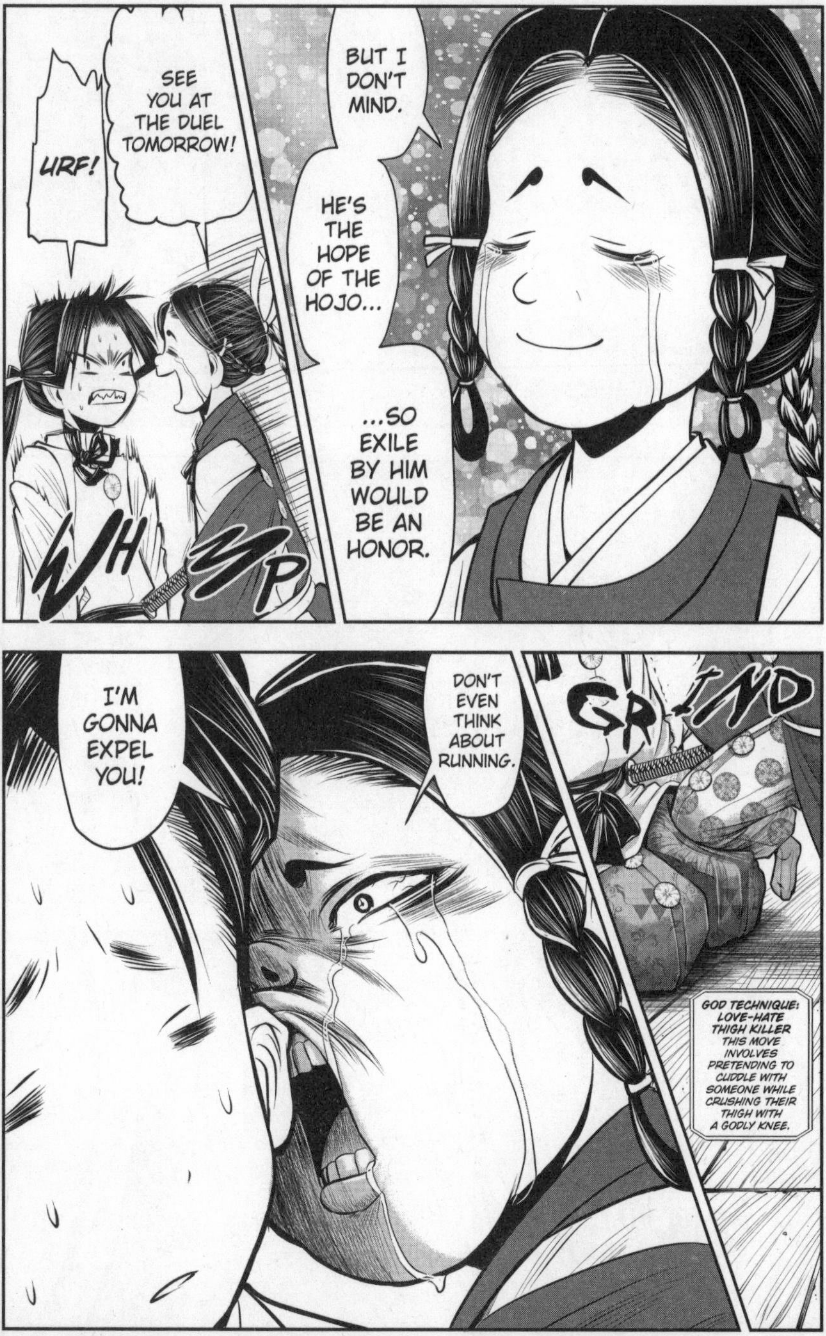
BUT I DON'T MIND.
HE'S THE HOPE OF THE HOJO...
...SO EXILE BY HIM WOULD BE AN HONOR.
SEE YOU AT THE DUEL TOMORROW!
URF!
WHUMP
GRIND
GOD TECHNIQUE: LOVE-HATE THIGH KILLER
THIS MOVE INVOLVES PRETENDING TO CUDDLE WITH SOMEONE WHILE CRUSHING THEIR THIGH WITH A GODLY KNEE.
DON'T EVEN THINK ABOUT RUNNING.
I'M GONNA EXPEL YOU!

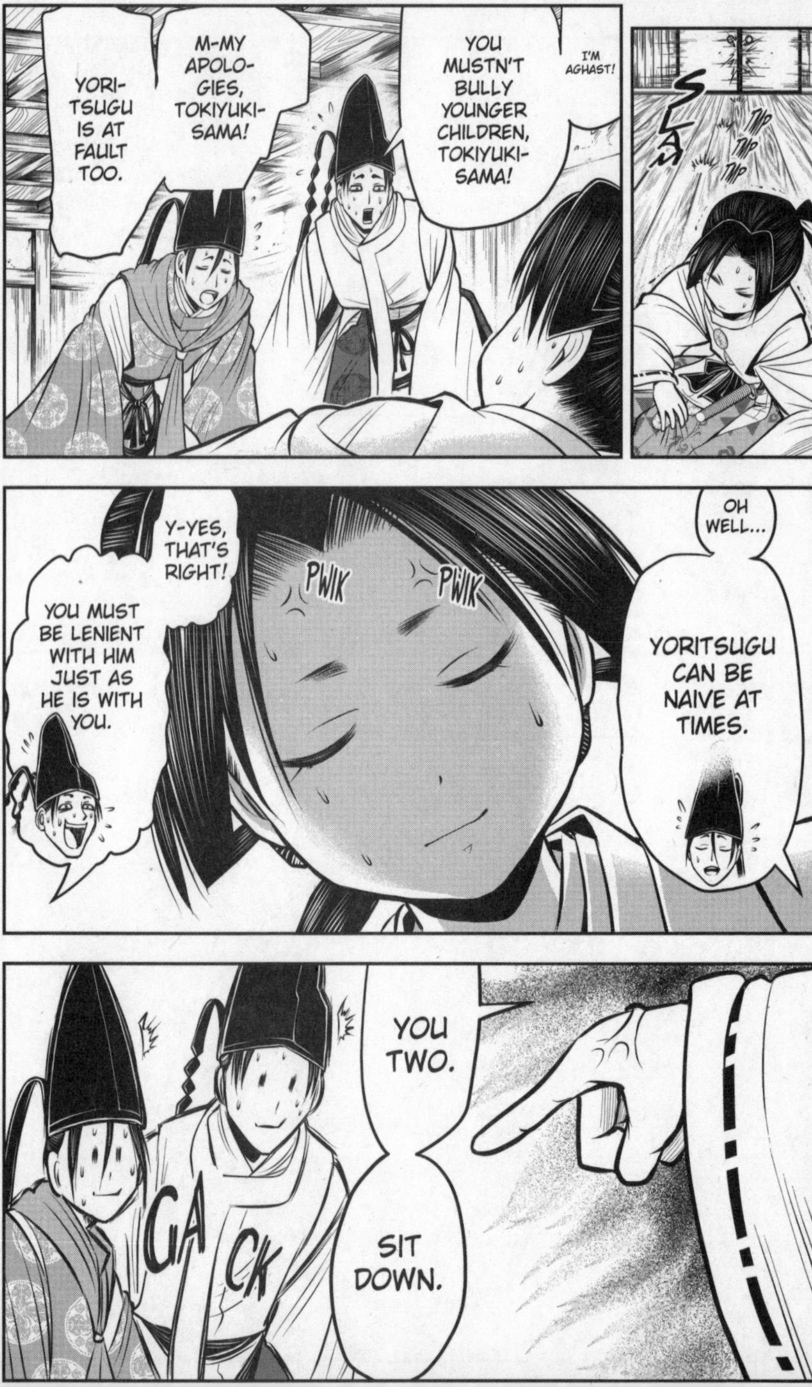
SLAM
TMP TMP TMP
I'M AGHAST!
YOU MUSTN'T BULLY YOUNGER CHILDREN, TOKIYUKI-SAMA!
M-MY APOLOGIES, TOKIYUKI-SAMA!
YORITSUGU IS AT FAULT TOO.
OH WELL...
YORITSUGU CAN BE NAIVE AT TIMES.
PWIK PWIK
Y-YES, THAT'S RIGHT!
YOU MUST BE LENIENT WITH HIM JUST AS HE IS WITH YOU.
YOU TWO.
SIT DOWN.
GACK

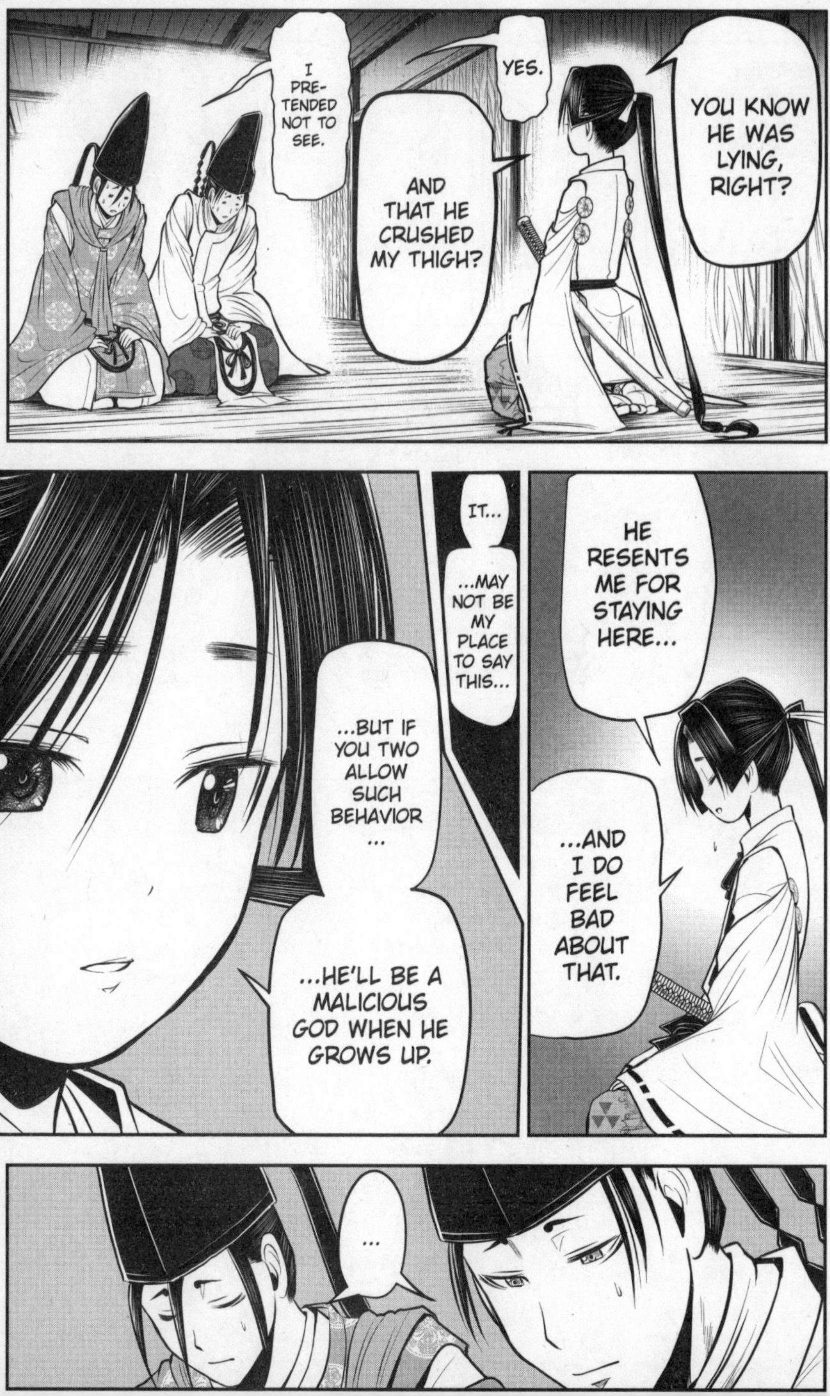
YOU KNOW HE WAS LYING, RIGHT?
YES.
AND THAT HE CRUSHED MY THIGH?
I PRETENDED NOT TO SEE.
HE RESENTS ME FOR STAYING HERE...
...AND I DO FEEL BAD ABOUT THAT.
IT...
...MAY NOT BE MY PLACE TO SAY THIS...
...BUT IF YOU TWO ALLOW SUCH BEHAVIOR...
...HE'LL BE A MALICIOUS GOD WHEN HE GROWS UP.
...

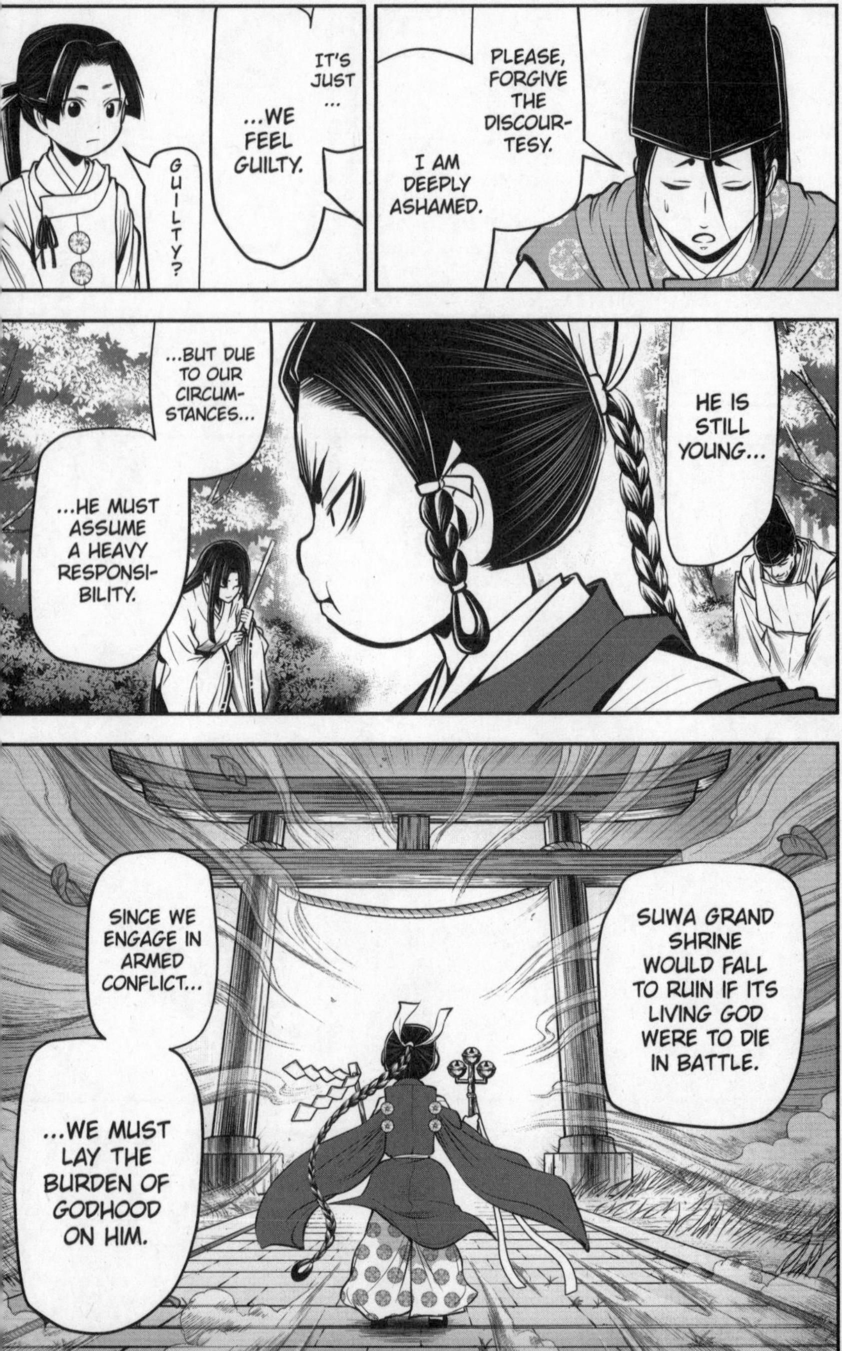
PLEASE, FORGIVE THE DISCOURTESY.
I AM DEEPLY ASHAMED.
IT'S JUST ...
...WE FEEL GUILTY.
GUILTY?
HE IS STILL YOUNG...
...BUT DUE TO OUR CIRCUMSTANCES...
...HE MUST ASSUME A HEAVY RESPONSIBILITY.
SUWA GRAND SHRINE WOULD FALL TO RUIN IF ITS LIVING GOD WERE TO DIE IN BATTLE.
SINCE WE ENGAGE IN ARMED CONFLICT...
...WE MUST LAY THE BURDEN OF GODHOOD ON HIM.

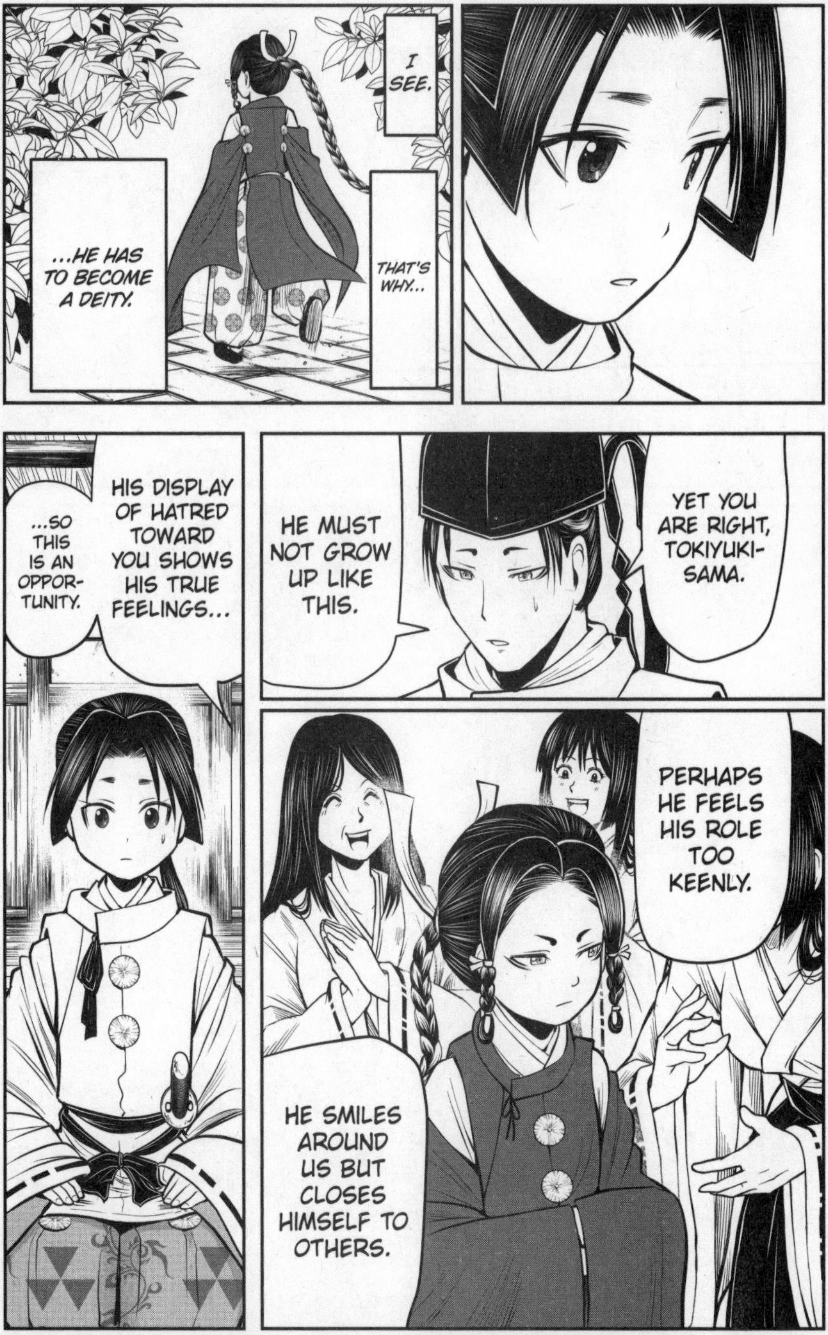
I SEE.
THAT'S WHY...
...HE HAS TO BECOME A DEITY.
YET YOU ARE RIGHT, TOKIYUKI-SAMA.
HE MUST NOT GROW UP LIKE THIS.
PERHAPS HE FEELS HIS ROLE TOO KEENLY.
HE SMILES AROUND US BUT CLOSES HIMSELF TO OTHERS.
HIS DISPLAY OF HATRED TOWARD YOU SHOWS HIS TRUE FEELINGS...
...SO THIS IS AN OPPOR-TUNITY.

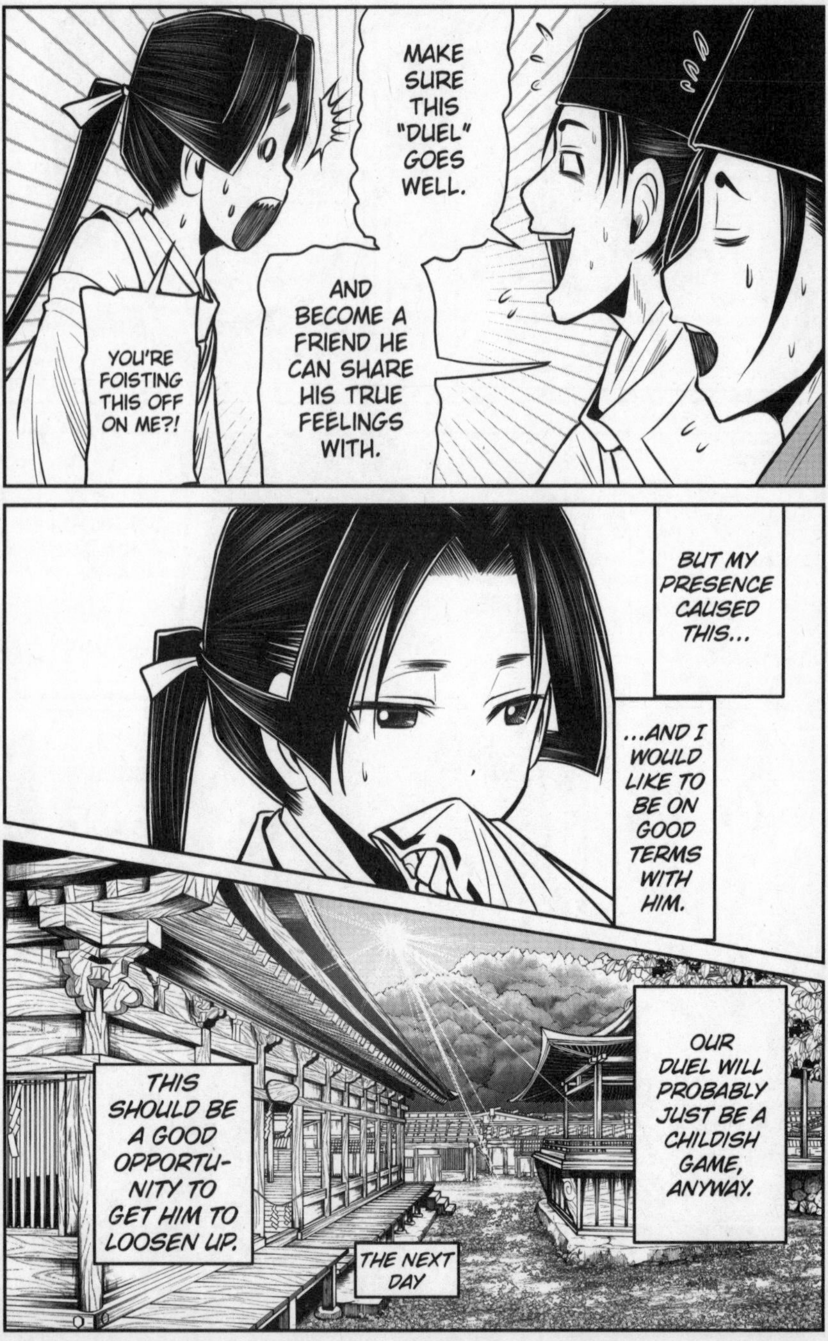
MAKE SURE THIS "DUEL" GOES WELL.
AND BECOME A FRIEND HE CAN SHARE HIS TRUE FEELINGS WITH.
YOU'RE FOISTING THIS OFF ON ME?!
BUT MY PRESENCE CAUSED THIS...
...AND I WOULD LIKE TO BE ON GOOD TERMS WITH HIM.
OUR DUEL WILL PROBABLY JUST BE A CHILDISH GAME, ANYWAY.
THIS SHOULD BE A GOOD OPPORTU-NITY TO GET HIM TO LOOSEN UP.
THE NEXT DAY

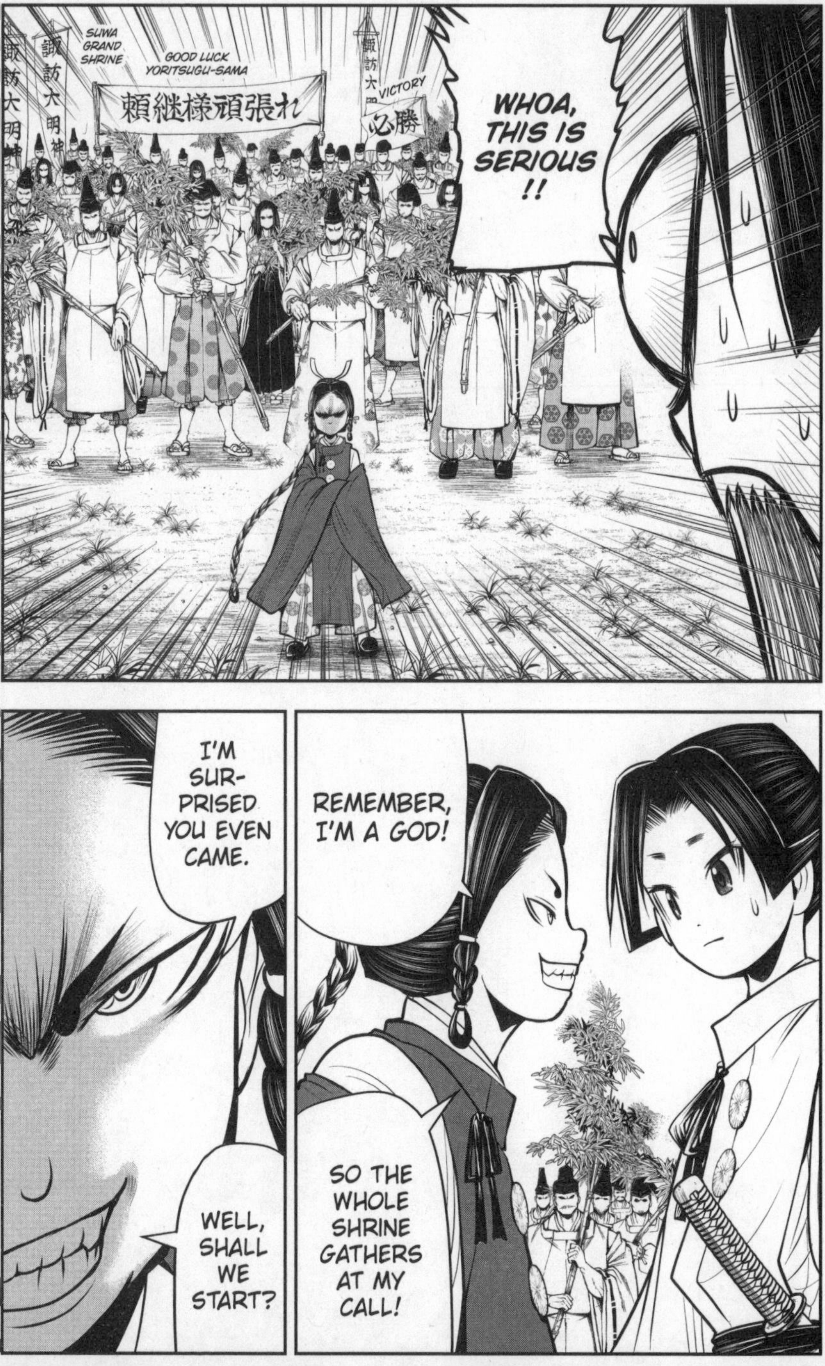

WHOA, THIS IS SERIOUS!!
諏訪大明
VICTORY
必勝
GOOD LUCK YORITSUGU-SAMA
頼継様頑張れ
SUWA GRAND SHRINE
諏訪大明神
諏訪大明神
REMEMBER, I'M A GOD!
SO THE WHOLE SHRINE GATHERS AT MY CALL!
I'M SURPRISED YOU EVEN CAME.
WELL, SHALL WE START?

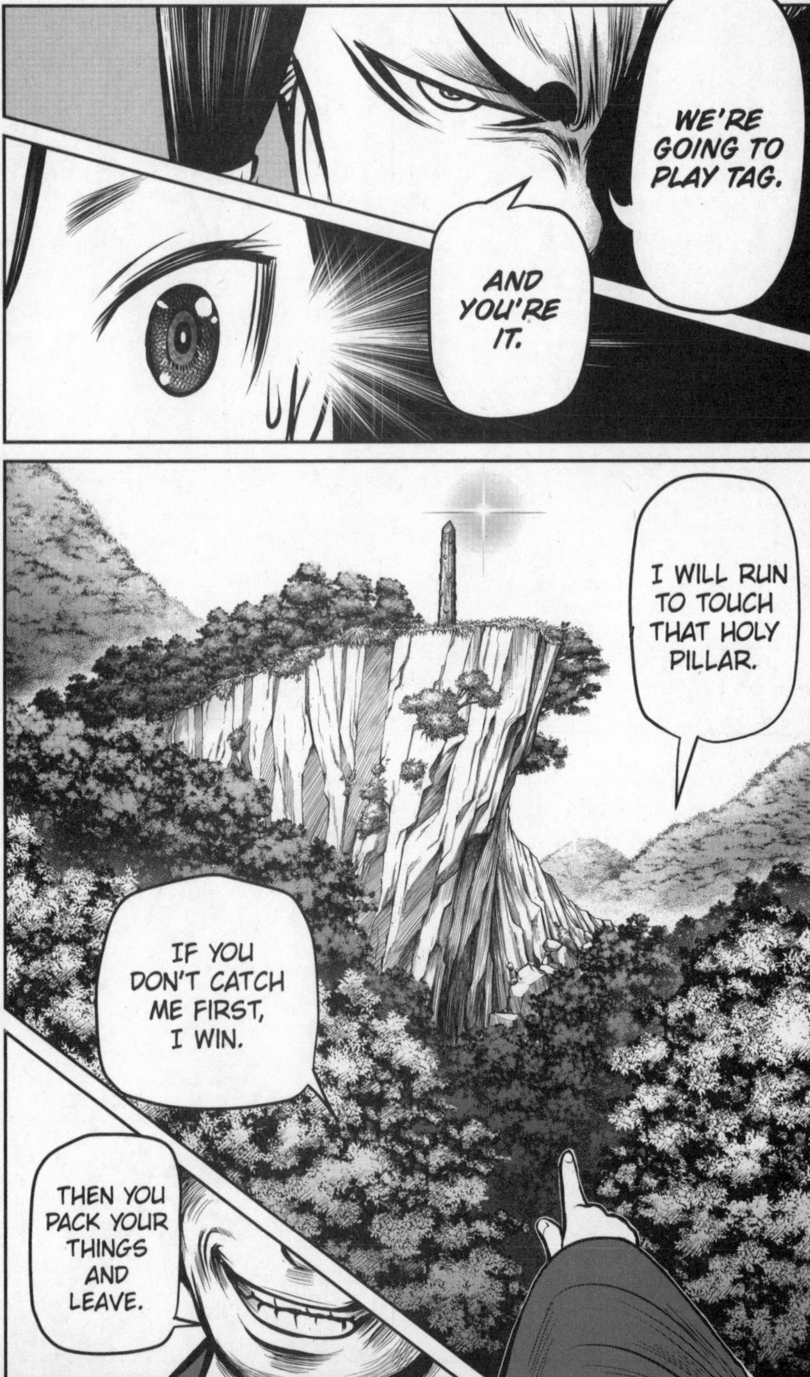
WE'RE GOING TO PLAY TAG.
AND YOU'RE IT.
I WILL RUN TO TOUCH THAT HOLY PILLAR.
IF YOU DON'T CATCH ME FIRST, I WIN.
THEN YOU PACK YOUR THINGS AND LEAVE.

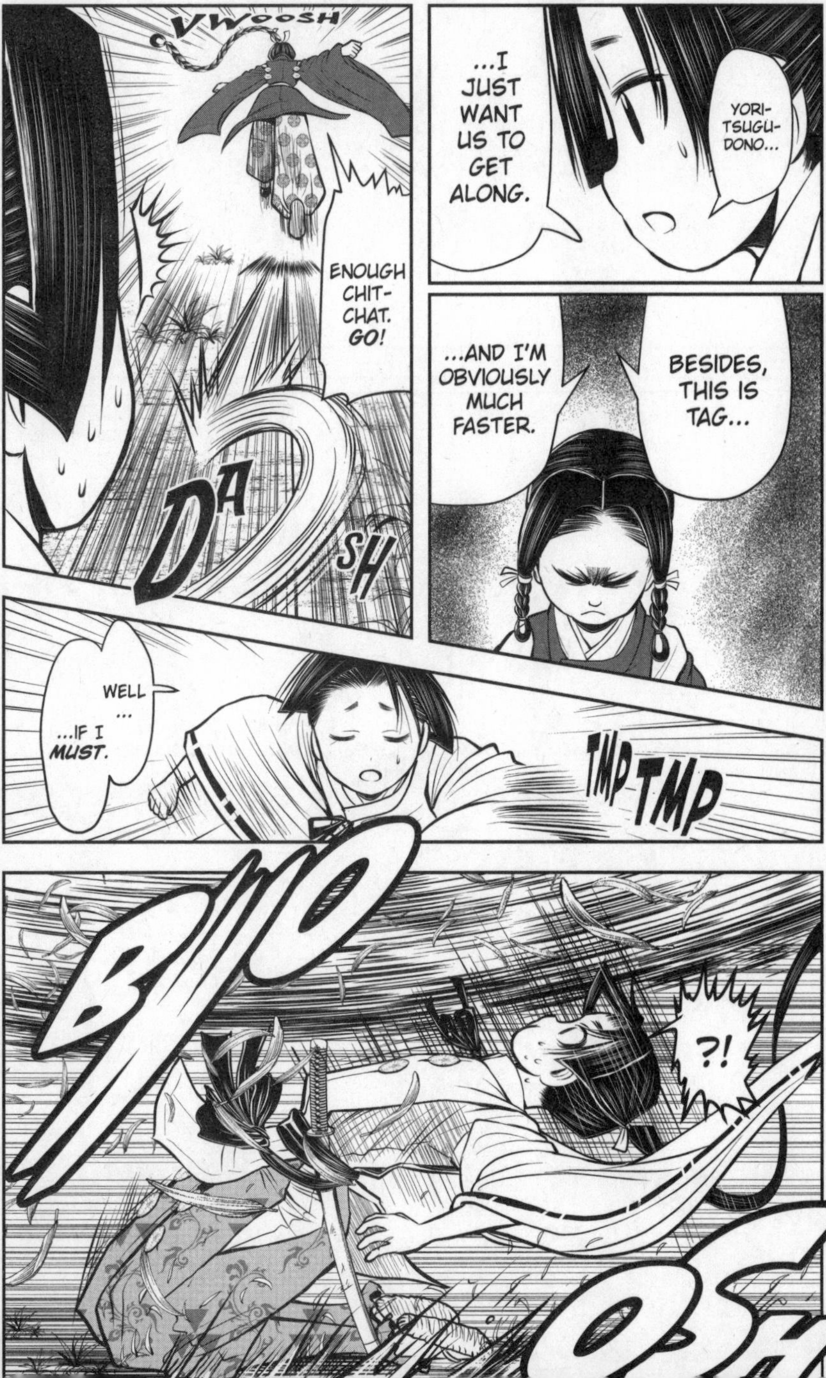
YORI-TSUGU-DONO...
...I JUST WANT US TO GET ALONG.
BESIDES, THIS IS TAG...
...AND I'M OBVIOUSLY MUCH FASTER.
VWOOSH
ENOUGH CHIT-CHAT. GO!
DASH
WELL... ...IF I MUST.
TMP TMP
BYO
?!
OSH

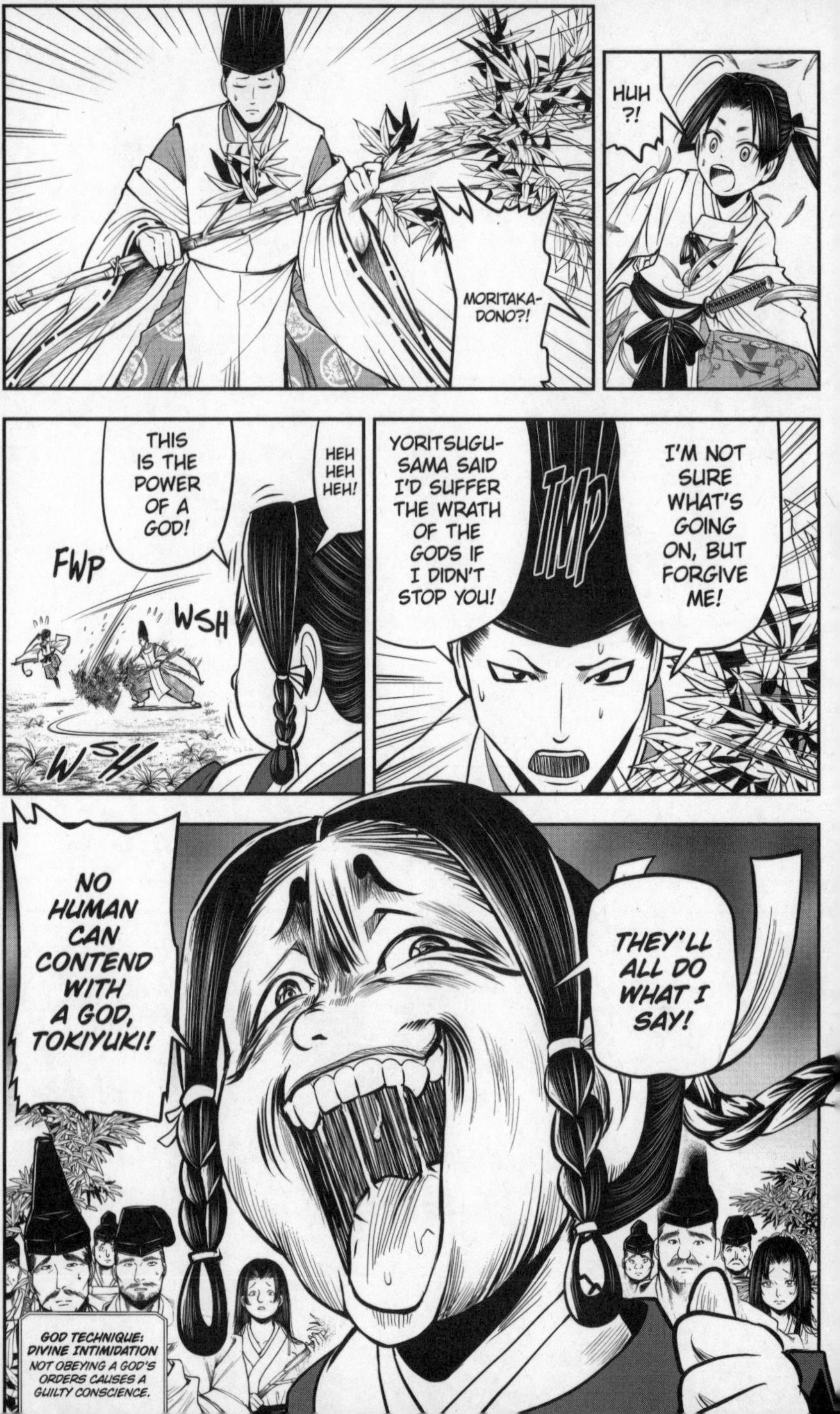
HUH?!
MORITAKA-DONO?!
I'M NOT SURE WHAT'S GOING ON, BUT FORGIVE ME!
YORITSUGU-SAMA SAID I'D SUFFER THE WRATH OF THE GODS IF I DIDN'T STOP YOU!
TMP
HEH HEH HEH!
THIS IS THE POWER OF A GOD!
FWP
WSH
WSH
THEY'LL ALL DO WHAT I SAY!
NO HUMAN CAN CONTEND WITH A GOD, TOKIYUKI!
GOD TECHNIQUE: DIVINE INTIMIDATION
NOT OBEYING A GOD'S ORDERS CAUSES A GUILTY CONSCIENCE.

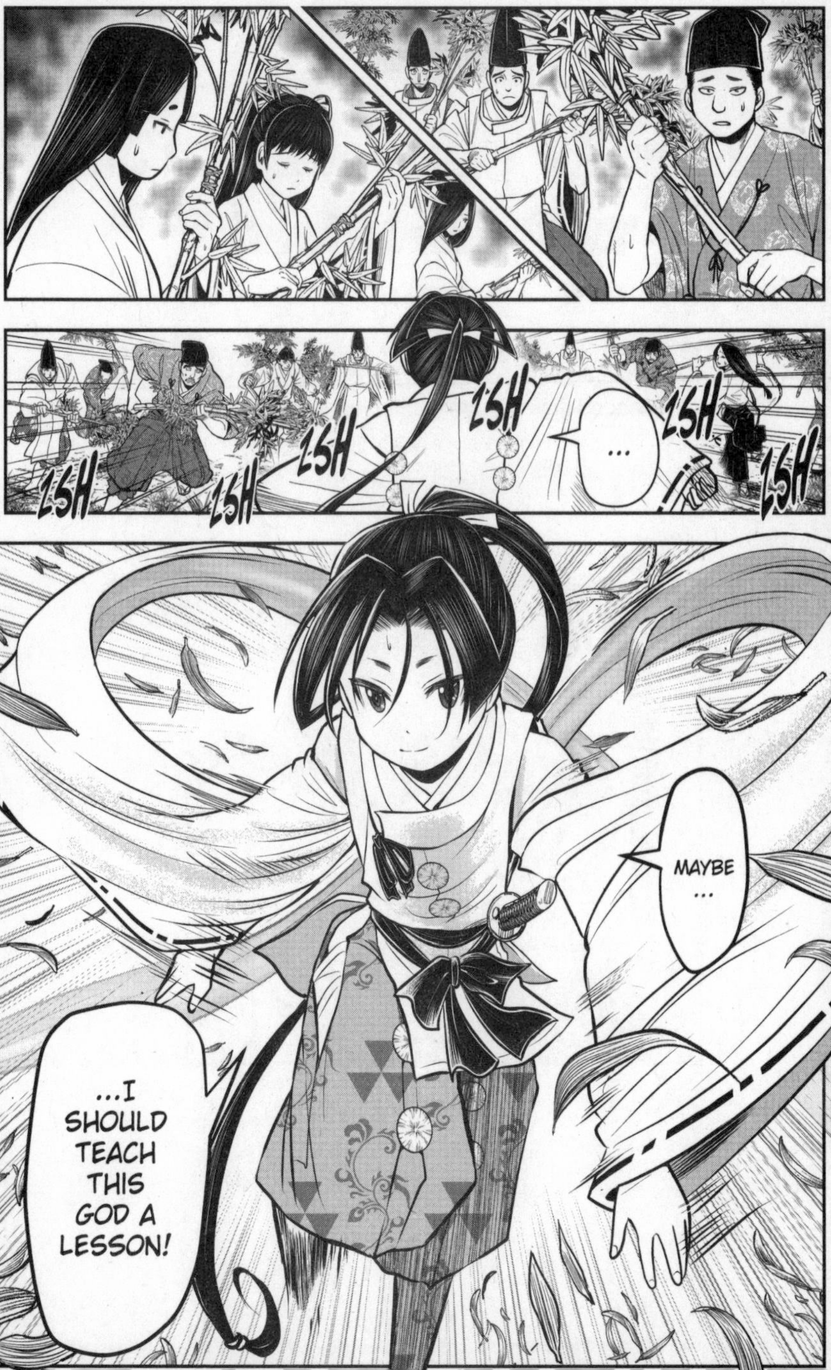

...
RUSH
RUSH
RUSH
RUSH
RUSH
RUSH
MAYBE ...
...I SHOULD TEACH THIS GOD A LESSON!

LAYER OF:

I've drawn a lot of weird faces, but I have special affection for this one. It's so snotty that looking at it cheers me up, and I think I managed it with the minimum number of lines.

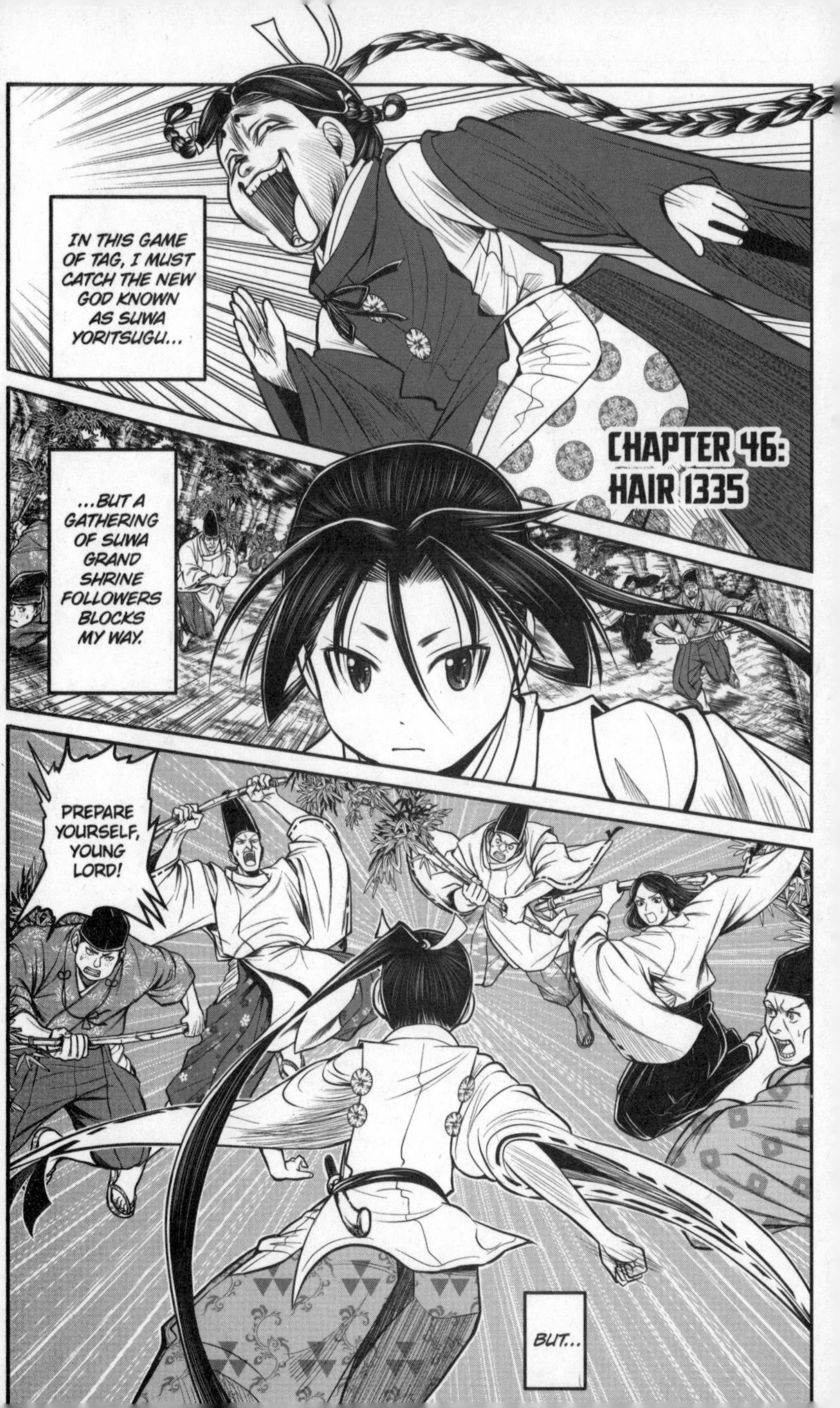
IN THIS GAME OF TAG, I MUST CATCH THE NEW GOD KNOWN AS SUWA YORITSUGU...
CHAPTER 46: HAIR 1335
...BUT A GATHERING OF SUWA GRAND SHRINE FOLLOWERS BLOCKS MY WAY.
PREPARE YOURSELF, YOUNG LORD!
BUT...

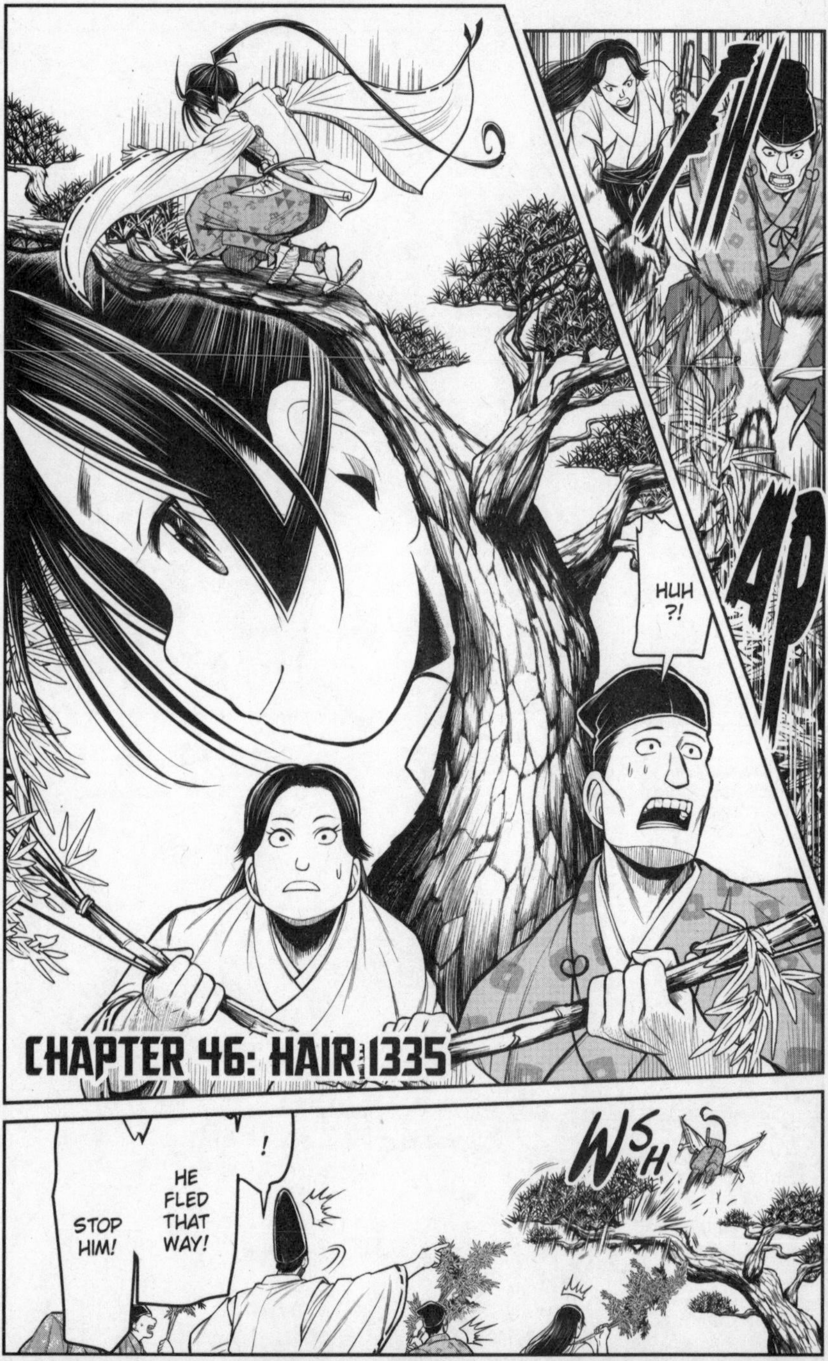
HUH ?!
CHAPTER 46: HAIR 1335
WSH
!
HE FLED THAT WAY!
STOP HIM!

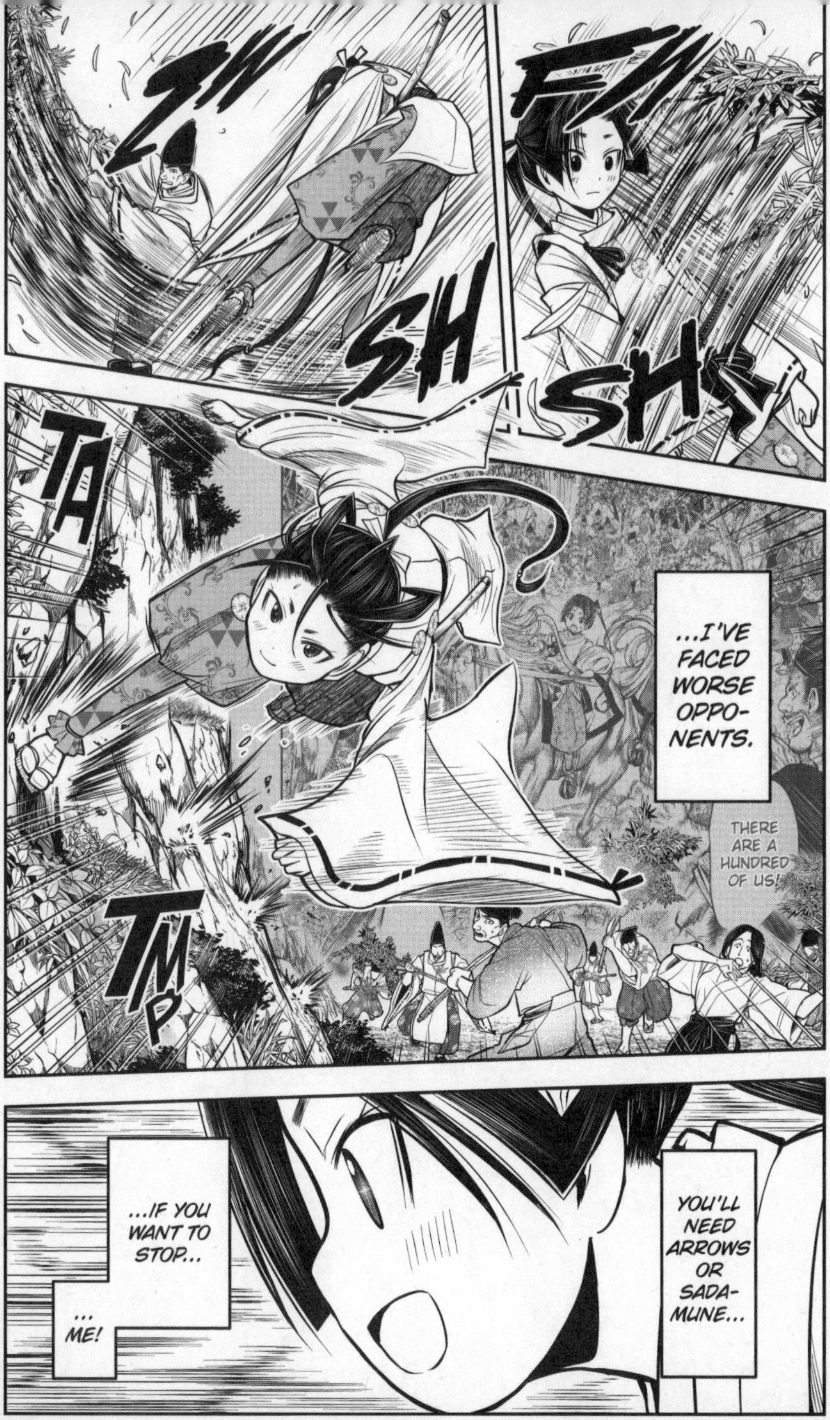
FWN
SH
ZWN
SH
...I'VE FACED WORSE OPPONENTS.
THERE ARE A HUNDRED OF US!
TA
TMP
YOU'LL NEED ARROWS OR SADAMUNE...
...IF YOU WANT TO STOP...
... ME!

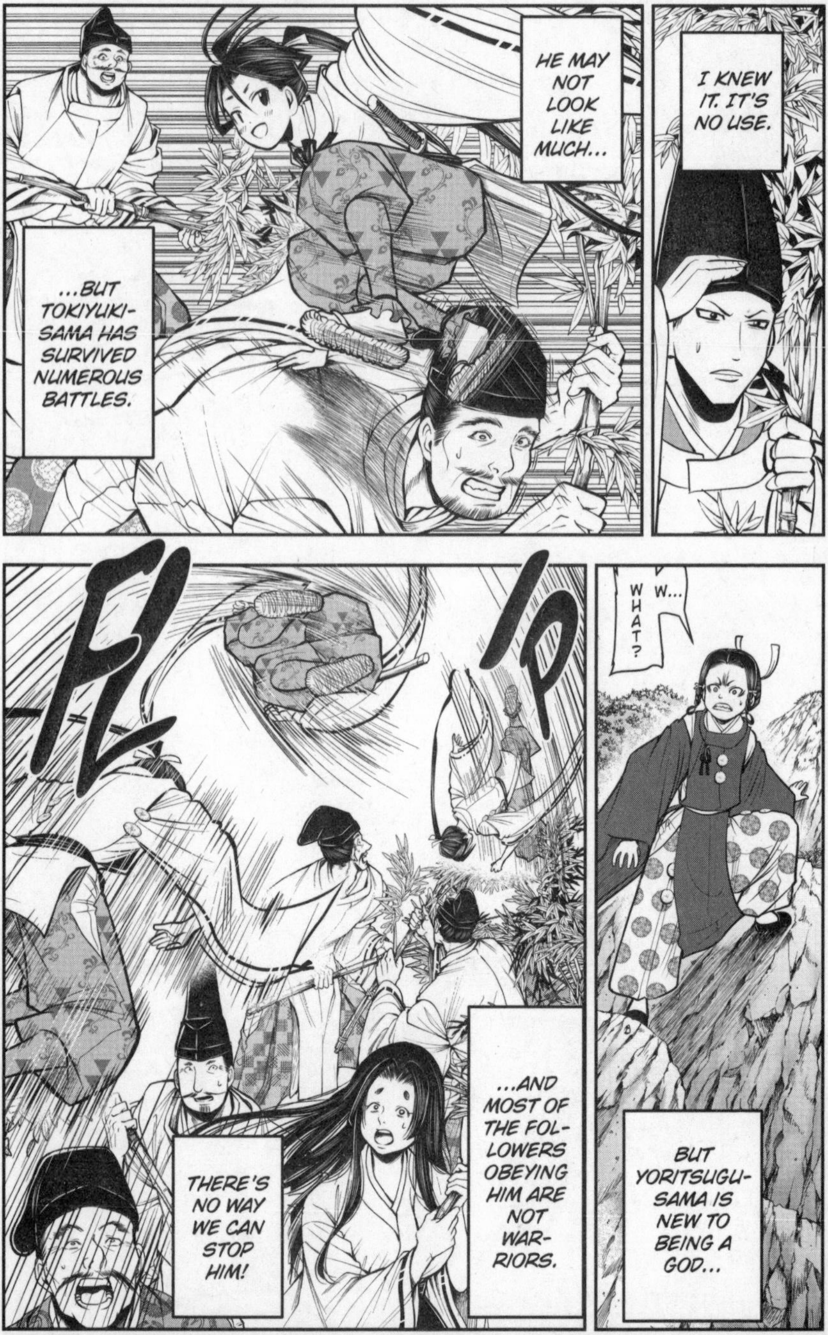
I KNEW IT. IT'S NO USE.
HE MAY NOT LOOK LIKE MUCH...
...BUT TOKIYUKI-SAMA HAS SURVIVED NUMEROUS BATTLES.
W...
WHAT?
BUT YORITSUGU-SAMA IS NEW TO BEING A GOD...
FLIP
...AND MOST OF THE FOL-LOWERS OBEYING HIM ARE NOT WAR-RIORS.
THERE'S NO WAY WE CAN STOP HIM!

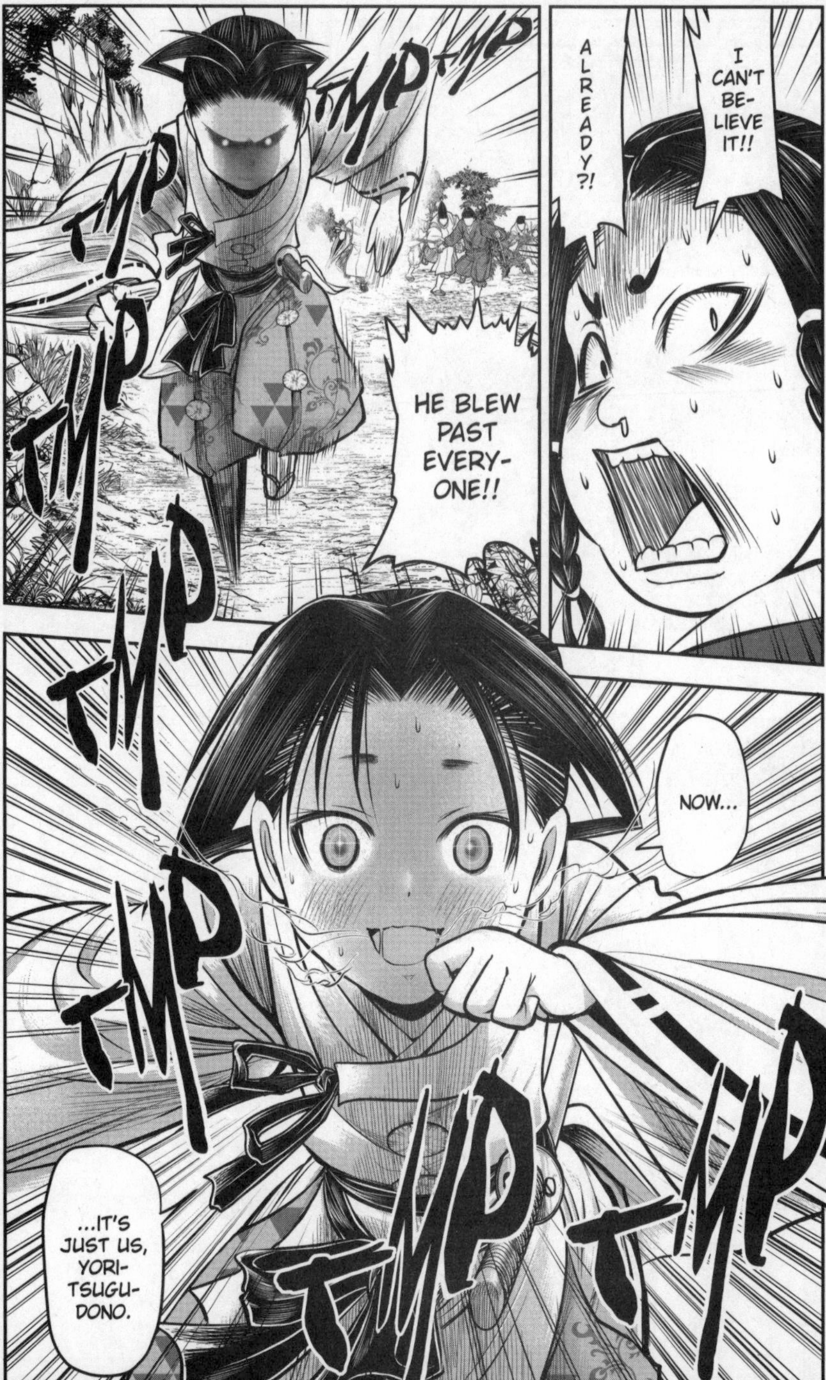
I CAN'T BE-LIEVE IT!!
ALREADY?!
TMP TMP
HE BLEW PAST EVERY-ONE!!
TMP
TMP
TMP
NOW...
TMP
...IT'S JUST US, YORI-TSUGU-DONO.
TMP TMP TMP

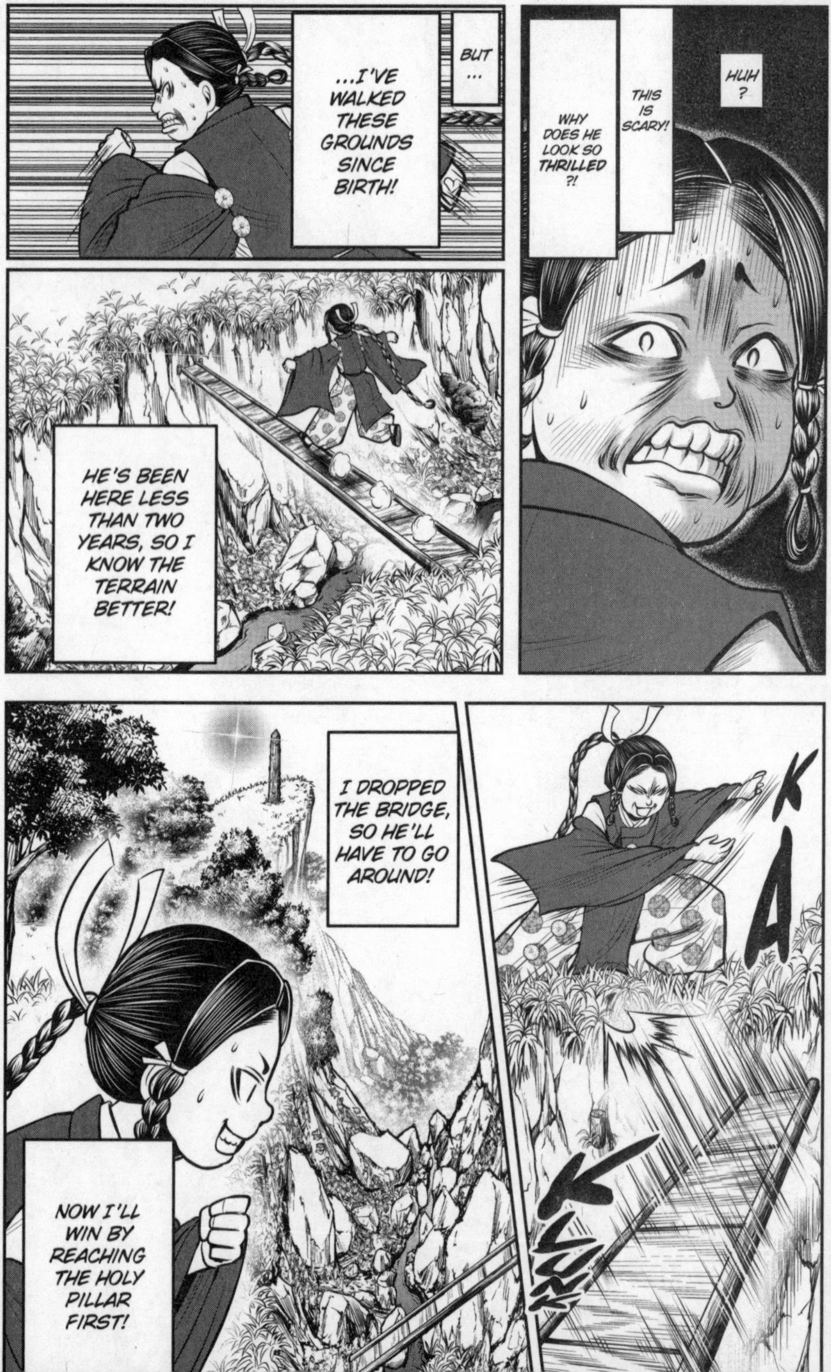
HUH?
THIS IS SCARY!
WHY DOES HE LOOK SO THRILLED?!
BUT...
...I'VE WALKED THESE GROUNDS SINCE BIRTH!
HE'S BEEN HERE LESS THAN TWO YEARS, SO I KNOW THE TERRAIN BETTER!
KA
KLUNK
I DROPPED THE BRIDGE, SO HE'LL HAVE TO GO AROUND!
NOW I'LL WIN BY REACHING THE HOLY PILLAR FIRST!

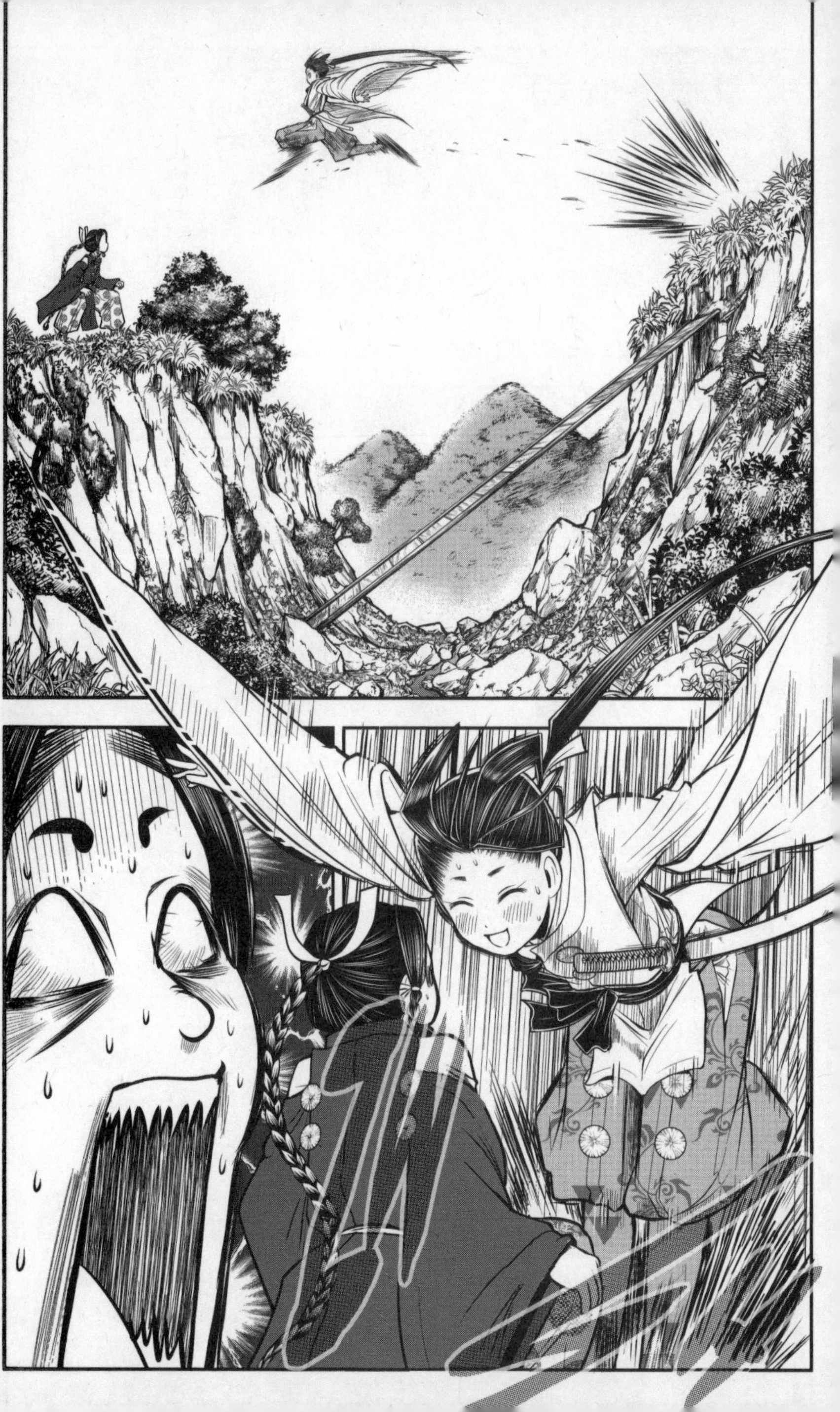

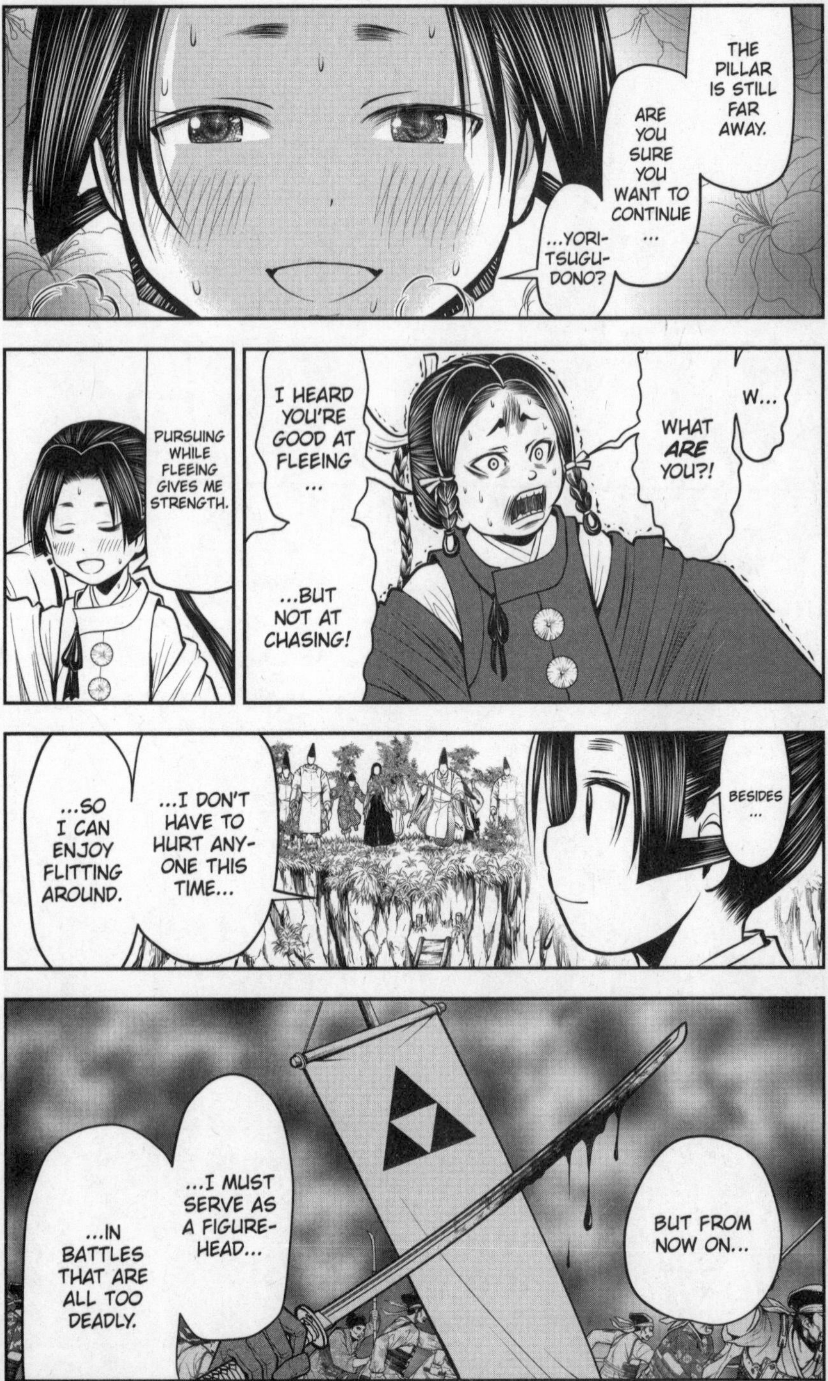
THE PILLAR IS STILL FAR AWAY.
ARE YOU SURE YOU WANT TO CONTINUE ...
...YORI-TSUGU-DONO?
W...
WHAT ARE YOU?!
I HEARD YOU'RE GOOD AT FLEEING ...
...BUT NOT AT CHASING!
PURSUING WHILE FLEEING GIVES ME STRENGTH.
BESIDES ...
...I DON'T HAVE TO HURT ANY-ONE THIS TIME...
...SO I CAN ENJOY FLITTING AROUND.
BUT FROM NOW ON...
...I MUST SERVE AS A FIGURE-HEAD...
...IN BATTLES THAT ARE ALL TOO DEADLY.

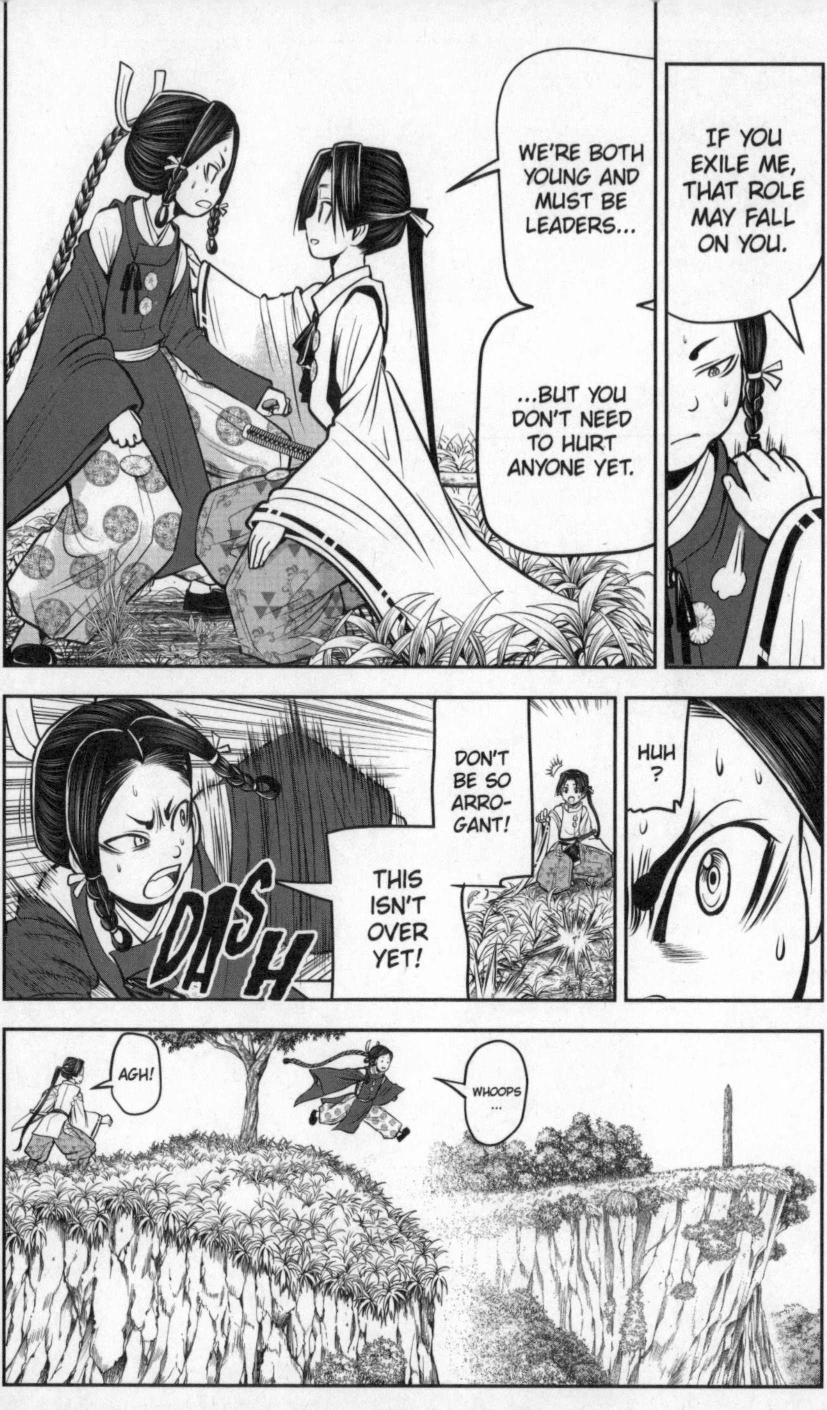
IF YOU EXILE ME, THAT ROLE MAY FALL ON YOU.
WE'RE BOTH YOUNG AND MUST BE LEADERS...
...BUT YOU DON'T NEED TO HURT ANYONE YET.
HUH ?
DON'T BE SO ARRO-GANT!
THIS ISN'T OVER YET!
DASH
WHOOPS ...
AGH!

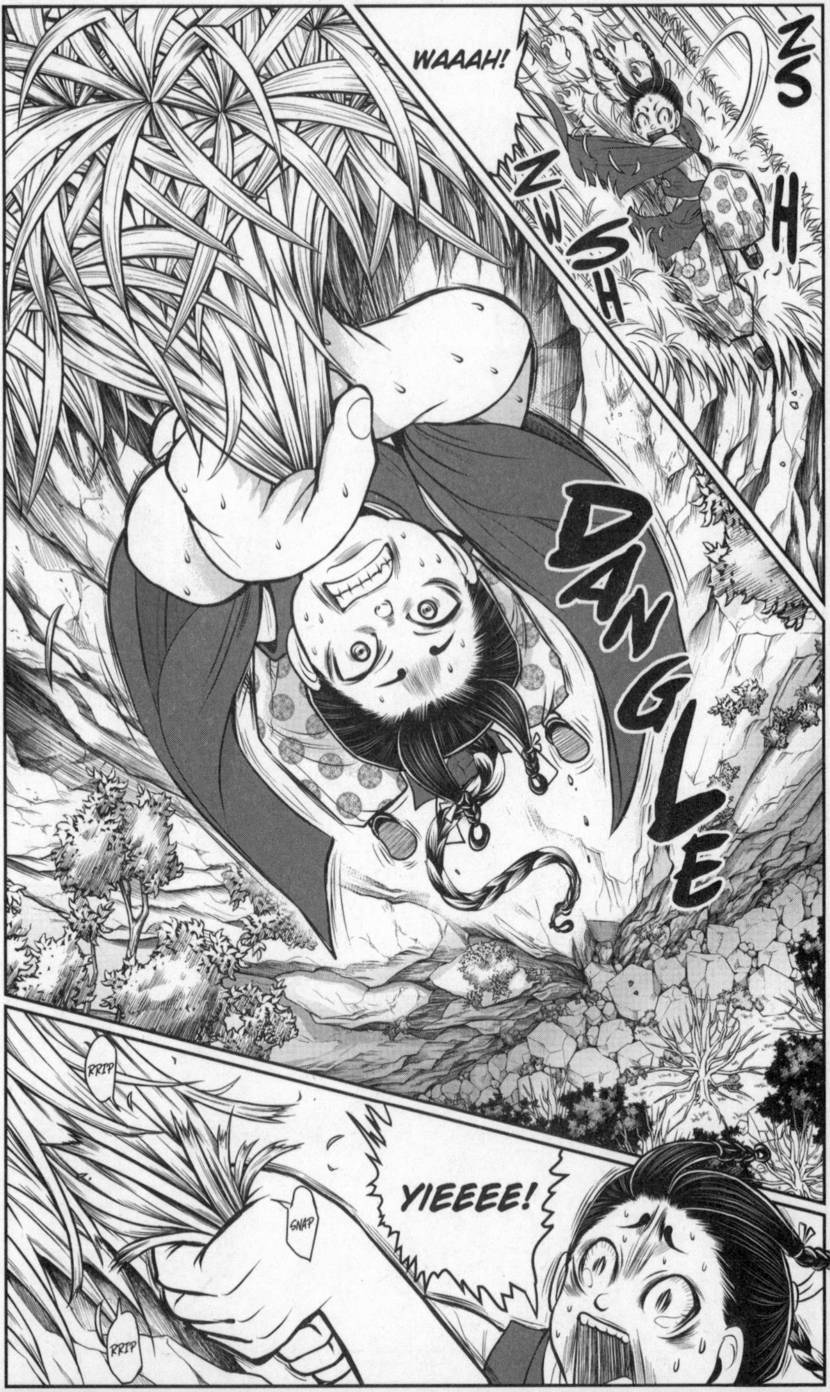
WAAAH!
ZSH
ZWSH
DANGLE
RRIP
YIEEEE!
SNAP
RRIP

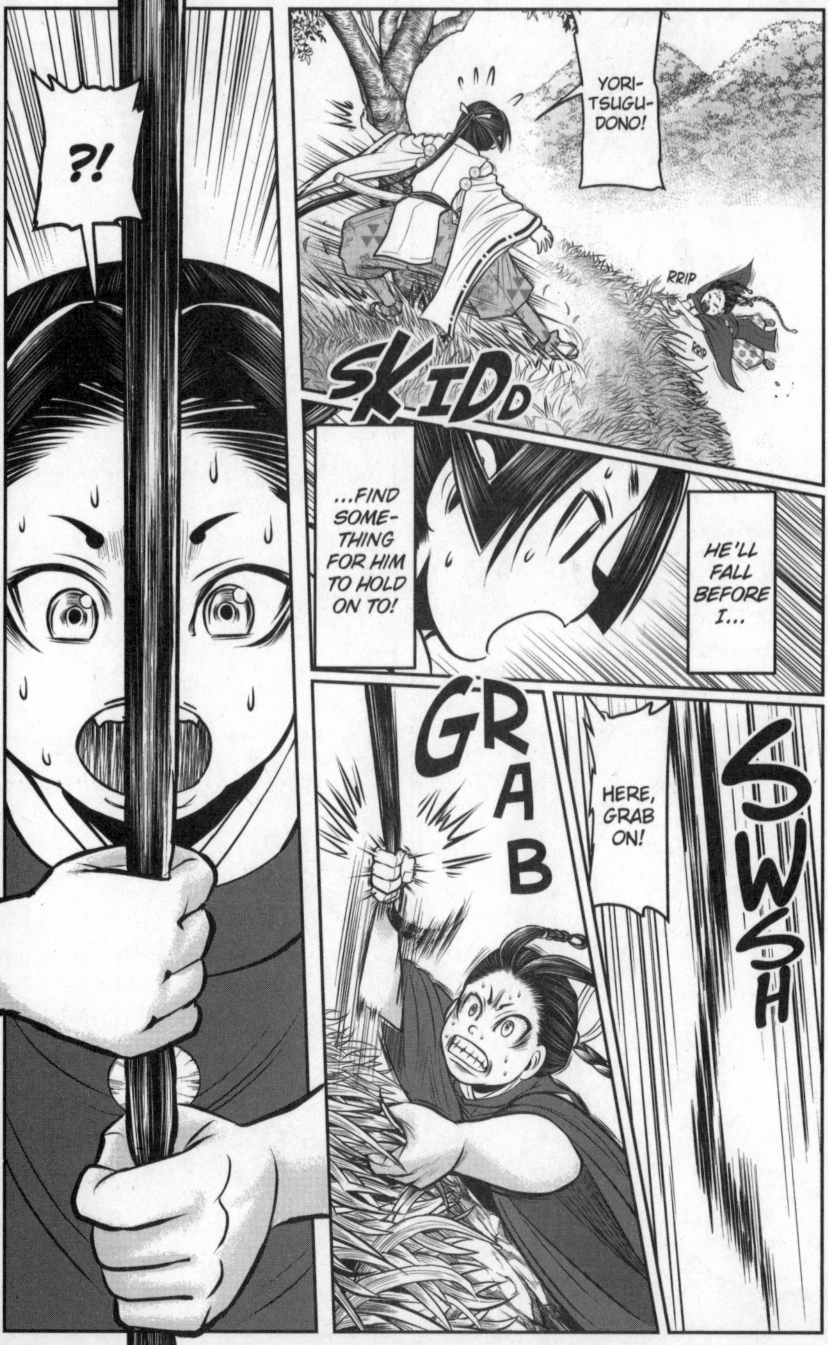
YORI-TSUGU-DONO!
RRIP
RRIP
SKIDD
HE'LL FALL BEFORE I...
...FIND SOMETHING FOR HIM TO HOLD ON TO!
SWSH
HERE, GRAB ON!
GRAB
?!

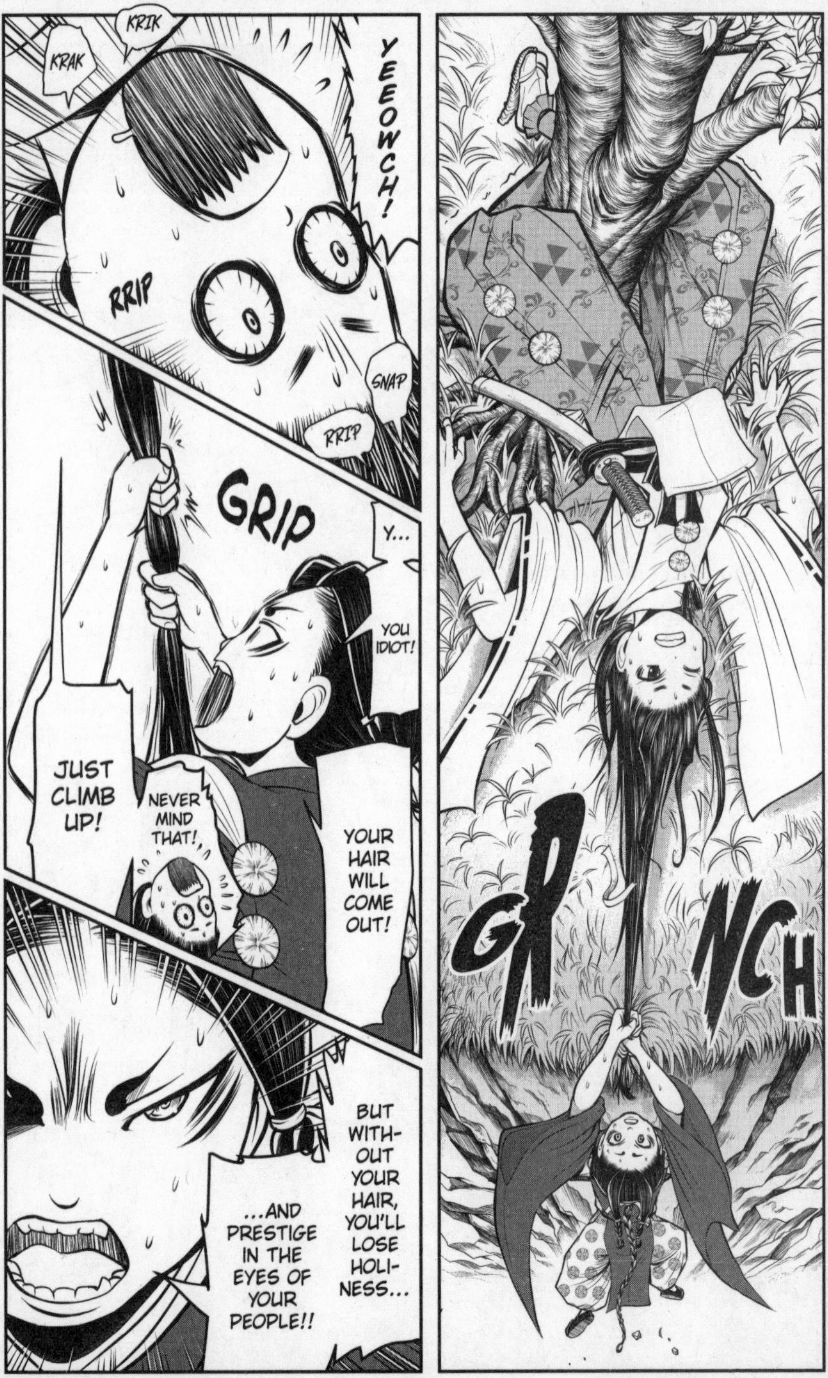
GRINCH
KRIK
KRAK
YEEEOWCH!
RRIP
SNAP
RRIP
GRIP
Y...
YOU IDIOT!
YOUR HAIR WILL COME OUT!
NEVER MIND THAT!
JUST CLIMB UP!
BUT WITH-OUT YOUR HAIR, YOU'LL LOSE HOLI-NESS...
...AND PRESTIGE IN THE EYES OF YOUR PEOPLE!!

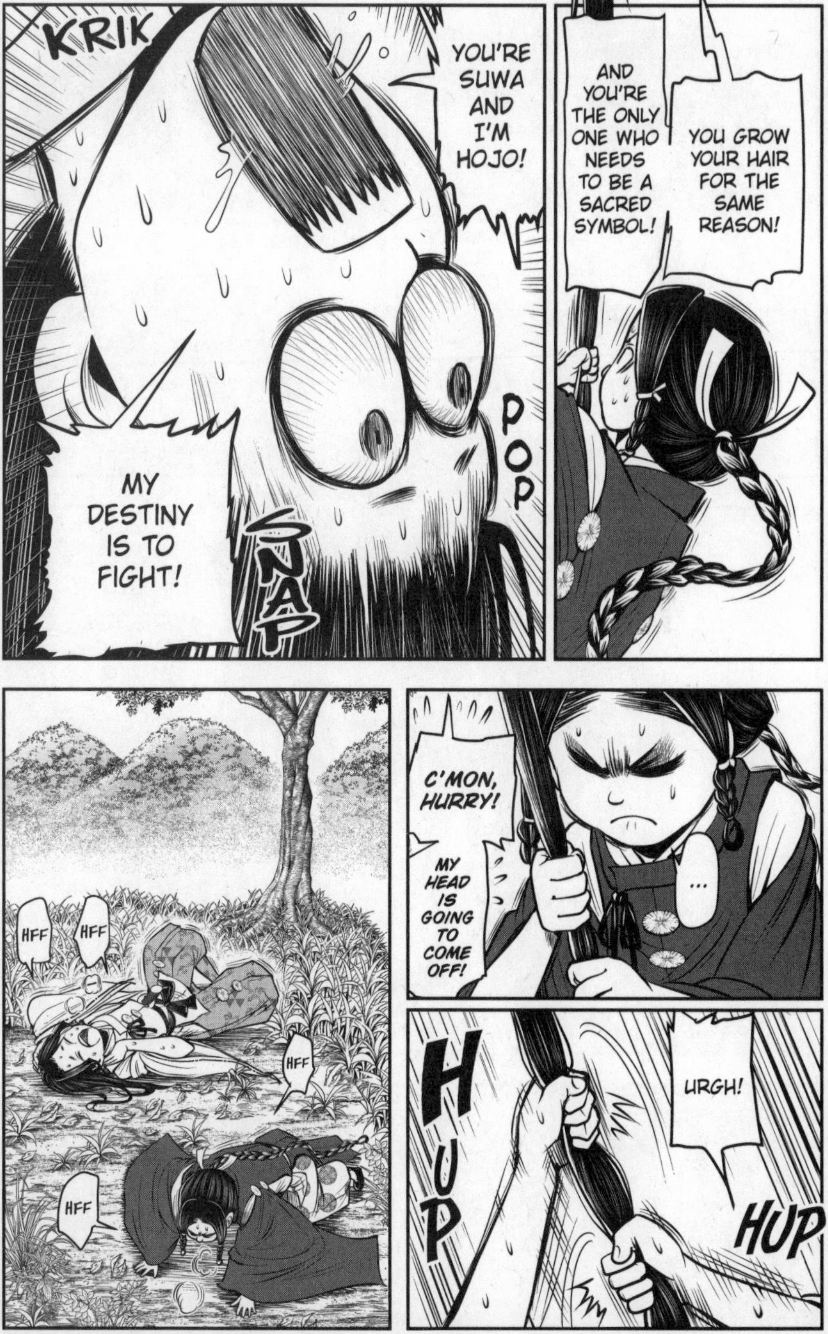
YOU GROW YOUR HAIR FOR THE SAME REASON!
AND YOU'RE THE ONLY ONE WHO NEEDS TO BE A SACRED SYMBOL!
KRIK
YOU'RE SUWA AND I'M HOJO!
POP
MY DESTINY IS TO FIGHT!
SNAP
C'MON, HURRY!
MY HEAD IS GOING TO COME OFF!
...
URGH!
HUP
HUP
HFF
HFF
HFF
HFF

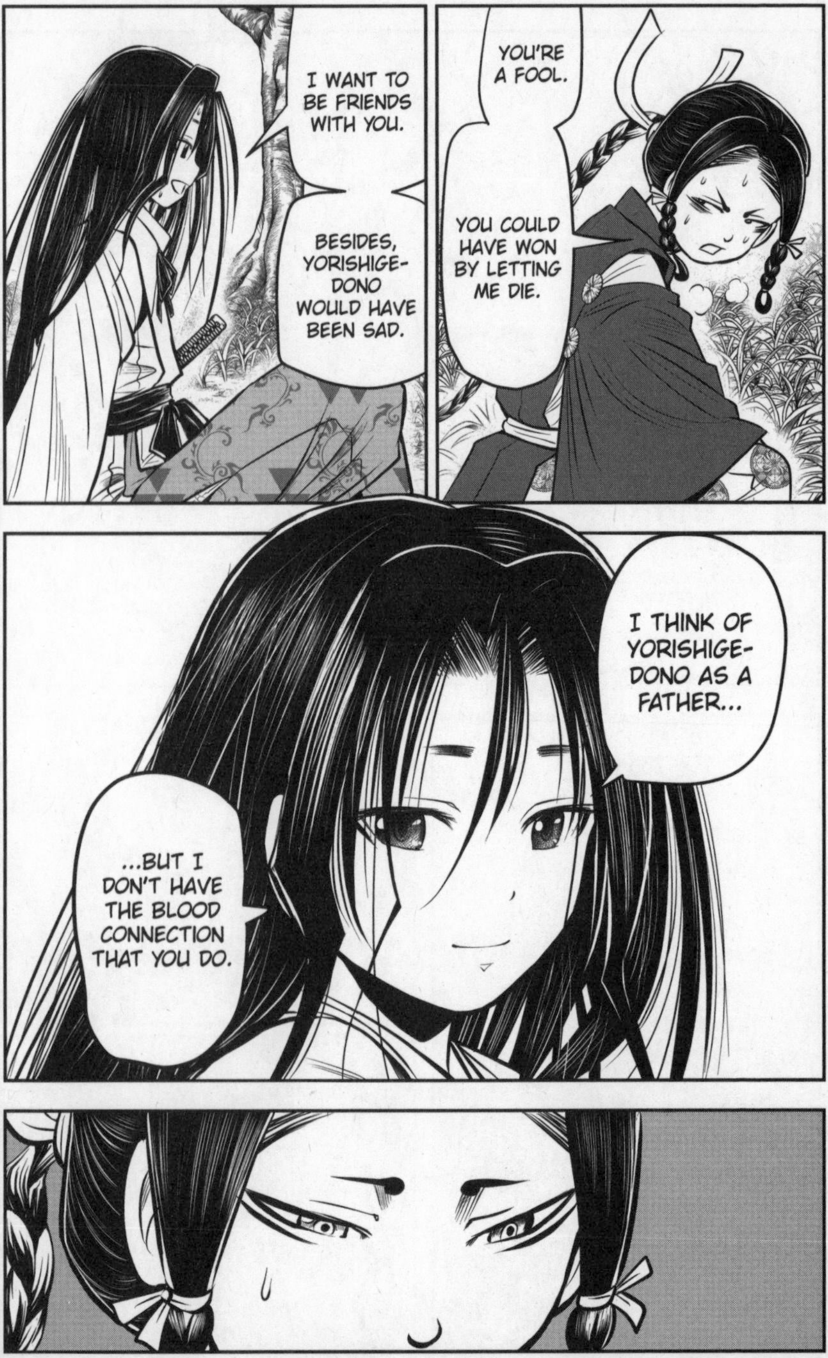
YOU'RE A FOOL.
YOU COULD HAVE WON BY LETTING ME DIE.
I WANT TO BE FRIENDS WITH YOU.
BESIDES, YORISHIGE-DONO WOULD HAVE BEEN SAD.
I THINK OF YORISHIGE-DONO AS A FATHER...
...BUT I DON'T HAVE THE BLOOD CONNECTION THAT YOU DO.

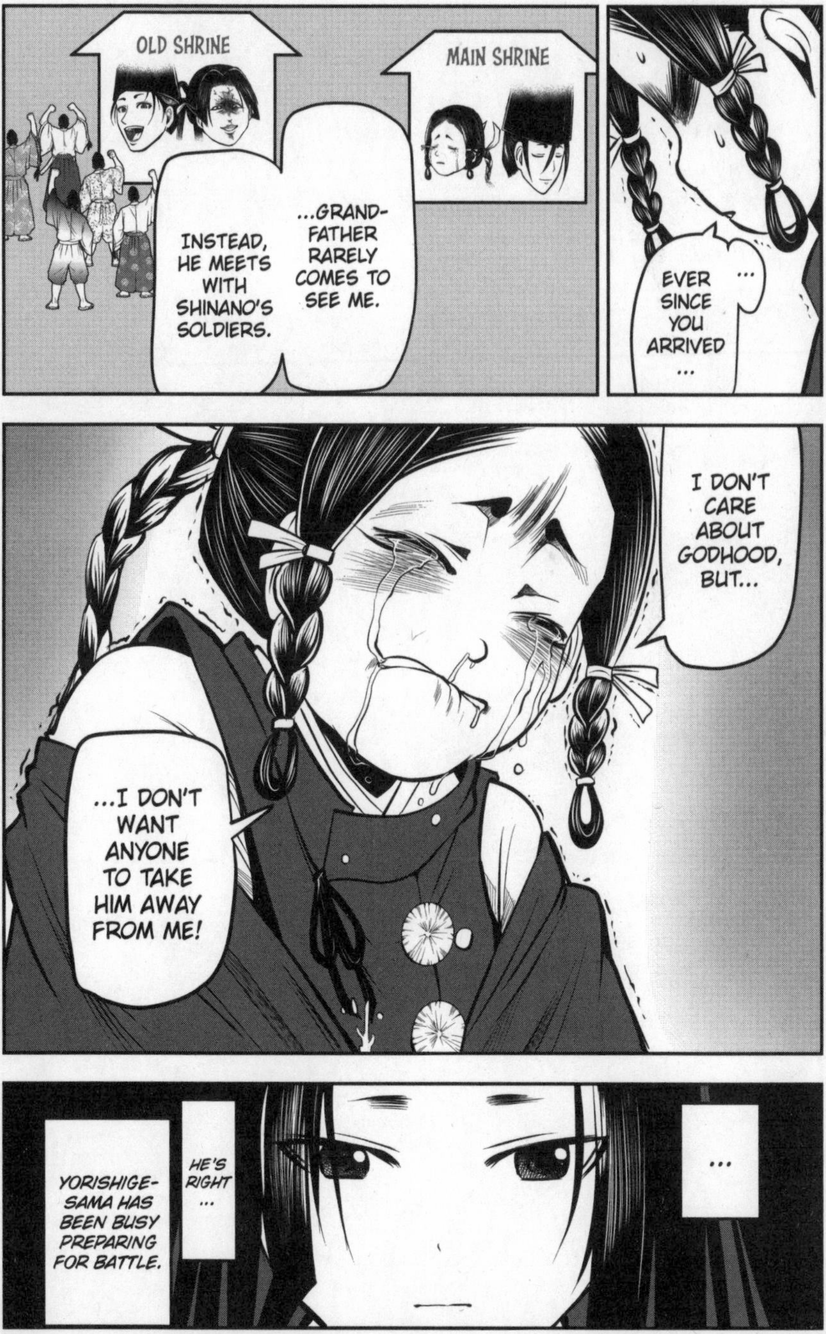
... EVER SINCE YOU ARRIVED ...
MAIN SHRINE
OLD SHRINE
...GRAND-FATHER RARELY COMES TO SEE ME.
INSTEAD, HE MEETS WITH SHINANO'S SOLDIERS.
I DON'T CARE ABOUT GODHOOD, BUT...
...I DON'T WANT ANYONE TO TAKE HIM AWAY FROM ME!
...
HE'S RIGHT ...
YORISHIGE-SAMA HAS BEEN BUSY PREPARING FOR BATTLE.

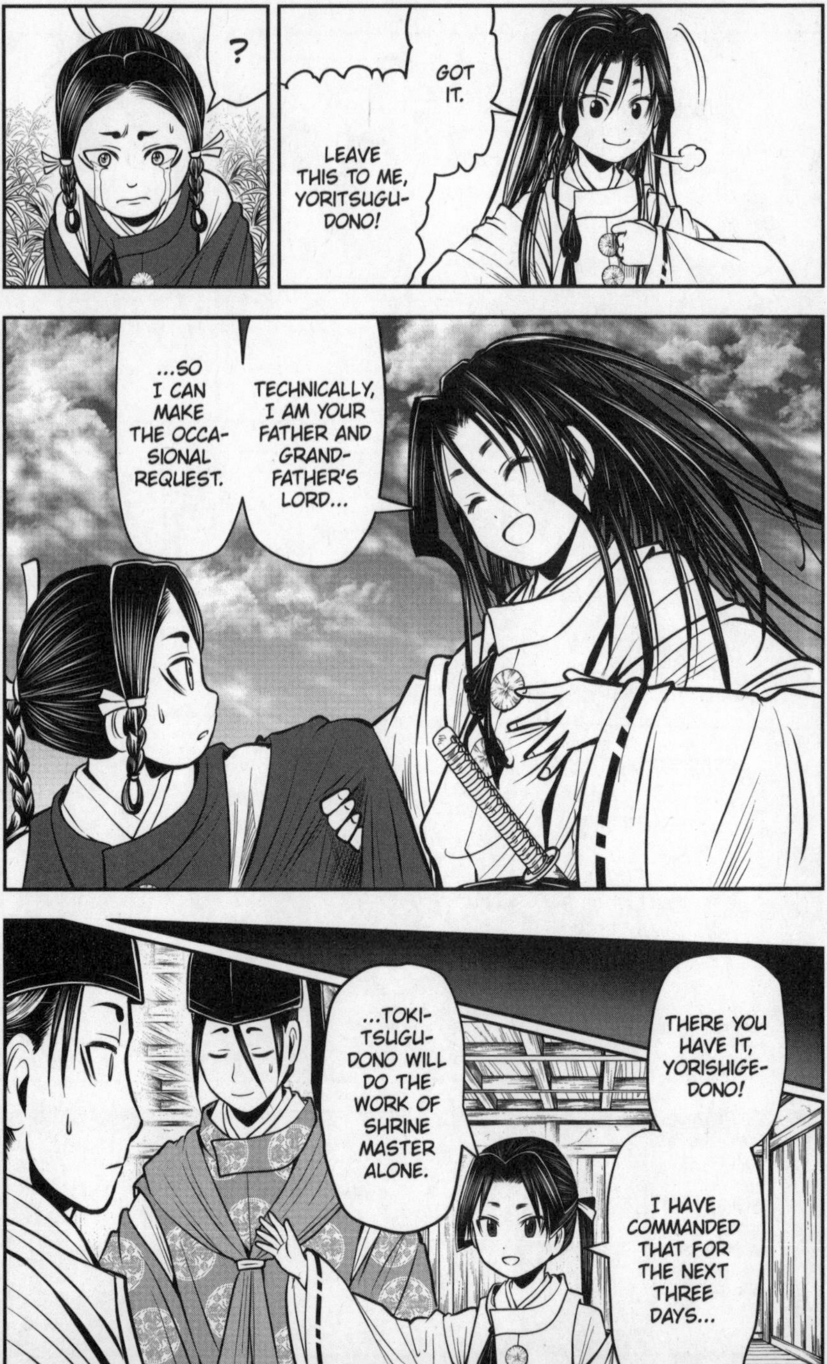
GOT IT.
LEAVE THIS TO ME, YORITSUGU-DONO!
?
TECHNICALLY, I AM YOUR FATHER AND GRAND-FATHER'S LORD...
...SO I CAN MAKE THE OCCA-SIONAL REQUEST.
THERE YOU HAVE IT, YORISHIGE-DONO!
I HAVE COMMANDED THAT FOR THE NEXT THREE DAYS...
...TOKI-TSUGU-DONO WILL DO THE WORK OF SHRINE MASTER ALONE.

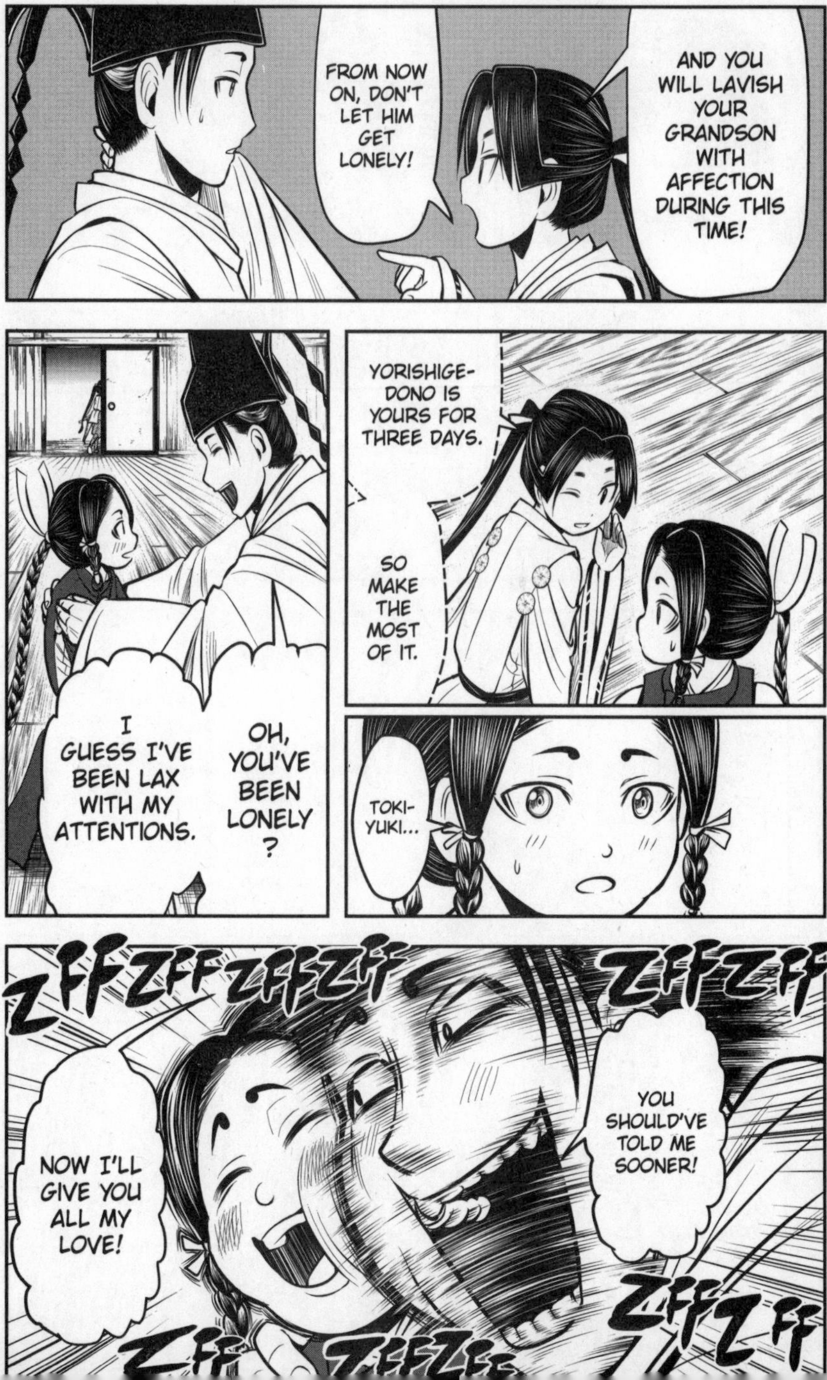
FROM NOW ON, DON'T LET HIM GET LONELY!
AND YOU WILL LAVISH YOUR GRANDSON WITH AFFECTION DURING THIS TIME!
YORISHIGE-DONO IS YOURS FOR THREE DAYS.
SO MAKE THE MOST OF IT.
TOKI-YUKI...
OH, YOU'VE BEEN LONELY?
I GUESS I'VE BEEN LAX WITH MY ATTENTIONS.
ZFF ZFF
YOU SHOULD'VE TOLD ME SOONER!
ZFF ZFF ZFF ZFF
NOW I'LL GIVE YOU ALL MY LOVE!
ZFF ZFF
ZFF ZFF ZFF

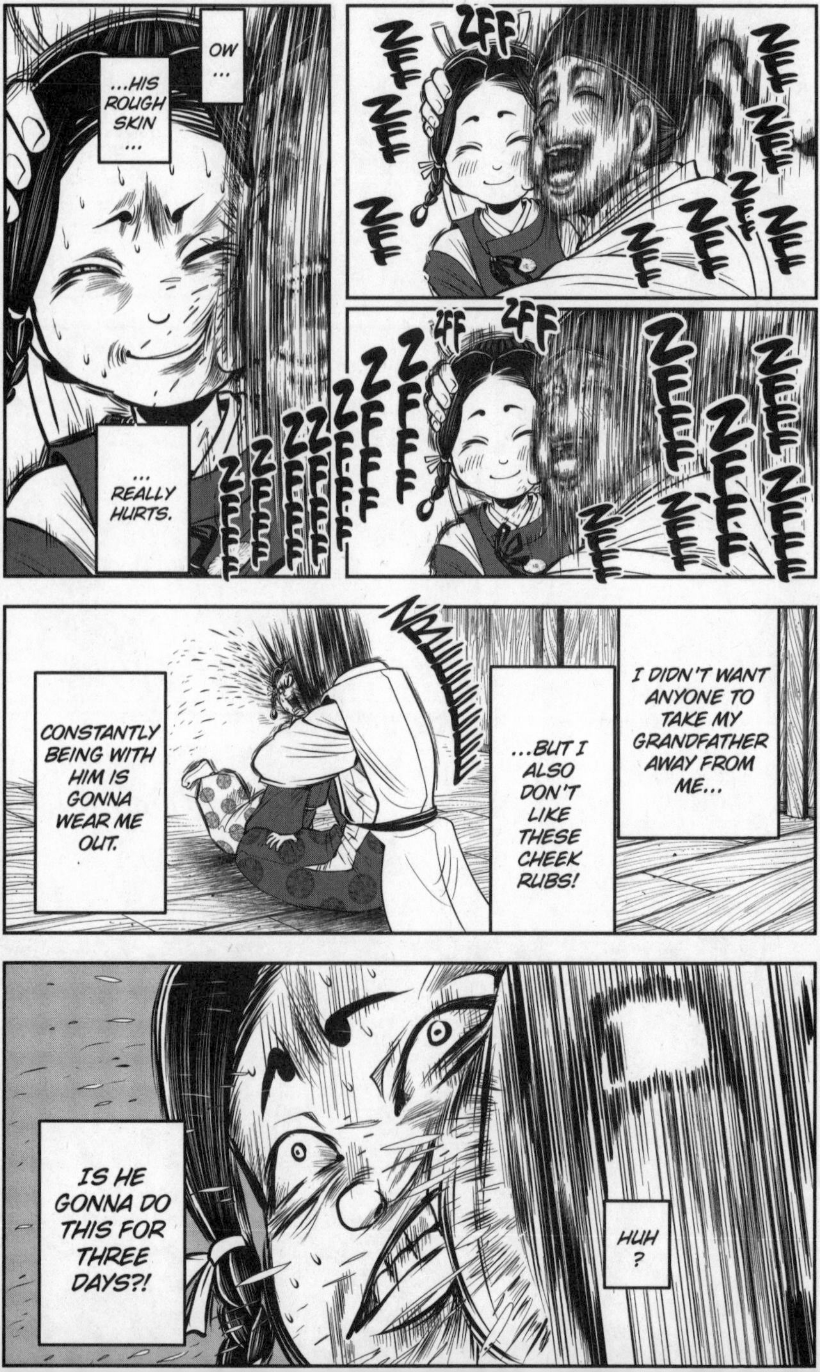

ZFF
ZEFF ZEFF ZEFF ZEFF ZEFF ZEFF ZEFF ZEFF ZEFF
ZFF ZFF
ZEFF ZEFF ZEFF ZEFF ZEFF ZEFF
ZFFF ZFFFF ZFFFF ZFFFF ZFFFF ZFFF ZFFF
OW ...
...HIS ROUGH SKIN ...
... REALLY HURTS.
I DIDN'T WANT ANYONE TO TAKE MY GRANDFATHER AWAY FROM ME...
...BUT I ALSO DON'T LIKE THESE CHEEK RUBS!
CONSTANTLY BEING WITH HIM IS GONNA WEAR ME OUT.
HUH ?
IS HE GONNA DO THIS FOR THREE DAYS?!

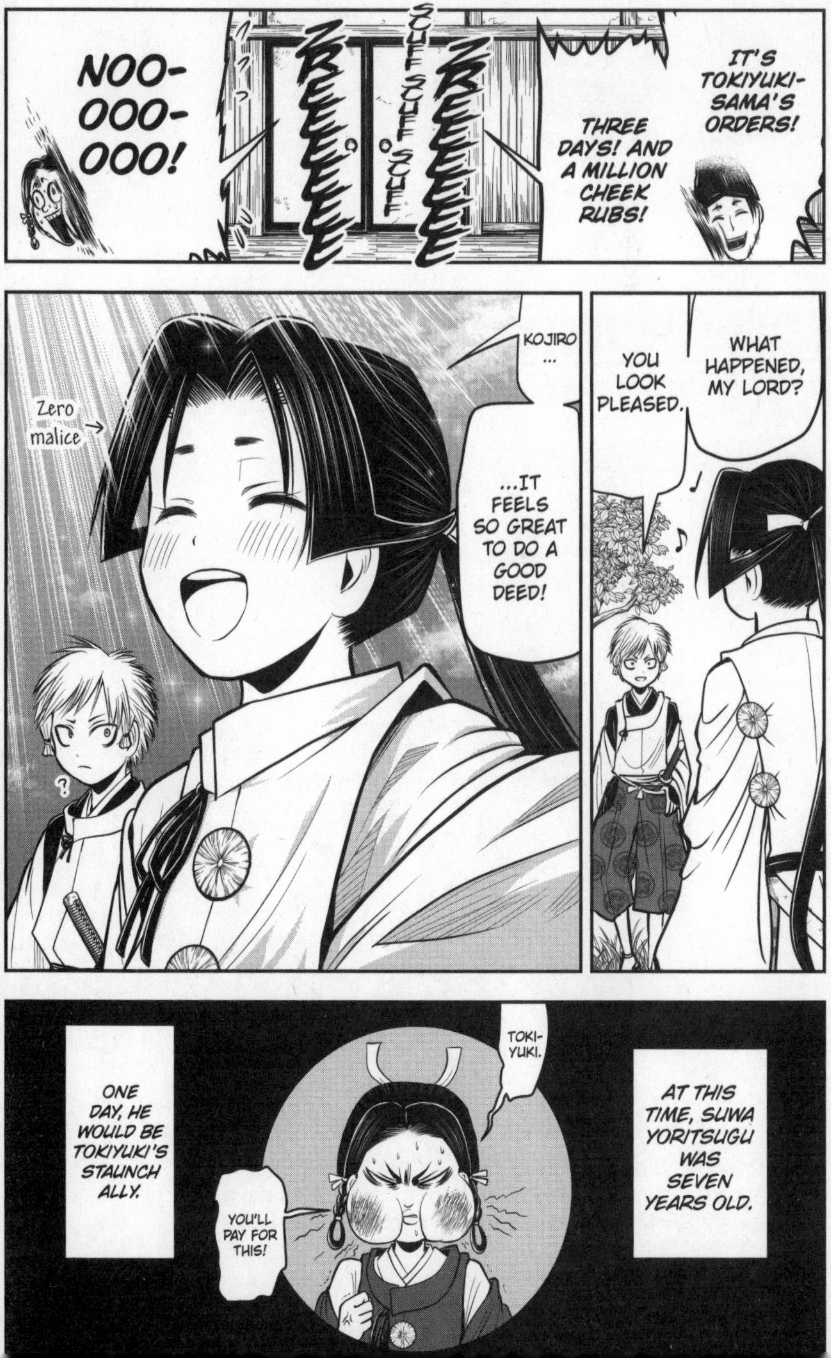
IT'S TOKIYUKI-SAMA'S ORDERS!
THREE DAYS! AND A MILLION CHEEK RUBS!
ZREEEEEEE
SCUFF SCUFF SCUFF
ZREEEEEEE
NOO-OOO-OOO!
WHAT HAPPENED, MY LORD?
YOU LOOK PLEASED.
KOJIRO ...
...IT FEELS SO GREAT TO DO A GOOD DEED!
Zero malice
AT THIS TIME, SUWA YORITSUGU WAS SEVEN YEARS OLD.
TOKI-YUKI.
YOU'LL PAY FOR THIS!
ONE DAY, HE WOULD BE TOKIYUKI'S STAUNCH ALLY.

YORISHIGE'S AGING SKIN

It's equal to about 1500-grit sandpaper. A cheek rub lasting a few minutes isn't so bad, but after three days and three nights, the victim's skin begins to tear, flesh rips, and bones break. Yorishige himself, however, has divine protection, so he suffers zero damage.

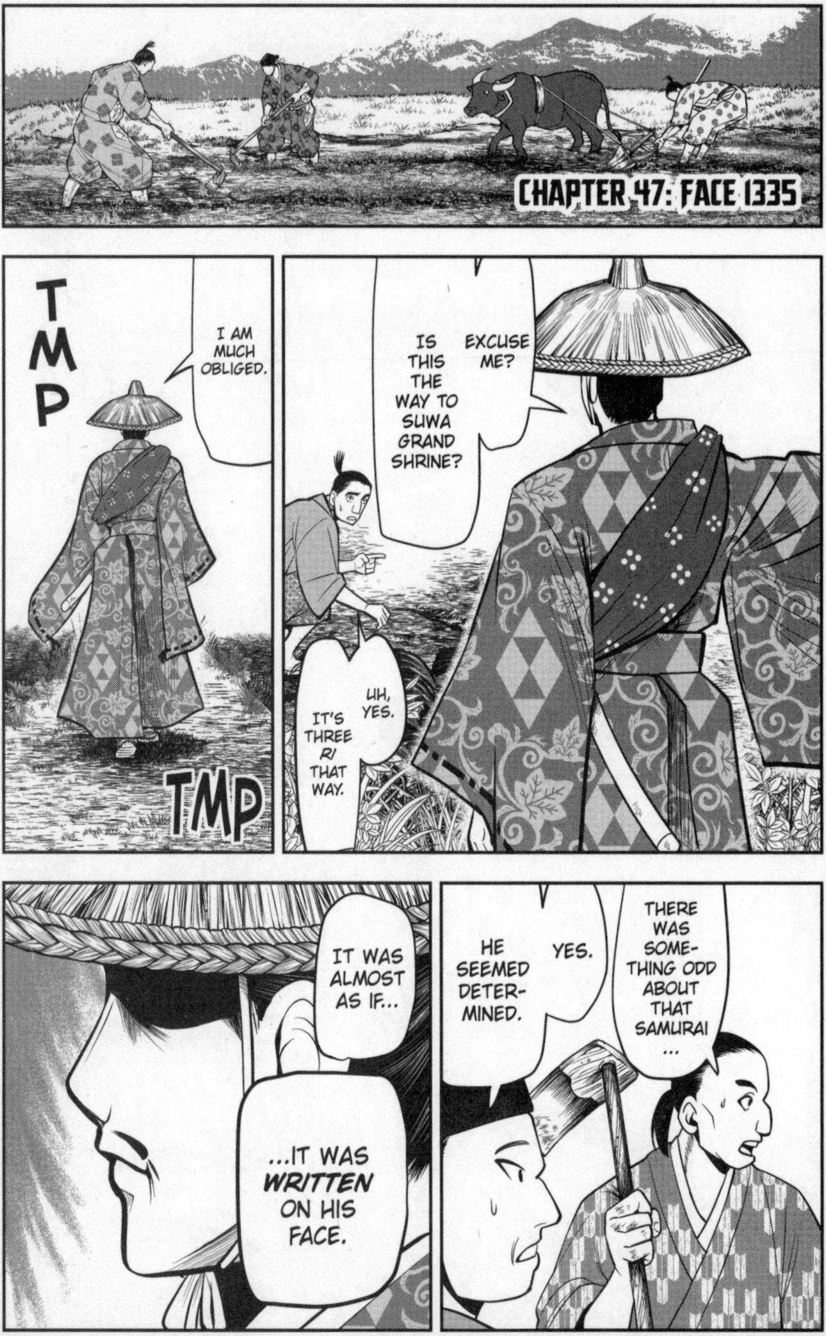
CHAPTER 47: FACE 1335
EXCUSE ME?
IS THIS THE WAY TO SUWA GRAND SHRINE?
UH, YES.
IT'S THREE *RI* THAT WAY.
I AM MUCH OBLIGED.
TMP
TMP
THERE WAS SOME-THING ODD ABOUT THAT SAMURAI ...
YES.
HE SEEMED DETER-MINED.
IT WAS ALMOST AS IF...
...IT WAS **WRITTEN** ON HIS FACE.

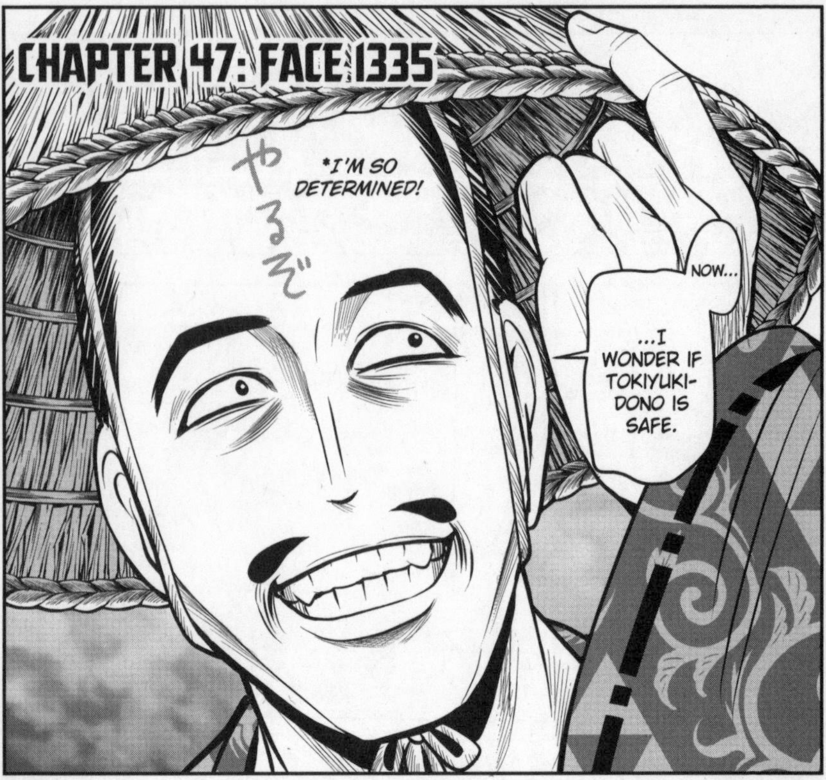
CHAPTER 47: FACE 1335
NOW...
...I WONDER IF TOKIYUKI-DONO IS SAFE.
やるぞ
*I'M SO DETERMINED!

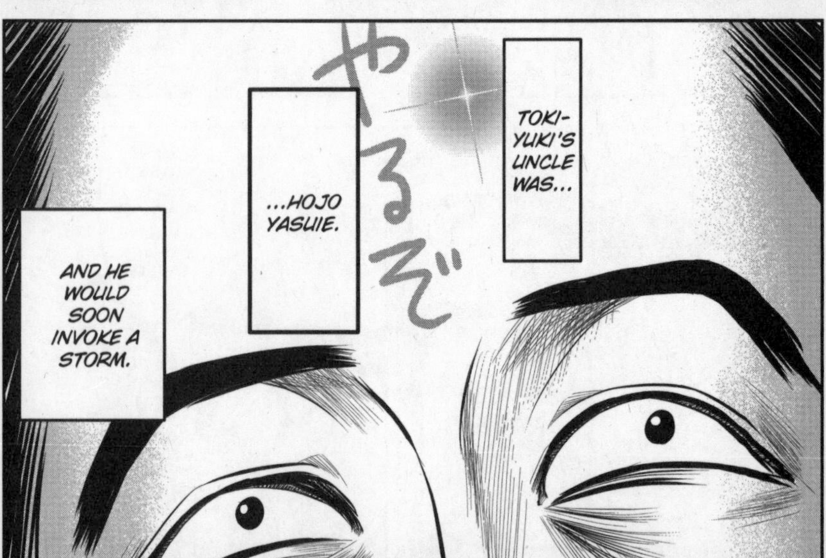
TOKI-YUKI'S UNCLE WAS...
...HOJO YASUIE.
やるぞ
AND HE WOULD SOON INVOKE A STORM.

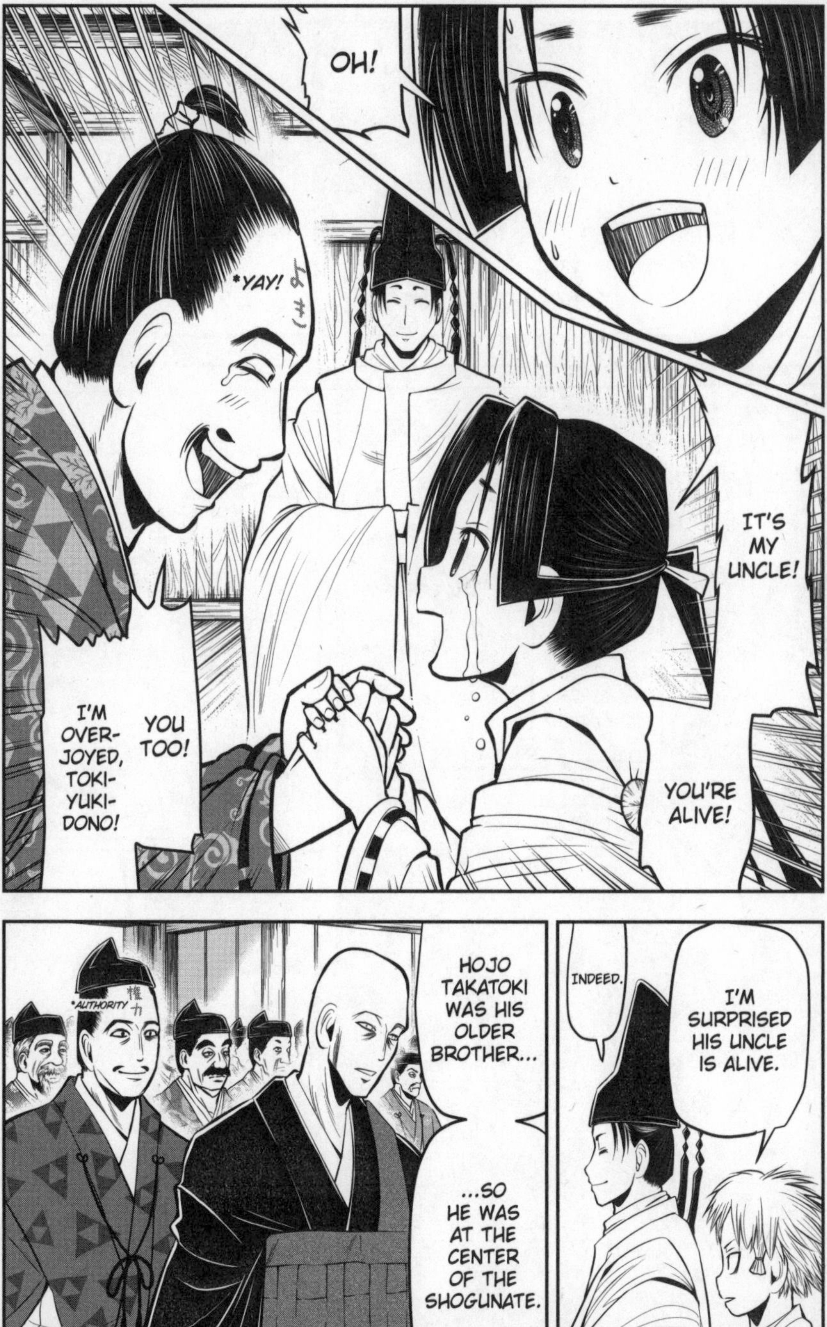
OH!
IT'S MY UNCLE!
YOU'RE ALIVE!
*YAY! よき
YOU TOO!
I'M OVER-JOYED, TOKI-YUKI-DONO!
I'M SURPRISED HIS UNCLE IS ALIVE.
INDEED.
HOJO TAKATOKI WAS HIS OLDER BROTHER...
...SO HE WAS AT THE CENTER OF THE SHOGUNATE.
*AUTHORITY 権力

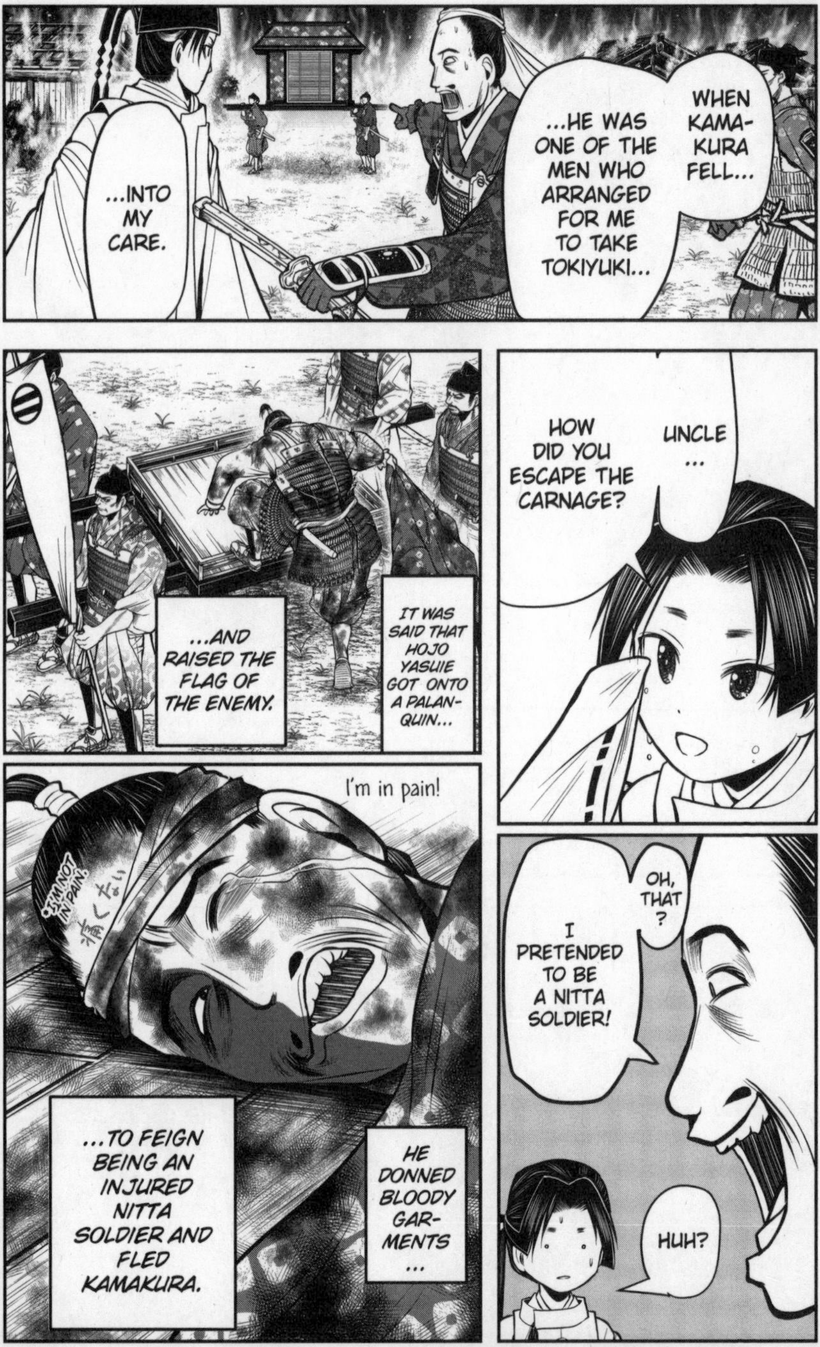
WHEN KAMA-KURA FELL...
...HE WAS ONE OF THE MEN WHO ARRANGED FOR ME TO TAKE TOKIYUKI...
...INTO MY CARE.
UNCLE...
HOW DID YOU ESCAPE THE CARNAGE?
IT WAS SAID THAT HOJO YASUIE GOT ONTO A PALAN-QUIN...
...AND RAISED THE FLAG OF THE ENEMY.
OH, THAT?
I PRETENDED TO BE A NITTA SOLDIER!
HUH?
I'm in pain!
痛くない
I'M NOT IN PAIN.
HE DONNED BLOODY GAR-MENTS...
...TO FEIGN BEING AN INJURED NITTA SOLDIER AND FLED KAMAKURA.

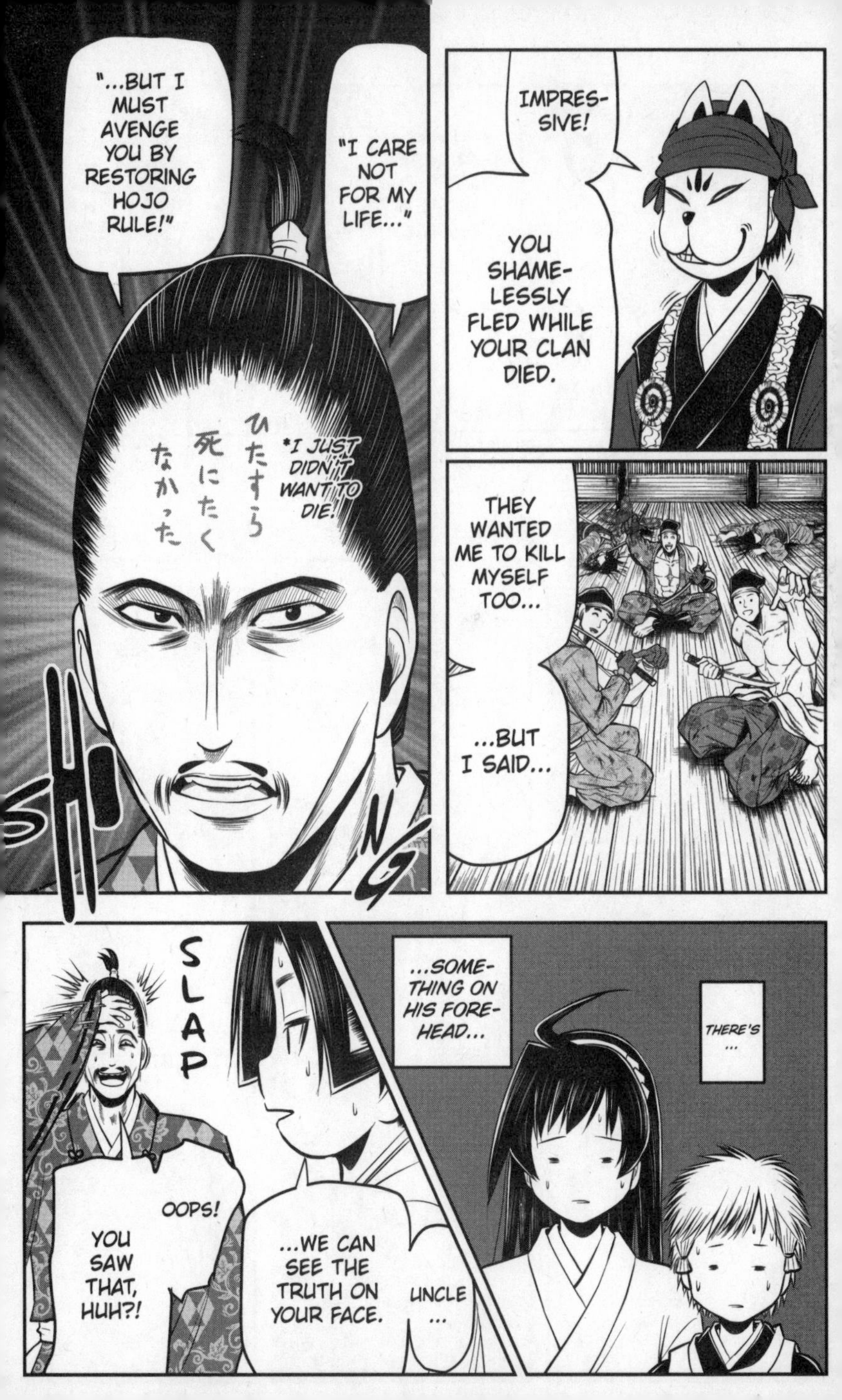
IMPRES-SIVE!
YOU SHAME-LESSLY FLED WHILE YOUR CLAN DIED.
THEY WANTED ME TO KILL MYSELF TOO...
...BUT I SAID...
"I CARE NOT FOR MY LIFE..."
"...BUT I MUST AVENGE YOU BY RESTORING HOJO RULE!"
ひたすら死にたくなかった
*I JUST DIDN'T WANT TO DIE!
SHING
THERE'S ...
...SOME-THING ON HIS FORE-HEAD...
UNCLE ...
...WE CAN SEE THE TRUTH ON YOUR FACE.
SLAP
OOPS!
YOU SAW THAT, HUH?!

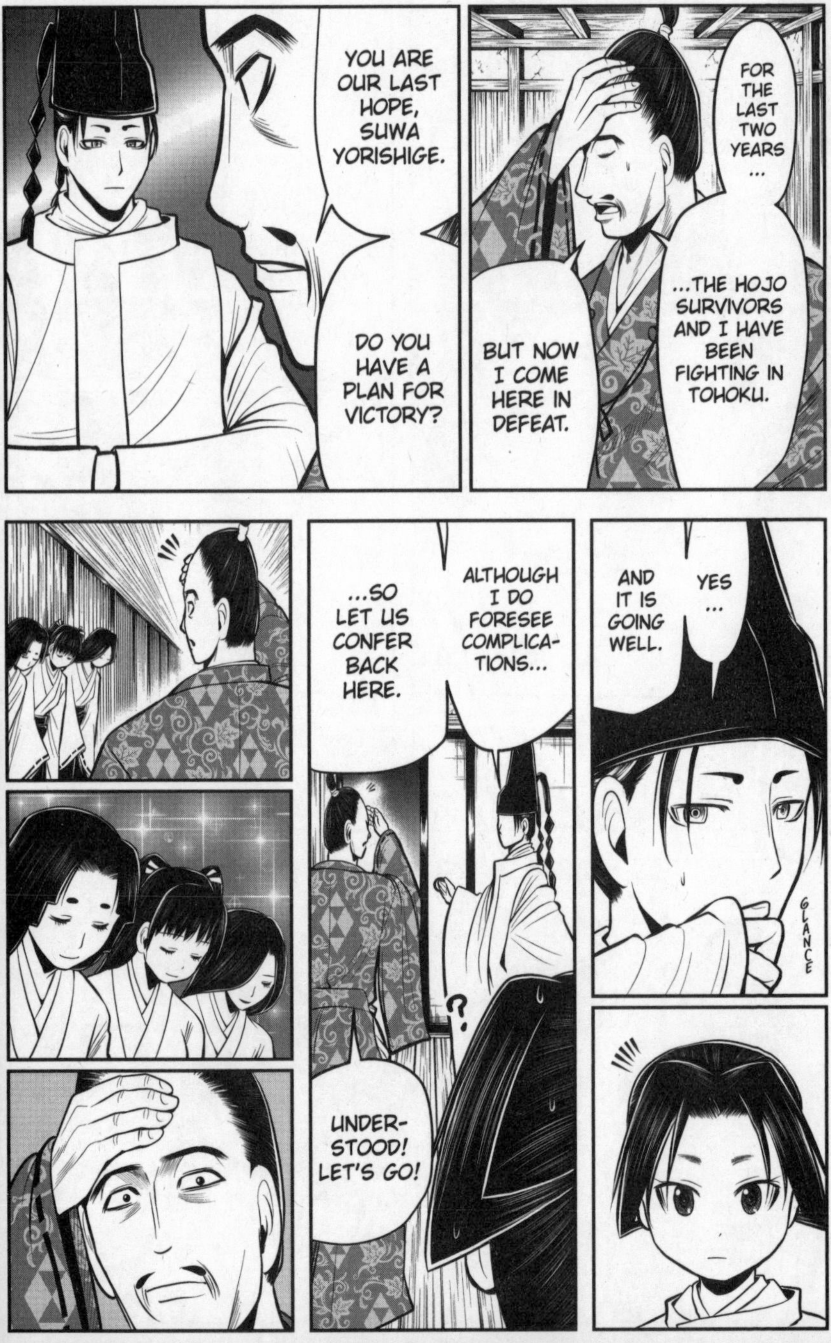
FOR THE LAST TWO YEARS...
...THE HOJO SURVIVORS AND I HAVE BEEN FIGHTING IN TOHOKU.
BUT NOW I COME HERE IN DEFEAT.
YOU ARE OUR LAST HOPE, SUWA YORISHIGE.
DO YOU HAVE A PLAN FOR VICTORY?
YES...
AND IT IS GOING WELL.
GLANCE
ALTHOUGH I DO FORESEE COMPLICATIONS...
...SO LET US CONFER BACK HERE.
?
UNDERSTOOD! LET'S GO!

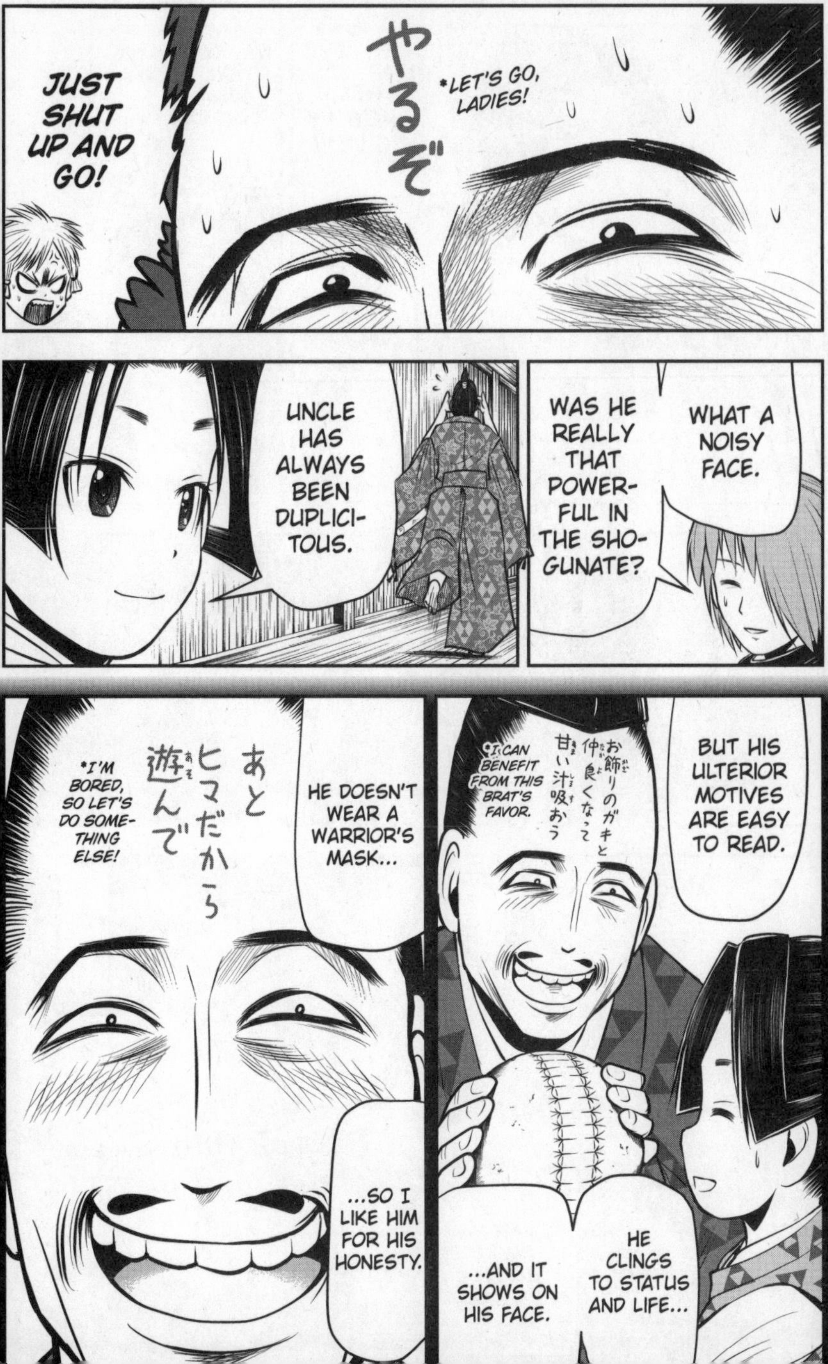
やるぞ
*LET'S GO, LADIES!
JUST SHUT UP AND GO!
WHAT A NOISY FACE.
WAS HE REALLY THAT POWERFUL IN THE SHOGUNATE?
UNCLE HAS ALWAYS BEEN DUPLICITOUS.
BUT HIS ULTERIOR MOTIVES ARE EASY TO READ.
お飾りのガキと仲良くなって甘い汁吸おう
*I CAN BENEFIT FROM THIS BRAT'S FAVOR.
HE CLINGS TO STATUS AND LIFE...
...AND IT SHOWS ON HIS FACE.
HE DOESN'T WEAR A WARRIOR'S MASK...
あとヒマだから遊んで
*I'M BORED, SO LET'S DO SOMETHING ELSE!
...SO I LIKE HIM FOR HIS HONESTY.

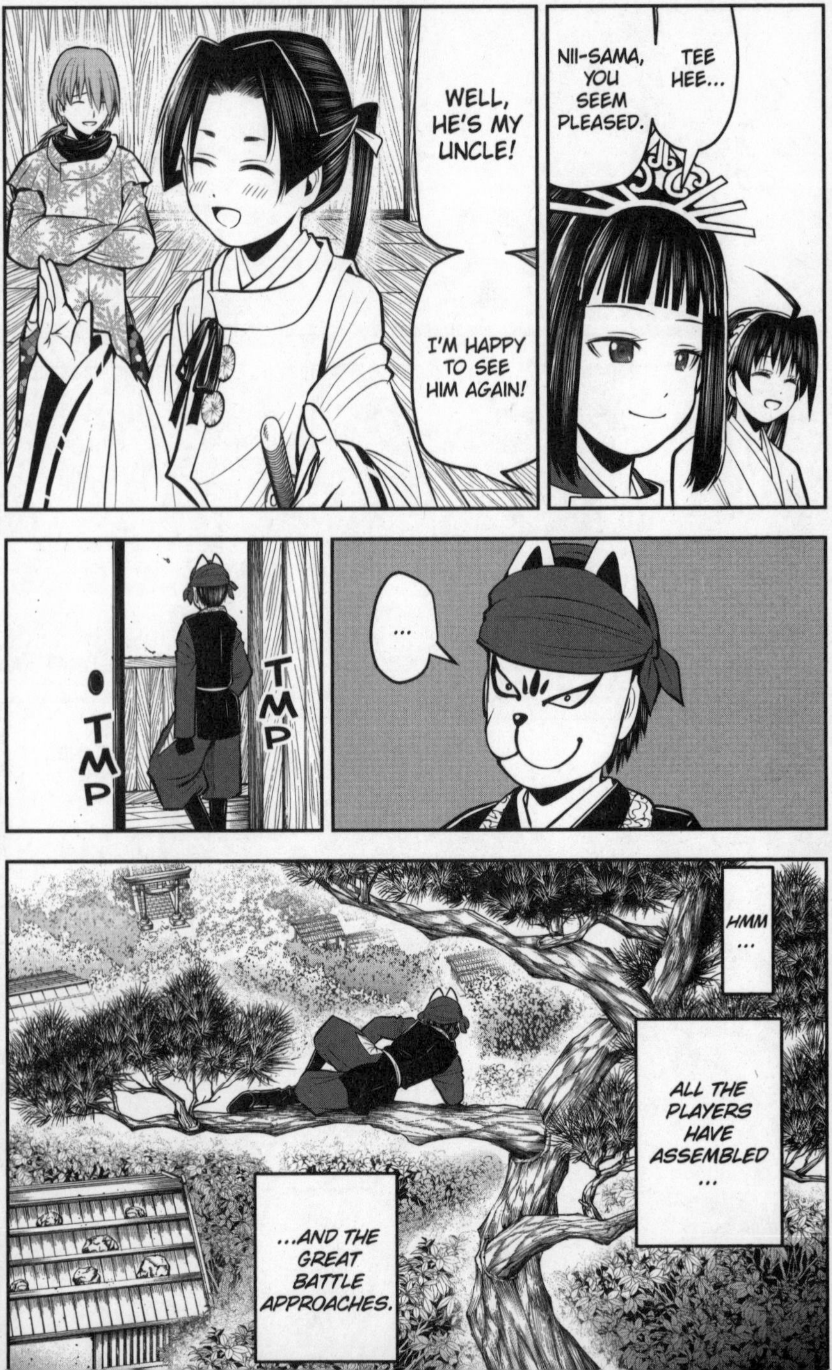
TEE HEE...
NII-SAMA, YOU SEEM PLEASED.
WELL, HE'S MY UNCLE!
I'M HAPPY TO SEE HIM AGAIN!
...
TMP
TMP
HMM...
ALL THE PLAYERS HAVE ASSEMBLED...
...AND THE GREAT BATTLE APPROACHES.

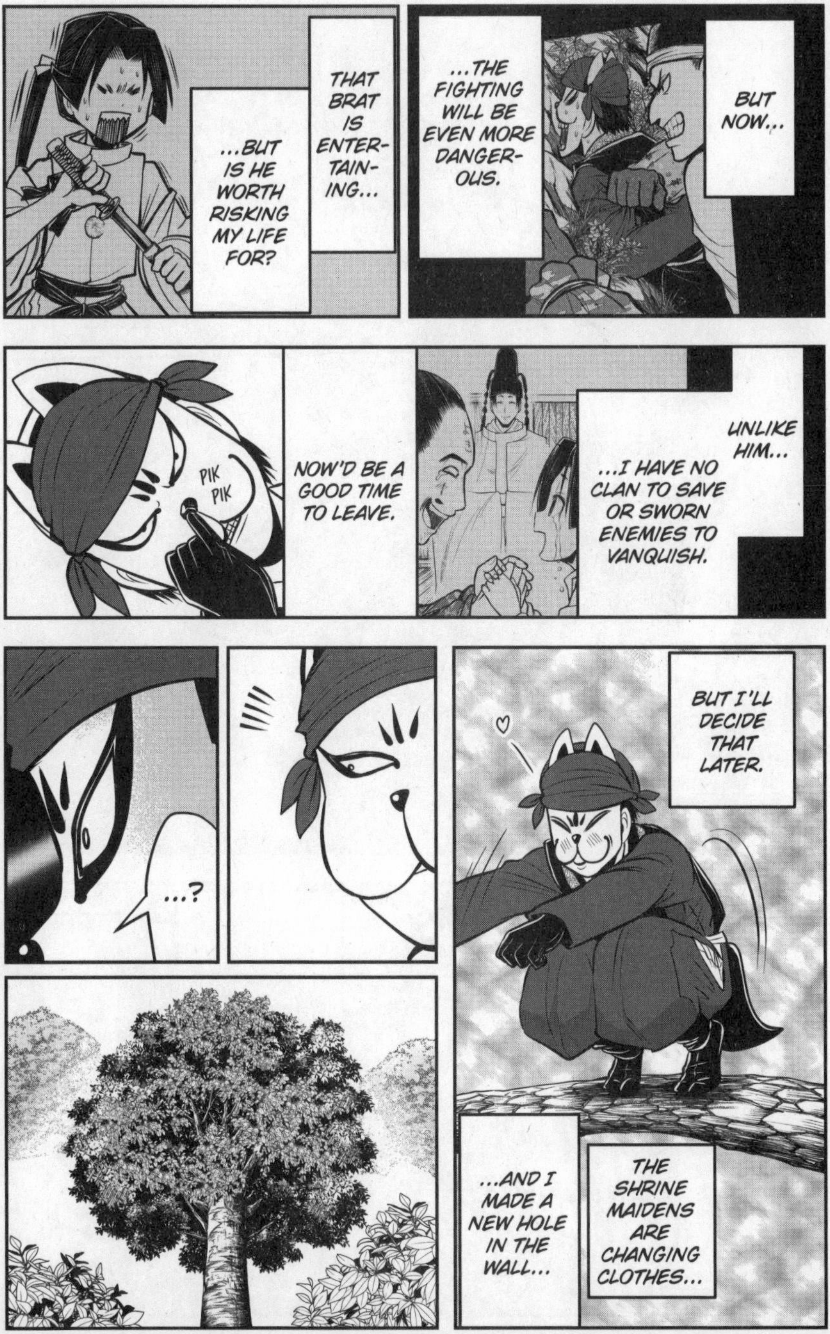

BUT NOW...
...THE FIGHTING WILL BE EVEN MORE DANGER-OUS.
THAT BRAT IS ENTER-TAIN-ING...
...BUT IS HE WORTH RISKING MY LIFE FOR?
UNLIKE HIM...
...I HAVE NO CLAN TO SAVE OR SWORN ENEMIES TO VANQUISH.
NOW'D BE A GOOD TIME TO LEAVE.
PIK PIK
BUT I'LL DECIDE THAT LATER.
THE SHRINE MAIDENS ARE CHANGING CLOTHES...
...AND I MADE A NEW HOLE IN THE WALL...
...?

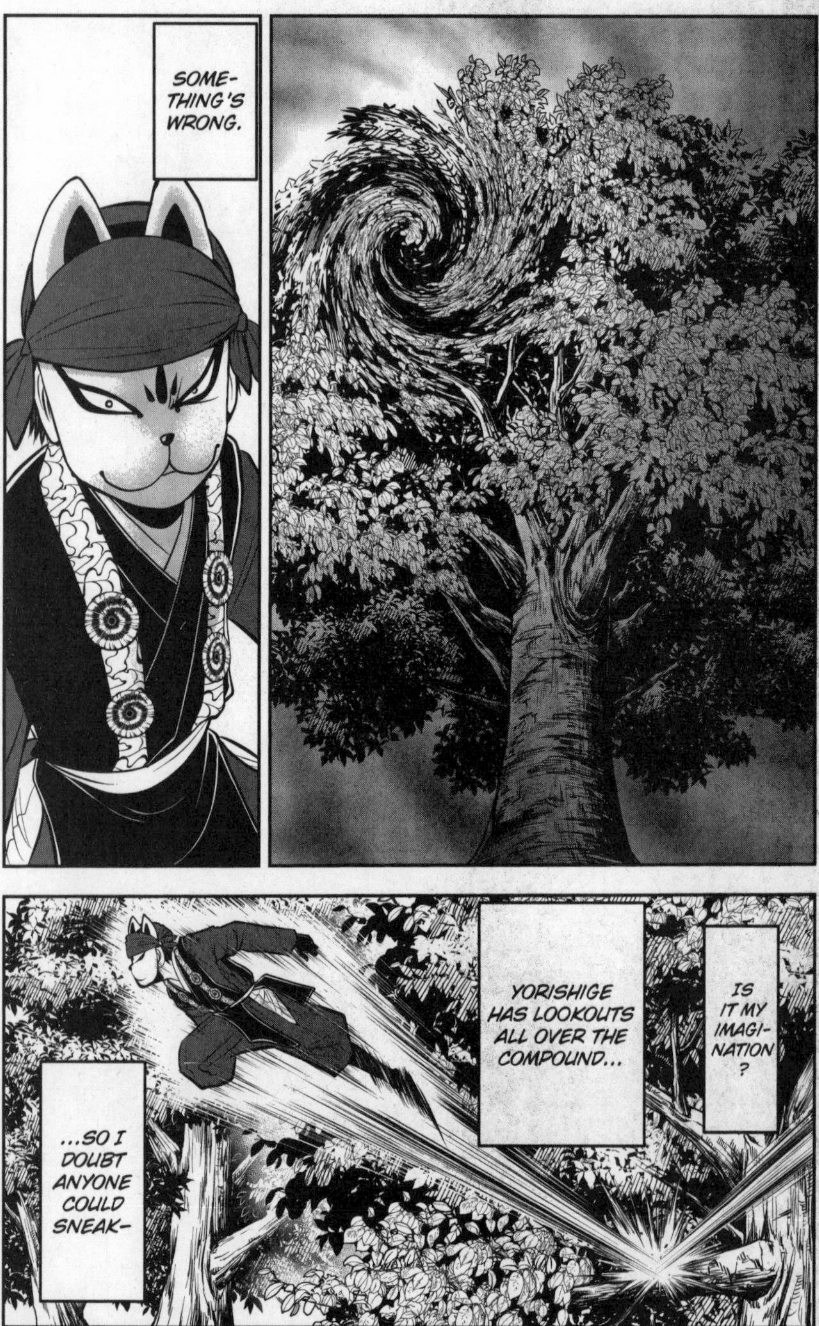
SOME-THING'S WRONG.
IS IT MY IMAGI-NATION?
YORISHIGE HAS LOOKOUTS ALL OVER THE COMPOUND...
...SO I DOUBT ANYONE COULD SNEAK-

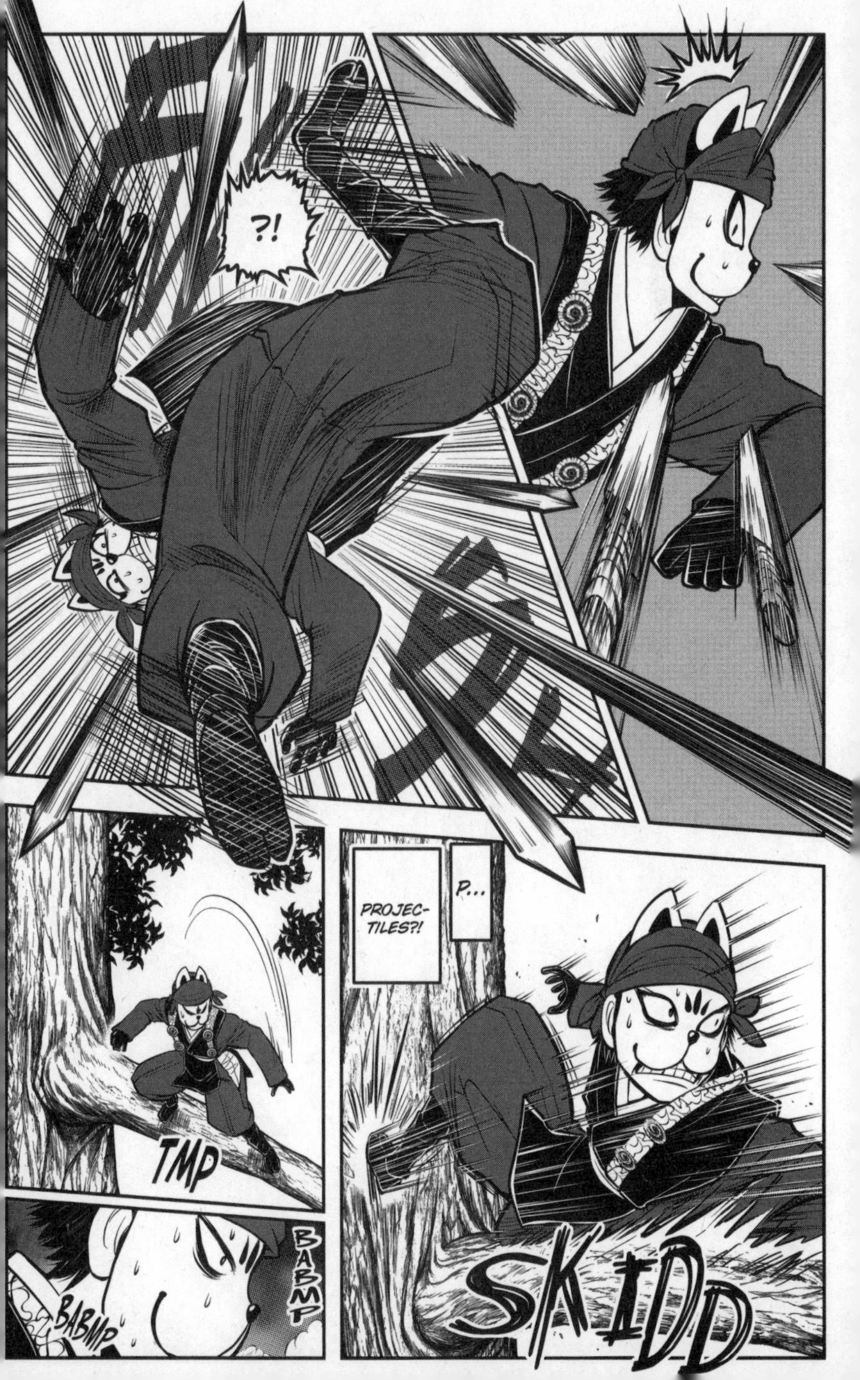
?!
P...
PROJEC-
TILES?!
SKIDD
TMP
BABMP
BABMP

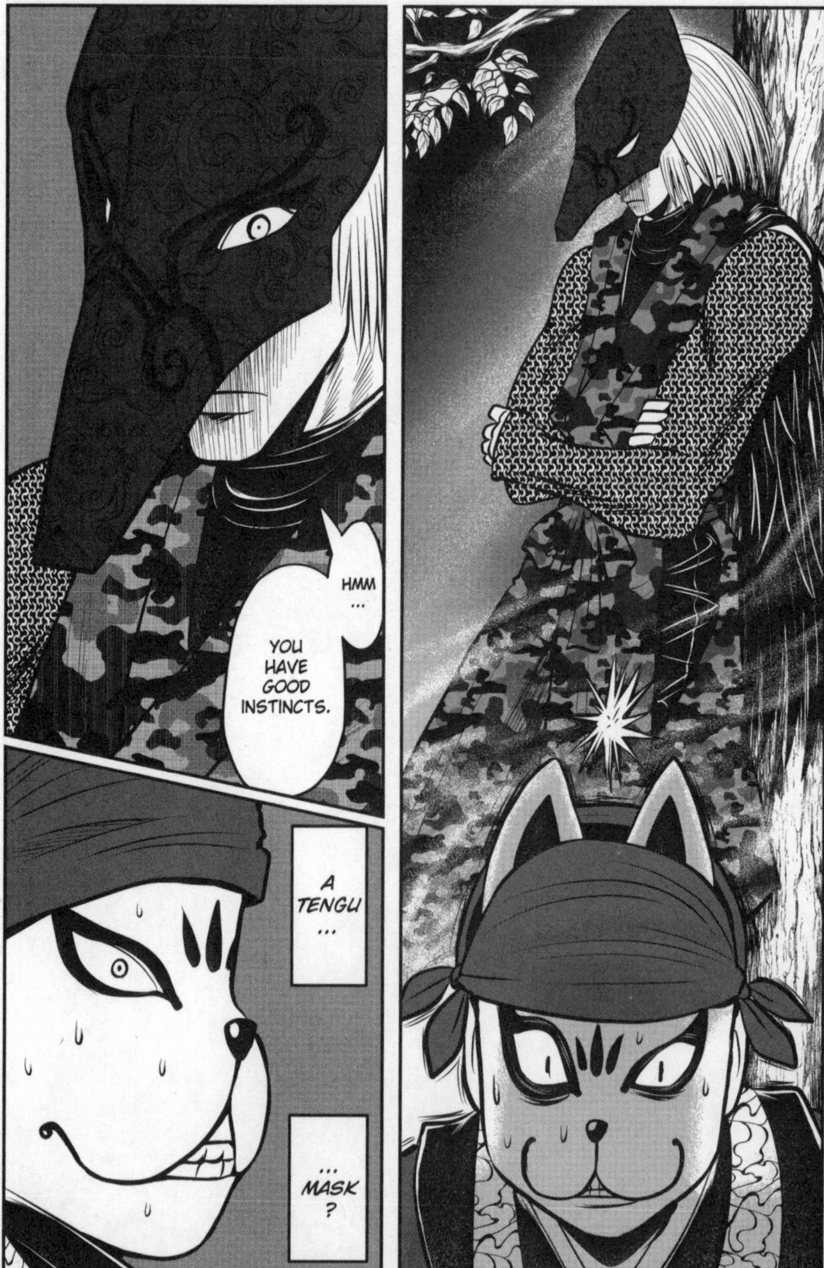
HMM ...
YOU HAVE GOOD INSTINCTS.
A TENGU ...
... MASK ?

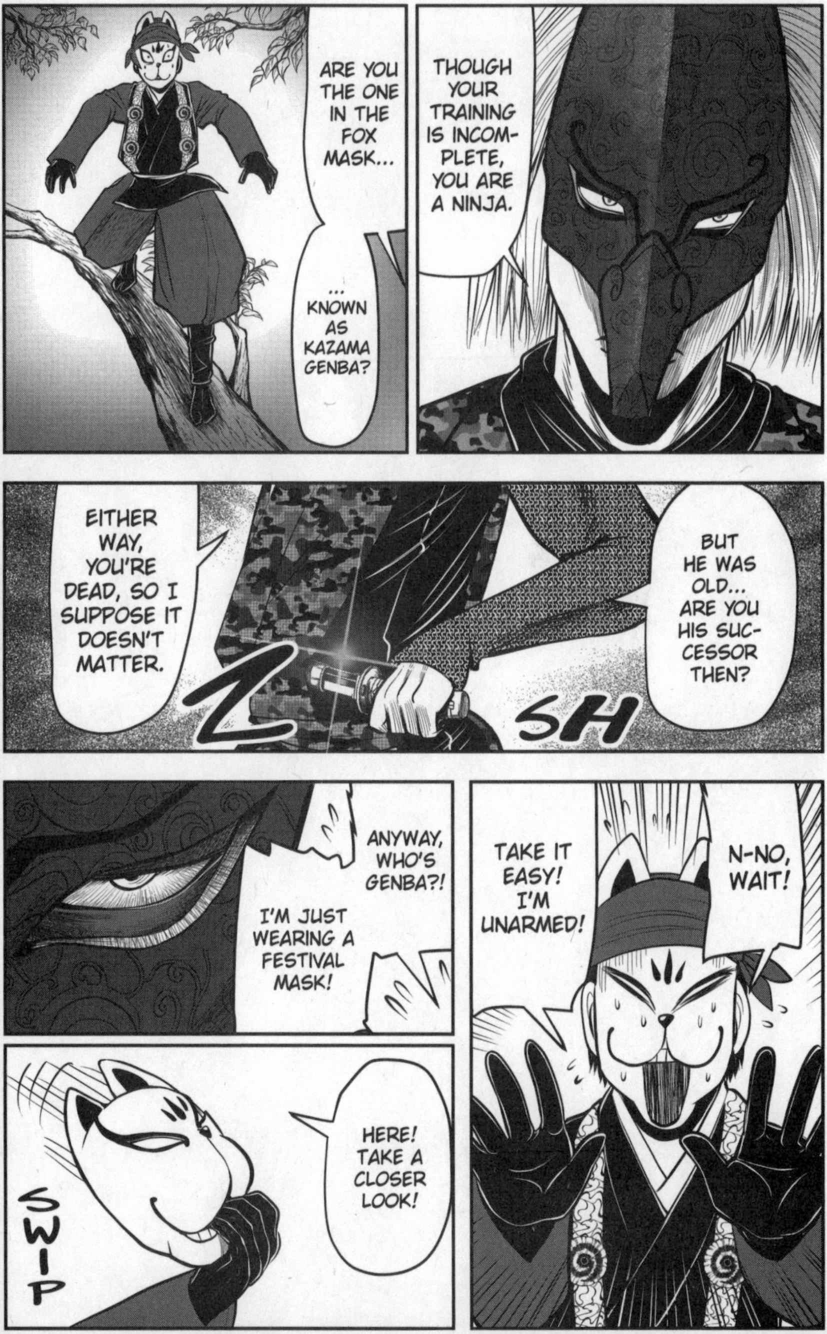
THOUGH YOUR TRAINING IS INCOMPLETE, YOU ARE A NINJA.
ARE YOU THE ONE IN THE FOX MASK...
...KNOWN AS KAZAMA GENBA?
BUT HE WAS OLD... ARE YOU HIS SUCCESSOR THEN?
ZSH
EITHER WAY, YOU'RE DEAD, SO I SUPPOSE IT DOESN'T MATTER.
N-NO, WAIT!
TAKE IT EASY! I'M UNARMED!
ANYWAY, WHO'S GENBA?!
I'M JUST WEARING A FESTIVAL MASK!
HERE! TAKE A CLOSER LOOK!
SWIP

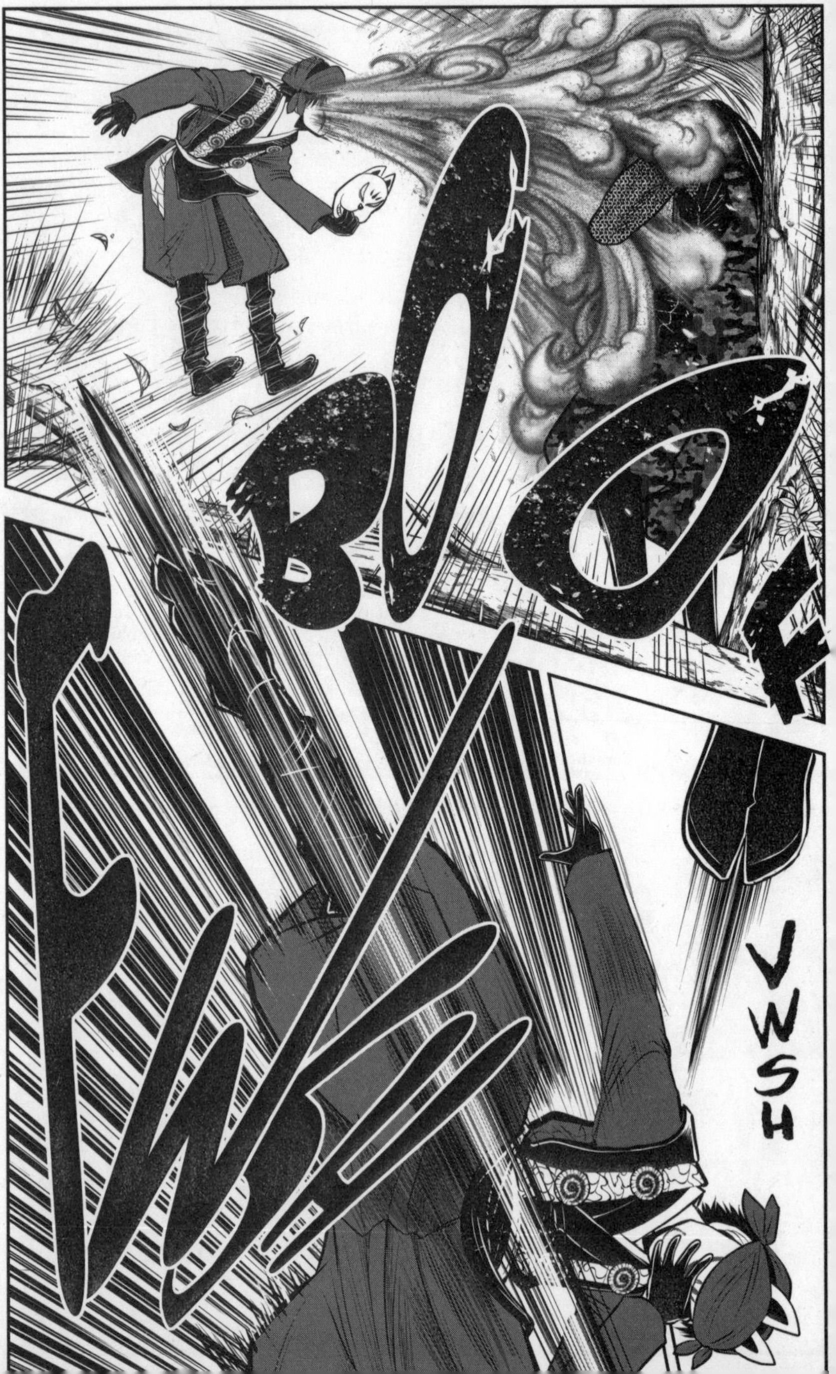

BLOOF
VWSH

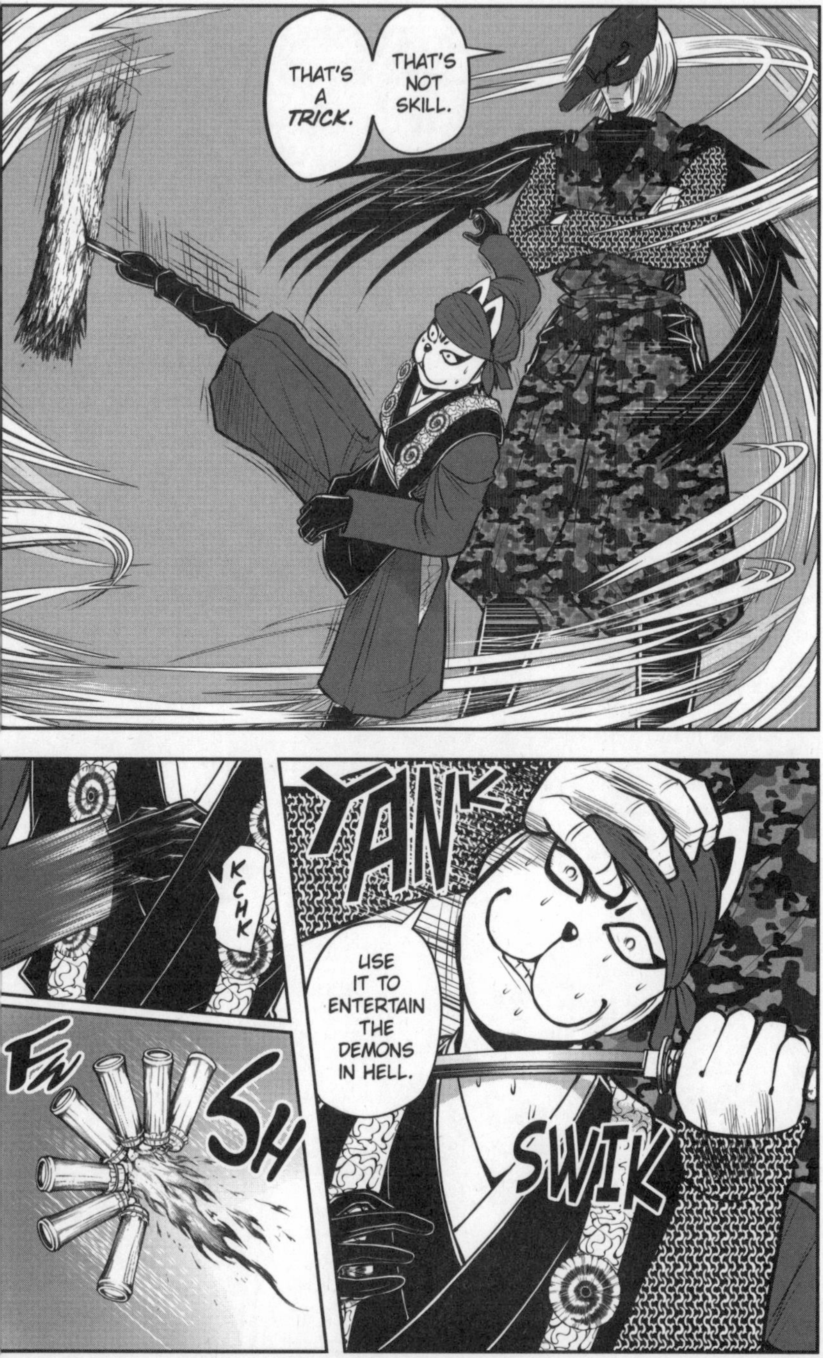
THAT'S NOT SKILL.
THAT'S A *TRICK*.
YANK
USE IT TO ENTERTAIN THE DEMONS IN HELL.
SWIK
KCHK
FWSH

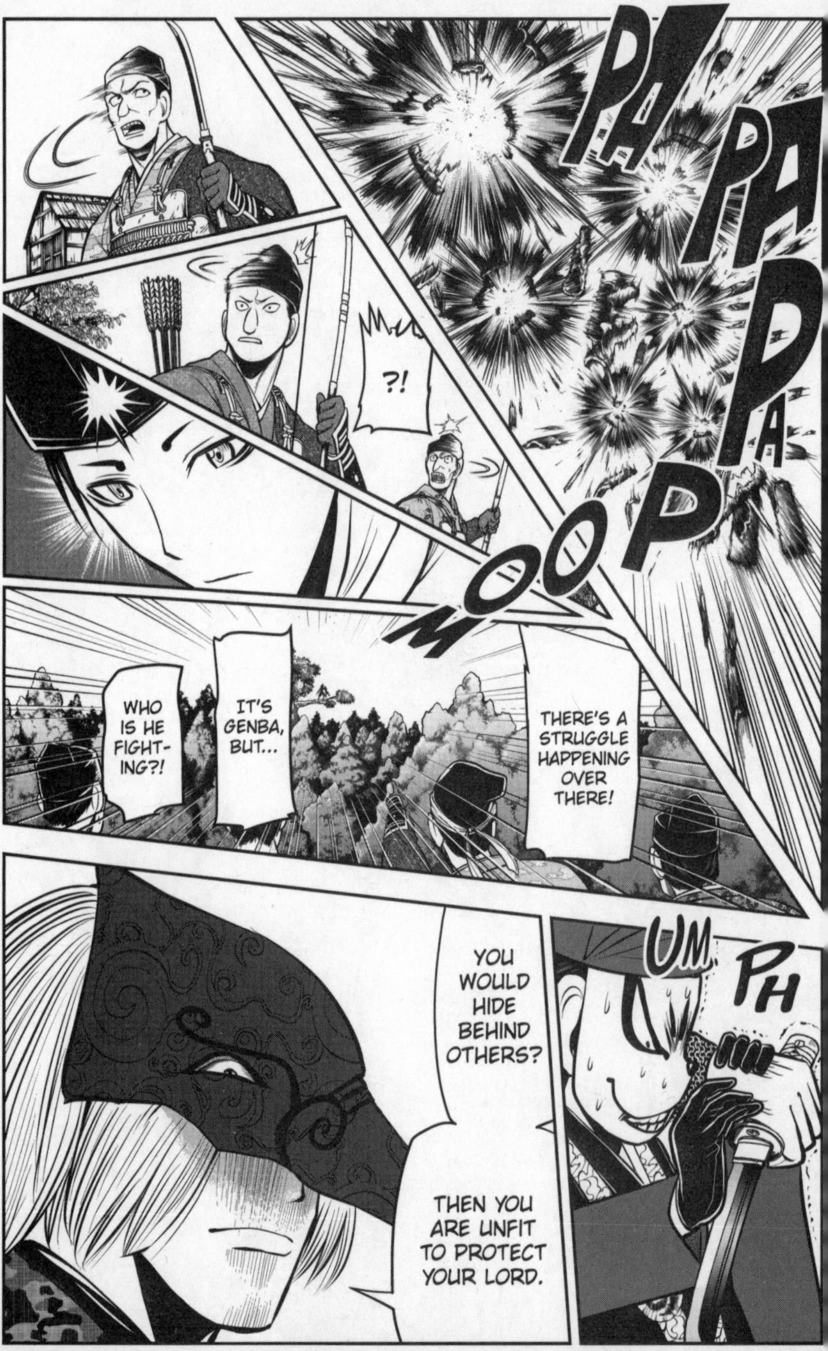
PAPAPAPA
?!
MOOOP
THERE'S A STRUGGLE HAPPENING OVER THERE!
IT'S GENBA, BUT...
WHO IS HE FIGHTING?!
UMPH
YOU WOULD HIDE BEHIND OTHERS?
THEN YOU ARE UNFIT TO PROTECT YOUR LORD.

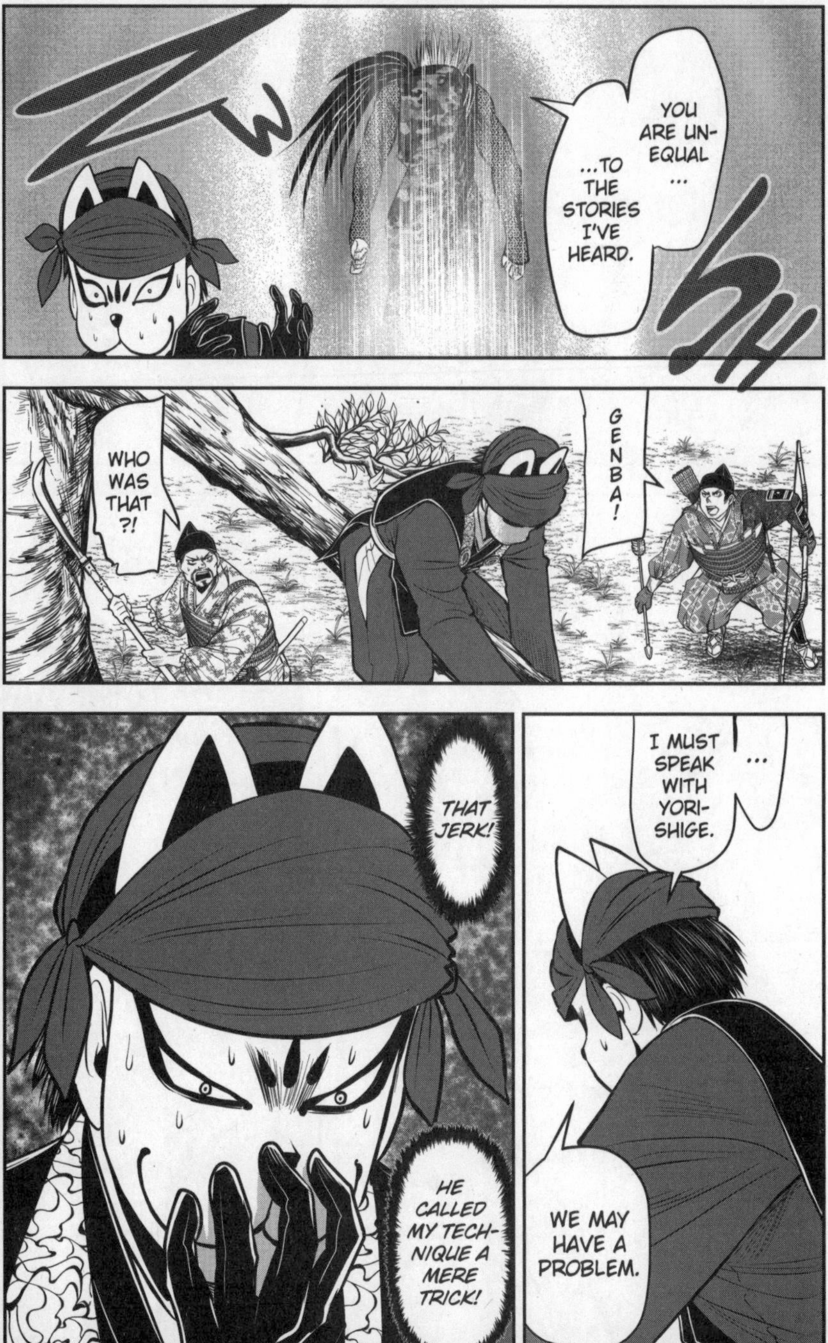
YOU ARE UN-EQUAL...
...TO THE STORIES I'VE HEARD.
GENBA!
WHO WAS THAT?!
I MUST SPEAK WITH YORI-SHIGE.
...
WE MAY HAVE A PROBLEM.
THAT JERK!
HE CALLED MY TECH-NIQUE A MERE TRICK!

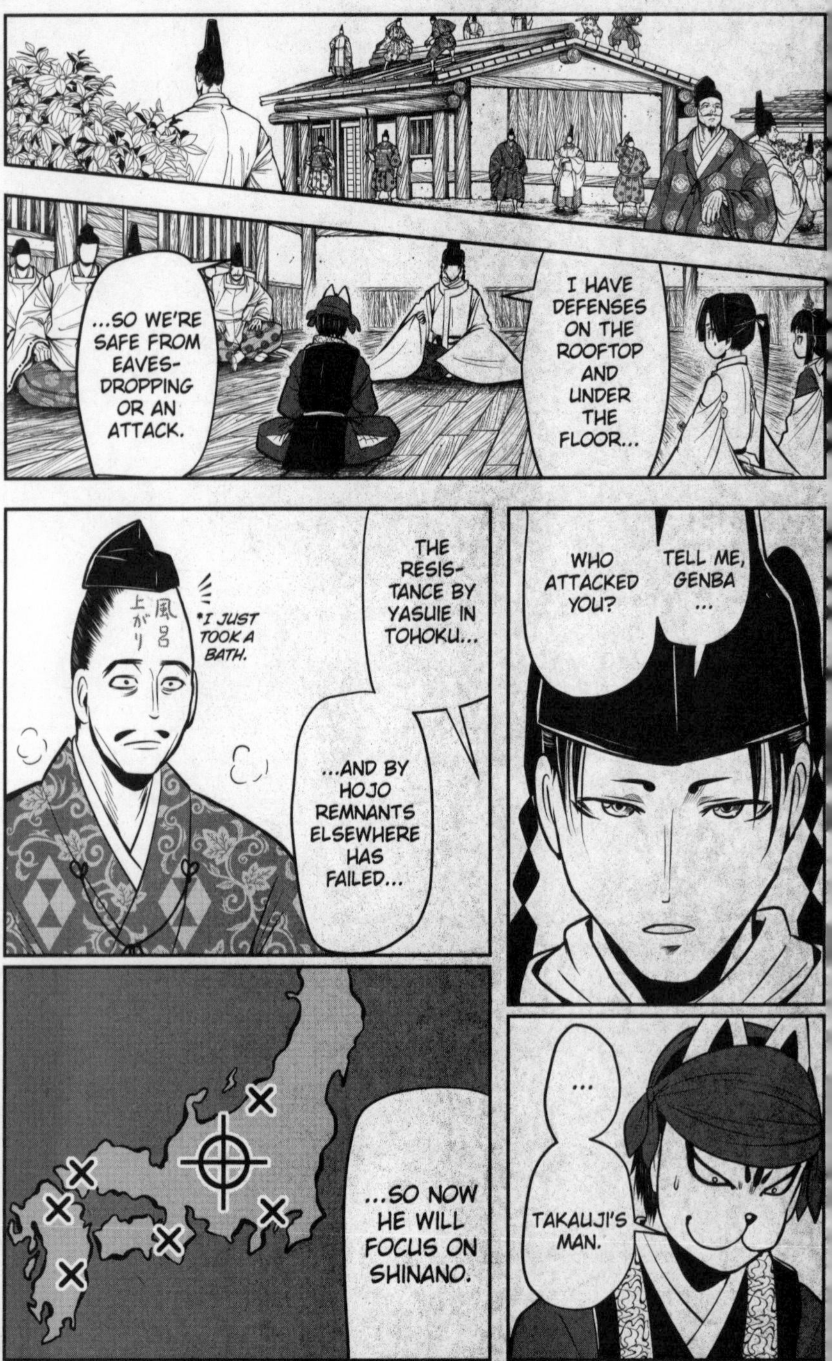
I HAVE DEFENSES ON THE ROOFTOP AND UNDER THE FLOOR...
...SO WE'RE SAFE FROM EAVES-DROPPING OR AN ATTACK.
TELL ME, GENBA ...
WHO ATTACKED YOU?
...
TAKAUJI'S MAN.
THE RESIS-TANCE BY YASUIE IN TOHOKU...
...AND BY HOJO REMNANTS ELSEWHERE HAS FAILED...
風呂上がり
*I JUST TOOK A BATH.
...SO NOW HE WILL FOCUS ON SHINANO.

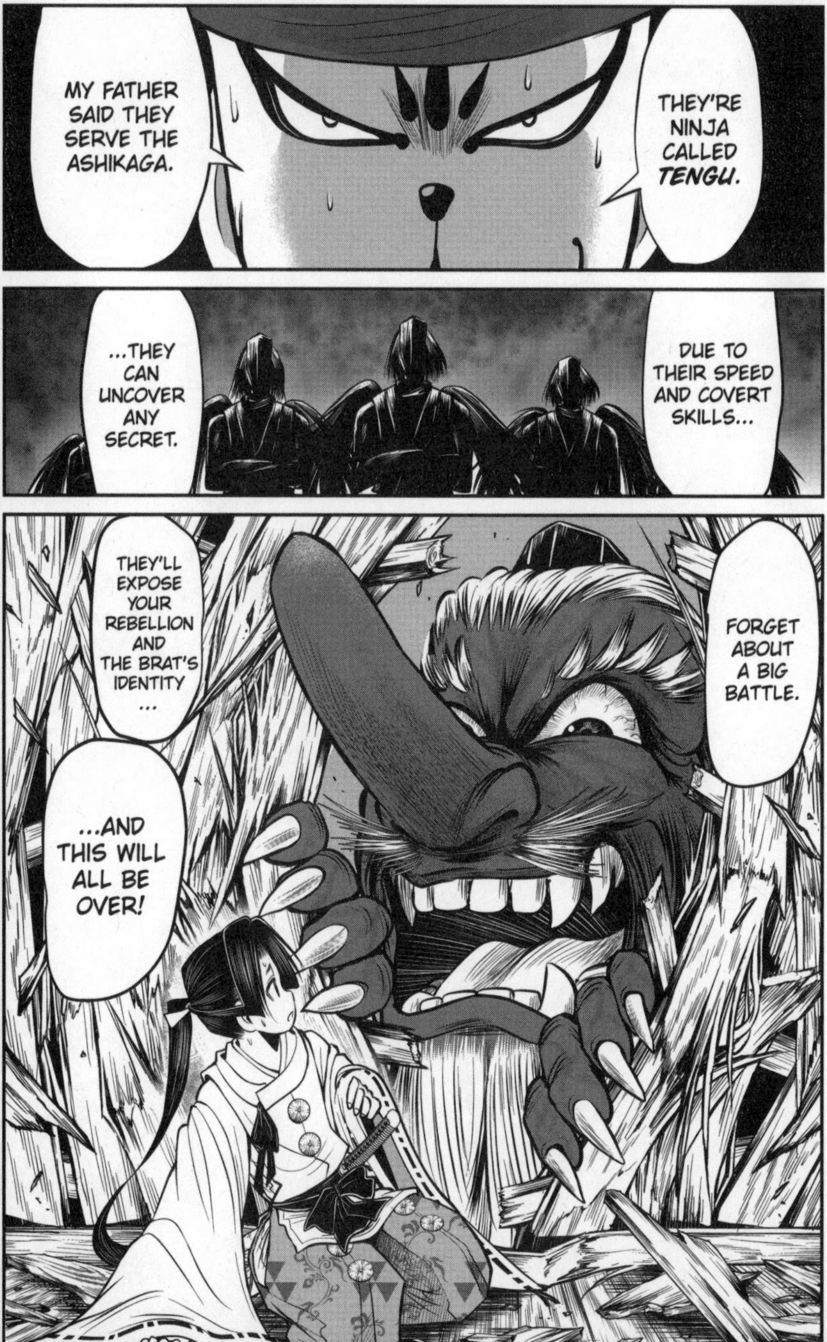
THEY'RE NINJA CALLED *TENGU*.
MY FATHER SAID THEY SERVE THE ASHIKAGA.
DUE TO THEIR SPEED AND COVERT SKILLS...
...THEY CAN UNCOVER ANY SECRET.
FORGET ABOUT A BIG BATTLE.
THEY'LL EXPOSE YOUR REBELLION AND THE BRAT'S IDENTITY ...
...AND THIS WILL ALL BE OVER!

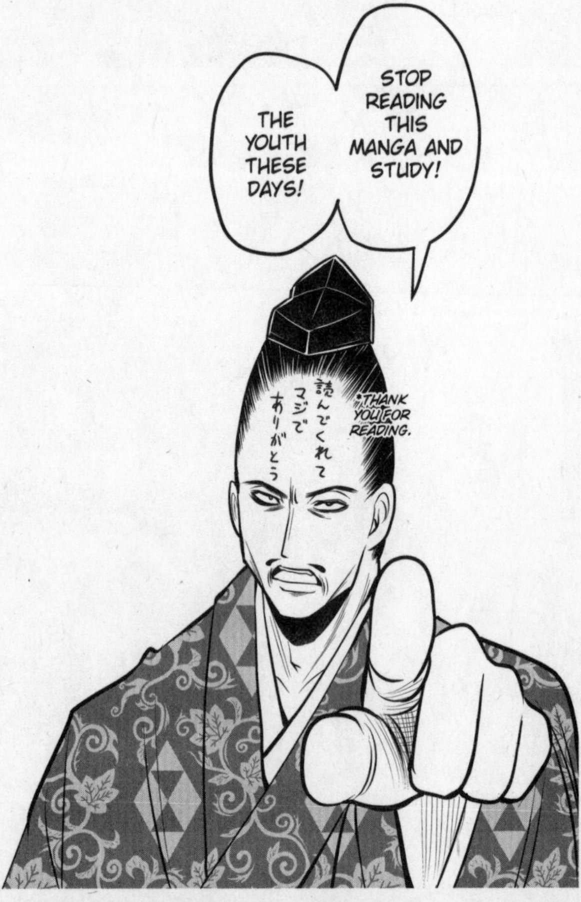
STOP READING THIS MANGA AND STUDY!
THE YOUTH THESE DAYS!
読んでくれてマジでありがとう
*THANK YOU FOR READING.

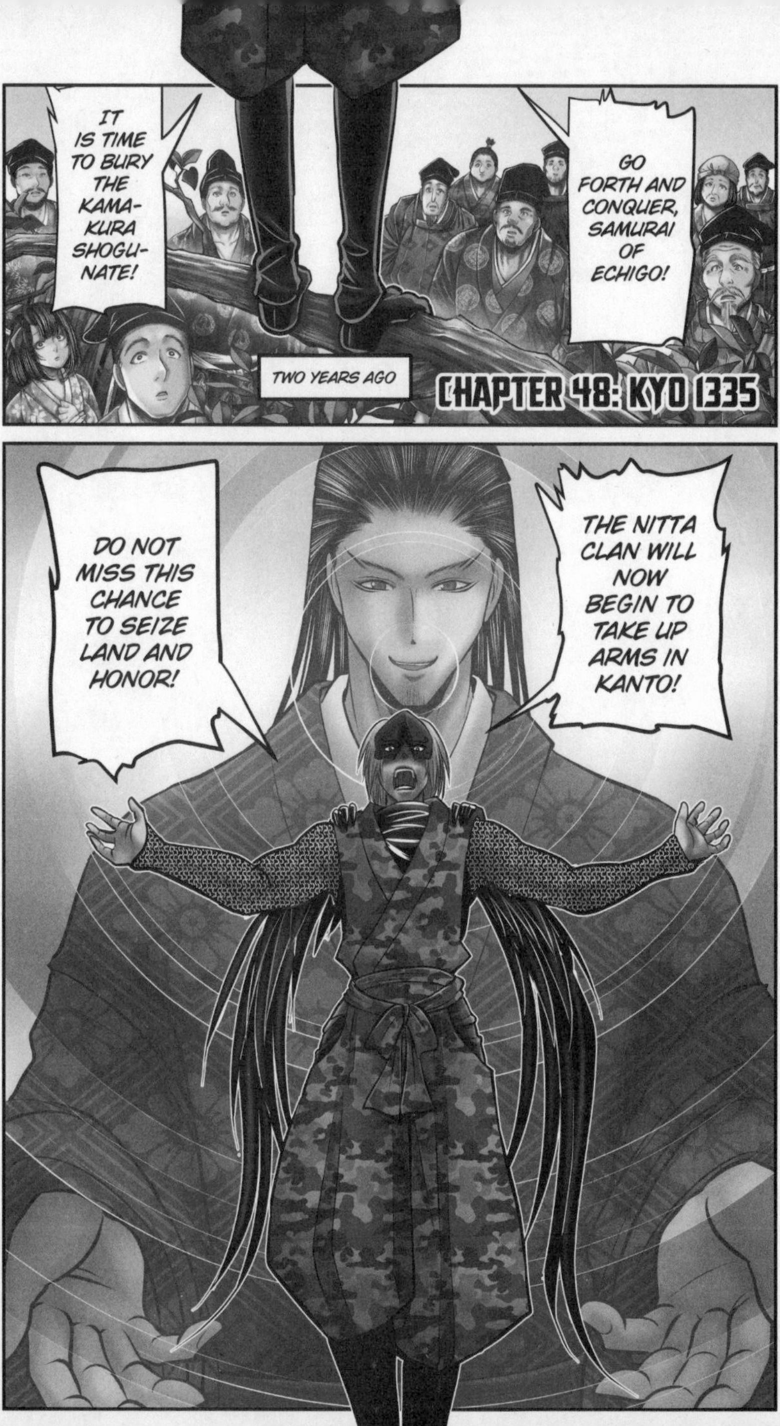
GO FORTH AND CONQUER, SAMURAI OF ECHIGO!
IT IS TIME TO BURY THE KAMAKURA SHOGUNATE!
TWO YEARS AGO
CHAPTER 48: KYO 1335
THE NITTA CLAN WILL NOW BEGIN TO TAKE UP ARMS IN KANTO!
DO NOT MISS THIS CHANCE TO SEIZE LAND AND HONOR!

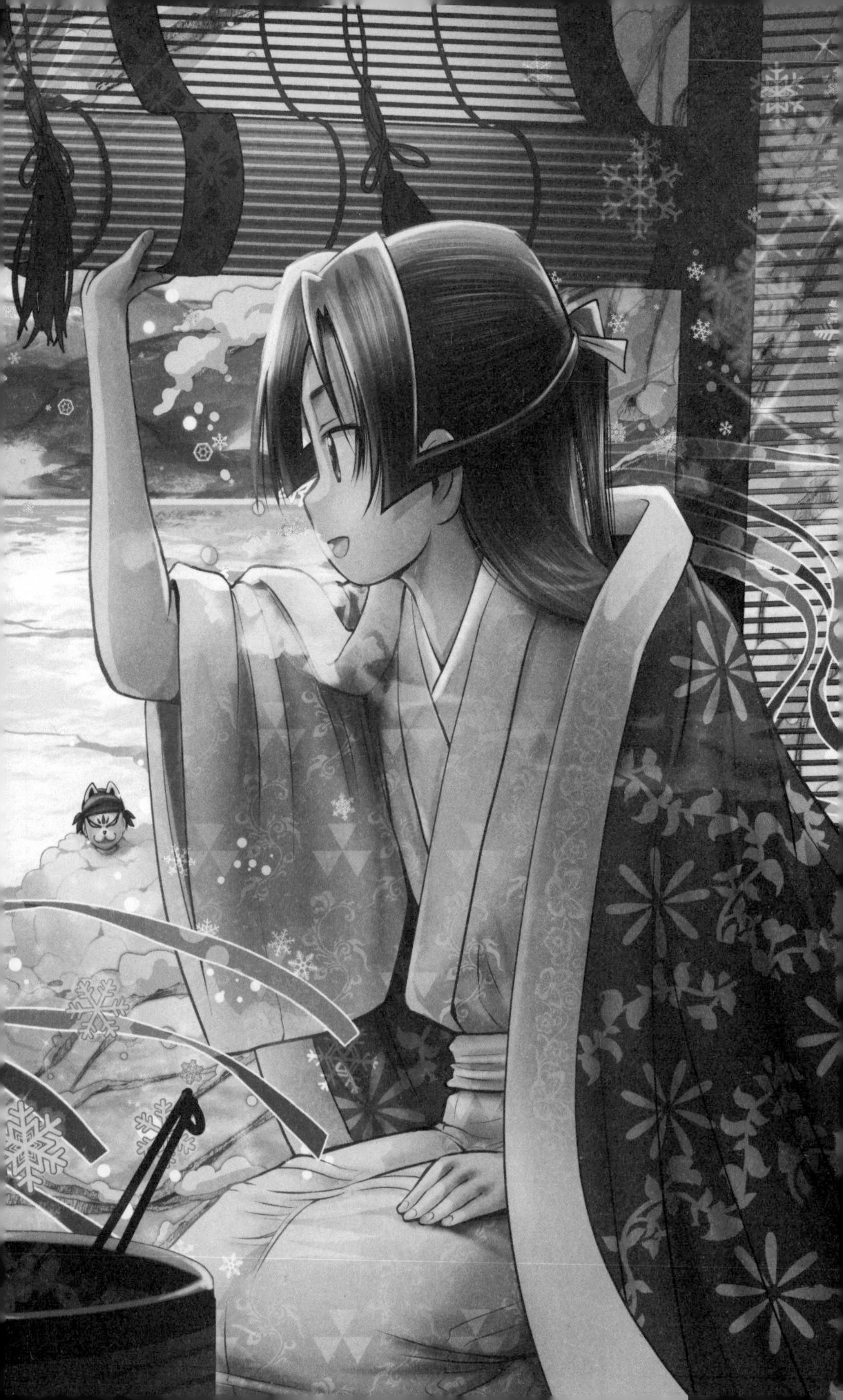

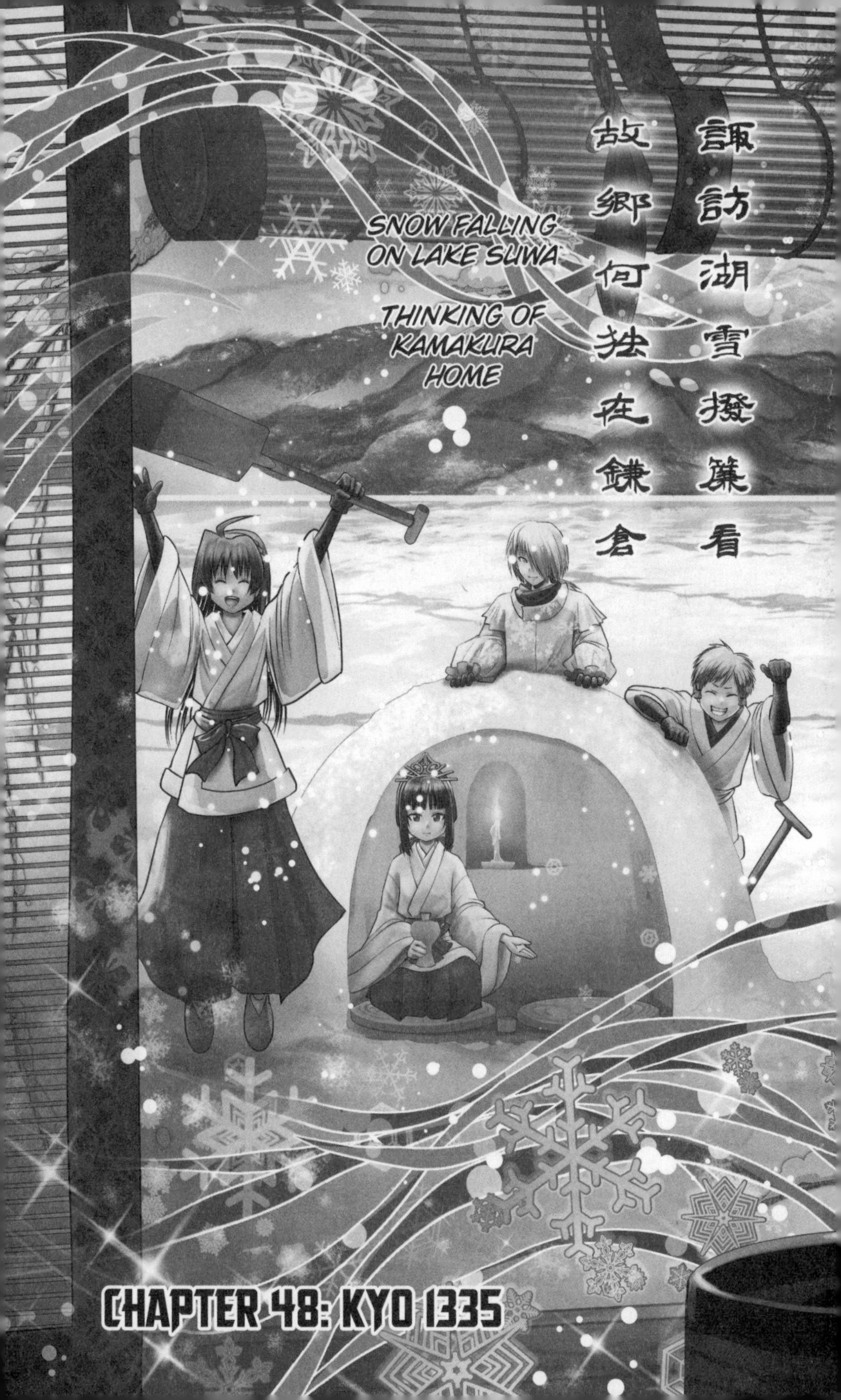
諏訪湖雪撥簾看
故郷何処在鎌倉
SNOW FALLING ON LAKE SUWA
THINKING OF KAMAKURA HOME
CHAPTER 48: KYO 1335

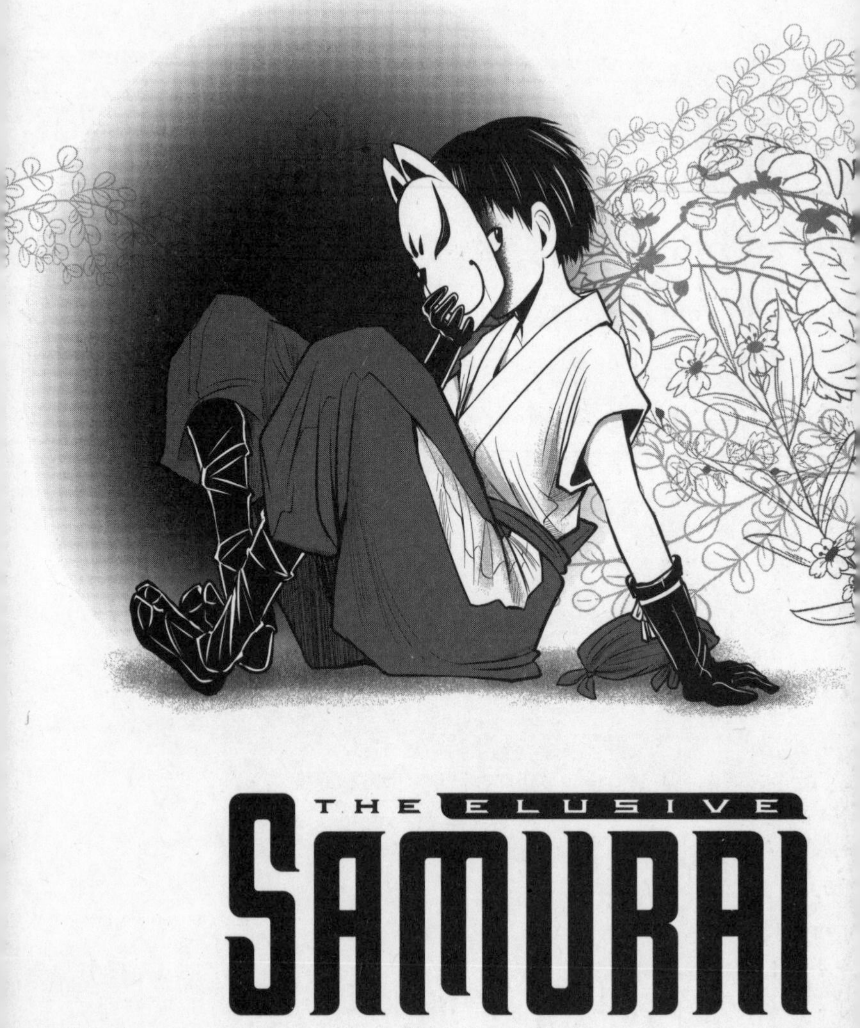

THE ELUSIVE SAMURAI

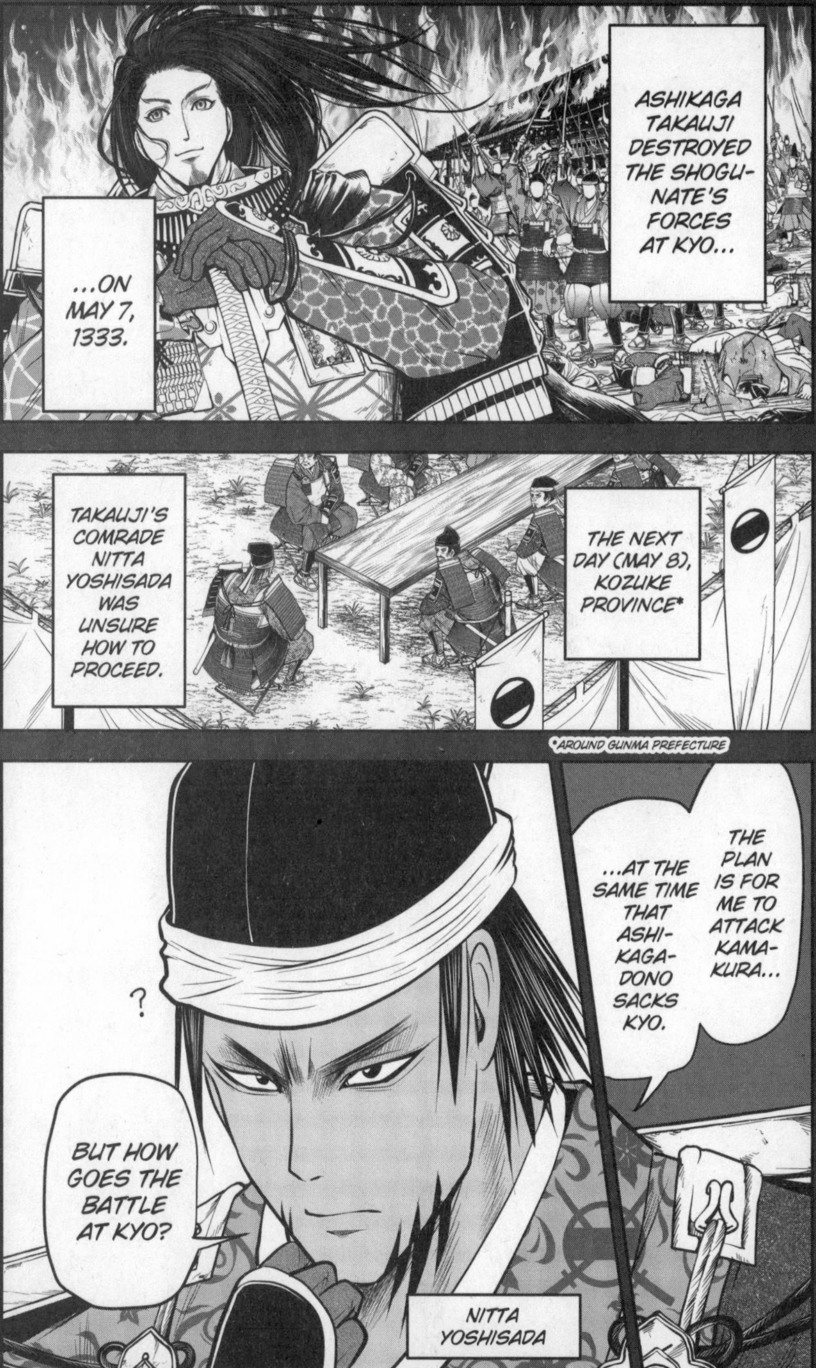
ASHIKAGA TAKAUJI DESTROYED THE SHOGUNATE'S FORCES AT KYO...
...ON MAY 7, 1333.
THE NEXT DAY (MAY 8), KOZUKE PROVINCE*
TAKAUJI'S COMRADE NITTA YOSHISADA WAS UNSURE HOW TO PROCEED.
*AROUND GUNMA PREFECTURE
THE PLAN IS FOR ME TO ATTACK KAMAKURA...
...AT THE SAME TIME THAT ASHIKAGA-DONO SACKS KYO.
?
BUT HOW GOES THE BATTLE AT KYO?
NITTA YOSHISADA

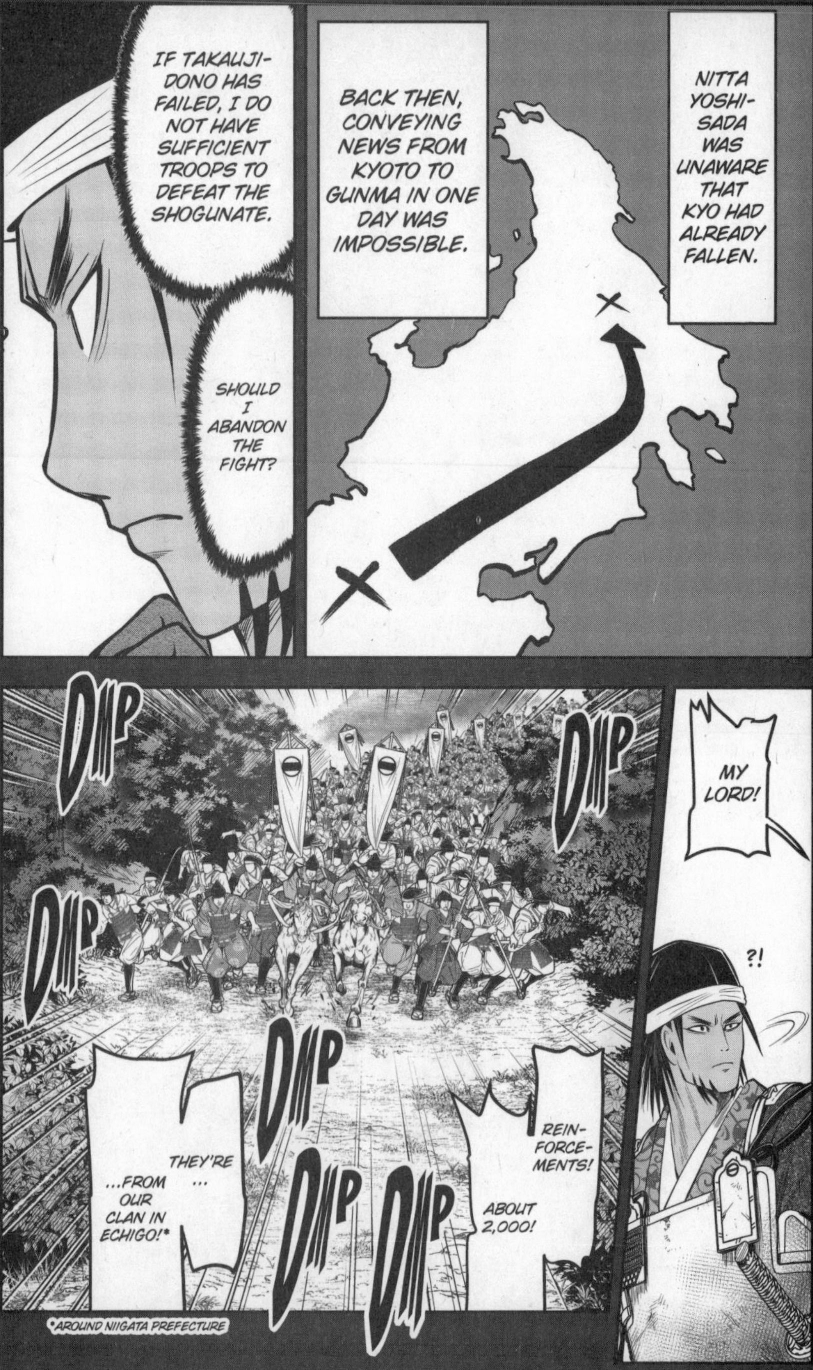
NITTA YOSHISADA WAS UNAWARE THAT KYO HAD ALREADY FALLEN.
BACK THEN, CONVEYING NEWS FROM KYOTO TO GUNMA IN ONE DAY WAS IMPOSSIBLE.
IF TAKAUJI-DONO HAS FAILED, I DO NOT HAVE SUFFICIENT TROOPS TO DEFEAT THE SHOGUNATE.
SHOULD I ABANDON THE FIGHT?
MY LORD!
?!
DMP
DMP
DMP
DMP
REIN-FORCEMENTS!
ABOUT 2,000!
THEY'RE ...
...FROM OUR CLAN IN ECHIGO!*
DMP
DMP
*AROUND NIIGATA PREFECTURE

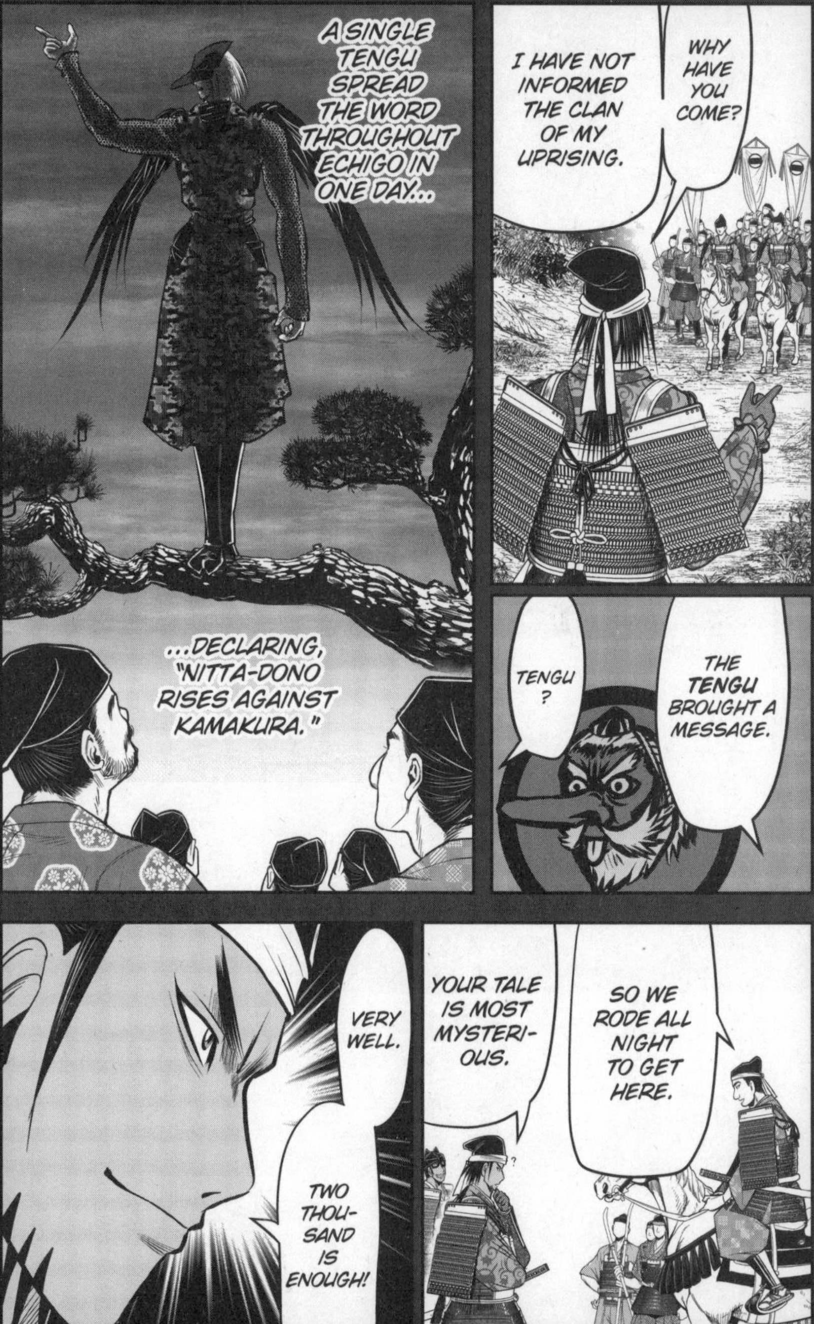
WHY HAVE YOU COME?
I HAVE NOT INFORMED THE CLAN OF MY UPRISING.
THE TENGU BROUGHT A MESSAGE.
TENGU?
A SINGLE TENGU SPREAD THE WORD THROUGHOUT ECHIGO IN ONE DAY...
...DECLARING, "NITTA-DONO RISES AGAINST KAMAKURA."
SO WE RODE ALL NIGHT TO GET HERE.
YOUR TALE IS MOST MYSTERIOUS.
VERY WELL.
TWO THOUSAND IS ENOUGH!

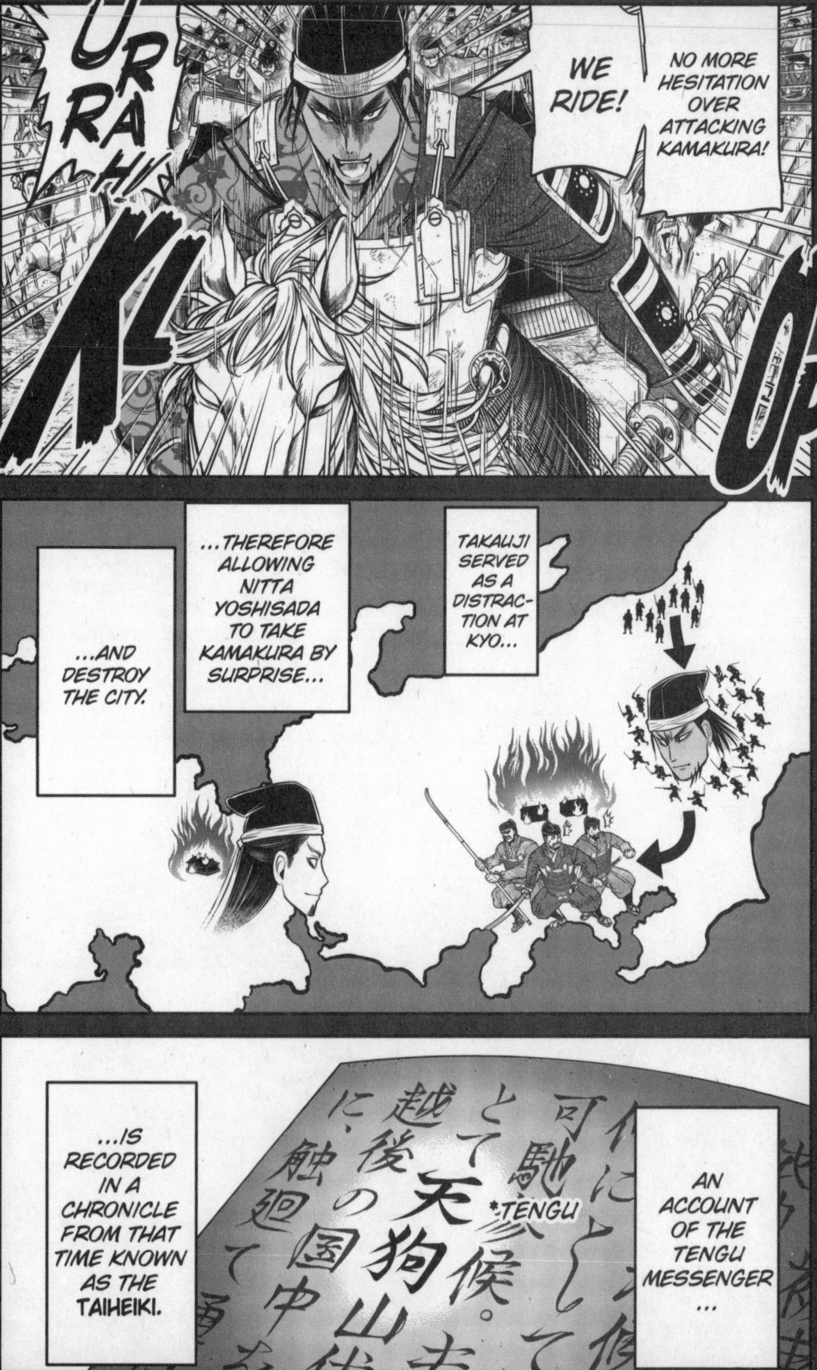
NO MORE HESITATION OVER ATTACKING KAMAKURA!
WE RIDE!
URRAHH!
KLOP
TAKAUJI SERVED AS A DISTRACTION AT KYO...
...THEREFORE ALLOWING NITTA YOSHISADA TO TAKE KAMAKURA BY SURPRISE...
...AND DESTROY THE CITY.
AN ACCOUNT OF THE TENGU MESSENGER...
可馳参候。
とて
越後の国中
に触廻て
天狗山伏
*TENGU
...IS RECORDED IN A CHRONICLE FROM THAT TIME KNOWN AS THE TAIHEIKI.

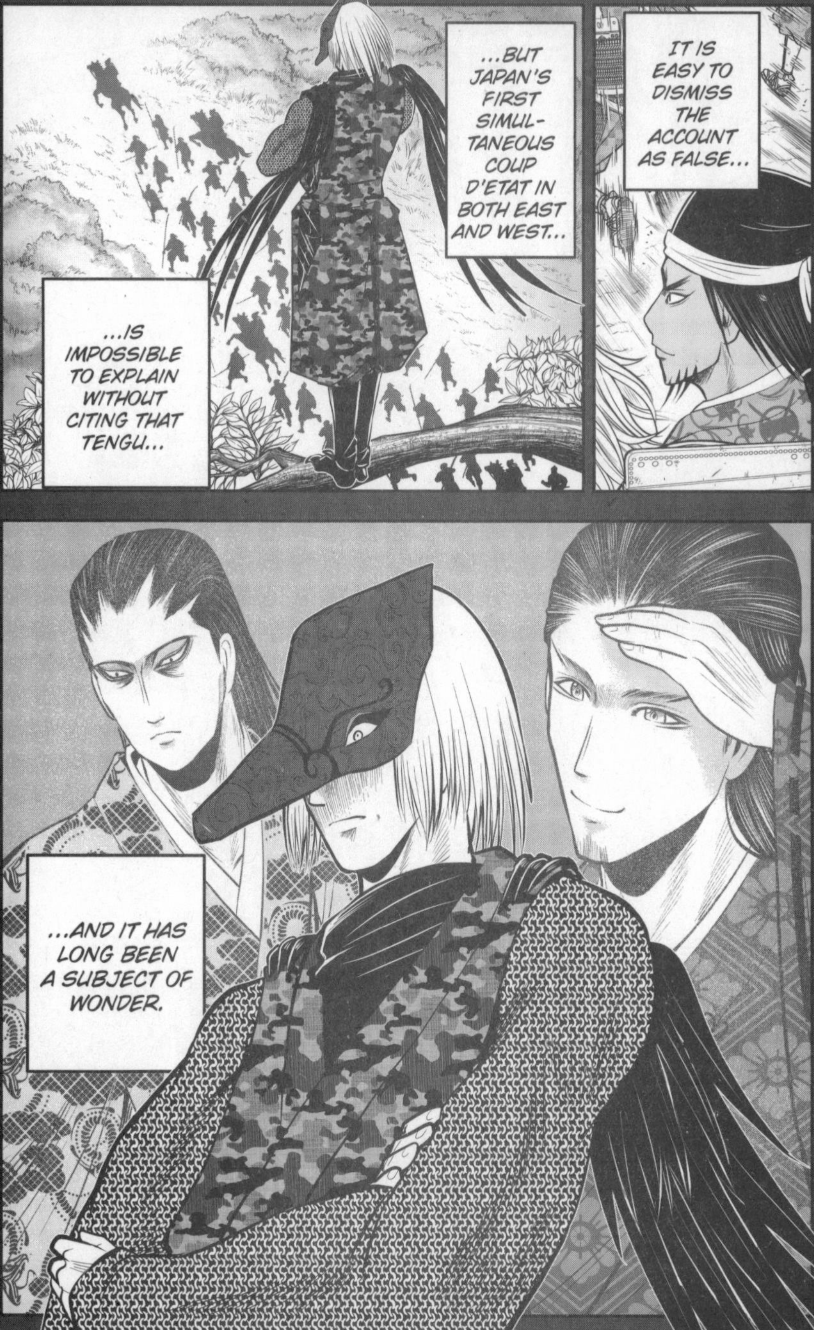
IT IS EASY TO DISMISS THE ACCOUNT AS FALSE...
...BUT JAPAN'S FIRST SIMUL-TANEOUS COUP D'ETAT IN BOTH EAST AND WEST...
...IS IMPOSSIBLE TO EXPLAIN WITHOUT CITING THAT TENGU...
...AND IT HAS LONG BEEN A SUBJECT OF WONDER.

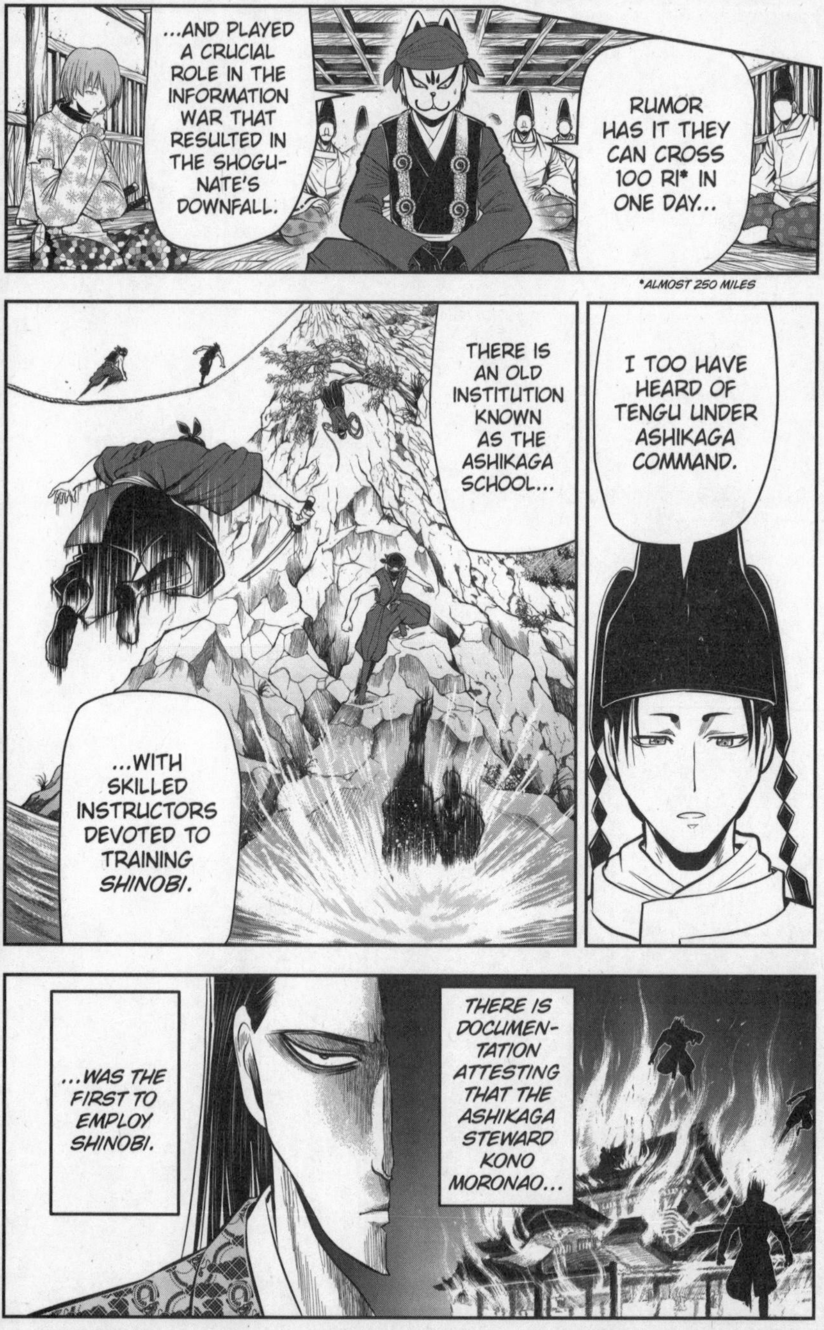

...AND PLAYED A CRUCIAL ROLE IN THE INFORMATION WAR THAT RESULTED IN THE SHOGUNATE'S DOWNFALL.
RUMOR HAS IT THEY CAN CROSS 100 RI* IN ONE DAY...
*ALMOST 250 MILES
I TOO HAVE HEARD OF TENGU UNDER ASHIKAGA COMMAND.
THERE IS AN OLD INSTITUTION KNOWN AS THE ASHIKAGA SCHOOL...
...WITH SKILLED INSTRUCTORS DEVOTED TO TRAINING *SHINOBI*.
THERE IS DOCUMENTATION ATTESTING THAT THE ASHIKAGA STEWARD KONO MORONAO...
...WAS THE FIRST TO EMPLOY SHINOBI.

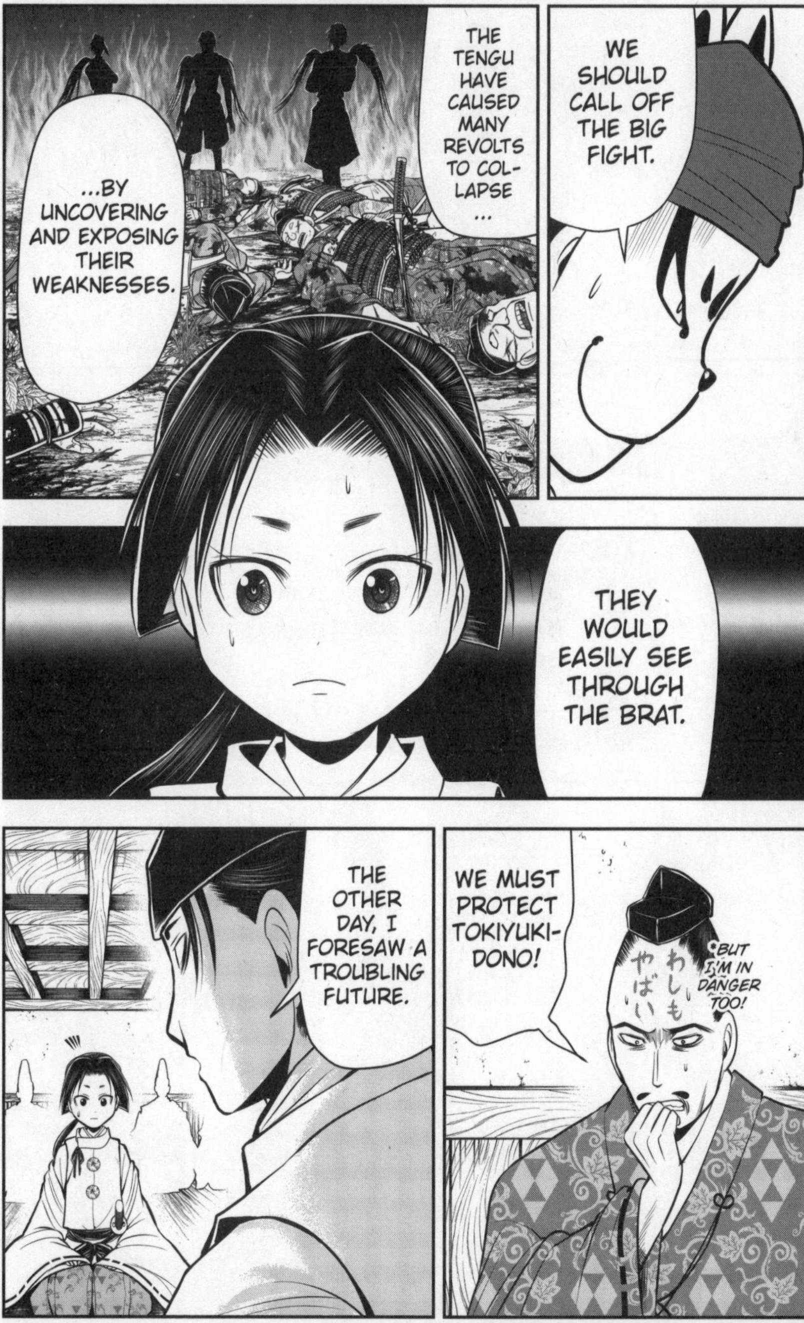
WE SHOULD CALL OFF THE BIG FIGHT.
THE TENGU HAVE CAUSED MANY REVOLTS TO COL-LAPSE ...
...BY UNCOVERING AND EXPOSING THEIR WEAKNESSES.
THEY WOULD EASILY SEE THROUGH THE BRAT.
WE MUST PROTECT TOKIYUKI-DONO!
わしもやばい
*BUT I'M IN DANGER TOO!
THE OTHER DAY, I FORESAW A TROUBLING FUTURE.

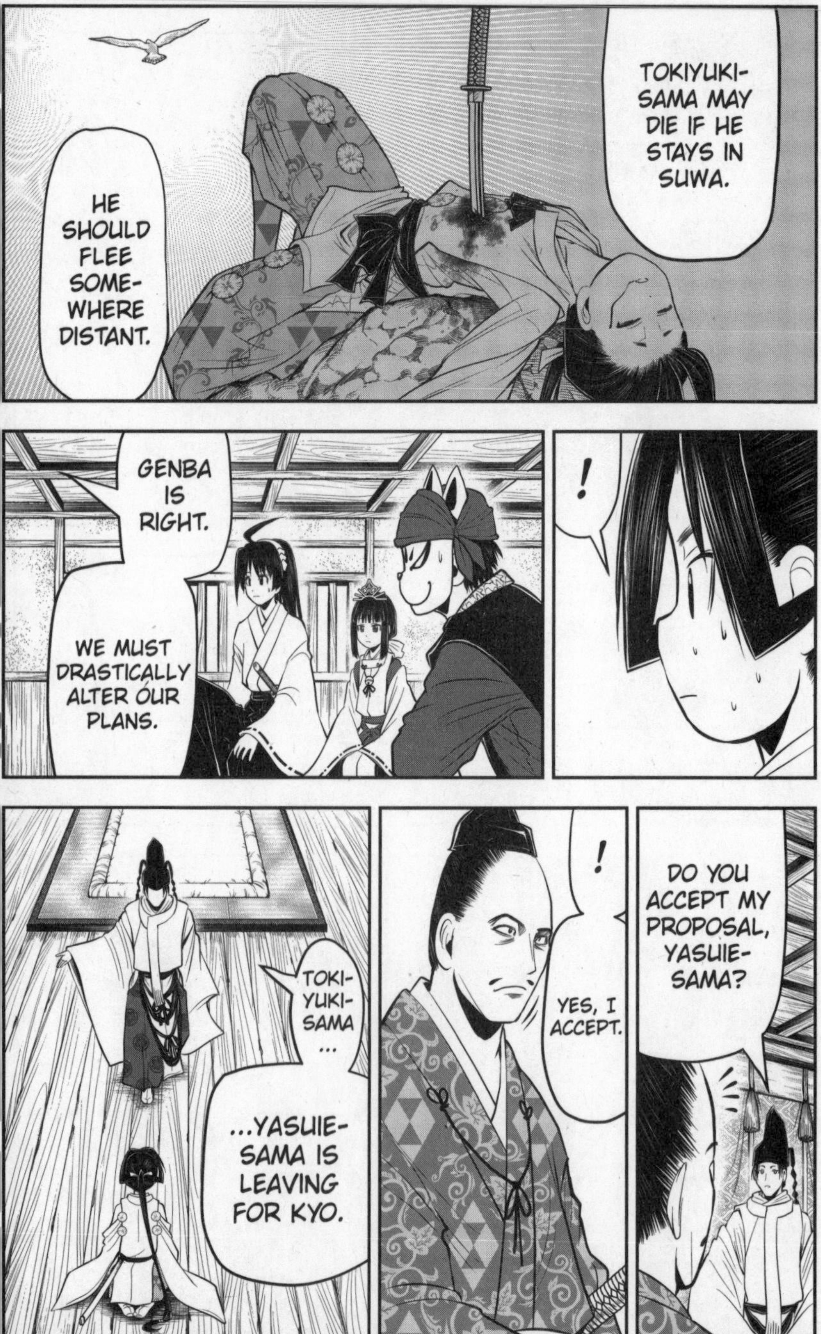
TOKIYUKI-SAMA MAY DIE IF HE STAYS IN SUWA.
HE SHOULD FLEE SOMEWHERE DISTANT.
!
GENBA IS RIGHT.
WE MUST DRASTICALLY ALTER OUR PLANS.
DO YOU ACCEPT MY PROPOSAL, YASUIE-SAMA?
!
YES, I ACCEPT.
TOKIYUKI-SAMA ...
...YASUIE-SAMA IS LEAVING FOR KYO.

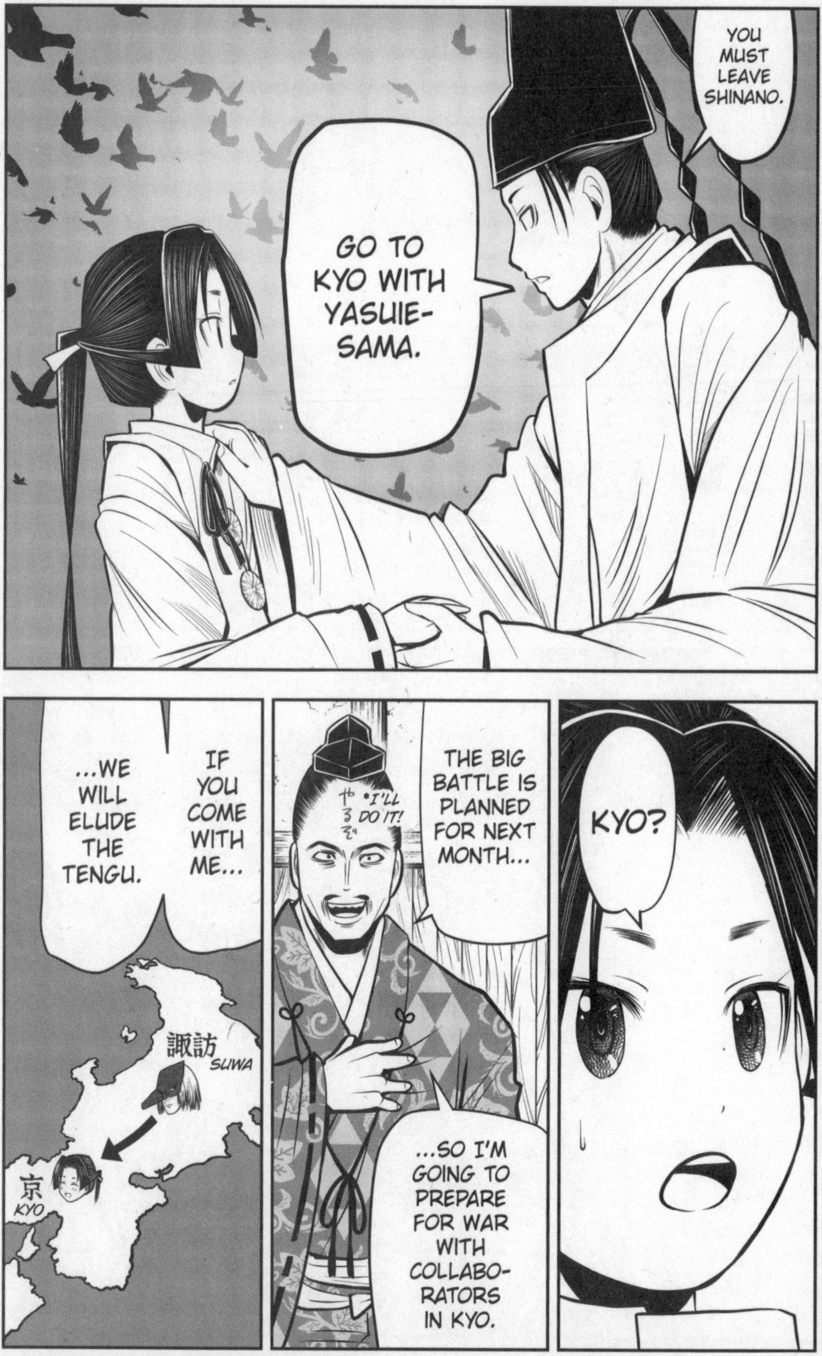
YOU MUST LEAVE SHINANO.
GO TO KYO WITH YASUIE-SAMA.
KYO?
THE BIG BATTLE IS PLANNED FOR NEXT MONTH...
やるぞ
*I'LL DO IT!
...SO I'M GOING TO PREPARE FOR WAR WITH COLLABO-RATORS IN KYO.
IF YOU COME WITH ME...
...WE WILL ELUDE THE TENGU.
諏訪
SUWA
京
KYO

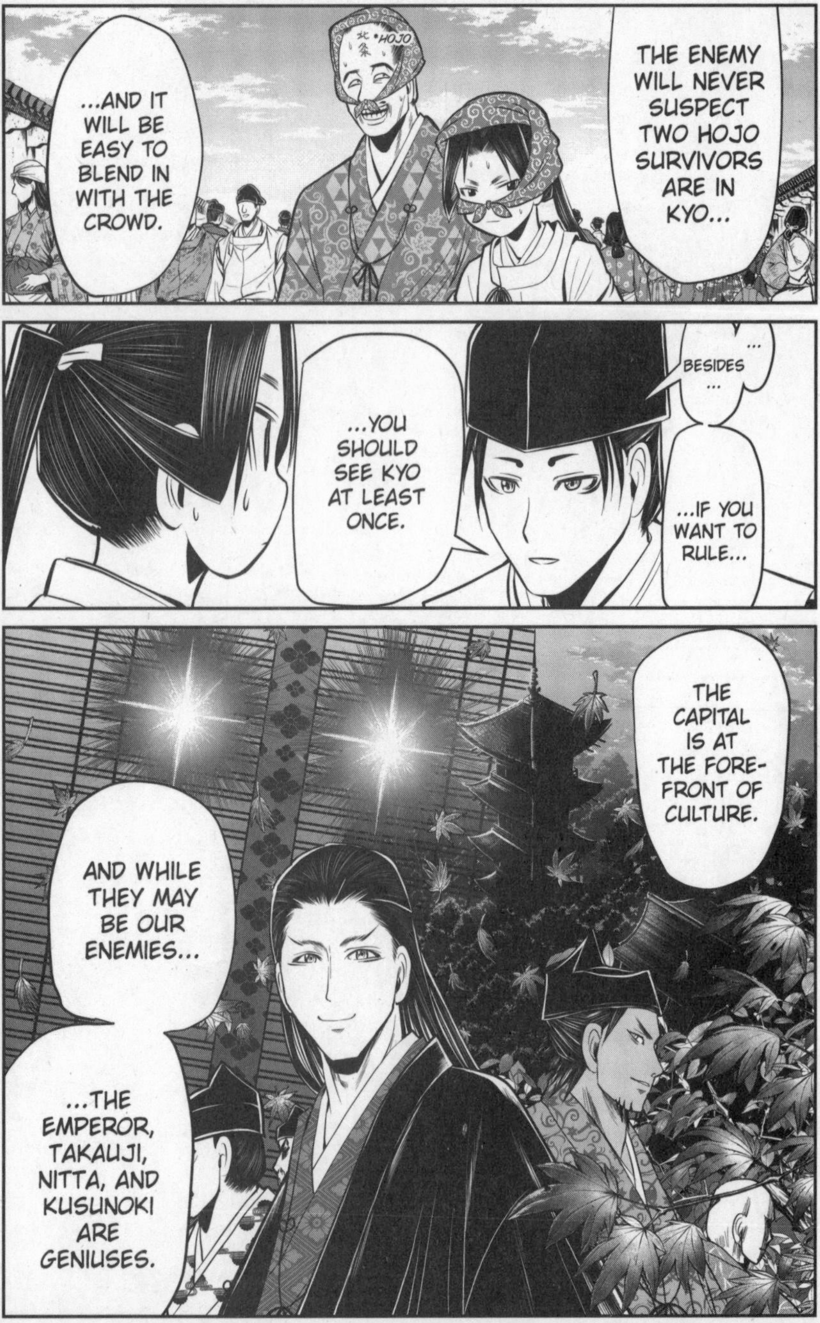
THE ENEMY WILL NEVER SUSPECT TWO HOJO SURVIVORS ARE IN KYO...
北条 HOJO
...AND IT WILL BE EASY TO BLEND IN WITH THE CROWD.
...BESIDES...
...IF YOU WANT TO RULE...
...YOU SHOULD SEE KYO AT LEAST ONCE.
THE CAPITAL IS AT THE FORE-FRONT OF CULTURE.
AND WHILE THEY MAY BE OUR ENEMIES...
...THE EMPEROR, TAKAUJI, NITTA, AND KUSUNOKI ARE GENIUSES.

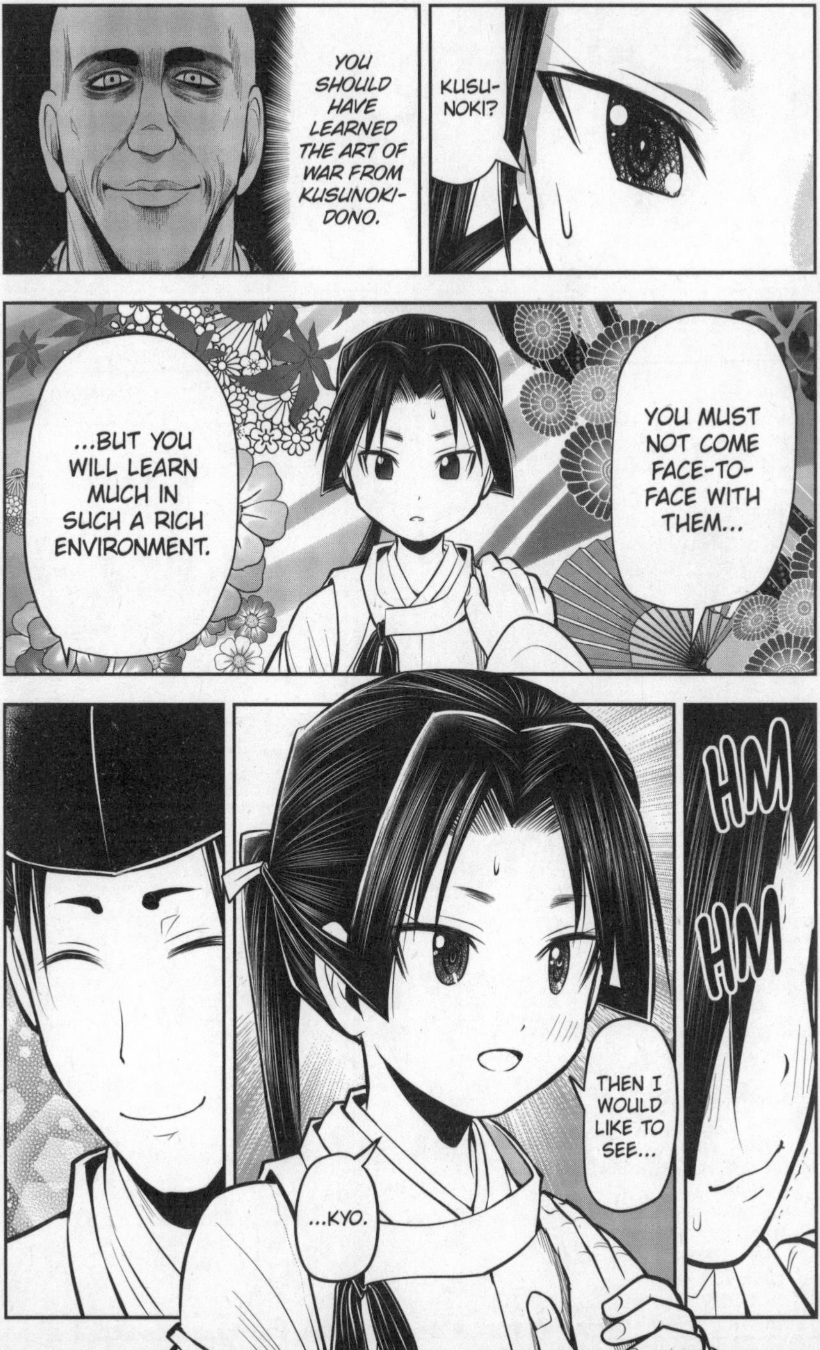
KUSU-NOKI?
YOU SHOULD HAVE LEARNED THE ART OF WAR FROM KUSUNOKI-DONO.
YOU MUST NOT COME FACE-TO-FACE WITH THEM...
...BUT YOU WILL LEARN MUCH IN SUCH A RICH ENVIRONMENT.
HM HM
THEN I WOULD LIKE TO SEE...
...KYO.

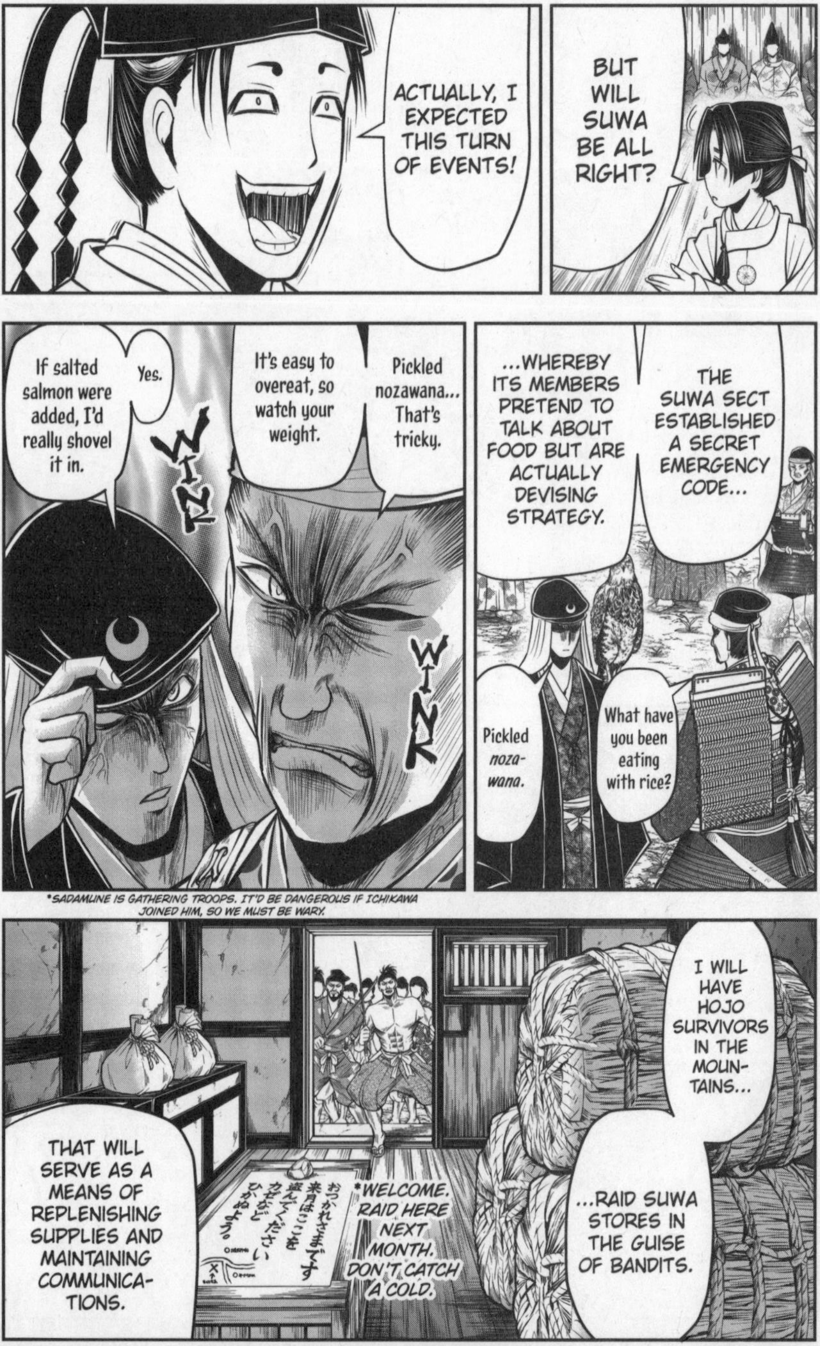
BUT WILL SUWA BE ALL RIGHT?
ACTUALLY, I EXPECTED THIS TURN OF EVENTS!
THE SUWA SECT ESTABLISHED A SECRET EMERGENCY CODE...
...WHEREBY ITS MEMBERS PRETEND TO TALK ABOUT FOOD BUT ARE ACTUALLY DEVISING STRATEGY.
What have you been eating with rice?
Pickled *nozawana.*
Pickled nozawana... That's tricky.
It's easy to overeat, so watch your weight.
WINK
Yes.
If salted salmon were added, I'd really shovel it in.
WINK
*SADAMUNE IS GATHERING TROOPS. IT'D BE DANGEROUS IF ICHIKAWA JOINED HIM, SO WE MUST BE WARY.
I WILL HAVE HOJO SURVIVORS IN THE MOUNTAINS...
...RAID SUWA STORES IN THE GUISE OF BANDITS.
おつかれさまです 来月はここを 盗んでください カゼなど ひかぬよう。
*WELCOME. RAID HERE NEXT MONTH. DON'T CATCH A COLD.
THAT WILL SERVE AS A MEANS OF REPLENISHING SUPPLIES AND MAINTAINING COMMUNICATIONS.

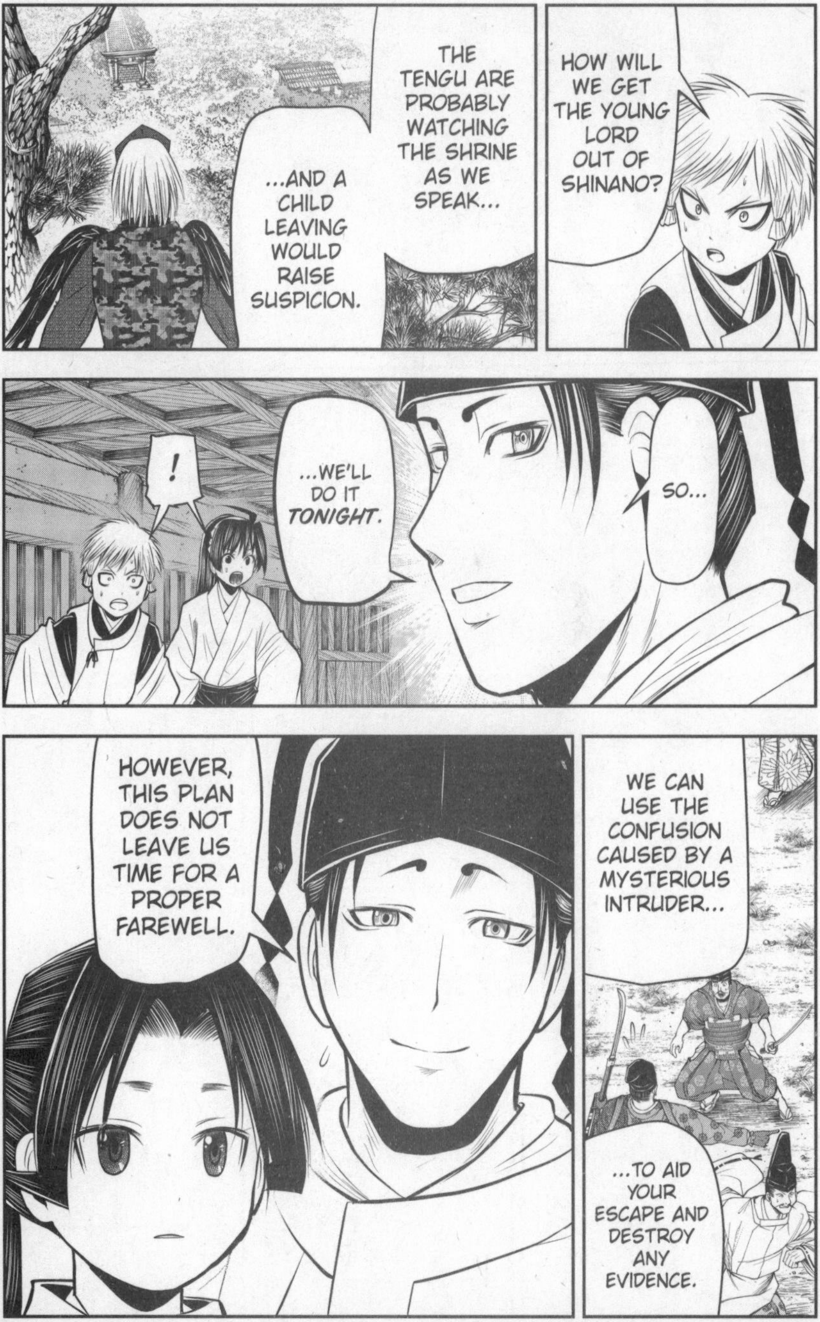
HOW WILL WE GET THE YOUNG LORD OUT OF SHINANO?
THE TENGU ARE PROBABLY WATCHING THE SHRINE AS WE SPEAK...
...AND A CHILD LEAVING WOULD RAISE SUSPICION.
SO...
...WE'LL DO IT *TONIGHT*.
!
WE CAN USE THE CONFUSION CAUSED BY A MYSTERIOUS INTRUDER...
...TO AID YOUR ESCAPE AND DESTROY ANY EVIDENCE.
HOWEVER, THIS PLAN DOES NOT LEAVE US TIME FOR A PROPER FAREWELL.

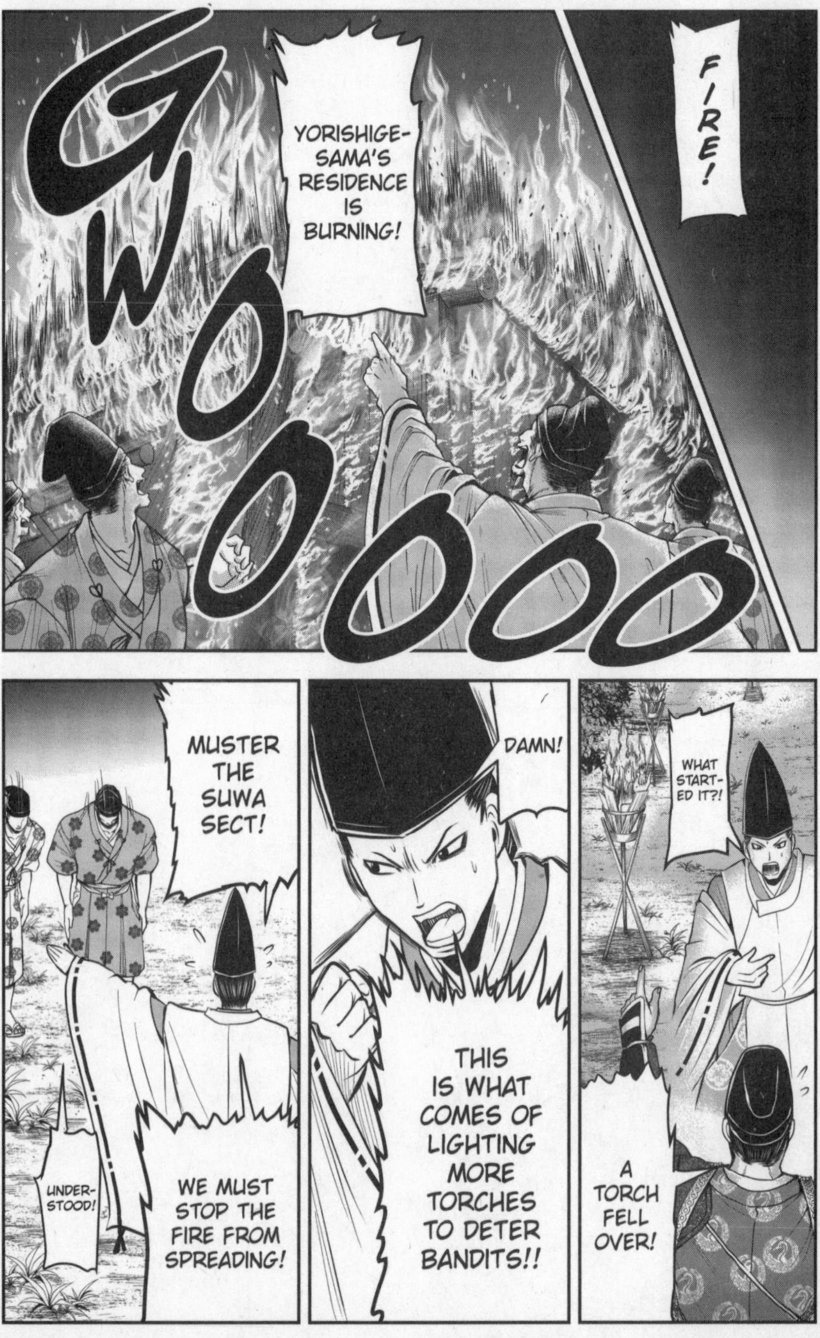
FIRE!
YORISHIGE-SAMA'S RESIDENCE IS BURNING!
GWOOOOOO
WHAT START-ED IT?!
A TORCH FELL OVER!
DAMN!
THIS IS WHAT COMES OF LIGHTING MORE TORCHES TO DETER BANDITS!!
MUSTER THE SUWA SECT!
WE MUST STOP THE FIRE FROM SPREADING!
UNDER-STOOD!

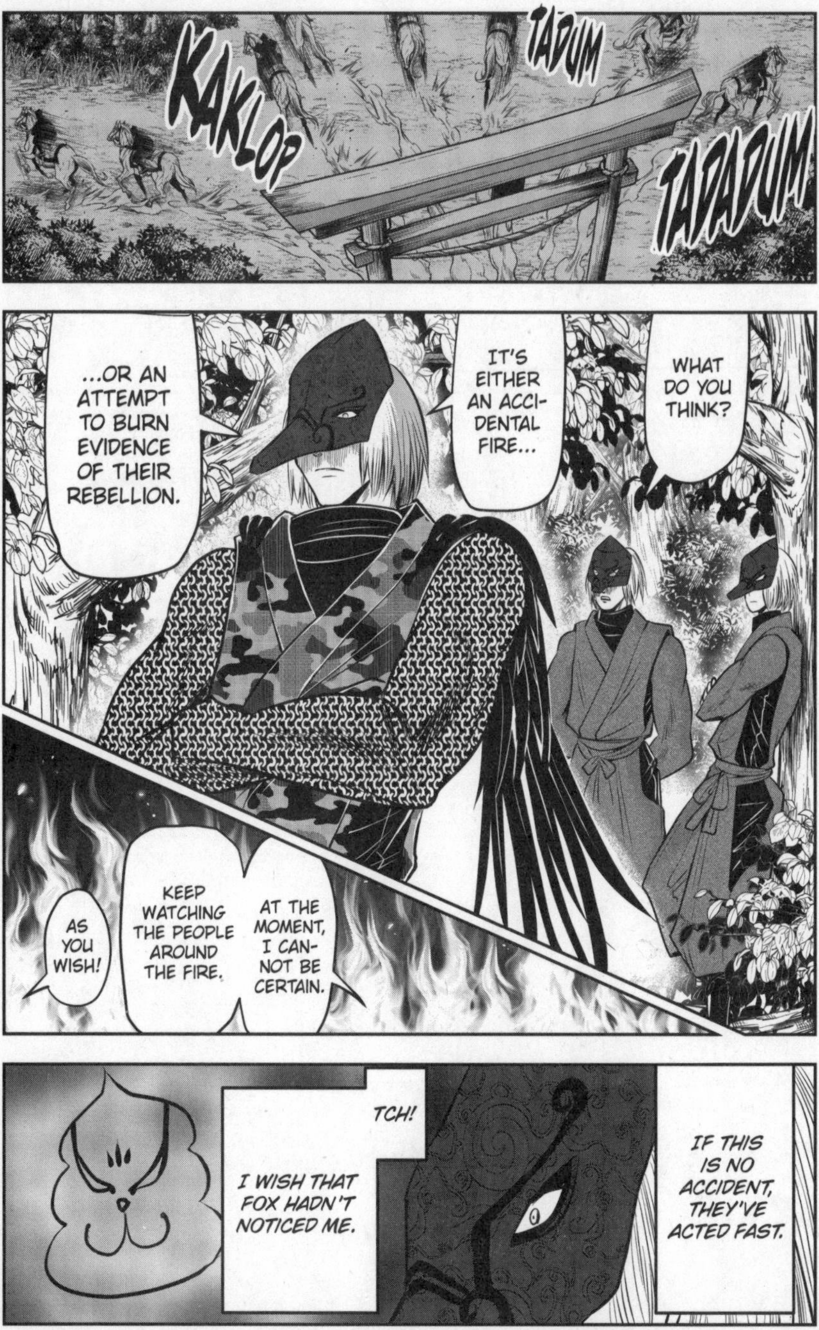
TADUM
TADADUM
KAKLOP
WHAT DO YOU THINK?
IT'S EITHER AN ACCI-DENTAL FIRE...
...OR AN ATTEMPT TO BURN EVIDENCE OF THEIR REBELLION.
AT THE MOMENT, I CAN-NOT BE CERTAIN.
KEEP WATCHING THE PEOPLE AROUND THE FIRE.
AS YOU WISH!
IF THIS IS NO ACCIDENT, THEY'VE ACTED FAST.
TCH!
I WISH THAT FOX HADN'T NOTICED ME.

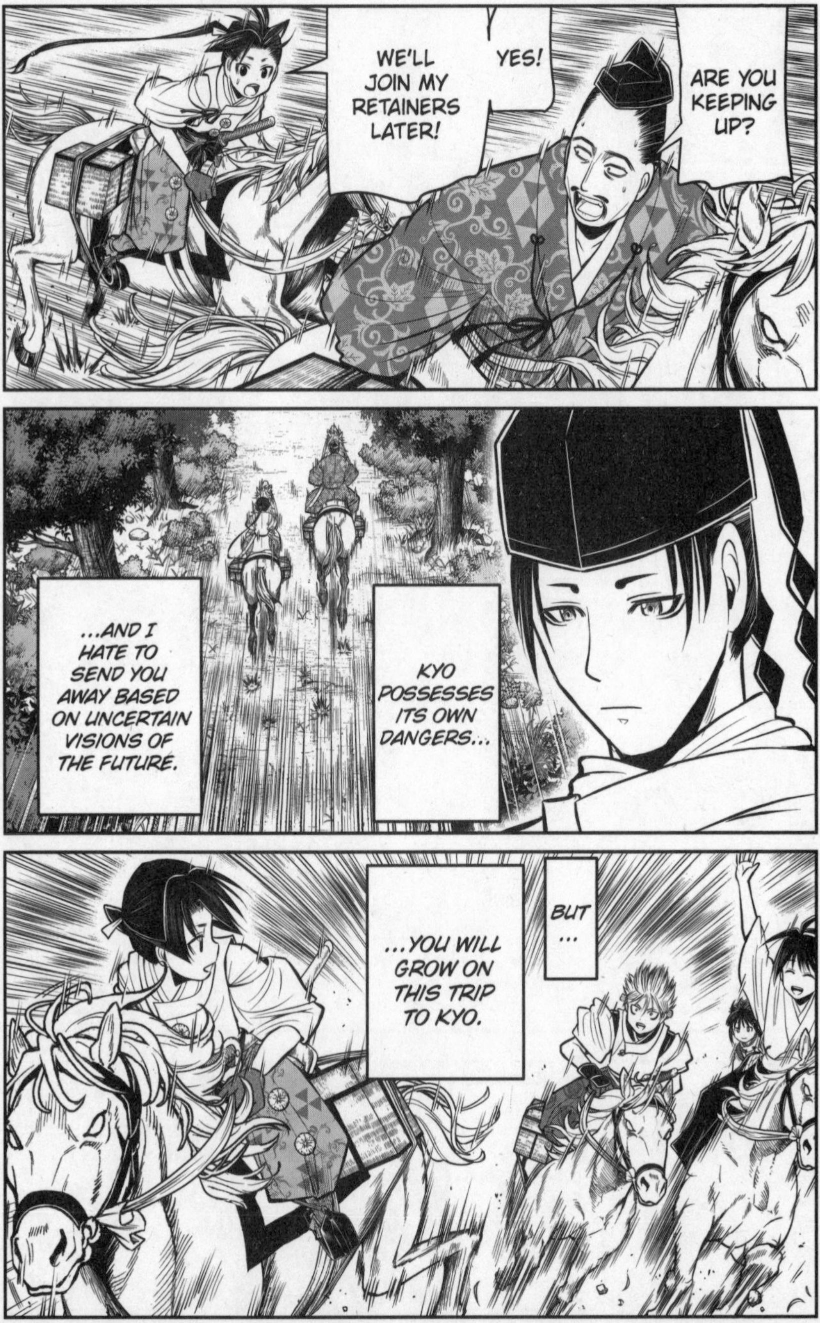
ARE YOU KEEPING UP?
YES!
WE'LL JOIN MY RETAINERS LATER!
KYO POSSESSES ITS OWN DANGERS...
...AND I HATE TO SEND YOU AWAY BASED ON UNCERTAIN VISIONS OF THE FUTURE.
BUT ...
...YOU WILL GROW ON THIS TRIP TO KYO.

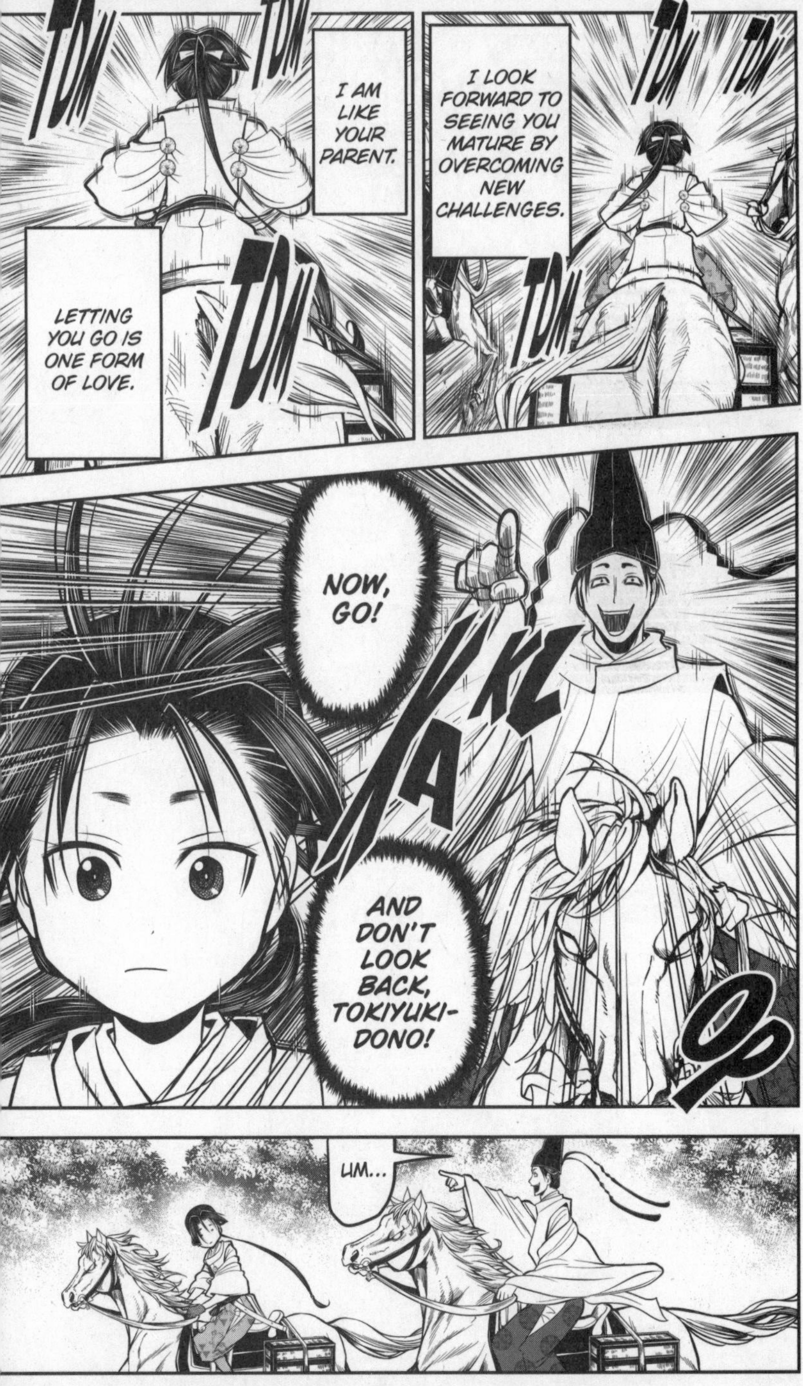
I LOOK FORWARD TO SEEING YOU MATURE BY OVERCOMING NEW CHALLENGES.
TDM TDM
TDM
I AM LIKE YOUR PARENT.
TDM TDM
LETTING YOU GO IS ONE FORM OF LOVE.
TDM
NOW, GO!
AND DON'T LOOK BACK, TOKIYUKI-DONO!
UM...

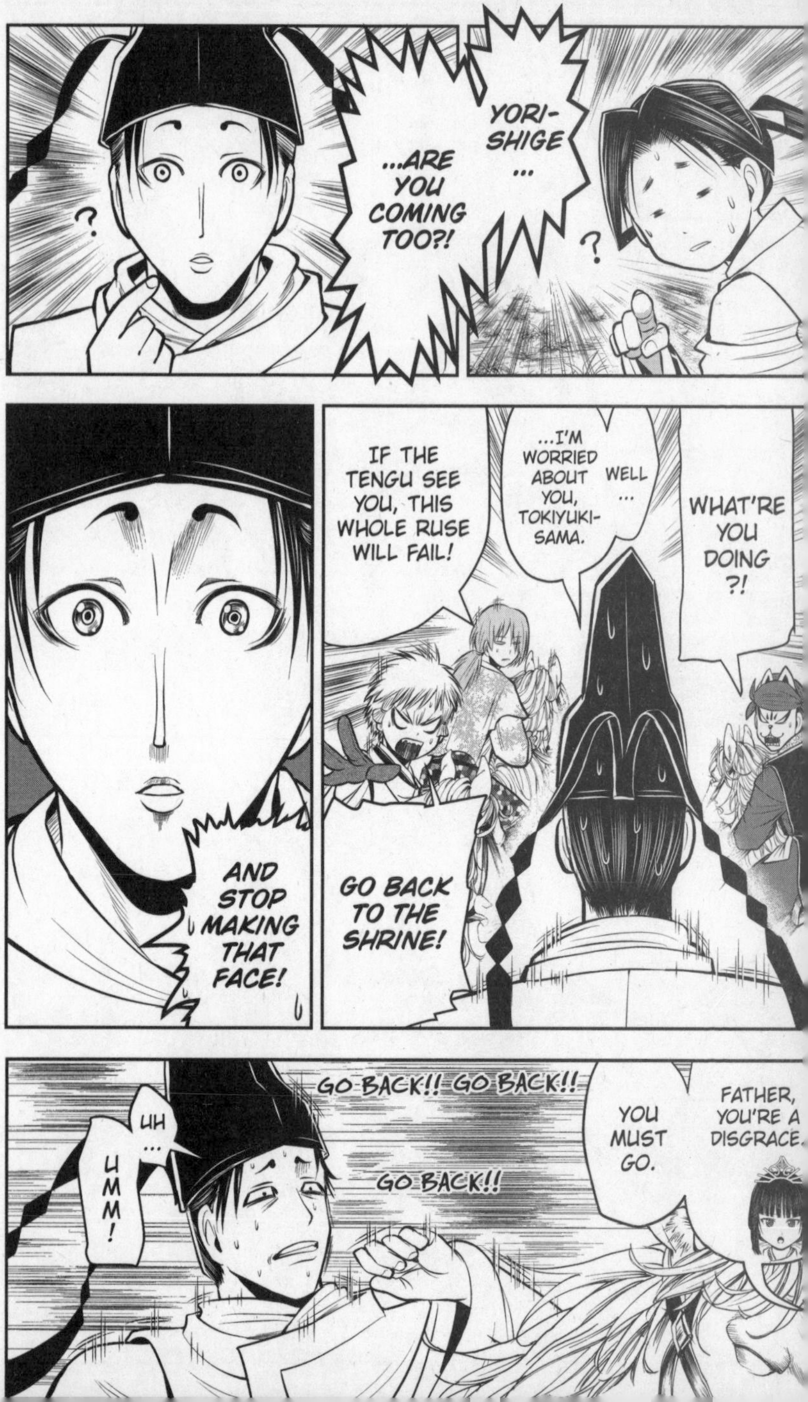
YORI-SHIGE ...
...ARE YOU COMING TOO?!
WHAT'RE YOU DOING ?!
WELL ...
...I'M WORRIED ABOUT YOU, TOKIYUKI-SAMA.
IF THE TENGU SEE YOU, THIS WHOLE RUSE WILL FAIL!
GO BACK TO THE SHRINE!
AND STOP MAKING THAT FACE!
FATHER, YOU'RE A DISGRACE.
YOU MUST GO.
GO BACK!! GO BACK!!
GO BACK!!
UH ... UMM!

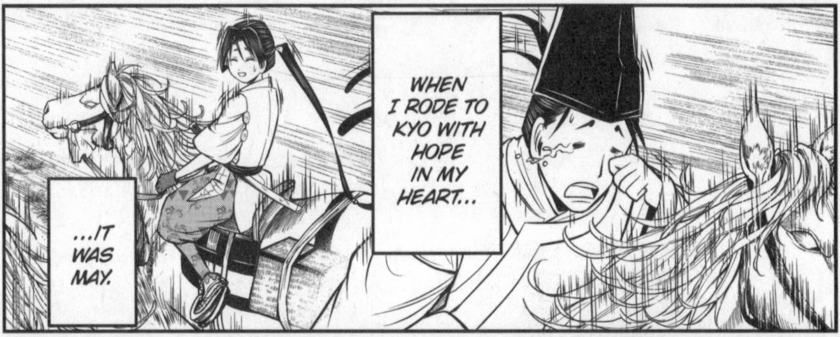
WHEN I RODE TO KYO WITH HOPE IN MY HEART...
...IT WAS MAY.
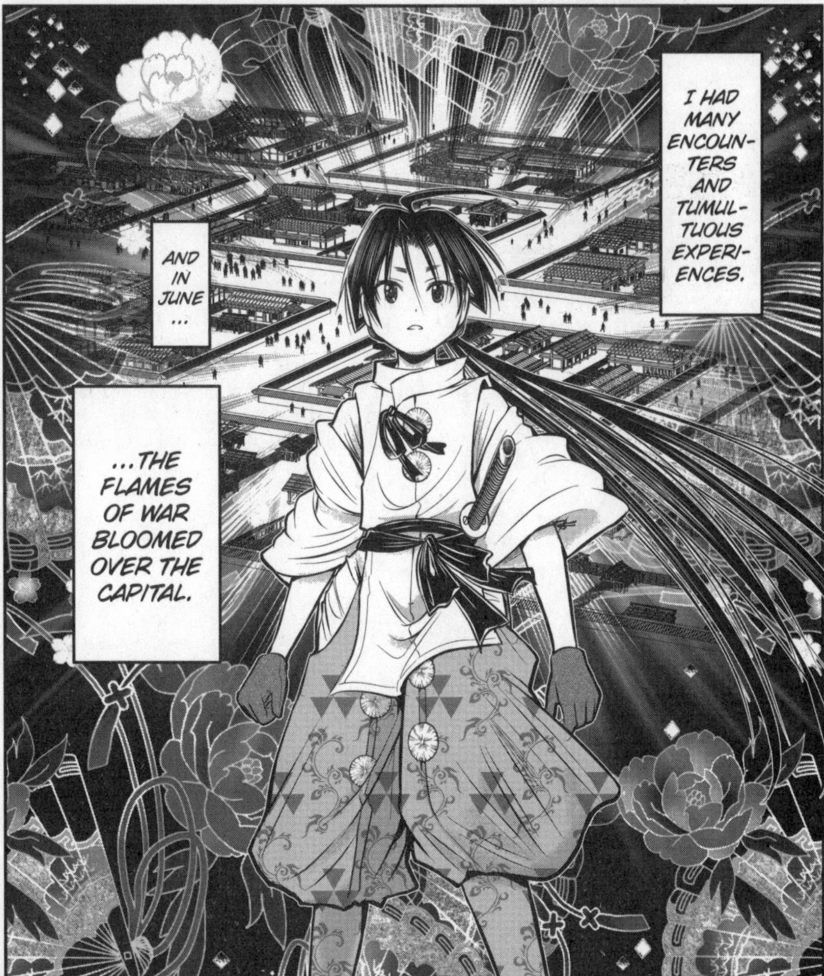
I HAD MANY ENCOUN-TERS AND TUMUL-TUOUS EXPERI-ENCES.
AND IN JUNE...
...THE FLAMES OF WAR BLOOMED OVER THE CAPITAL.

1335

KOJIRO

★ N

ABILITIES		NANBOKU-CHO COMPATIBILITY	
MARTIAL ARTS	63	SAVAGERY	90
INTELLIGENCE	37	LOYALTY	95
POLITICS	5	CHAOS	59
LEADERSHIP	61	INGENUITY	31
CHARM	42	RUNNING AND HIDING	43

CREST

MULBERRY LEAVES, MOON, AND THORNS

SKILL SWORD FIGHTING *(CHEI)*: 20 PERCENT INCREASE TO SWORDSMANSHIP

SKILL GENERALSHIP *(TEI)*: 5 PERCENT INCREASE TO LEADERSHIP

SKILL WARRIOR ESSENCE *(TEI)*: 5 PERCENT INCREASE TO MARTIAL ARTS, LOYALTY AND SAVAGERY

SKILL BANTER: LEADERSHIP, CHAOS, AND RESPONSE SPEED INCREASE ALONG WITH HIS LORD'S AIRHEADEDNESS

RELATIONSHIP WITH TOKIYUKI
LORD: 30 PERCENT, FRIEND: 70 PERCENT

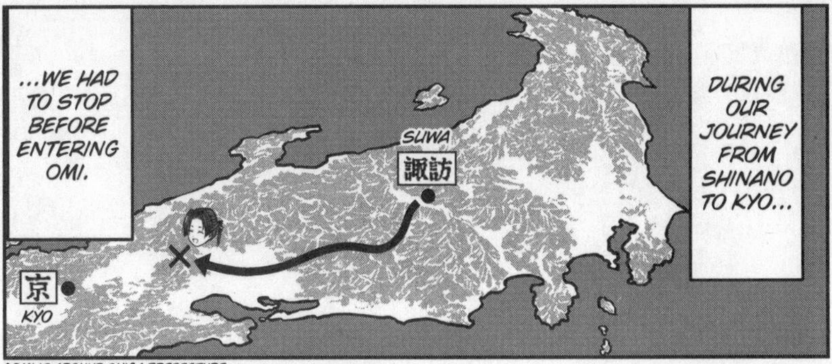
DURING OUR JOURNEY FROM SHINANO TO KYO...
SUWA
諏訪
京
KYO
...WE HAD TO STOP BEFORE ENTERING OMI.

*OMI IS AROUND SHIGA PREFECTURE

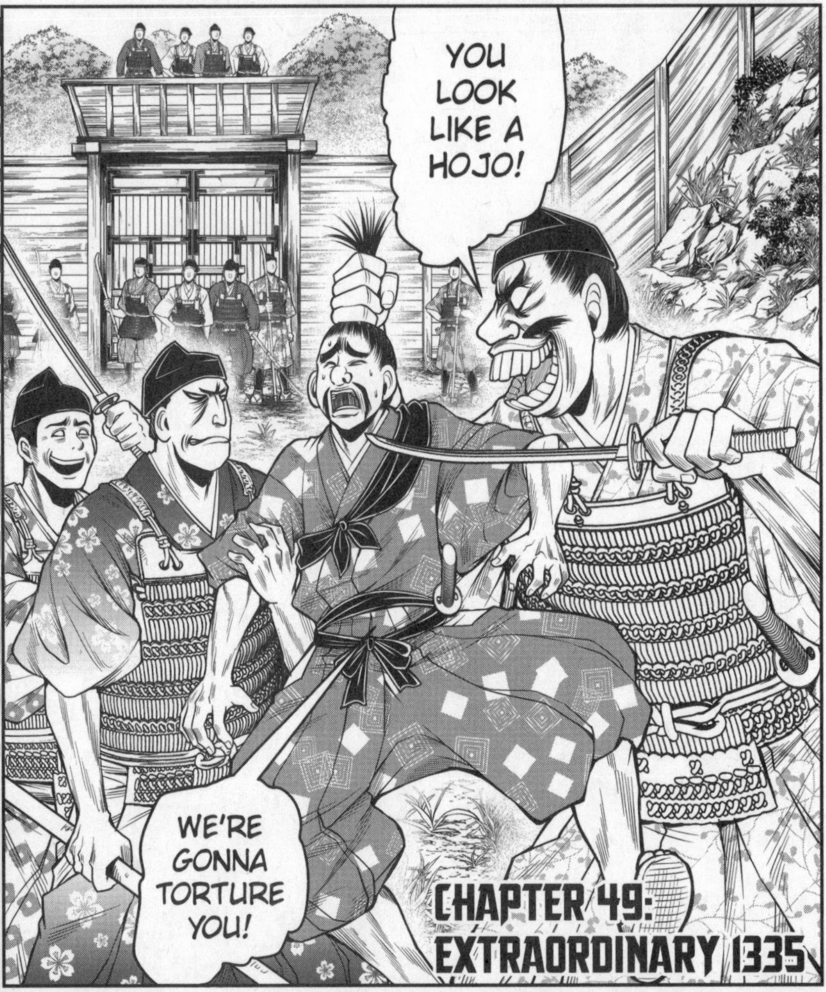
YOU LOOK LIKE A HOJO!
WE'RE GONNA TORTURE YOU!
CHAPTER 49: EXTRAORDINARY 1335

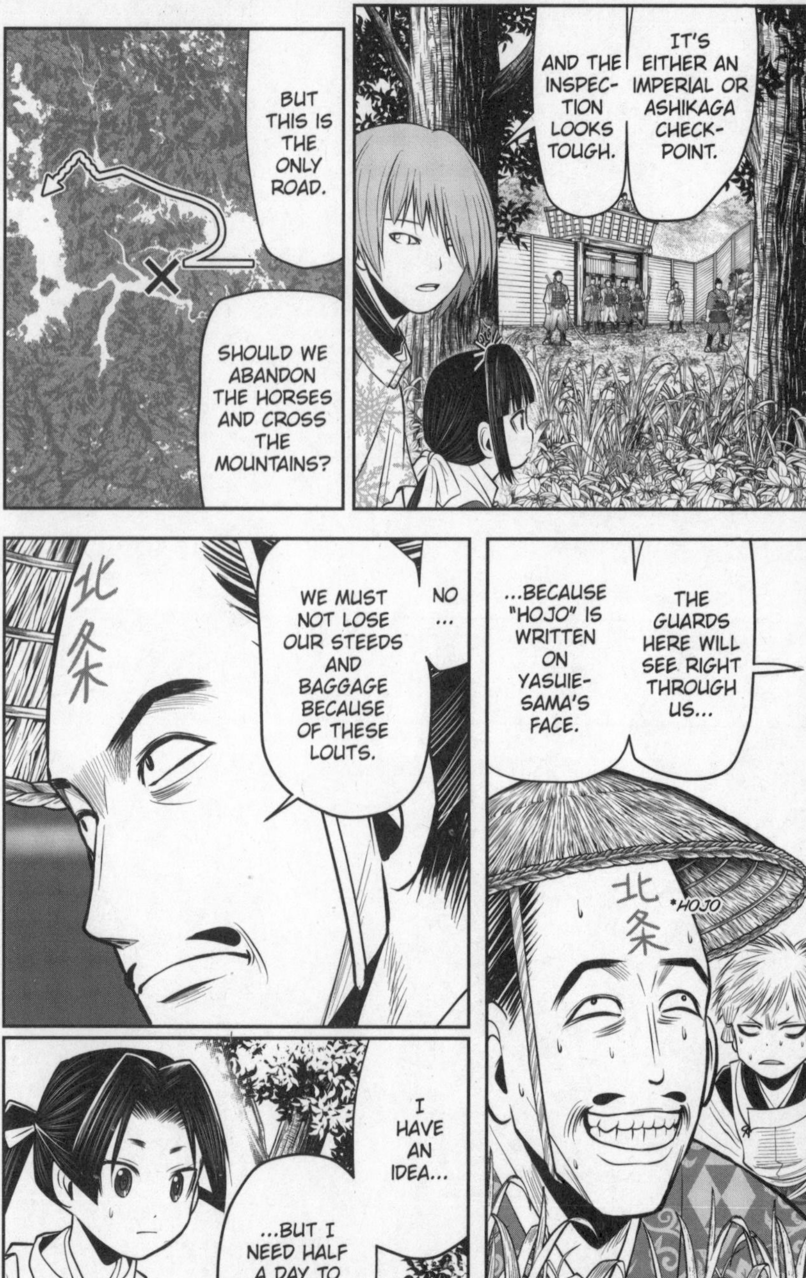
IT'S EITHER AN IMPERIAL OR ASHIKAGA CHECKPOINT.
AND THE INSPECTION LOOKS TOUGH.
BUT THIS IS THE ONLY ROAD.
SHOULD WE ABANDON THE HORSES AND CROSS THE MOUNTAINS?
THE GUARDS HERE WILL SEE RIGHT THROUGH US...
...BECAUSE "HOJO" IS WRITTEN ON YASUIE-SAMA'S FACE.
北条
*HOJO
NO...
WE MUST NOT LOSE OUR STEEDS AND BAGGAGE BECAUSE OF THESE LOUTS.
北条
I HAVE AN IDEA...
...BUT I NEED HALF A DAY TO PREPARE.

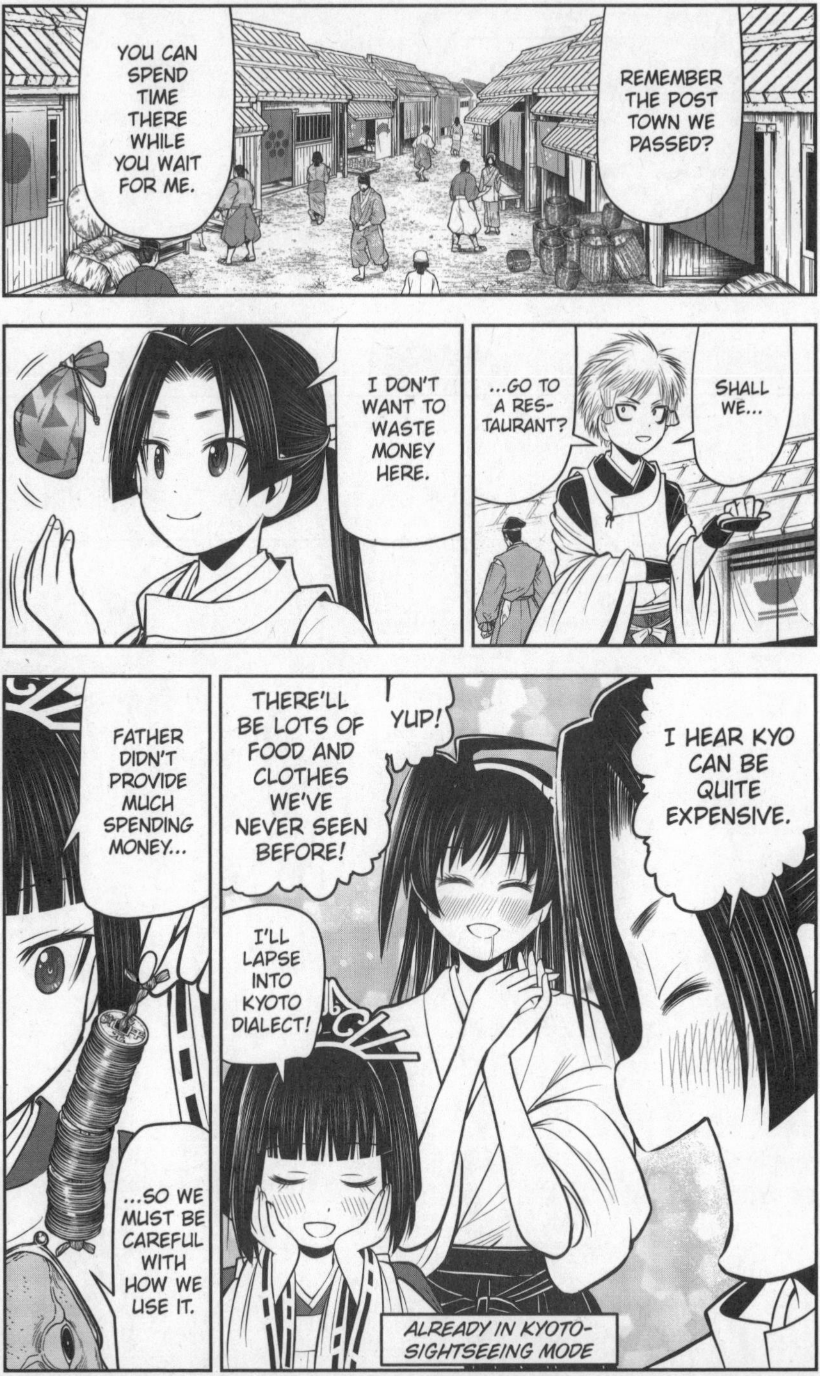
REMEMBER THE POST TOWN WE PASSED?
YOU CAN SPEND TIME THERE WHILE YOU WAIT FOR ME.
SHALL WE...
...GO TO A RES-TAURANT?
I DON'T WANT TO WASTE MONEY HERE.
I HEAR KYO CAN BE QUITE EXPENSIVE.
YUP!
THERE'LL BE LOTS OF FOOD AND CLOTHES WE'VE NEVER SEEN BEFORE!
I'LL LAPSE INTO KYOTO DIALECT!
ALREADY IN KYOTO-SIGHTSEEING MODE
FATHER DIDN'T PROVIDE MUCH SPENDING MONEY...
...SO WE MUST BE CAREFUL WITH HOW WE USE IT.

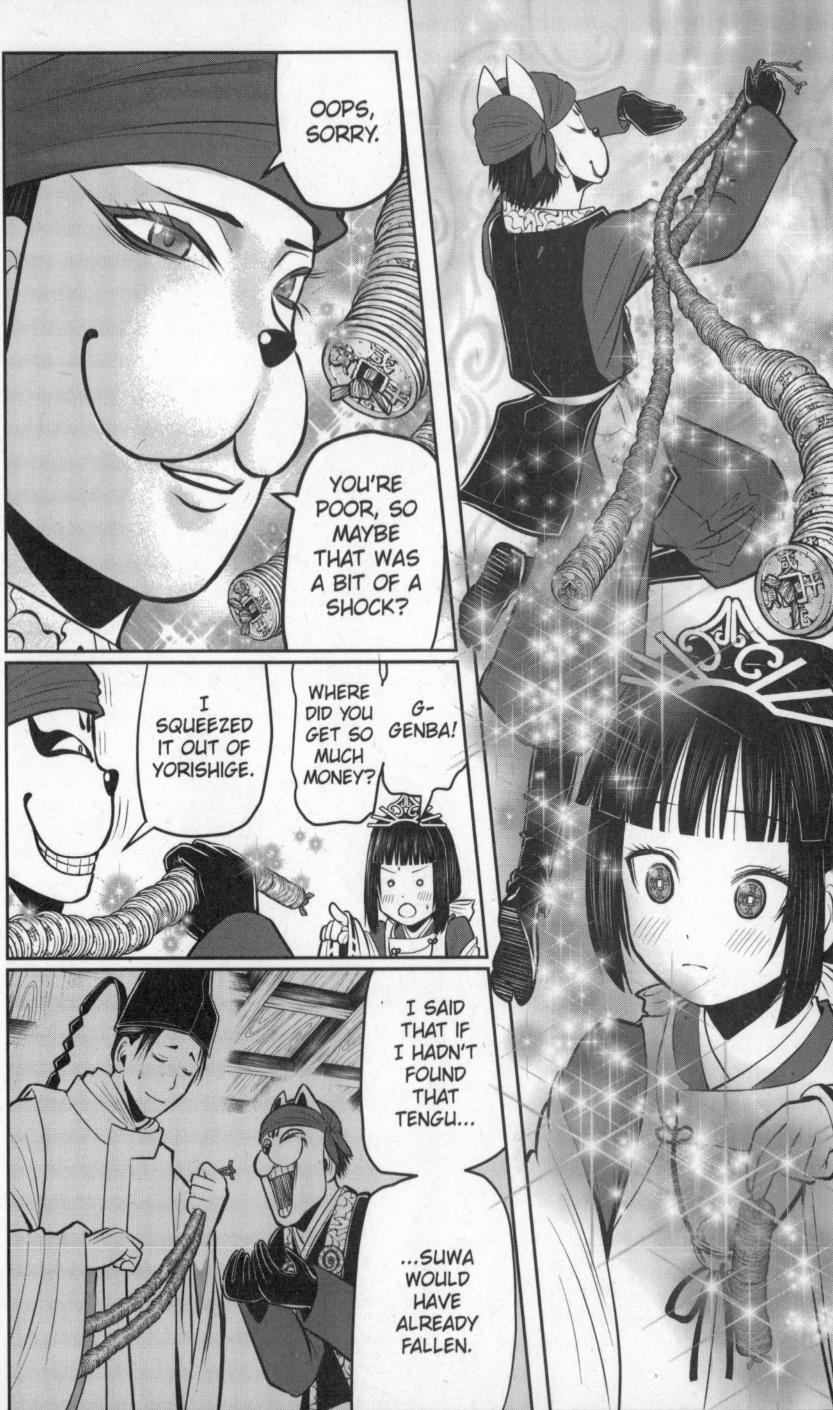
OOPS, SORRY.
YOU'RE POOR, SO MAYBE THAT WAS A BIT OF A SHOCK?
G- GENBA!
WHERE DID YOU GET SO MUCH MONEY?
I SQUEEZED IT OUT OF YORISHIGE.
I SAID THAT IF I HADN'T FOUND THAT TENGU...
...SUWA WOULD HAVE ALREADY FALLEN.

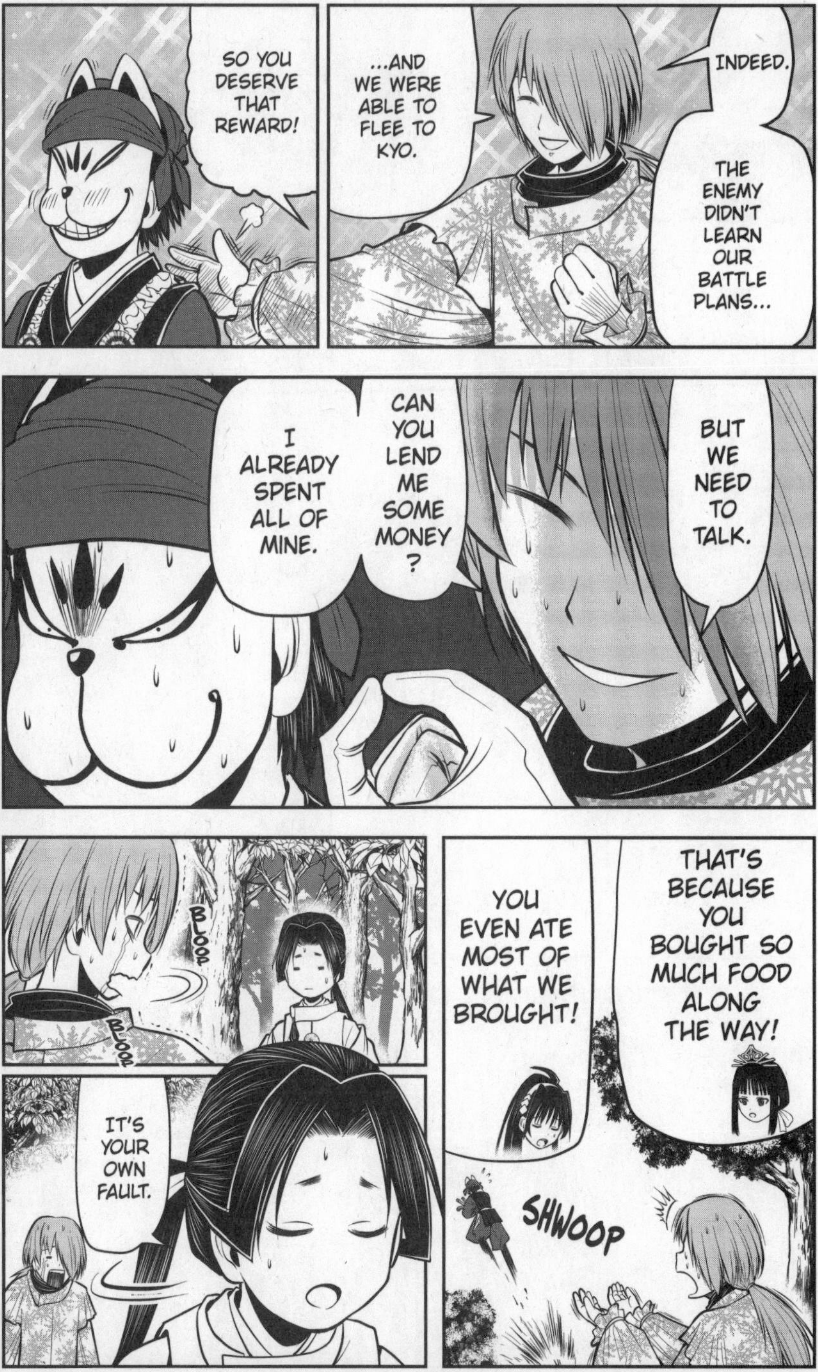
INDEED.
THE ENEMY DIDN'T LEARN OUR BATTLE PLANS...
...AND WE WERE ABLE TO FLEE TO KYO.
SO YOU DESERVE THAT REWARD!
BUT WE NEED TO TALK.
CAN YOU LEND ME SOME MONEY?
I ALREADY SPENT ALL OF MINE.
THAT'S BECAUSE YOU BOUGHT SO MUCH FOOD ALONG THE WAY!
YOU EVEN ATE MOST OF WHAT WE BROUGHT!
SHWOOP
BLOOP
BLOOP
IT'S YOUR OWN FAULT.

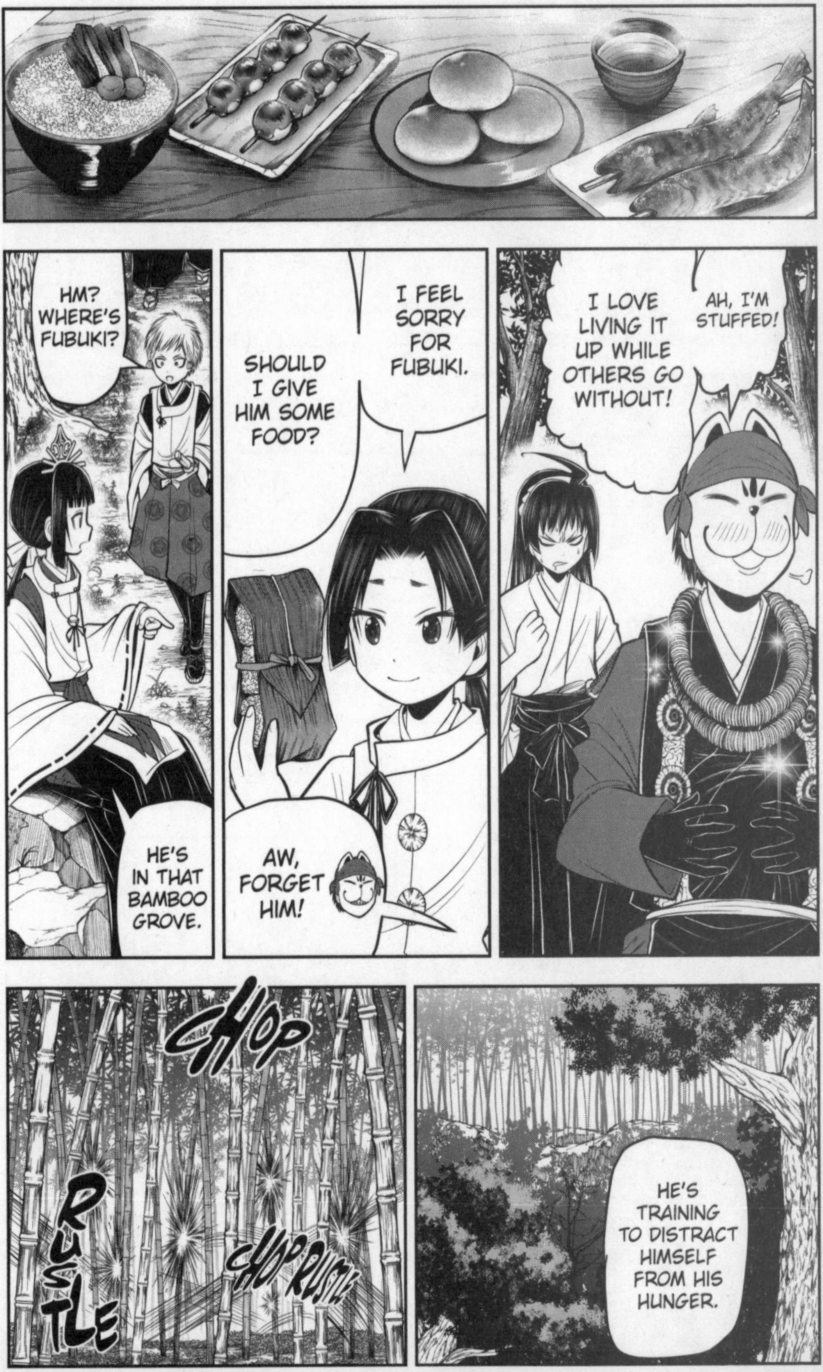
AH, I'M STUFFED!
I LOVE LIVING IT UP WHILE OTHERS GO WITHOUT!
I FEEL SORRY FOR FUBUKI.
SHOULD I GIVE HIM SOME FOOD?
AW, FORGET HIM!
HM? WHERE'S FUBUKI?
HE'S IN THAT BAMBOO GROVE.
HE'S TRAINING TO DISTRACT HIMSELF FROM HIS HUNGER.
CHOP
RUSTLE
CHOP RUSTLE

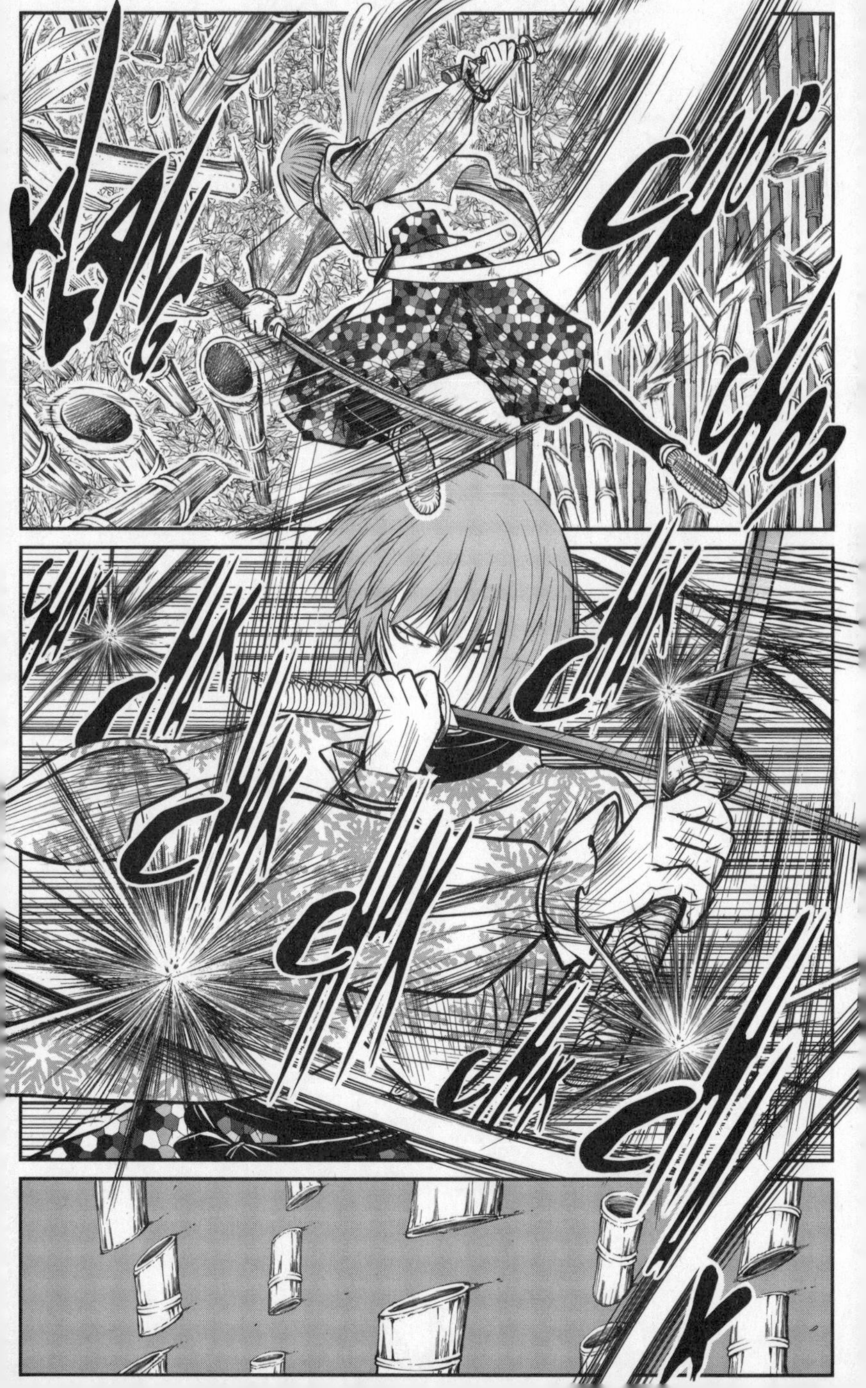

CHOP
CHOP
KLANG
CHAK
CHAK
CHAK
CHAK
CHAK
CHAK
CHAK
CHAK

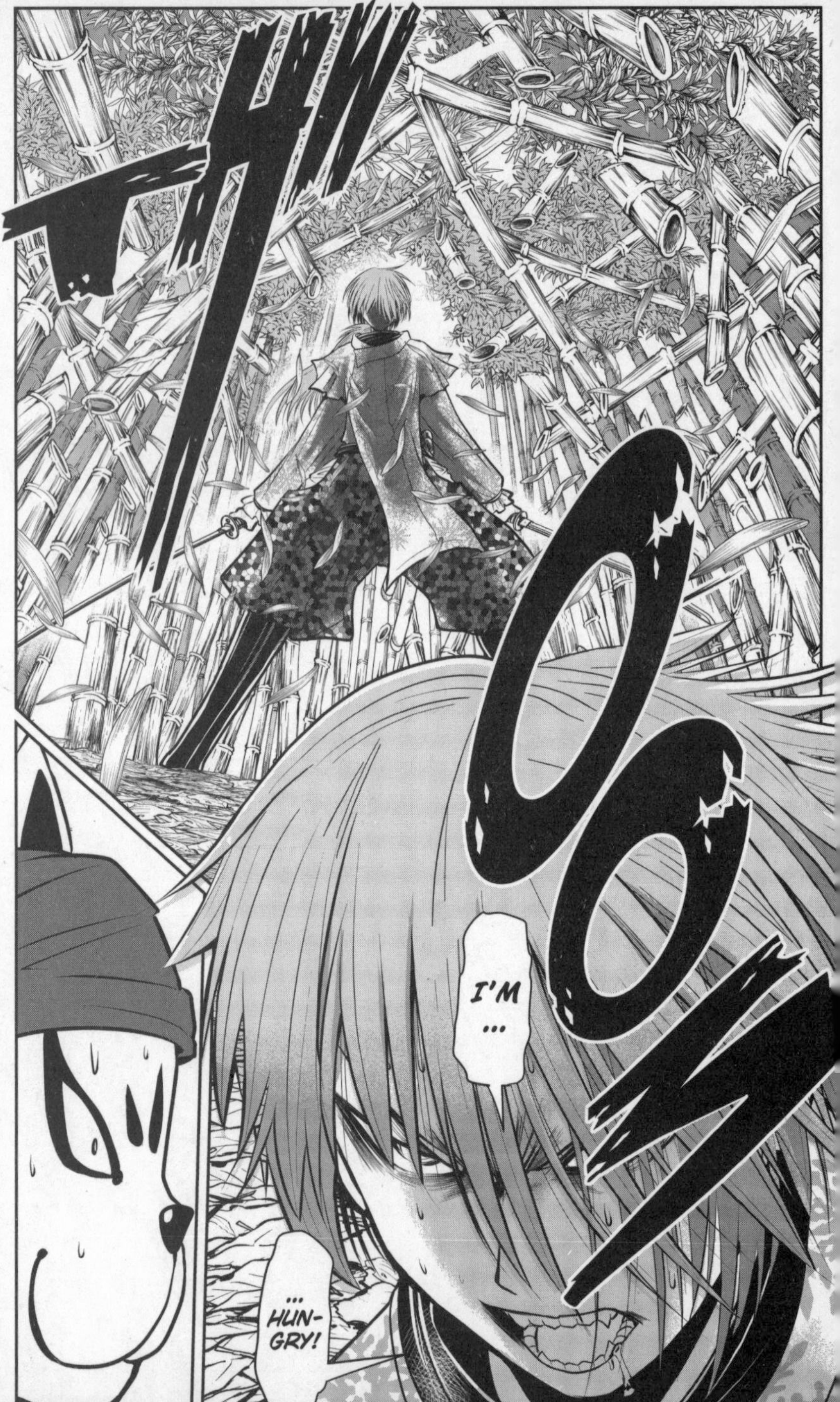
I'M ...
... HUN-GRY!

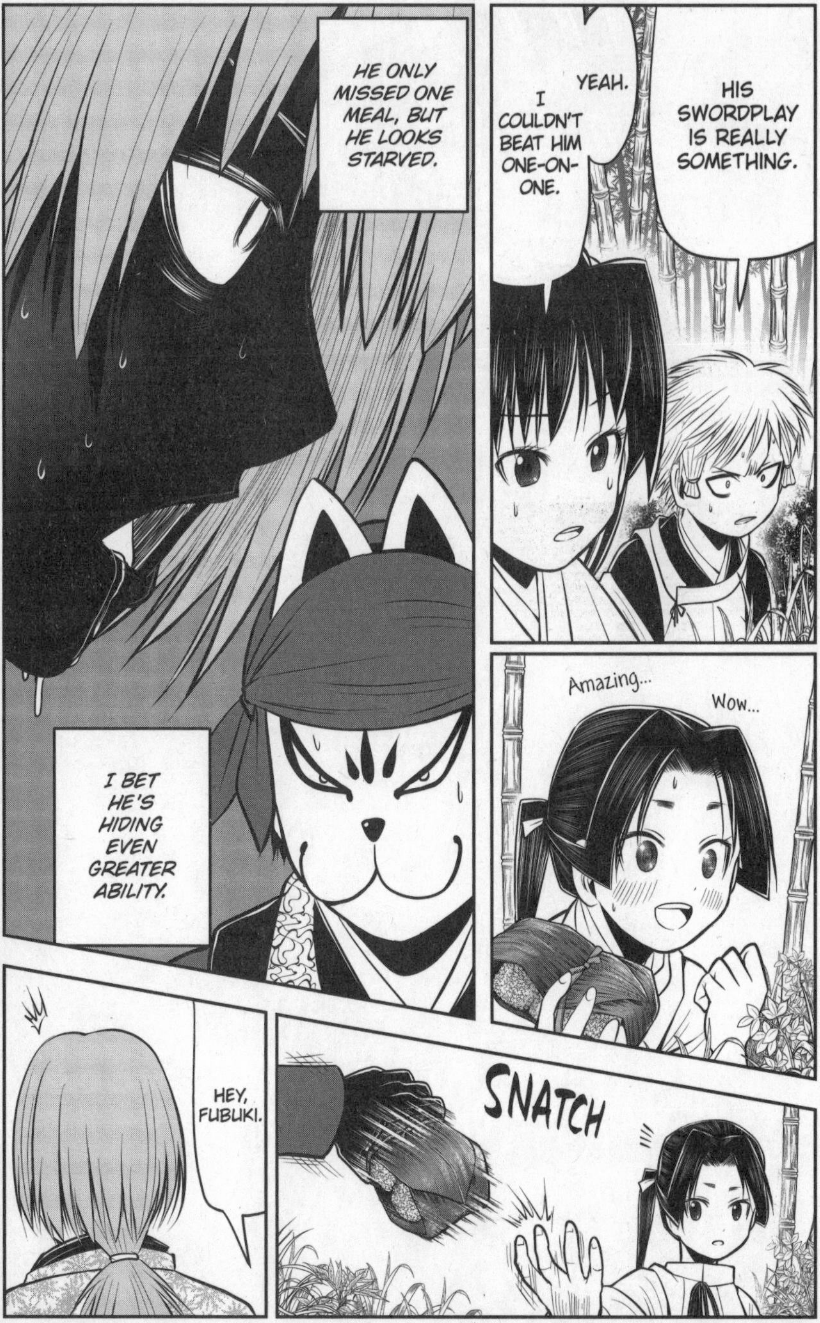
HIS SWORDPLAY IS REALLY SOMETHING.
YEAH.
I COULDN'T BEAT HIM ONE-ON-ONE.
Wow...
Amazing...
HE ONLY MISSED ONE MEAL, BUT HE LOOKS STARVED.
I BET HE'S HIDING EVEN GREATER ABILITY.
SNATCH
HEY, FUBUKI.

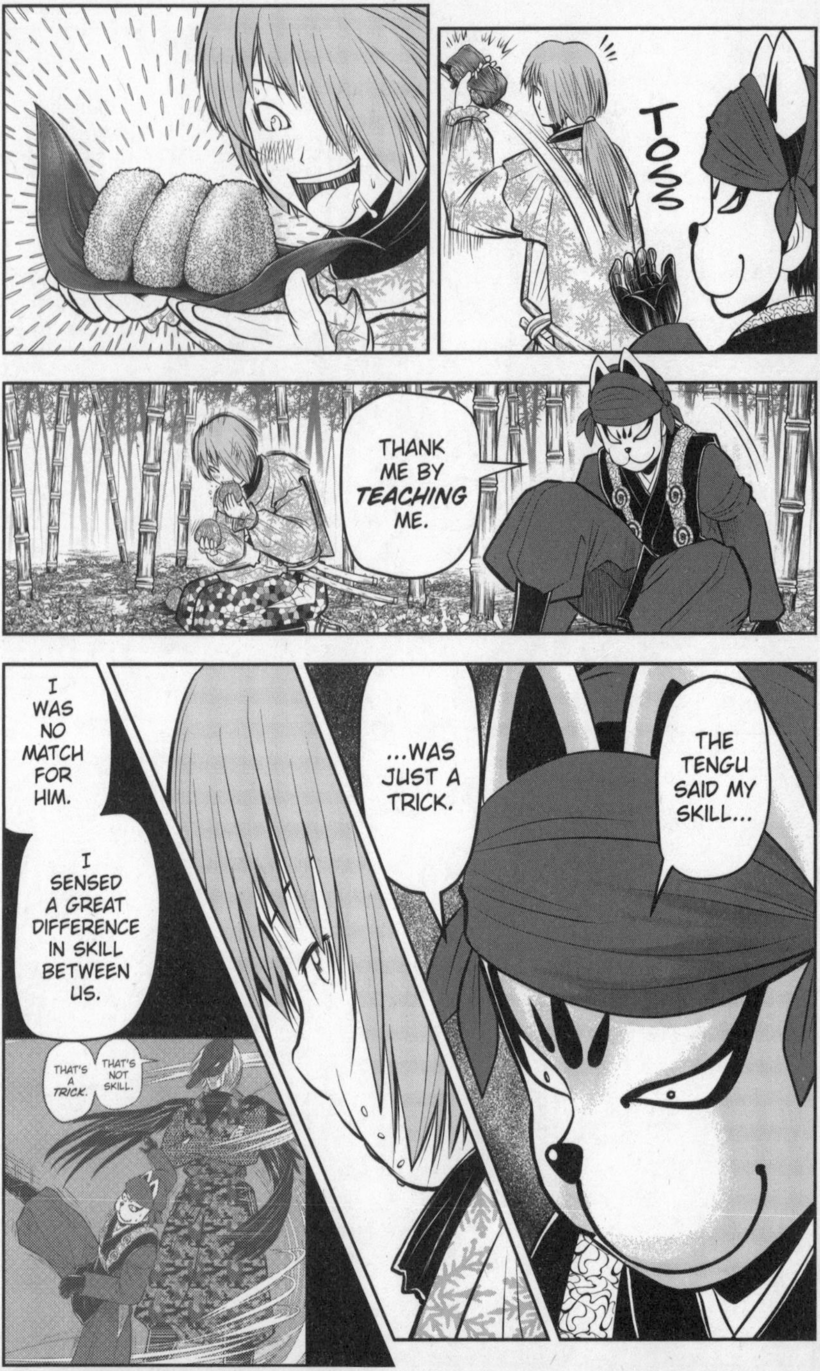
TOSS
THANK ME BY *TEACHING* ME.
THE TENGU SAID MY SKILL...
...WAS JUST A TRICK.
I WAS NO MATCH FOR HIM.
I SENSED A GREAT DIFFERENCE IN SKILL BETWEEN US.
THAT'S NOT SKILL.
THAT'S A *TRICK*.

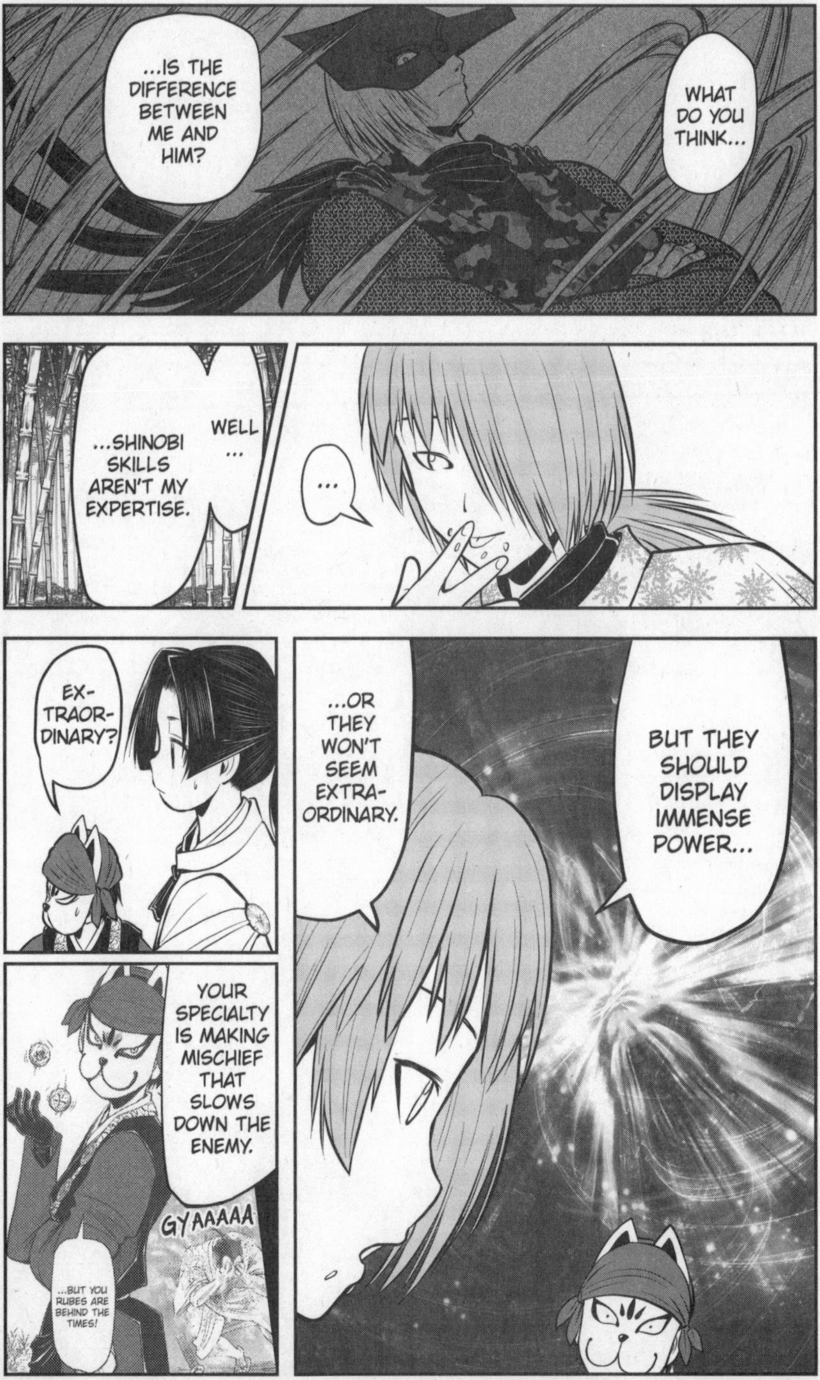
WHAT DO YOU THINK...
...IS THE DIFFERENCE BETWEEN ME AND HIM?
...
WELL ...
...SHINOBI SKILLS AREN'T MY EXPERTISE.
BUT THEY SHOULD DISPLAY IMMENSE POWER...
...OR THEY WON'T SEEM EXTRA-ORDINARY.
EX-TRAOR-DINARY?
YOUR SPECIALTY IS MAKING MISCHIEF THAT SLOWS DOWN THE ENEMY.
GYAAAAA
...BUT YOU RUBES ARE BEHIND THE TIMES!

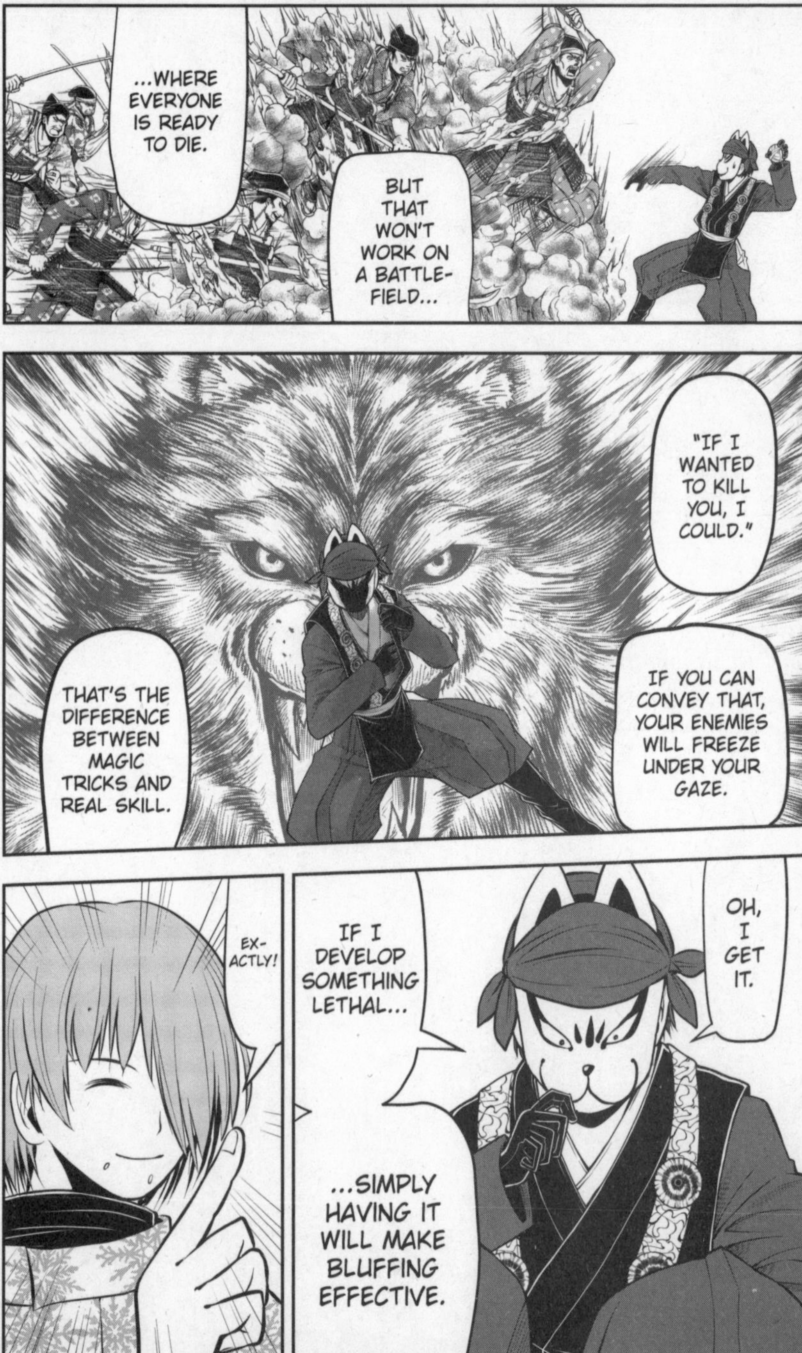
...WHERE EVERYONE IS READY TO DIE.
BUT THAT WON'T WORK ON A BATTLE-FIELD...
"IF I WANTED TO KILL YOU, I COULD."
IF YOU CAN CONVEY THAT, YOUR ENEMIES WILL FREEZE UNDER YOUR GAZE.
THAT'S THE DIFFERENCE BETWEEN MAGIC TRICKS AND REAL SKILL.
OH, I GET IT.
IF I DEVELOP SOMETHING LETHAL...
...SIMPLY HAVING IT WILL MAKE BLUFFING EFFECTIVE.
EX-ACTLY!

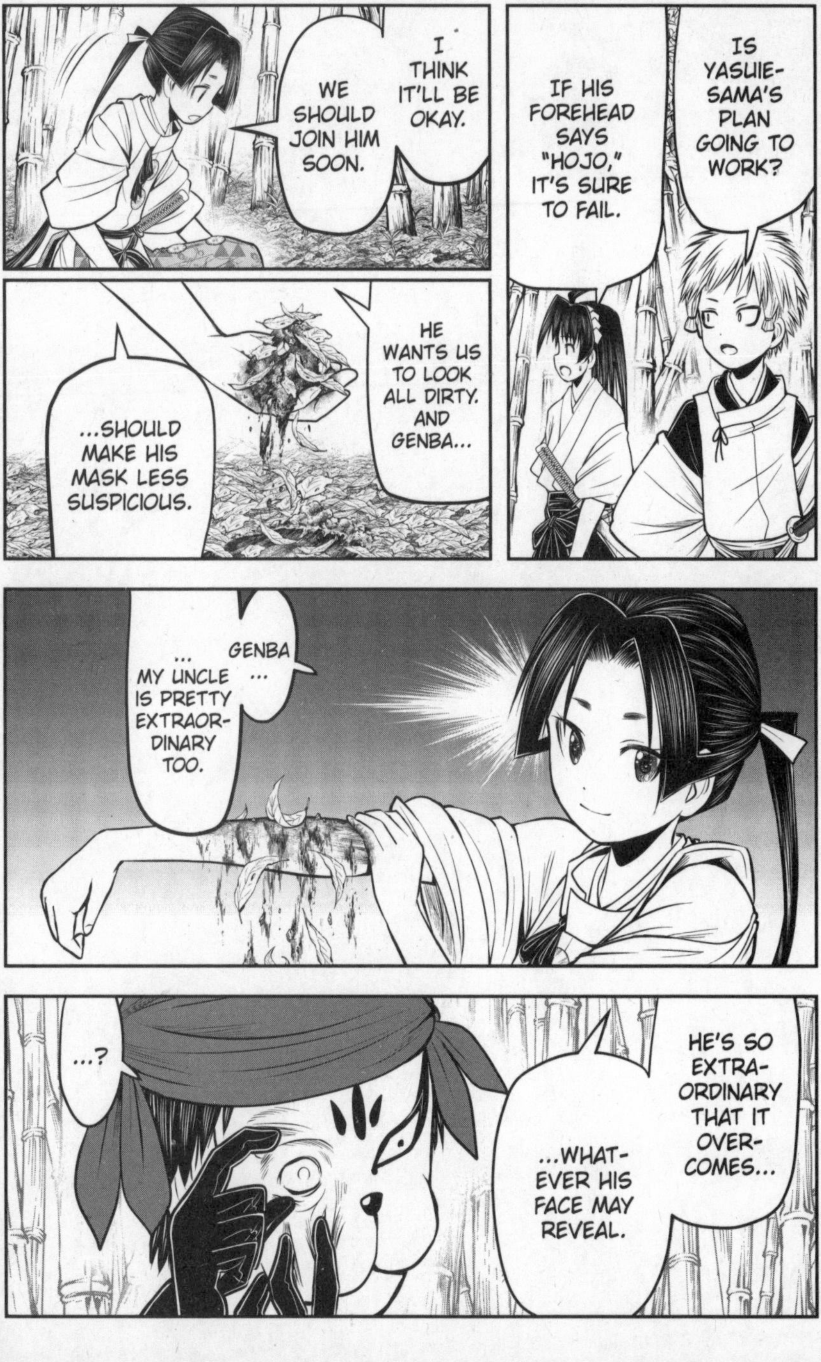
IS YASUIE-SAMA'S PLAN GOING TO WORK?
IF HIS FOREHEAD SAYS "HOJO," IT'S SURE TO FAIL.
I THINK IT'LL BE OKAY.
WE SHOULD JOIN HIM SOON.
HE WANTS US TO LOOK ALL DIRTY. AND GENBA...
...SHOULD MAKE HIS MASK LESS SUSPICIOUS.
GENBA ...
... MY UNCLE IS PRETTY EXTRAOR-DINARY TOO.
HE'S SO EXTRA-ORDINARY THAT IT OVER-COMES...
...WHAT-EVER HIS FACE MAY REVEAL.
...?

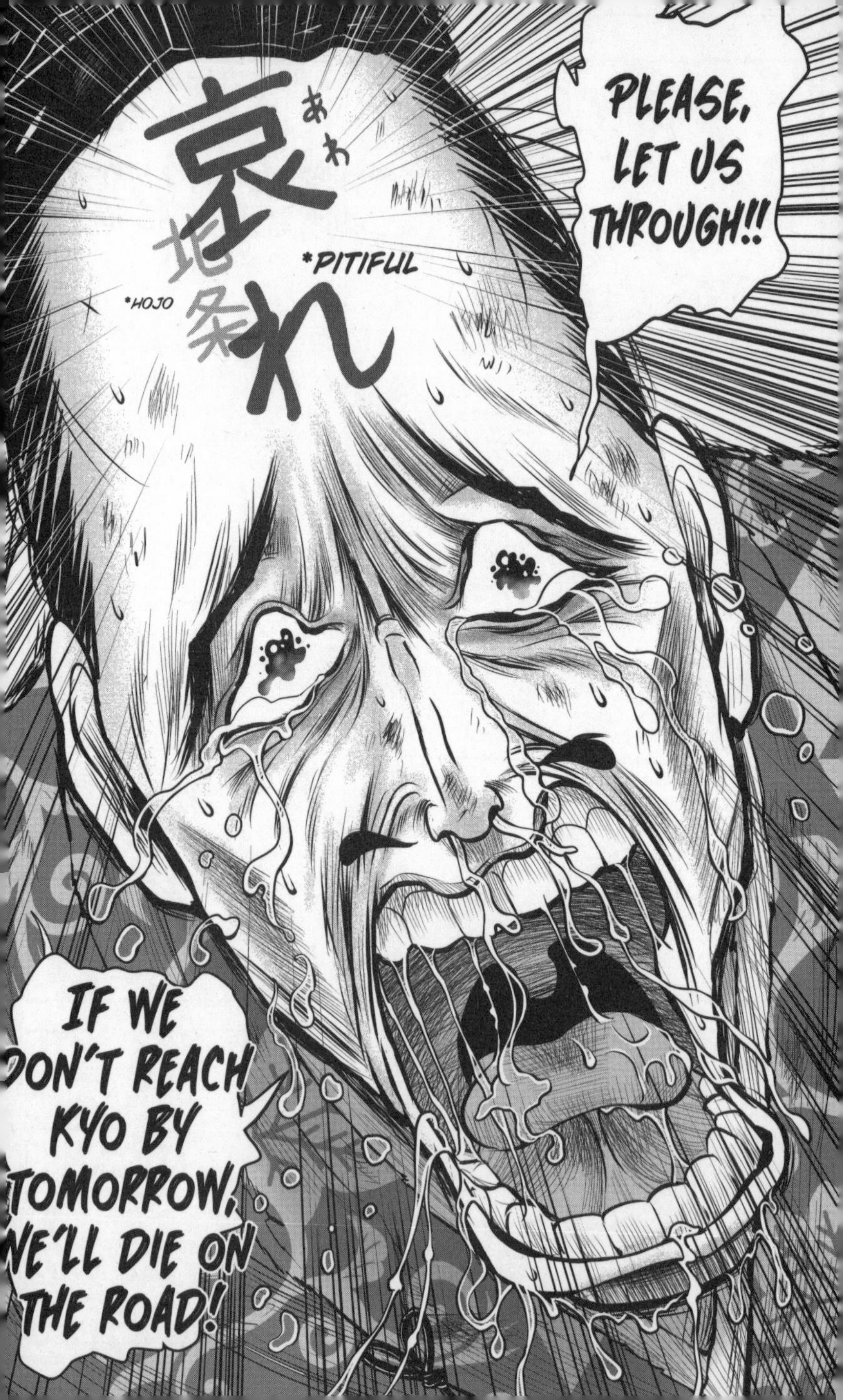
PLEASE, LET US THROUGH!!
哀れ
あわ
*PITIFUL
北条
*HOJO
IF WE DON'T REACH KYO BY TOMORROW, WE'LL DIE ON THE ROAD!

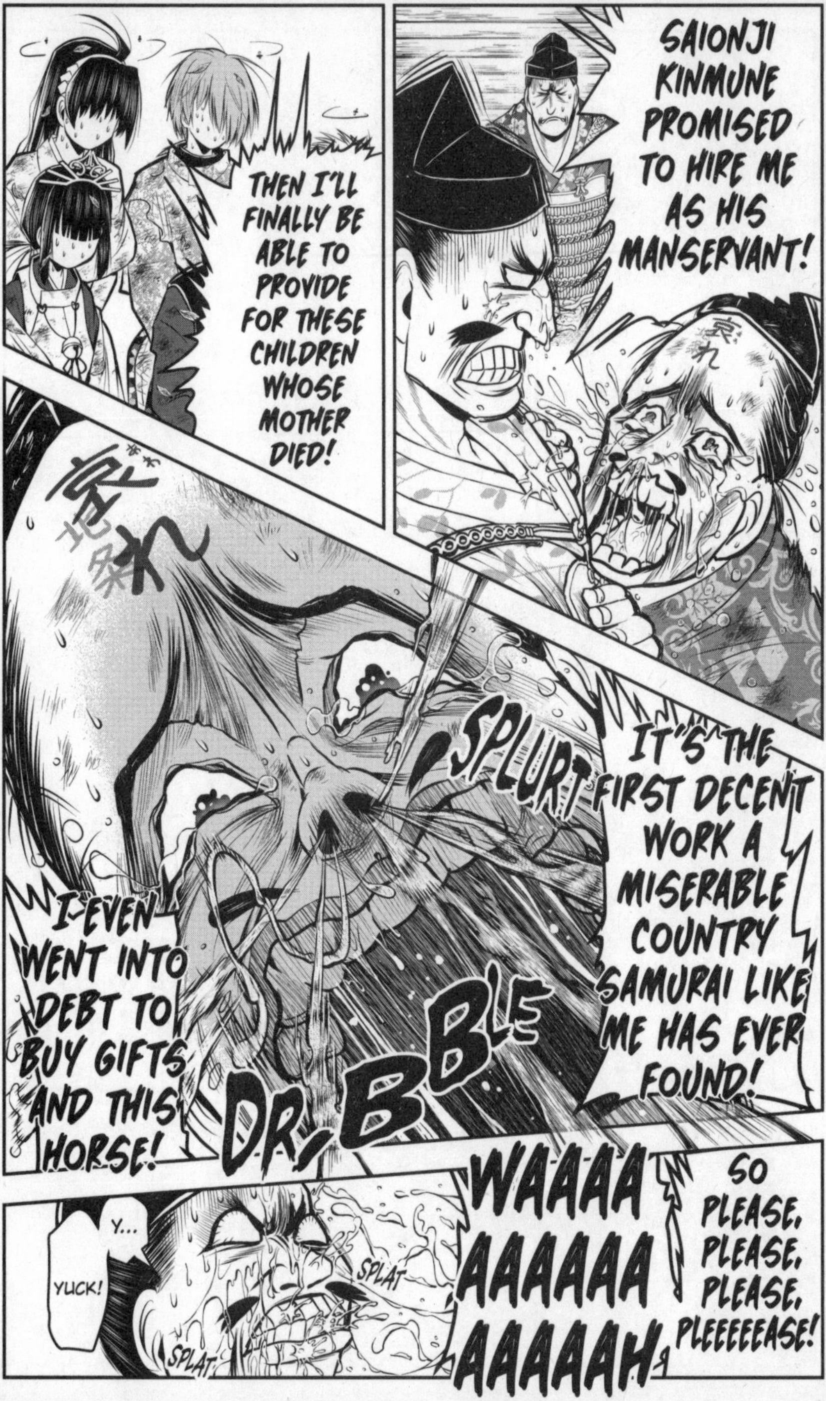
SAIONJI KINMUNE PROMISED TO HIRE ME AS HIS MANSERVANT!
THEN I'LL FINALLY BE ABLE TO PROVIDE FOR THESE CHILDREN WHOSE MOTHER DIED!
IT'S THE FIRST DECENT WORK A MISERABLE COUNTRY SAMURAI LIKE ME HAS EVER FOUND!
SPLURT
I-EVEN WENT INTO DEBT TO BUY GIFTS AND THIS HORSE!
DRIBBLE
SO PLEASE, PLEASE, PLEASE, PLEEEEEASE!
WAAAAAAAAAAAAAAAH
SPLAT
Y...
YUCK!
SPLAT

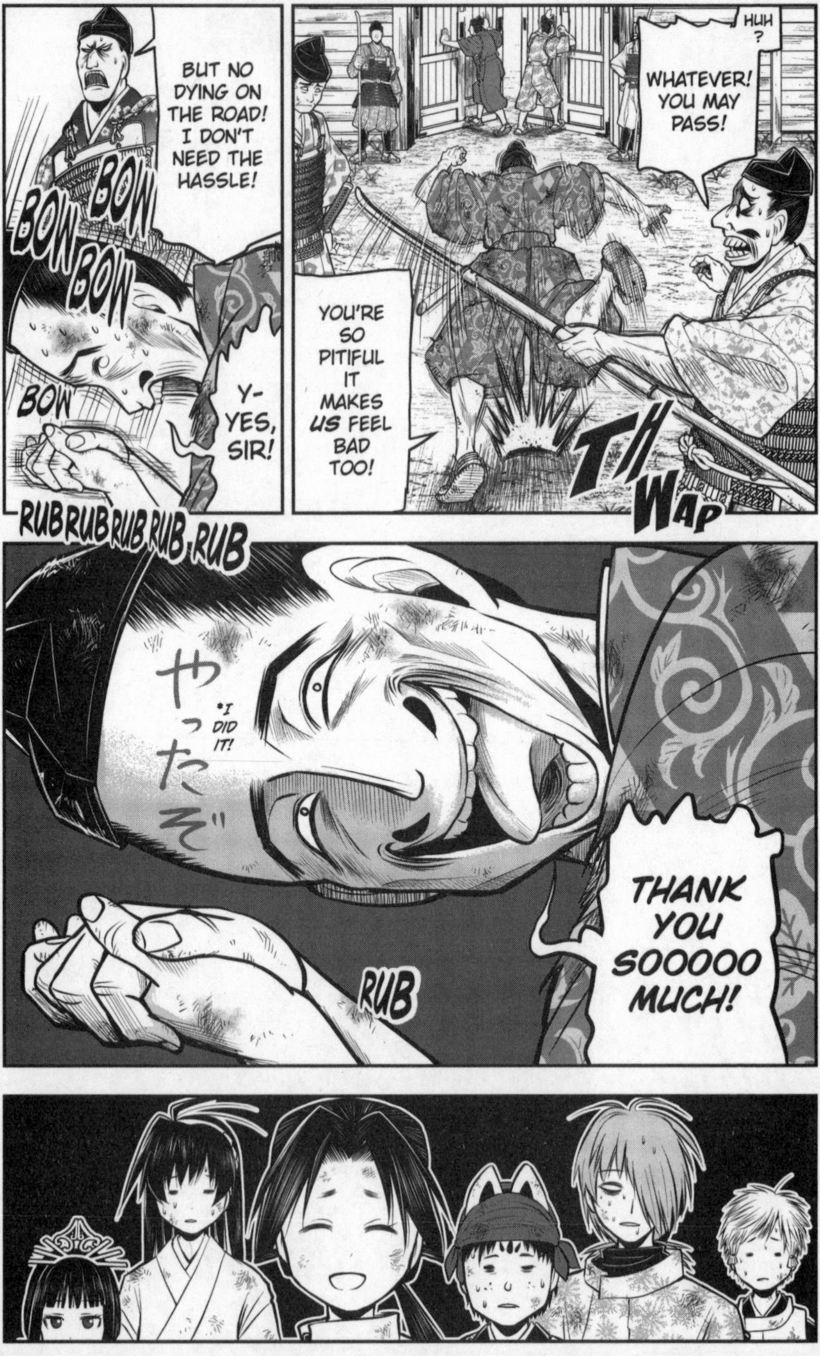
HUH?
WHATEVER! YOU MAY PASS!
YOU'RE SO PITIFUL IT MAKES US FEEL BAD TOO!
THWAP
BUT NO DYING ON THE ROAD! I DON'T NEED THE HASSLE!
BOW BOW BOW BOW BOW
Y-YES, SIR!
RUB RUB RUB RUB RUB
やったぞ
*I DID IT!
THANK YOU SOOOOO MUCH!
RUB

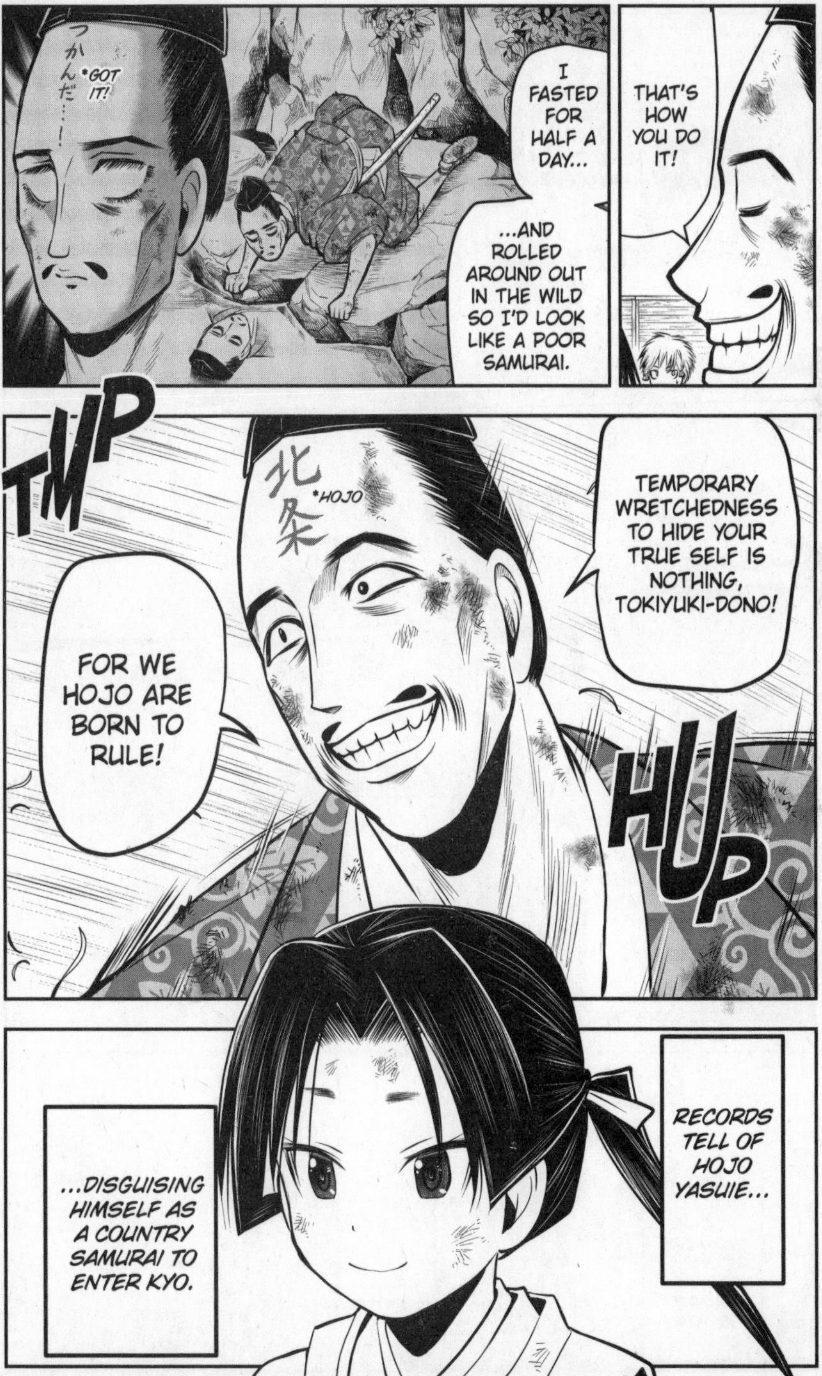
THAT'S HOW YOU DO IT!
I FASTED FOR HALF A DAY...
...AND ROLLED AROUND OUT IN THE WILD SO I'D LOOK LIKE A POOR SAMURAI.
つかんだ…!
*GOT IT!
TEMPORARY WRETCHEDNESS TO HIDE YOUR TRUE SELF IS NOTHING, TOKIYUKI-DONO!
TMP
北条
*HOJO
HUP
FOR WE HOJO ARE BORN TO RULE!
RECORDS TELL OF HOJO YASUIE...
...DISGUISING HIMSELF AS A COUNTRY SAMURAI TO ENTER KYO.

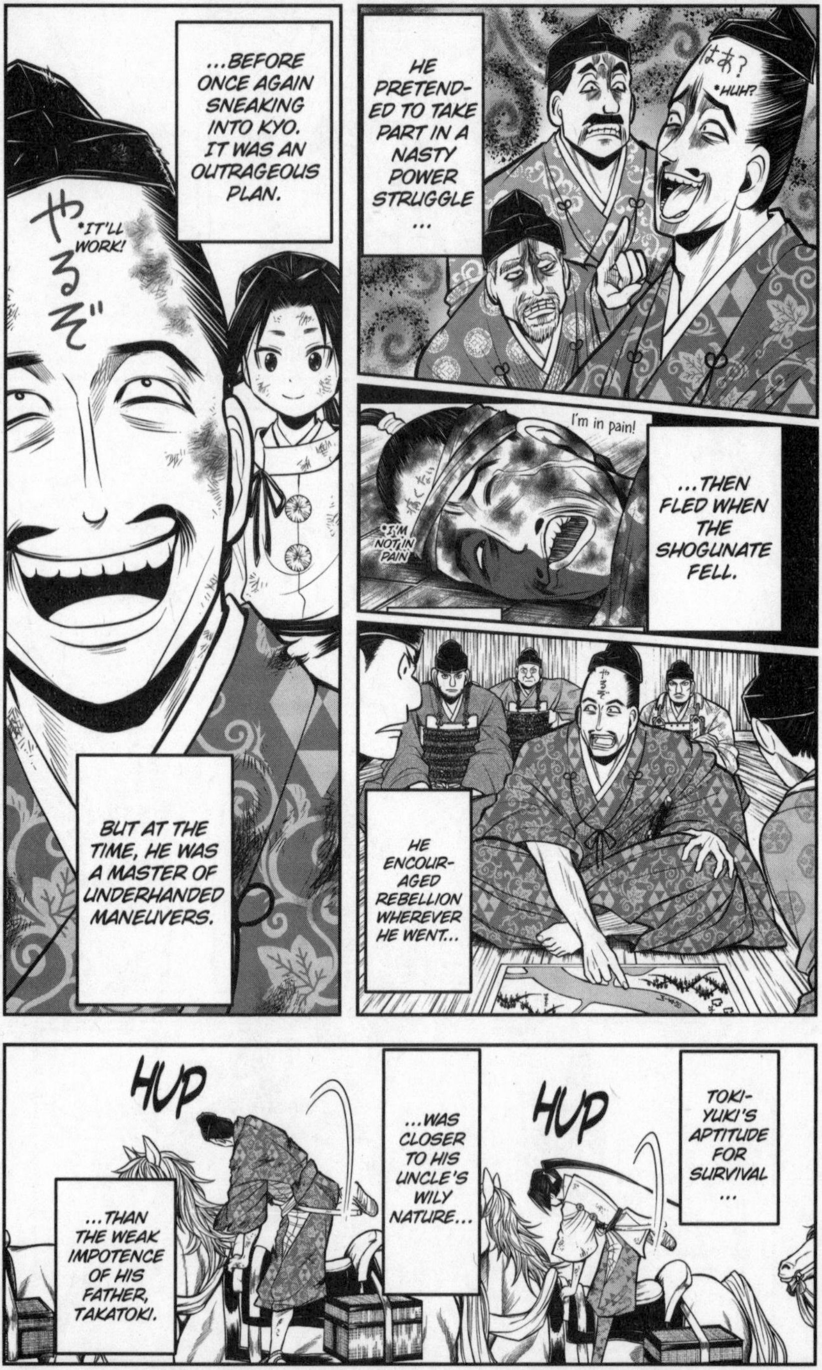
HE PRETENDED TO TAKE PART IN A NASTY POWER STRUGGLE...
はあ?
*HUH?
...THEN FLED WHEN THE SHOGUNATE FELL.
I'm in pain!
痛くない
*I'M NOT IN PAIN
HE ENCOURAGED REBELLION WHEREVER HE WENT...
...BEFORE ONCE AGAIN SNEAKING INTO KYO. IT WAS AN OUTRAGEOUS PLAN.
やるぞ
*IT'LL WORK!
BUT AT THE TIME, HE WAS A MASTER OF UNDERHANDED MANEUVERS.
TOKIYUKI'S APTITUDE FOR SURVIVAL...
HUP
...WAS CLOSER TO HIS UNCLE'S WILY NATURE...
HUP
...THAN THE WEAK IMPOTENCE OF HIS FATHER, TAKATOKI.

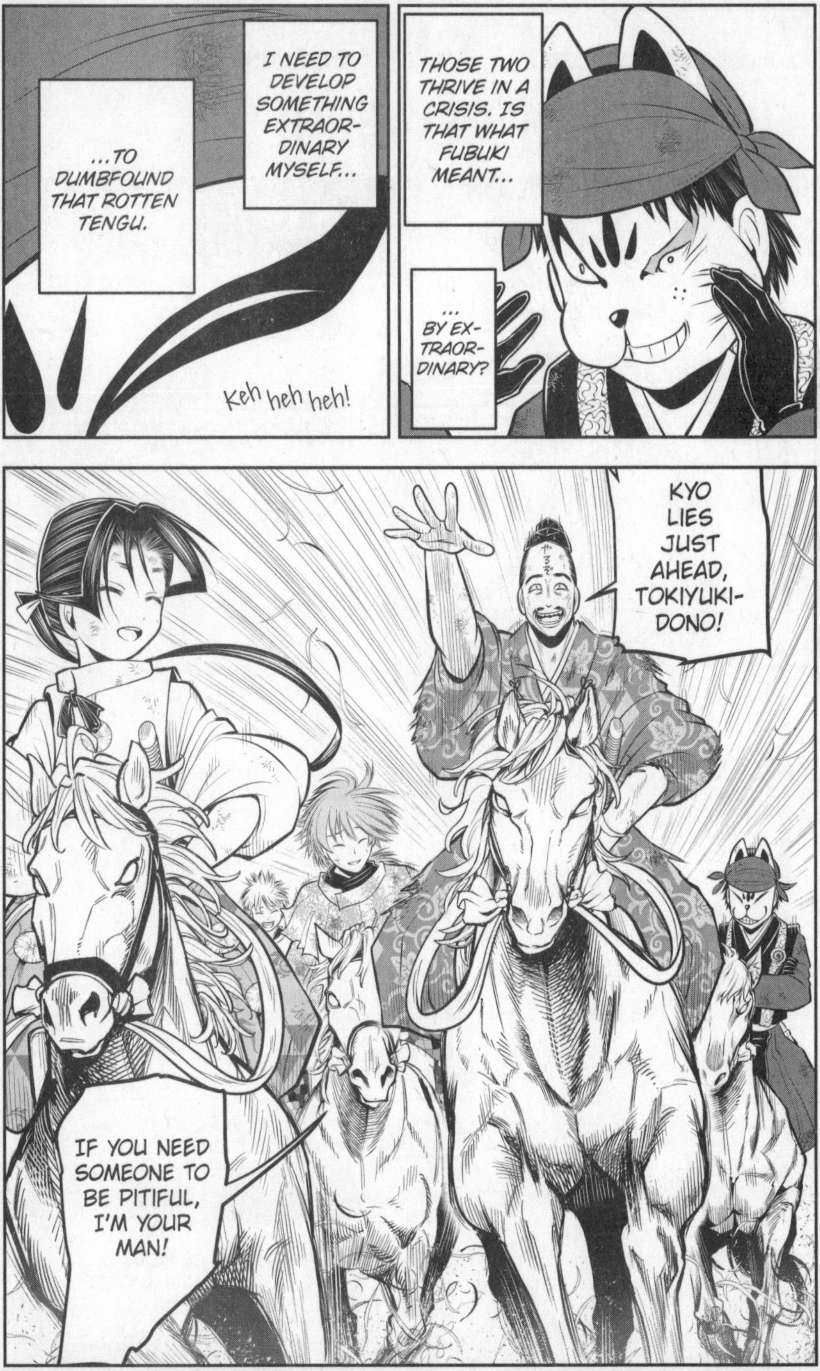
THOSE TWO THRIVE IN A CRISIS. IS THAT WHAT FUBUKI MEANT...
...BY EXTRAORDINARY?
I NEED TO DEVELOP SOMETHING EXTRAORDINARY MYSELF...
...TO DUMBFOUND THAT ROTTEN TENGU.
Keh heh heh!
KYO LIES JUST AHEAD, TOKIYUKI-DONO!
IF YOU NEED SOMEONE TO BE PITIFUL, I'M YOUR MAN!

1335

HOJO YASUIE

★★★ SR

この長崎親子は
眼の上のたんこぶ
追い落とすには
どうすればいいか
THE NAGASAKI FATHER AND SON FOIL MY RISE. WHAT CAN I DO TO RID MYSELF OF THEM?
まず手始めに
奴等が決めた
新しい執権は
殺すふりをして
脅し追い出す
I'LL PRETEND TO KILL THE NEW REGENT THEY'VE PICKED.
だが狡猾な奴等は
わしに謀反の罪を
着せかねないから
大義名分を考える
必要があるな
BUT THEY'RE CRAFTY. THEY MIGHT ACCUSE ME OF TREASON, SO I NEED A GOOD EXCUSE.
はぁー面倒くさ
一端仕切り直しだ
酒飲みながら
時行殿とでも遊ぼう
AW, WHAT A PAIN! I JUST WANNA DRINK AND GOOF OFF WITH TOKIYUKI-DONO!

ABILITIES		NANBOKU-CHO COMPATIBILITY	
MARTIAL ARTS	64	SAVAGERY	57
INTELLIGENCE	86	LOYALTY	45
POLITICS	79	CHAOS	90
LEADERSHIP	70	INGENUITY	38
CHARM	67	RUNNING AND HIDING	91

CREST

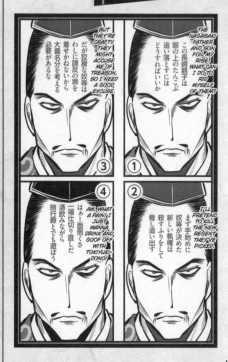

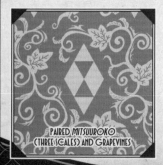

PAIRED MITSUUROKO (THREE SCALES) AND GRAPEVINES

SKILL WANDERING COMMUNICATION: HE CAN INSTIGATE AN UPRISING WHEREVER HE LURKS, REGARDLESS OF THE POLITICAL CONDITIONS.

SKILL MANIFOLD SCHEMES: 10 PERCENT INCREASE TO POLITICS

SKILL INCITEMENT: 15 PERCENT INCREASE TO CHARM AND NEGOTIATION

HIS FACE DURING POWER STRUGGLES

HIS THOUGHTS STILL APPEAR ON HIS FACE. AS PICTURED ABOVE, HOWEVER, THEY CHANGE SO QUICKLY THAT HIS POLITICAL OPPONENTS DON'T HAVE TIME TO READ THEM.

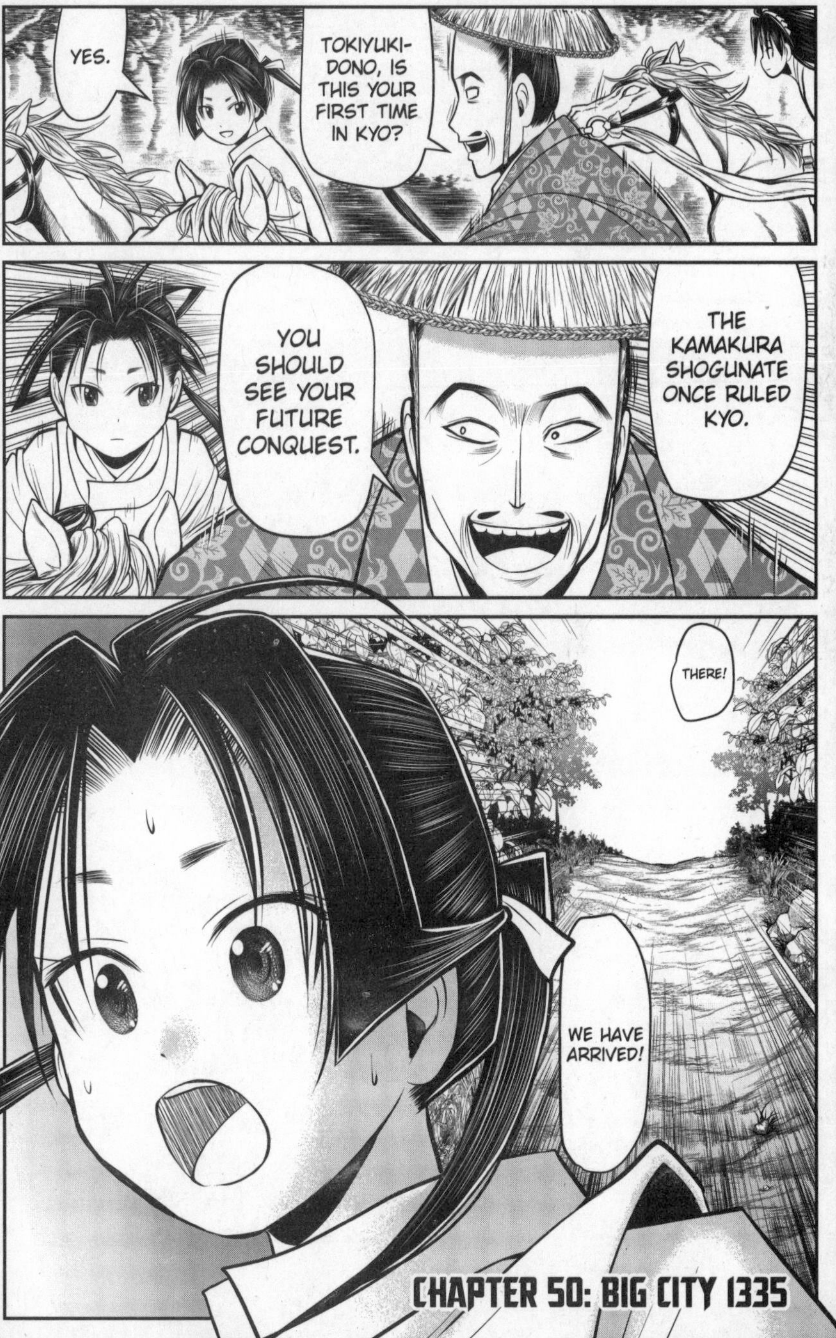
TOKIYUKI-DONO, IS THIS YOUR FIRST TIME IN KYO?
YES.
THE KAMAKURA SHOGUNATE ONCE RULED KYO.
YOU SHOULD SEE YOUR FUTURE CONQUEST.
THERE!
WE HAVE ARRIVED!
CHAPTER 50: BIG CITY 1335

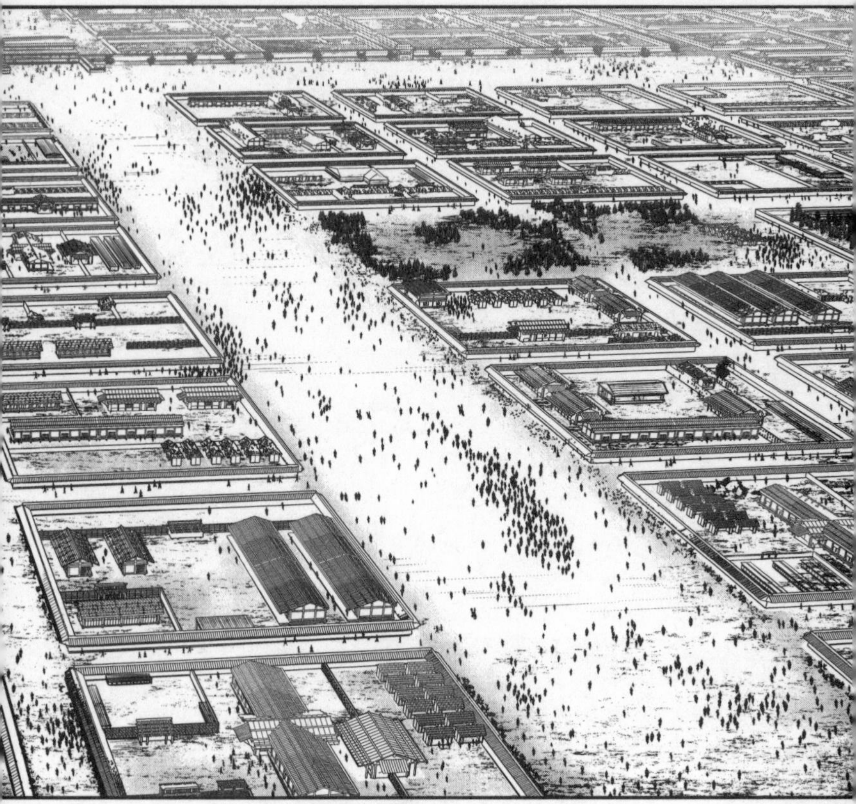

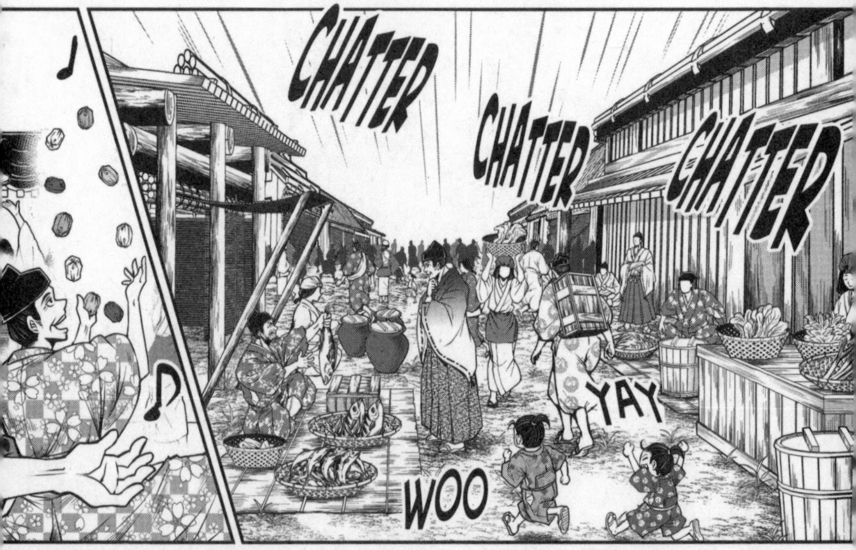
CHATTER
CHATTER
CHATTER
YAY
WOO

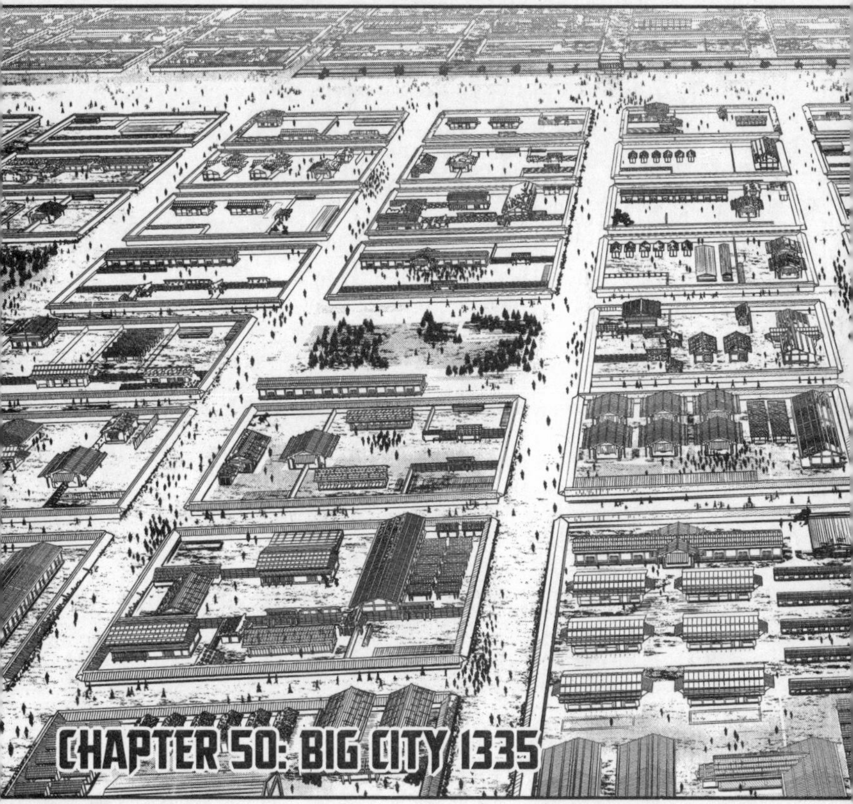
CHAPTER 50: BIG CITY 1335

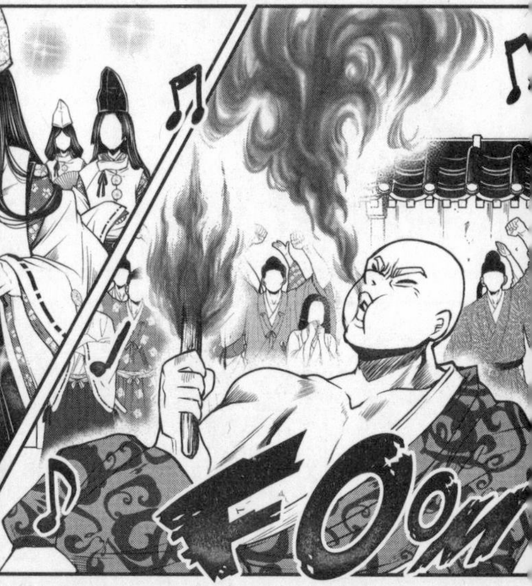
FOOM

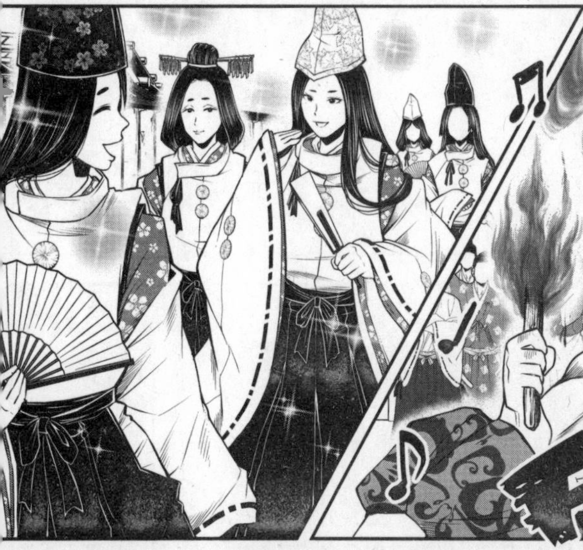

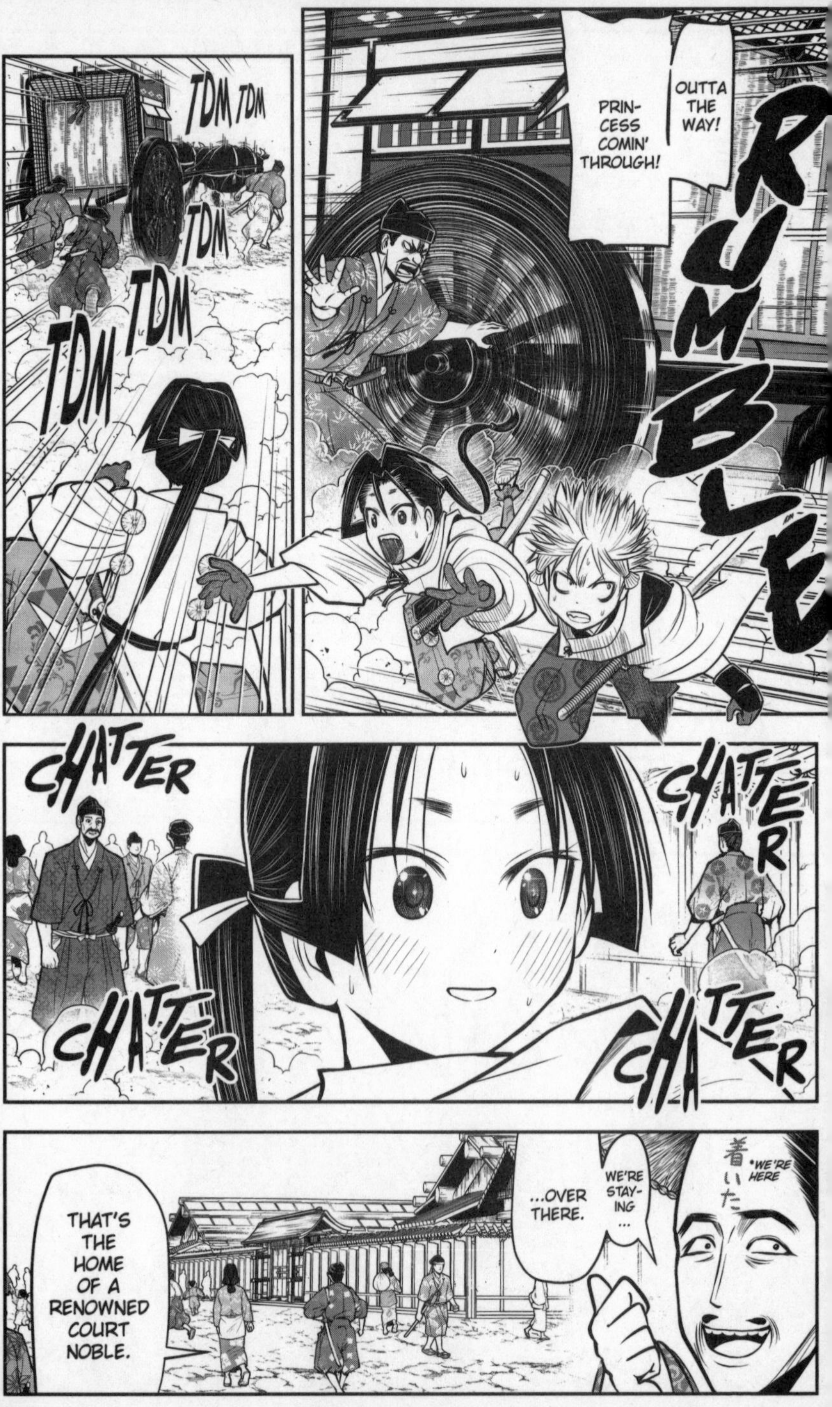

OUTTA THE WAY!
PRIN-CESS COMIN' THROUGH!
RUMBLE
TDM TDM
TDM
TDM
TDM
CHATTER
CHATTER
CHATTER
CHATTER
着いた
*WE'RE HERE
WE'RE STAYING ...
...OVER THERE.
THAT'S THE HOME OF A RENOWNED COURT NOBLE.

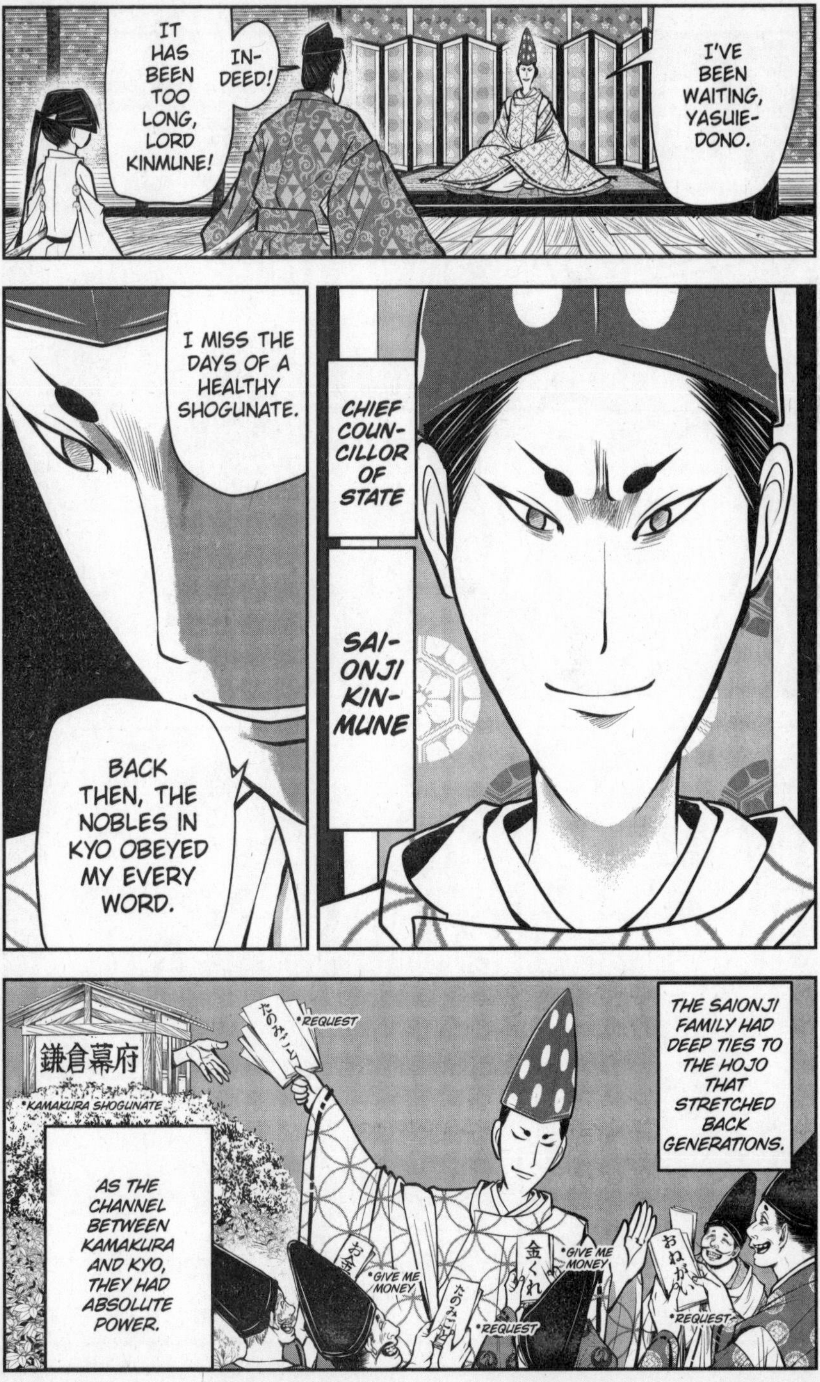
I'VE BEEN WAITING, YASUIE-DONO.
IN-DEED!
IT HAS BEEN TOO LONG, LORD KINMUNE!
CHIEF COUN-CILLOR OF STATE
SAI-ONJI KIN-MUNE
I MISS THE DAYS OF A HEALTHY SHOGUNATE.
BACK THEN, THE NOBLES IN KYO OBEYED MY EVERY WORD.
THE SAIONJI FAMILY HAD DEEP TIES TO THE HOJO THAT STRETCHED BACK GENERATIONS.
たのみごと
*REQUEST
鎌倉幕府
*KAMAKURA SHOGUNATE
おねがい
*REQUEST
金くれ
*GIVE ME MONEY
たのみごと
*REQUEST
お金
*GIVE ME MONEY
AS THE CHANNEL BETWEEN KAMAKURA AND KYO, THEY HAD ABSOLUTE POWER.

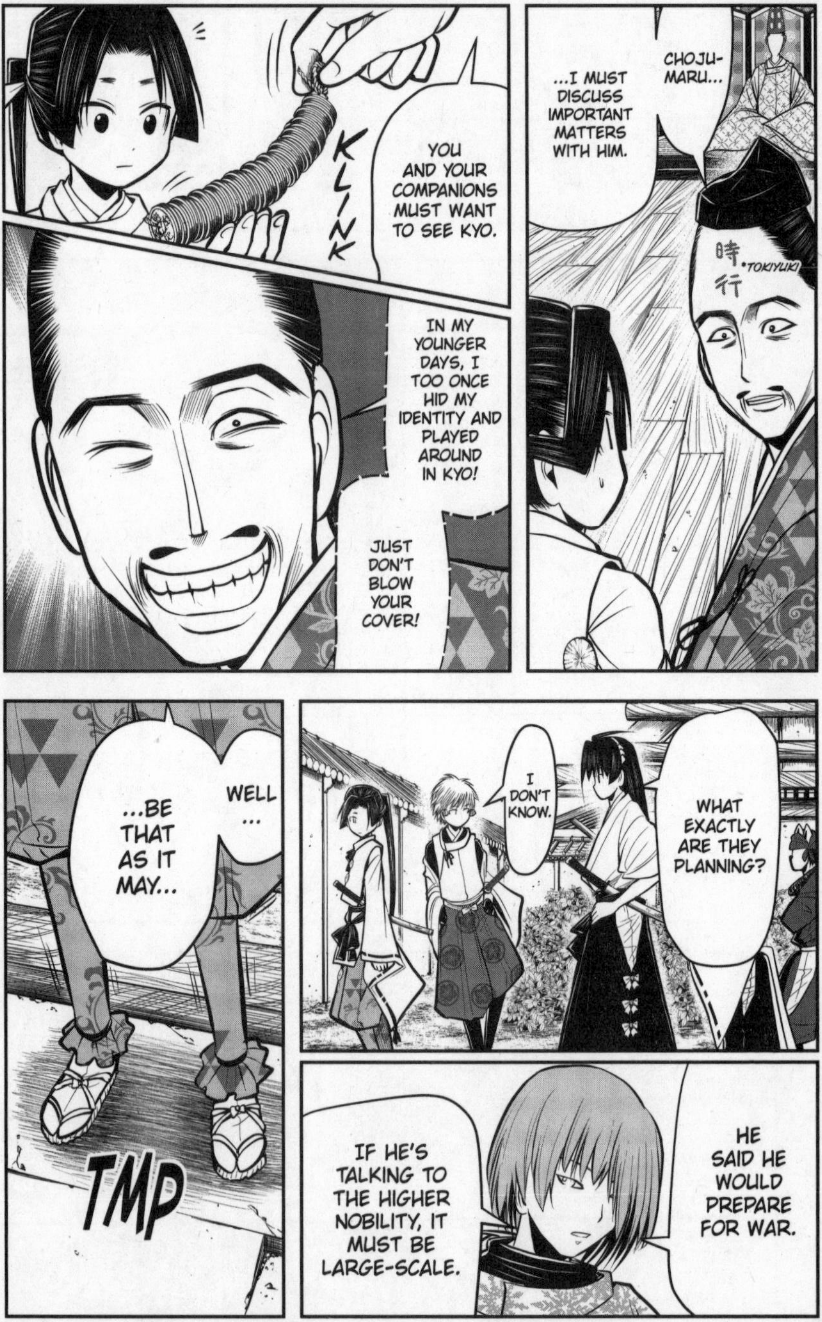
CHOJU-MARU...
...I MUST DISCUSS IMPORTANT MATTERS WITH HIM.
時行 TOKIYUKI
YOU AND YOUR COMPANIONS MUST WANT TO SEE KYO.
KLINK
IN MY YOUNGER DAYS, I TOO ONCE HID MY IDENTITY AND PLAYED AROUND IN KYO!
JUST DON'T BLOW YOUR COVER!
WHAT EXACTLY ARE THEY PLANNING?
I DON'T KNOW.
HE SAID HE WOULD PREPARE FOR WAR.
IF HE'S TALKING TO THE HIGHER NOBILITY, IT MUST BE LARGE-SCALE.
WELL ...
...BE THAT AS IT MAY...
TMP

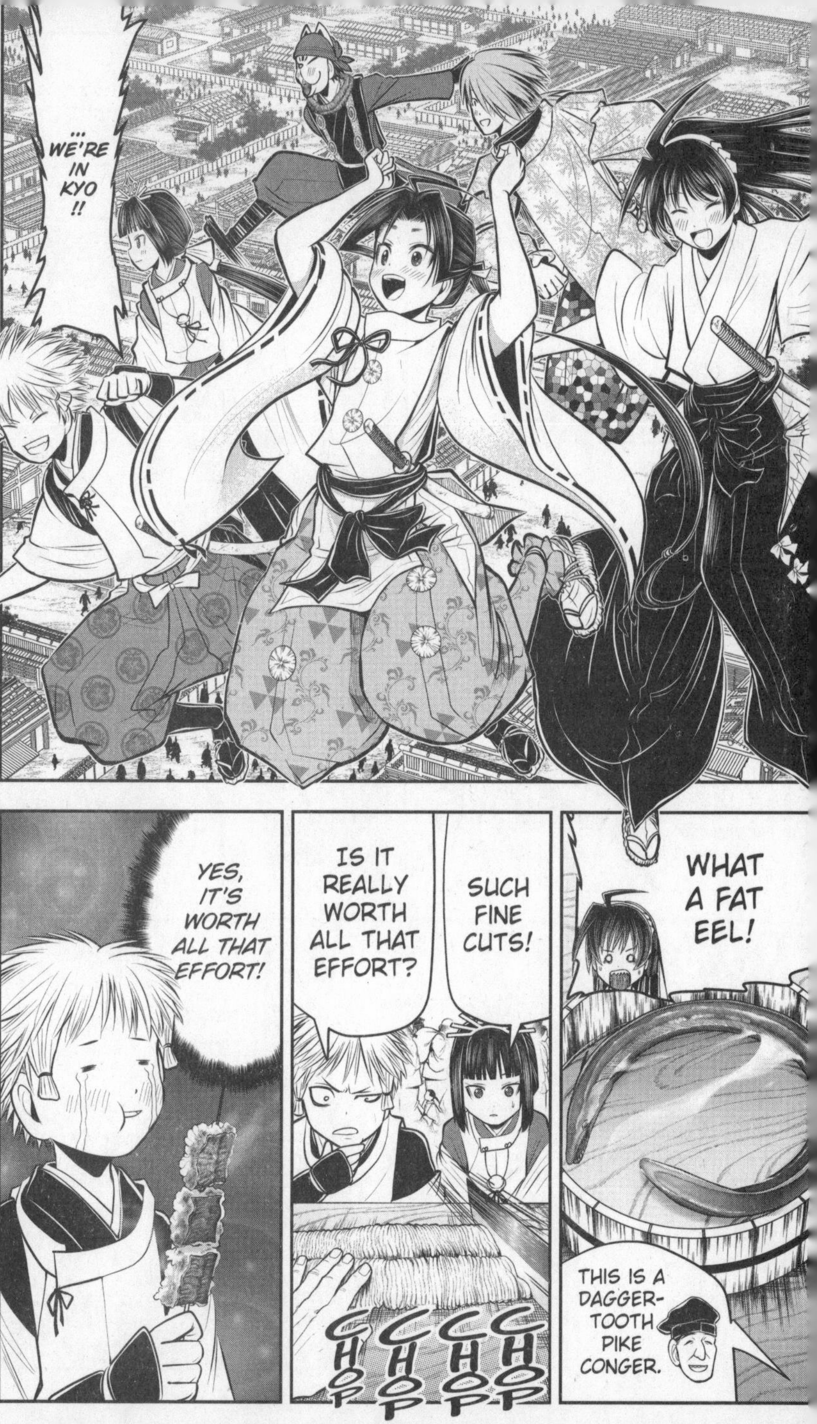
...WE'RE IN KYO!!
WHAT A FAT EEL!
THIS IS A DAGGER-TOOTH PIKE CONGER.
SUCH FINE CUTS!
IS IT REALLY WORTH ALL THAT EFFORT?
CHOP CHOP CHOP CHOP
YES, IT'S WORTH ALL THAT EFFORT!

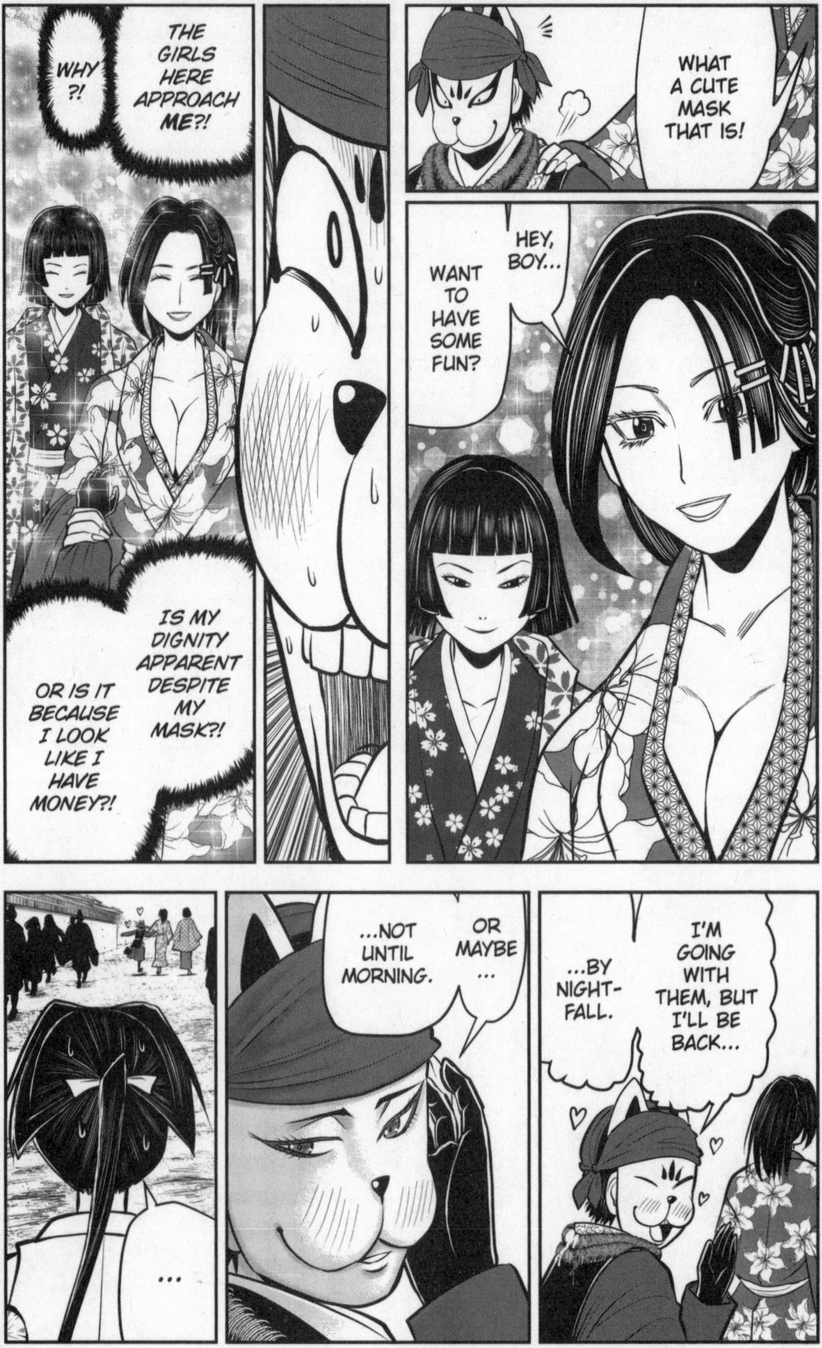
WHAT A CUTE MASK THAT IS!
HEY, BOY...
WANT TO HAVE SOME FUN?
THE GIRLS HERE APPROACH ME?!
WHY ?!
IS MY DIGNITY APPARENT DESPITE MY MASK?!
OR IS IT BECAUSE I LOOK LIKE I HAVE MONEY?!
I'M GOING WITH THEM, BUT I'LL BE BACK...
...BY NIGHT-FALL.
OR MAYBE ...
...NOT UNTIL MORNING.
...

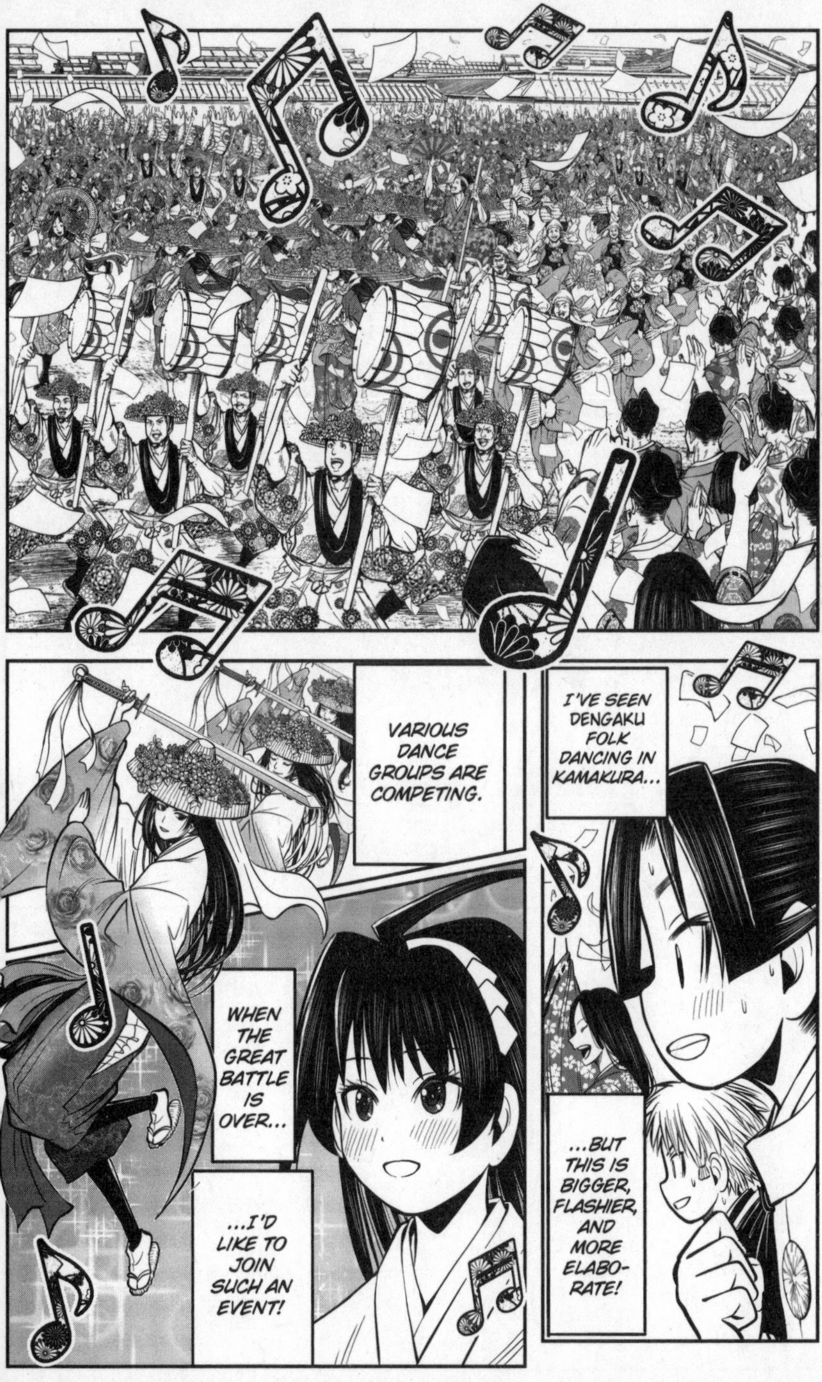
I'VE SEEN DENGAKU FOLK DANCING IN KAMAKURA...
...BUT THIS IS BIGGER, FLASHIER, AND MORE ELABO-RATE!
VARIOUS DANCE GROUPS ARE COMPETING.
WHEN THE GREAT BATTLE IS OVER...
...I'D LIKE TO JOIN SUCH AN EVENT!

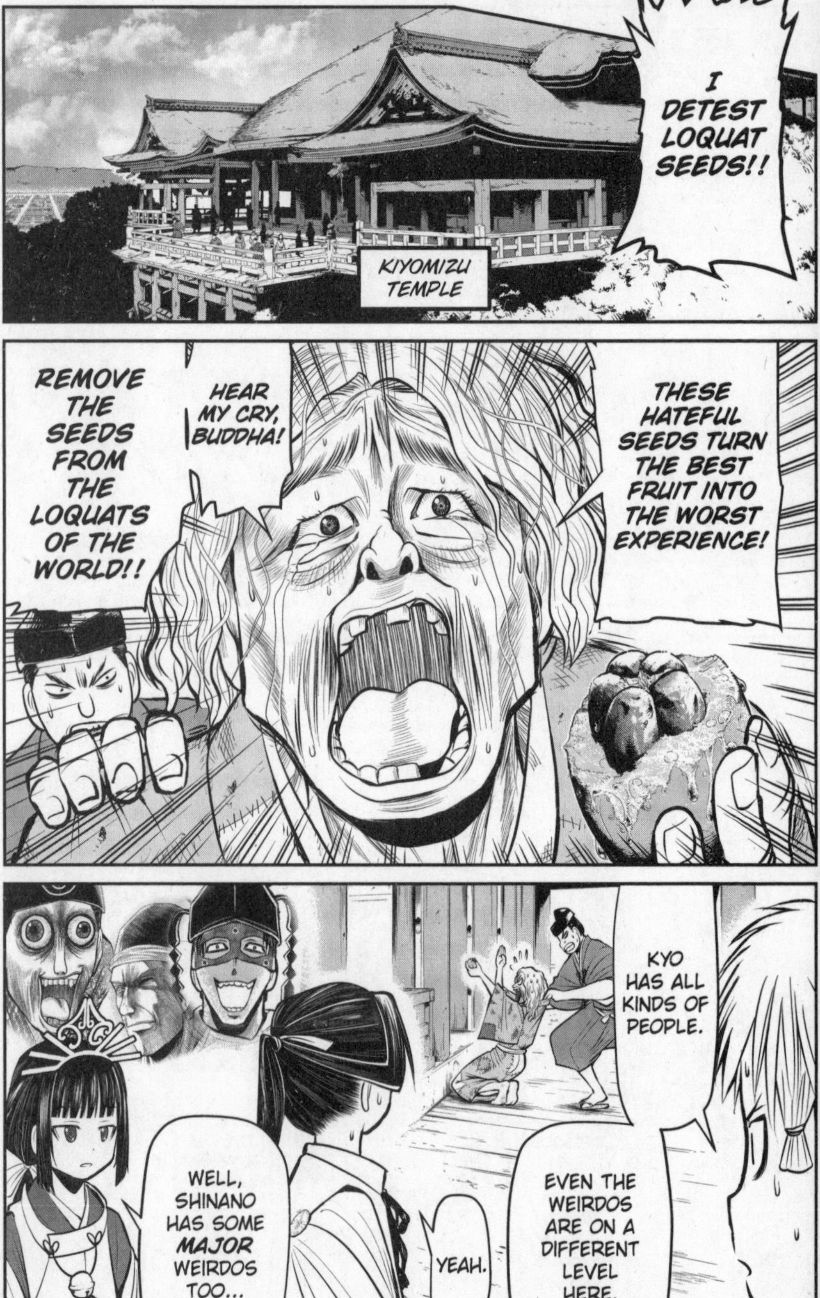
I DETEST LOQUAT SEEDS!!
KIYOMIZU TEMPLE
THESE HATEFUL SEEDS TURN THE BEST FRUIT INTO THE WORST EXPERIENCE!
HEAR MY CRY, BUDDHA!
REMOVE THE SEEDS FROM THE LOQUATS OF THE WORLD!!
KYO HAS ALL KINDS OF PEOPLE.
EVEN THE WEIRDOS ARE ON A DIFFERENT LEVEL HERE.
YEAH.
WELL, SHINANO HAS SOME MAJOR WEIRDOS TOO...

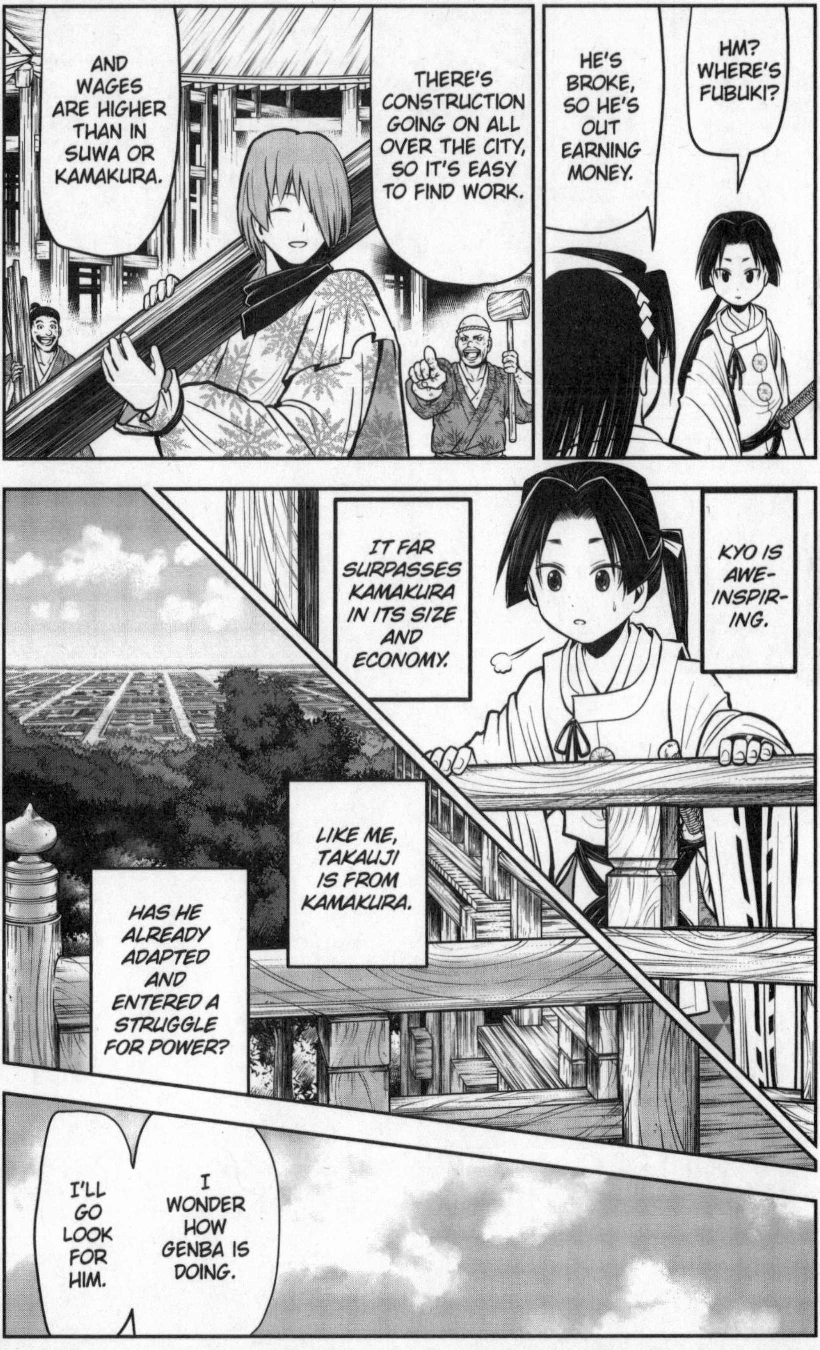
HM? WHERE'S FUBUKI?
HE'S BROKE, SO HE'S OUT EARNING MONEY.
THERE'S CONSTRUCTION GOING ON ALL OVER THE CITY, SO IT'S EASY TO FIND WORK.
AND WAGES ARE HIGHER THAN IN SUWA OR KAMAKURA.
KYO IS AWE-INSPIRING.
IT FAR SURPASSES KAMAKURA IN ITS SIZE AND ECONOMY.
LIKE ME, TAKAUJI IS FROM KAMAKURA.
HAS HE ALREADY ADAPTED AND ENTERED A STRUGGLE FOR POWER?
I WONDER HOW GENBA IS DOING.
I'LL GO LOOK FOR HIM.

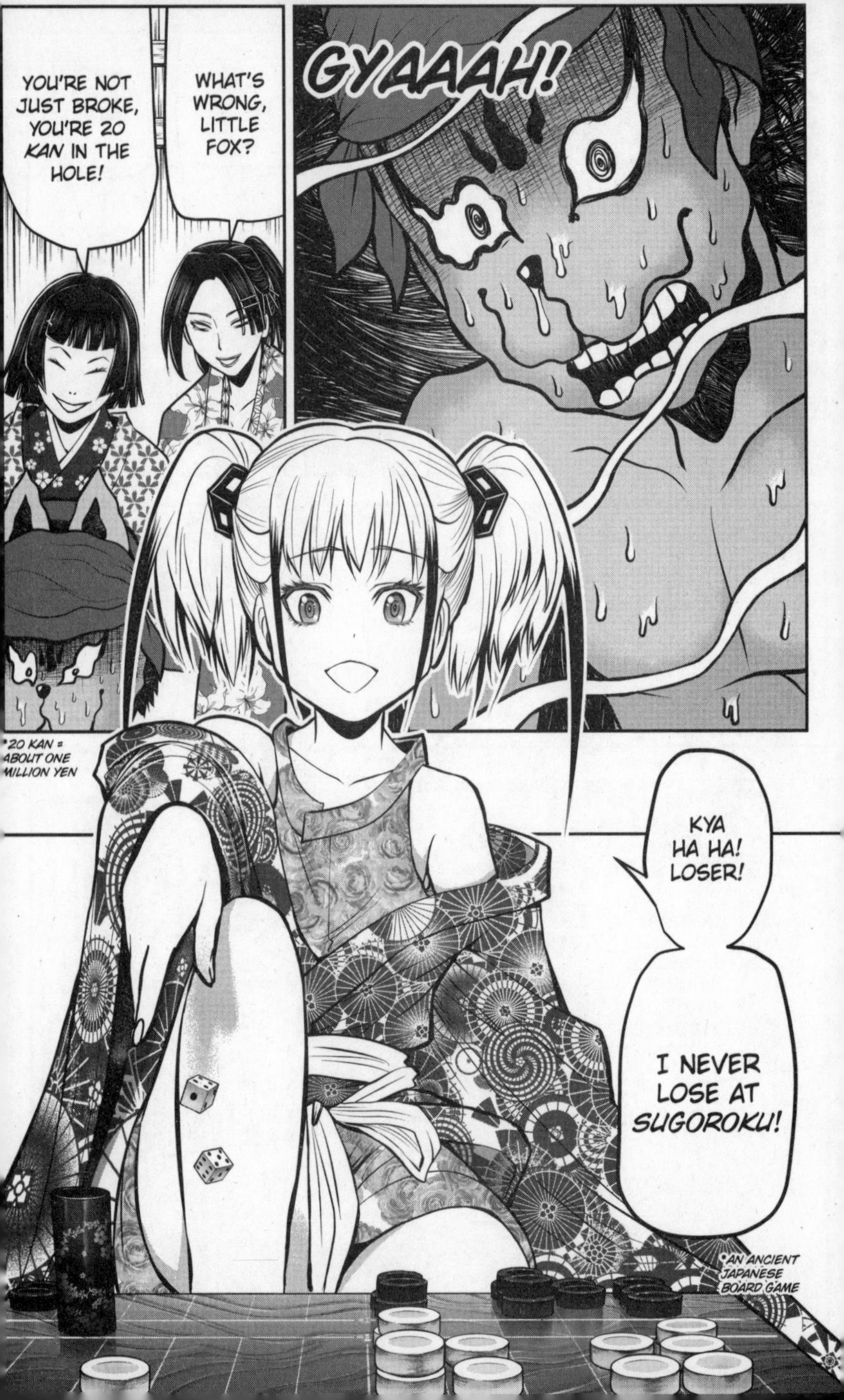
GYAAAH!
WHAT'S WRONG, LITTLE FOX?
YOU'RE NOT JUST BROKE, YOU'RE 20 KAN IN THE HOLE!
*20 KAN = ABOUT ONE MILLION YEN
KYA HA HA! LOSER!
I NEVER LOSE AT SUGOROKU!
*AN ANCIENT JAPANESE BOARD GAME

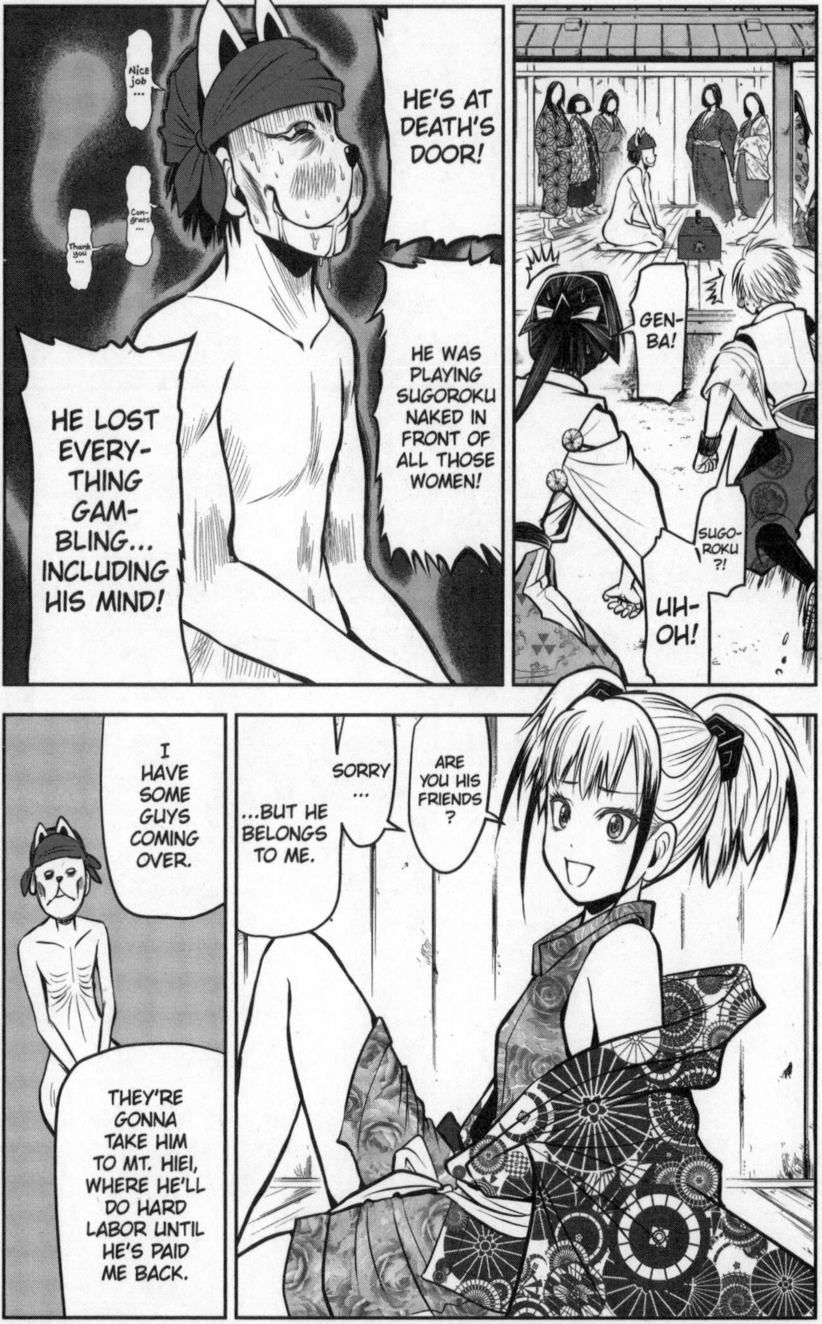
GEN-BA!
SUGO-ROKU?!
UH-OH!
HE'S AT DEATH'S DOOR!
HE WAS PLAYING SUGOROKU NAKED IN FRONT OF ALL THOSE WOMEN!
Nice job...
Congrats...
Thank you...
HE LOST EVERY-THING GAM-BLING... INCLUDING HIS MIND!
ARE YOU HIS FRIENDS?
SORRY...
...BUT HE BELONGS TO ME.
I HAVE SOME GUYS COMING OVER.
THEY'RE GONNA TAKE HIM TO MT. HIEI, WHERE HE'LL DO HARD LABOR UNTIL HE'S PAID ME BACK.

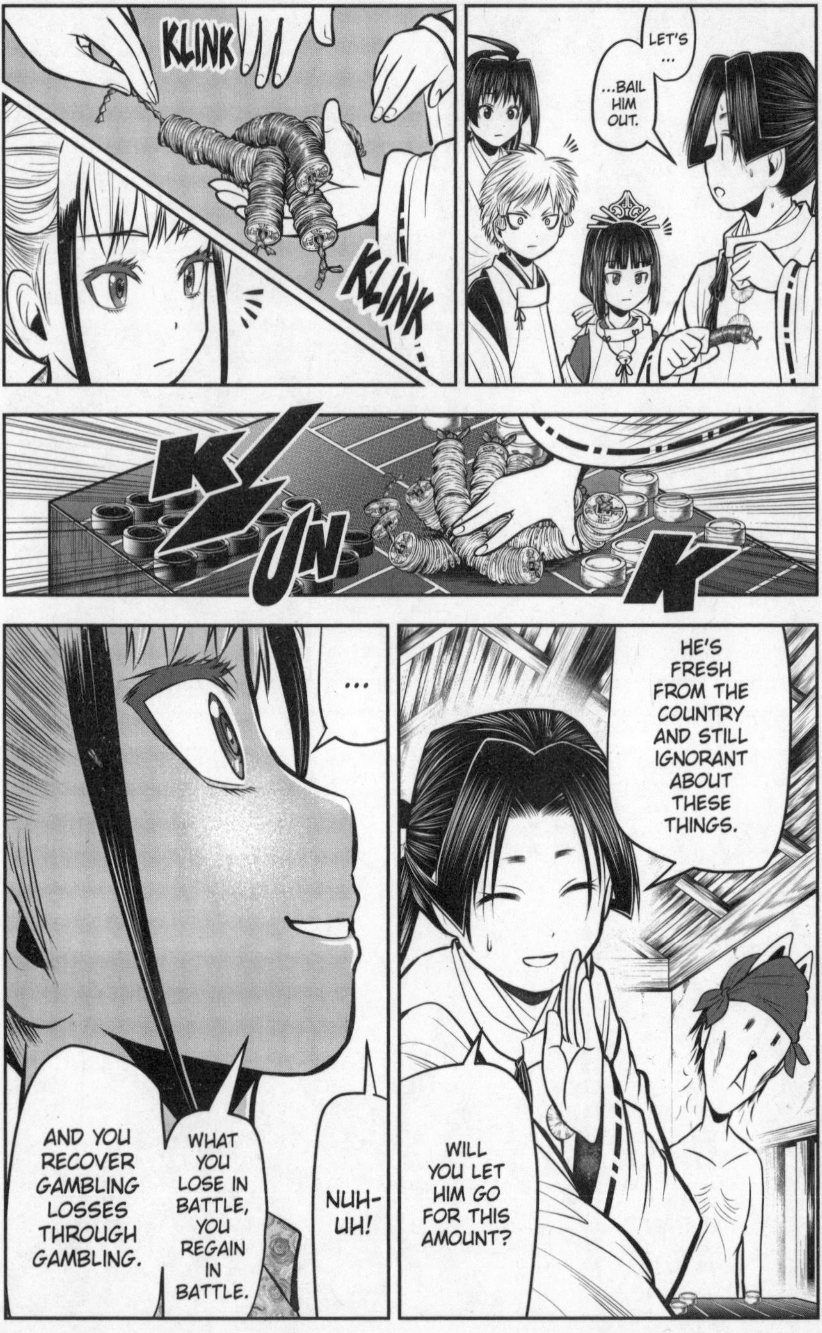

LET'S ...
...BAIL HIM OUT.
KLINK
KLINK
KLUNK
HE'S FRESH FROM THE COUNTRY AND STILL IGNORANT ABOUT THESE THINGS.
WILL YOU LET HIM GO FOR THIS AMOUNT?
...
NUH-UH!
WHAT YOU LOSE IN BATTLE, YOU REGAIN IN BATTLE.
AND YOU RECOVER GAMBLING LOSSES THROUGH GAMBLING.

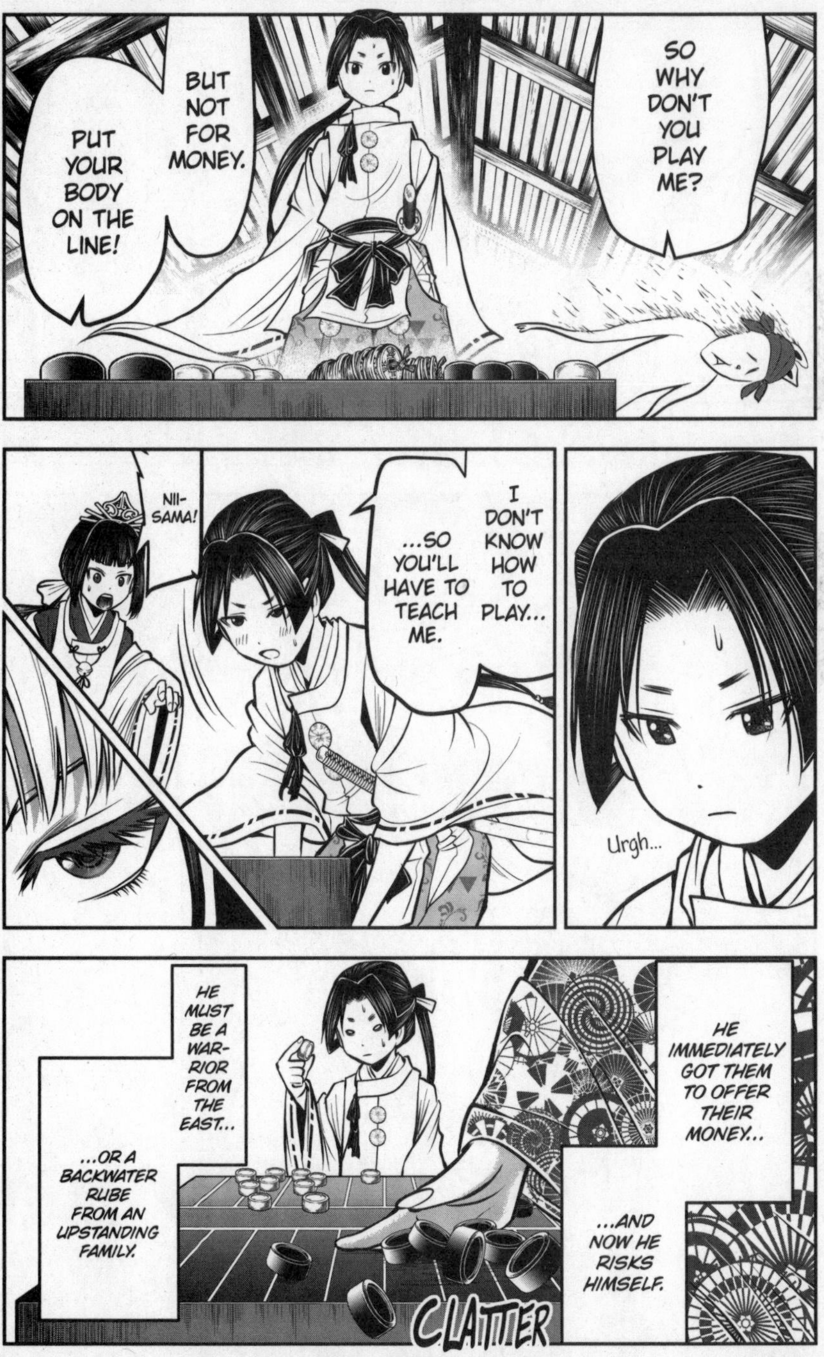
SO WHY DON'T YOU PLAY ME?
BUT NOT FOR MONEY.
PUT YOUR BODY ON THE LINE!
Urgh...
I DON'T KNOW HOW TO PLAY...
...SO YOU'LL HAVE TO TEACH ME.
NII-SAMA!
HE IMMEDIATELY GOT THEM TO OFFER THEIR MONEY...
...AND NOW HE RISKS HIMSELF.
HE MUST BE A WARRIOR FROM THE EAST...
...OR A BACKWATER RUBE FROM AN UPSTANDING FAMILY.
CLATTER

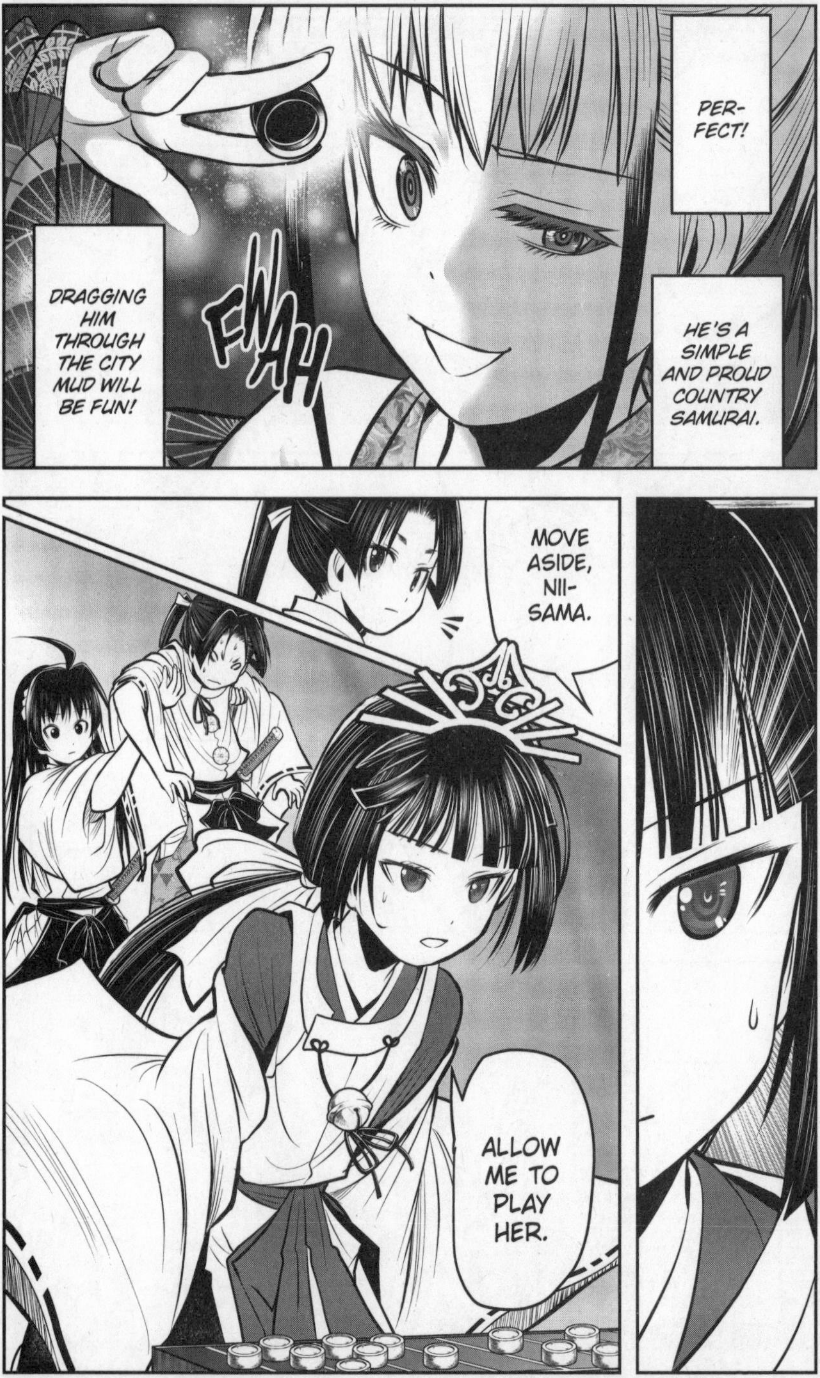
PER-FECT!
HE'S A SIMPLE AND PROUD COUNTRY SAMURAI.
FWAH
DRAGGING HIM THROUGH THE CITY MUD WILL BE FUN!
MOVE ASIDE, NII-SAMA.
ALLOW ME TO PLAY HER.

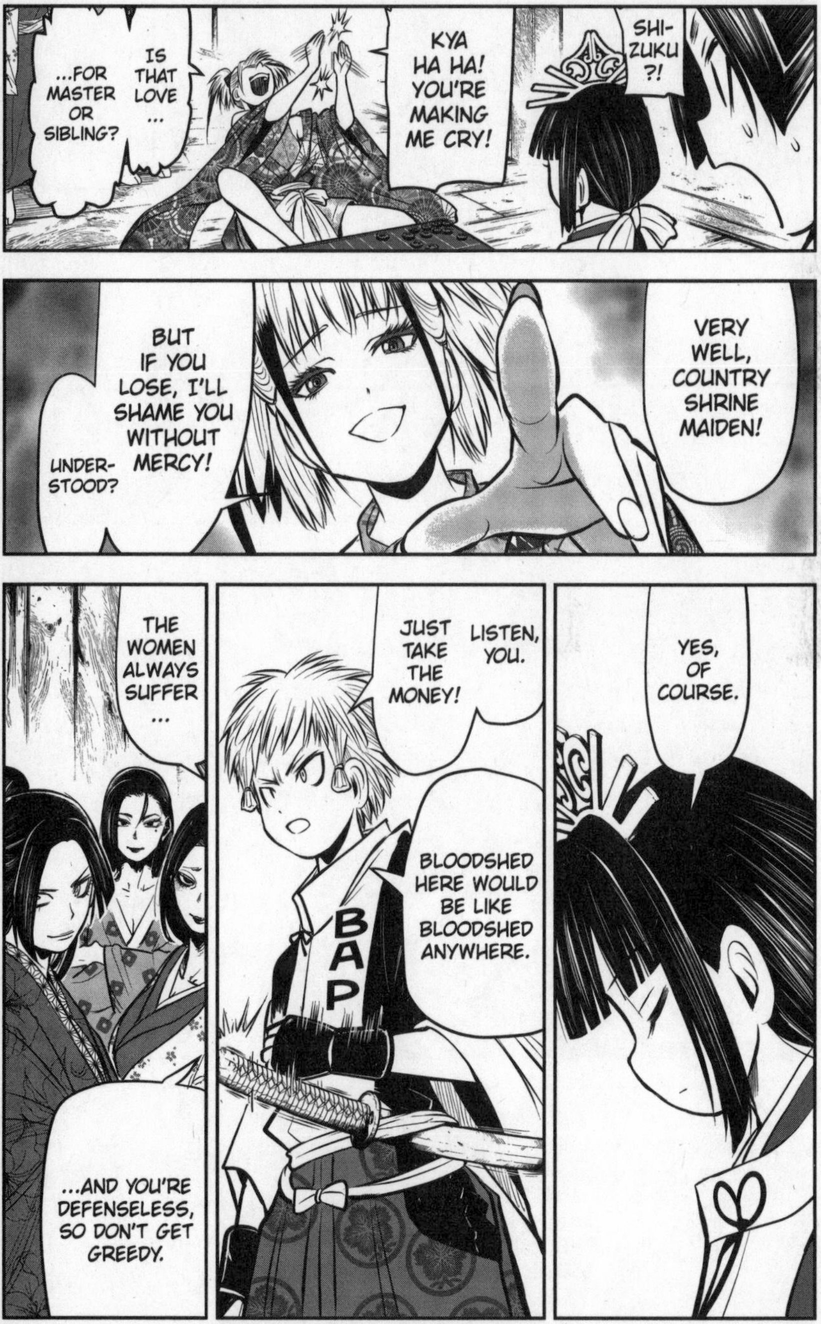
SHI-ZUKU?!
KYA HA HA! YOU'RE MAKING ME CRY!
IS THAT LOVE...
...FOR MASTER OR SIBLING?
VERY WELL, COUNTRY SHRINE MAIDEN!
BUT IF YOU LOSE, I'LL SHAME YOU WITHOUT MERCY!
UNDER-STOOD?
YES, OF COURSE.
LISTEN, YOU.
JUST TAKE THE MONEY!
BLOODSHED HERE WOULD BE LIKE BLOODSHED ANYWHERE.
BAP
THE WOMEN ALWAYS SUFFER...
...AND YOU'RE DEFENSELESS, SO DON'T GET GREEDY.

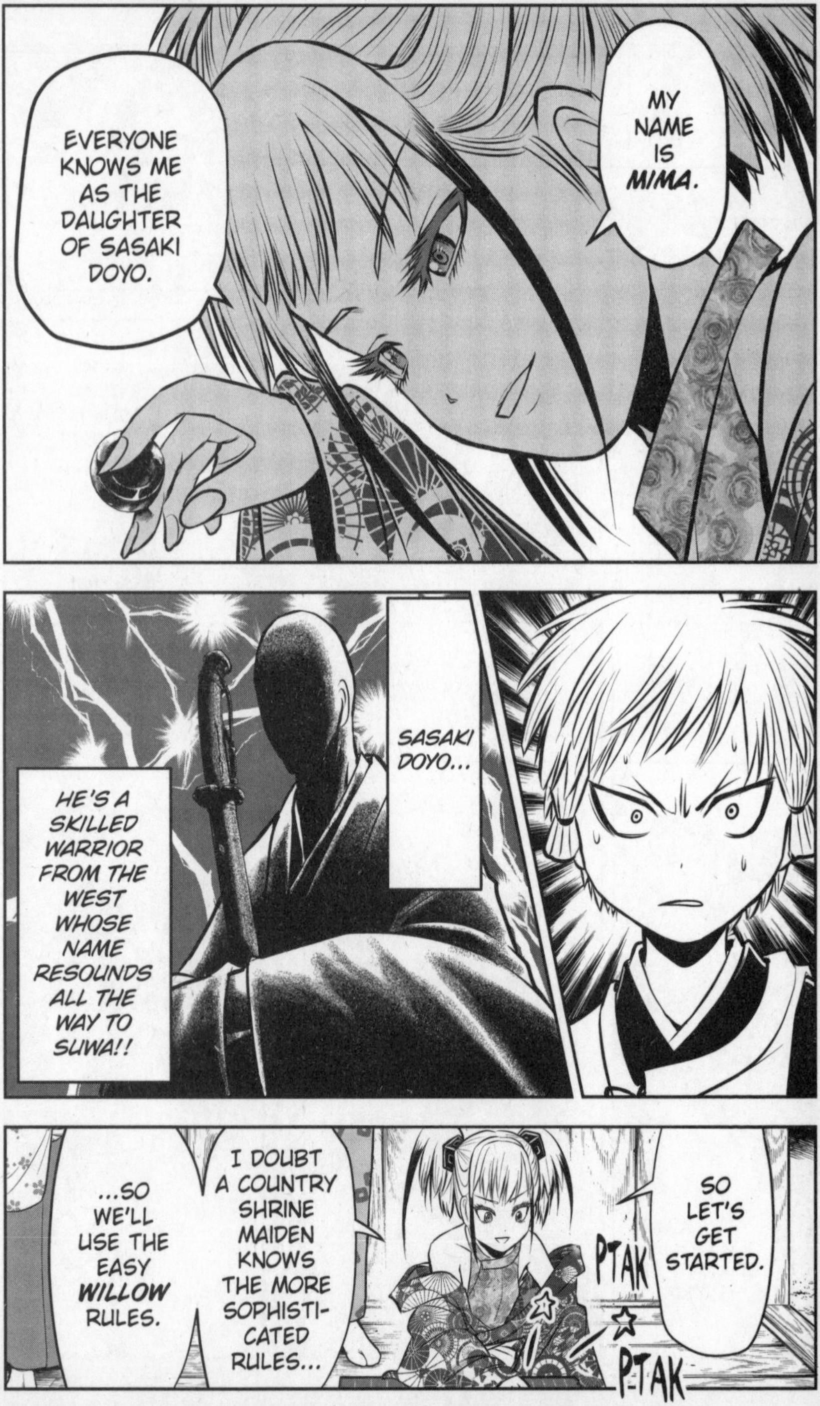
MY NAME IS MIMA.
EVERYONE KNOWS ME AS THE DAUGHTER OF SASAKI DOYO.
SASAKI DOYO...
HE'S A SKILLED WARRIOR FROM THE WEST WHOSE NAME RESOUNDS ALL THE WAY TO SUWA!!
SO LET'S GET STARTED.
PTAK
P-TAK
I DOUBT A COUNTRY SHRINE MAIDEN KNOWS THE MORE SOPHISTI-CATED RULES...
...SO WE'LL USE THE EASY WILLOW RULES.

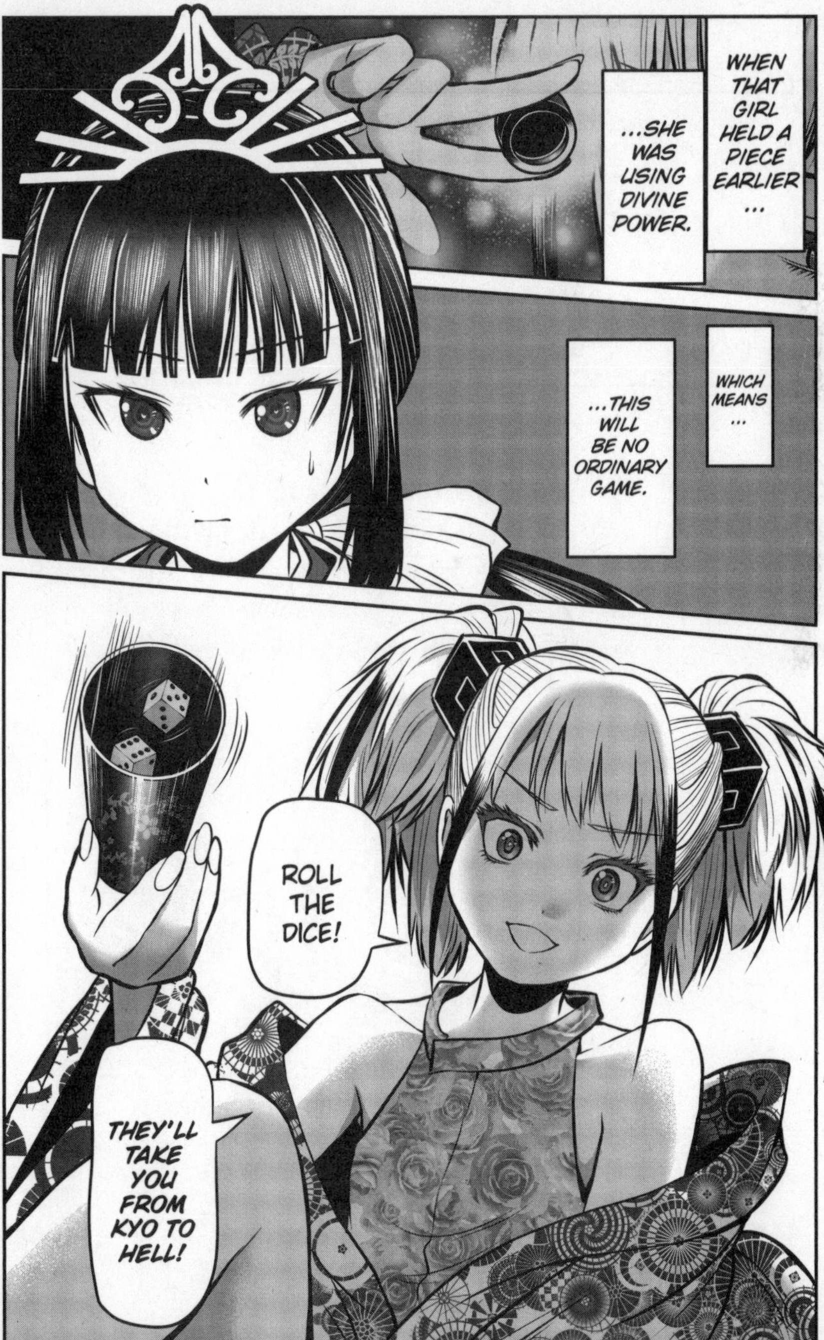
WHEN THAT GIRL HELD A PIECE EARLIER...
...SHE WAS USING DIVINE POWER.
WHICH MEANS...
...THIS WILL BE NO ORDINARY GAME.
ROLL THE DICE!
THEY'LL TAKE YOU FROM KYO TO HELL!

LOQUAT OLD WOMAN

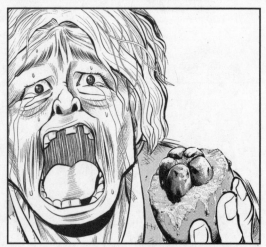

From the *Muchū Mondō-shū*
by Muso Soseki
A nameless old woman who existed 700
years ago.

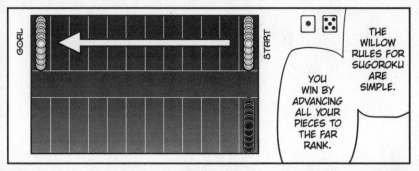

THE WILLOW RULES FOR SUGOROKU ARE SIMPLE.

YOU WIN BY ADVANCING ALL YOUR PIECES TO THE FAR RANK.

GOAL

START

BUT YOU HAVE TO LAND WITH AN EXACT ROLL OR MOVE BACK BY THE AMOUNT YOU WENT OVER.

IT ALL DEPENDS ON LUCK.

CHAPTER 51: SUGOROKU 1335

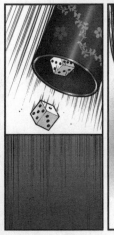

KOSS

PLUNK

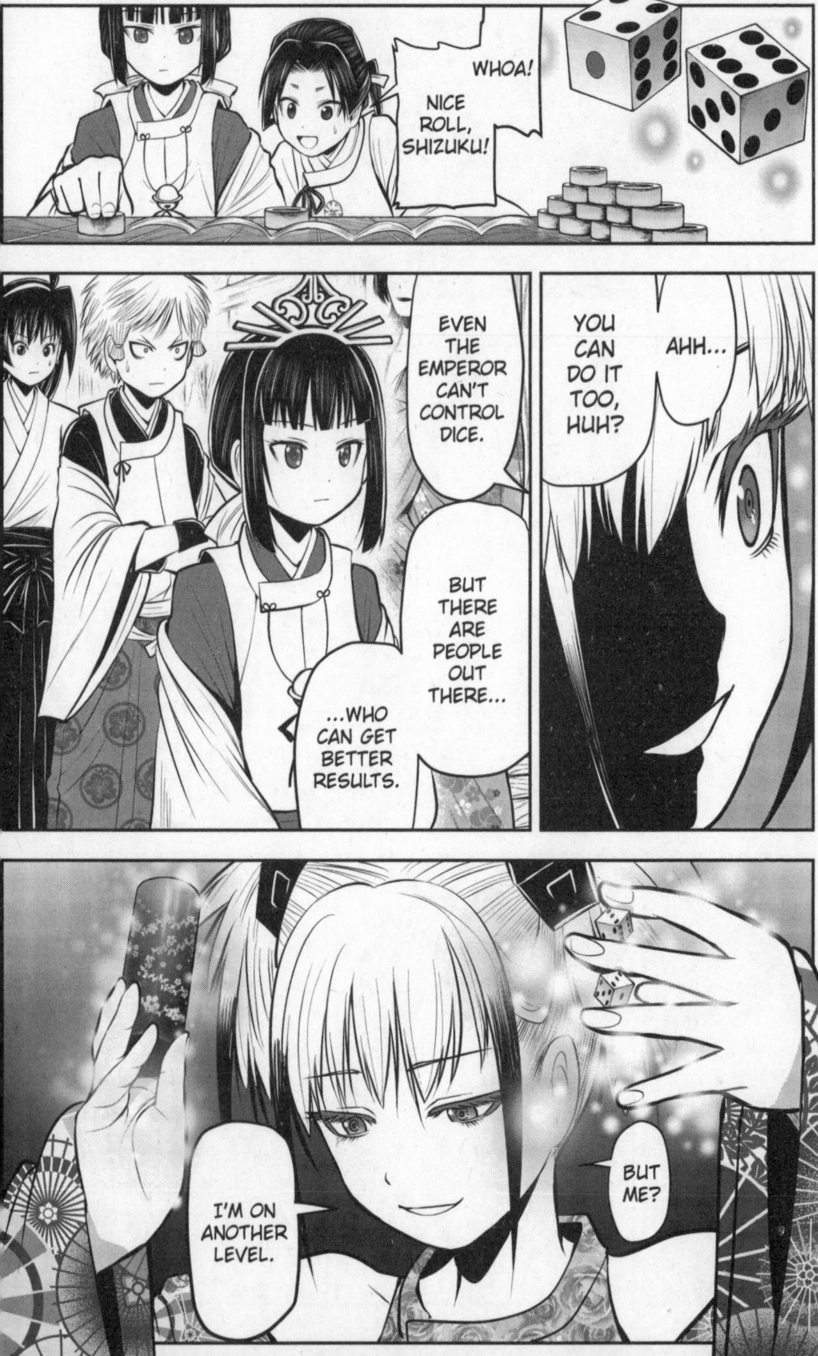
WHOA!
NICE ROLL, SHIZUKU!
AHH...
YOU CAN DO IT TOO, HUH?
EVEN THE EMPEROR CAN'T CONTROL DICE.
BUT THERE ARE PEOPLE OUT THERE...
...WHO CAN GET BETTER RESULTS.
BUT ME?
I'M ON ANOTHER LEVEL.

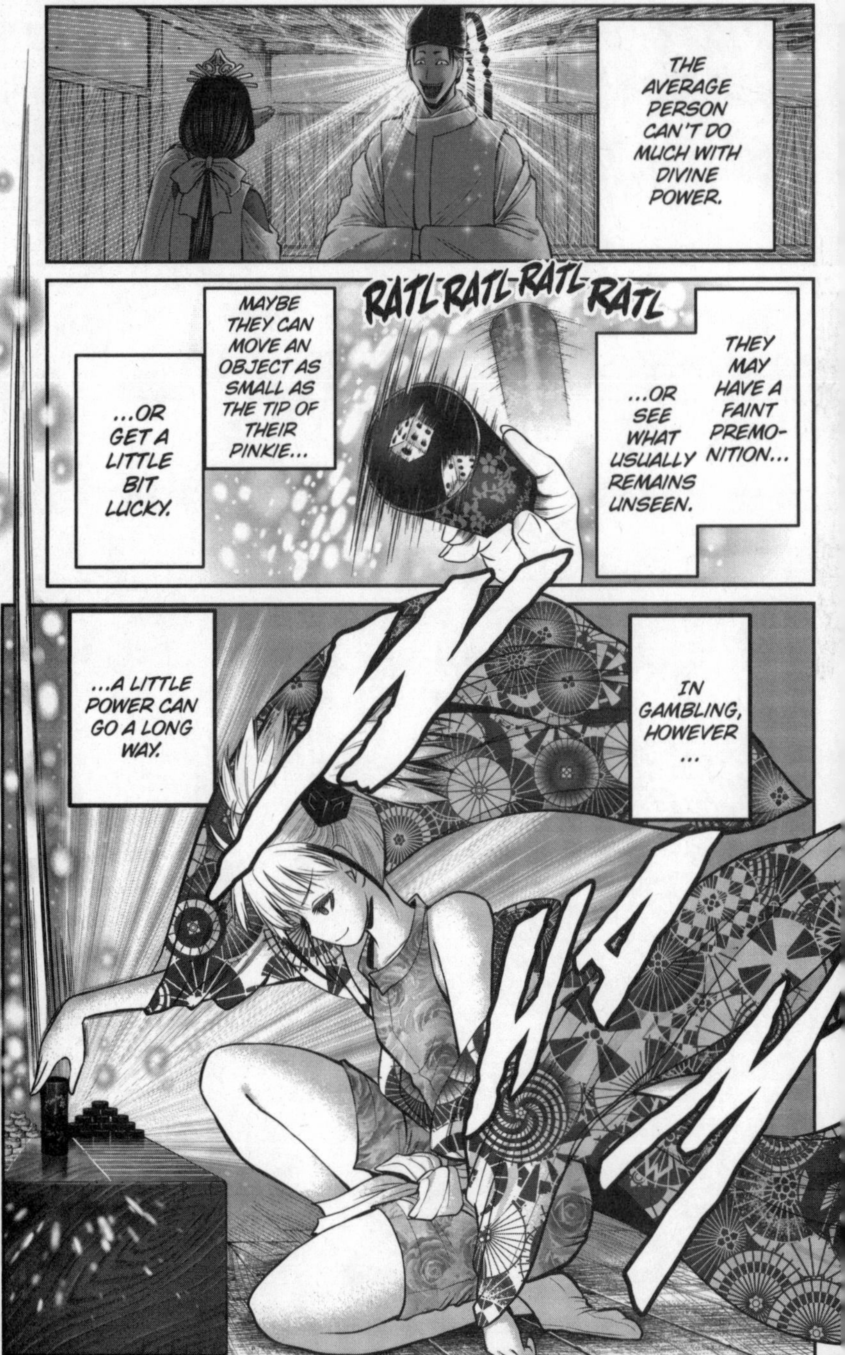
THE AVERAGE PERSON CAN'T DO MUCH WITH DIVINE POWER.
RATL-RATL-RATL-RATL
THEY MAY HAVE A FAINT PREMONITION...
...OR SEE WHAT USUALLY REMAINS UNSEEN.
MAYBE THEY CAN MOVE AN OBJECT AS SMALL AS THE TIP OF THEIR PINKIE...
...OR GET A LITTLE BIT LUCKY.
IN GAMBLING, HOWEVER...
...A LITTLE POWER CAN GO A LONG WAY.
WHAM

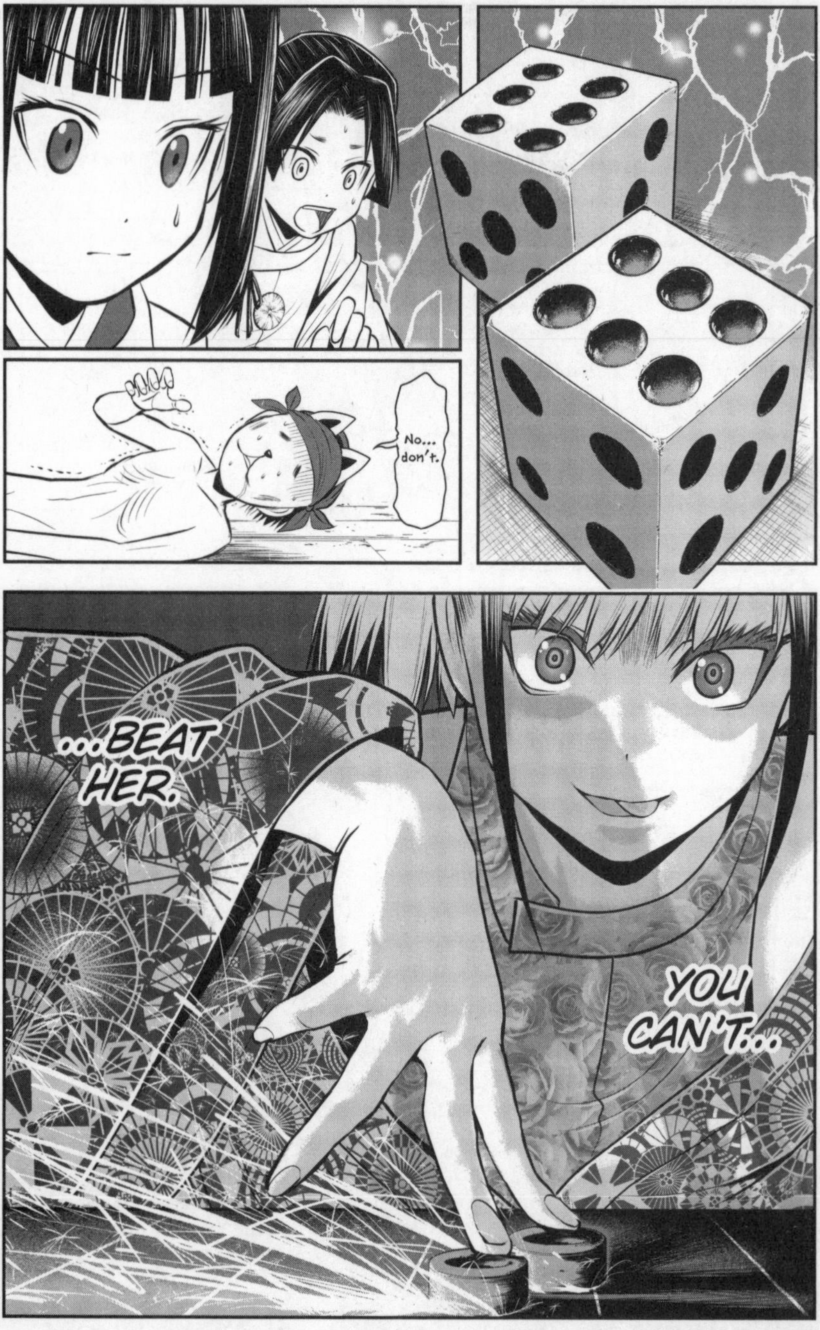
No... don't.
YOU CAN'T...
...BEAT HER.

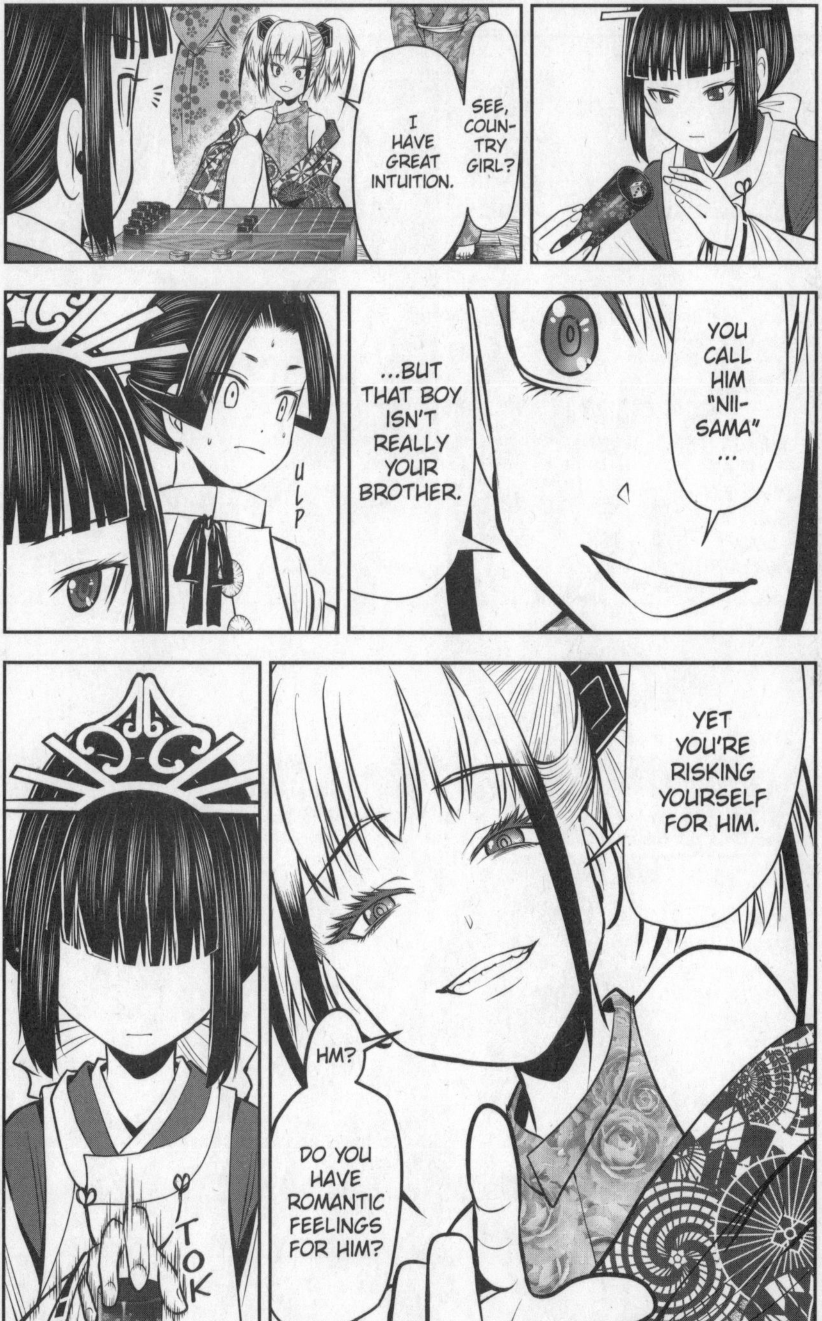
SEE, COUNTRY GIRL?
I HAVE GREAT INTUITION.
YOU CALL HIM "NII-SAMA"...
...BUT THAT BOY ISN'T REALLY YOUR BROTHER.
ULP
YET YOU'RE RISKING YOURSELF FOR HIM.
HM?
DO YOU HAVE ROMANTIC FEELINGS FOR HIM?
TOK

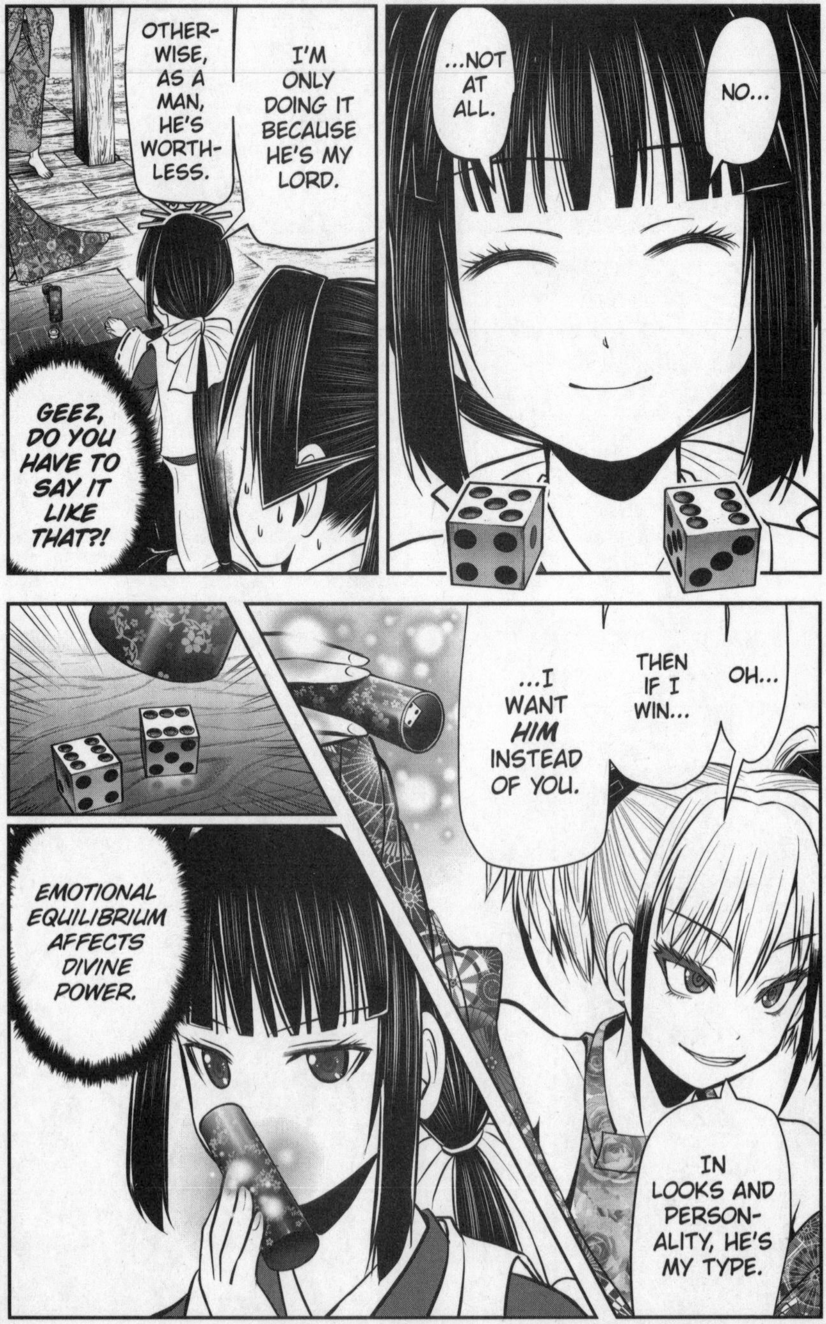
NO...
...NOT AT ALL.
I'M ONLY DOING IT BECAUSE HE'S MY LORD.
OTHER-WISE, AS A MAN, HE'S WORTH-LESS.
GEEZ, DO YOU HAVE TO SAY IT LIKE THAT?!
OH...
THEN IF I WIN...
...I WANT *HIM* INSTEAD OF YOU.
IN LOOKS AND PERSON-ALITY, HE'S MY TYPE.
EMOTIONAL EQUILIBRIUM AFFECTS DIVINE POWER.

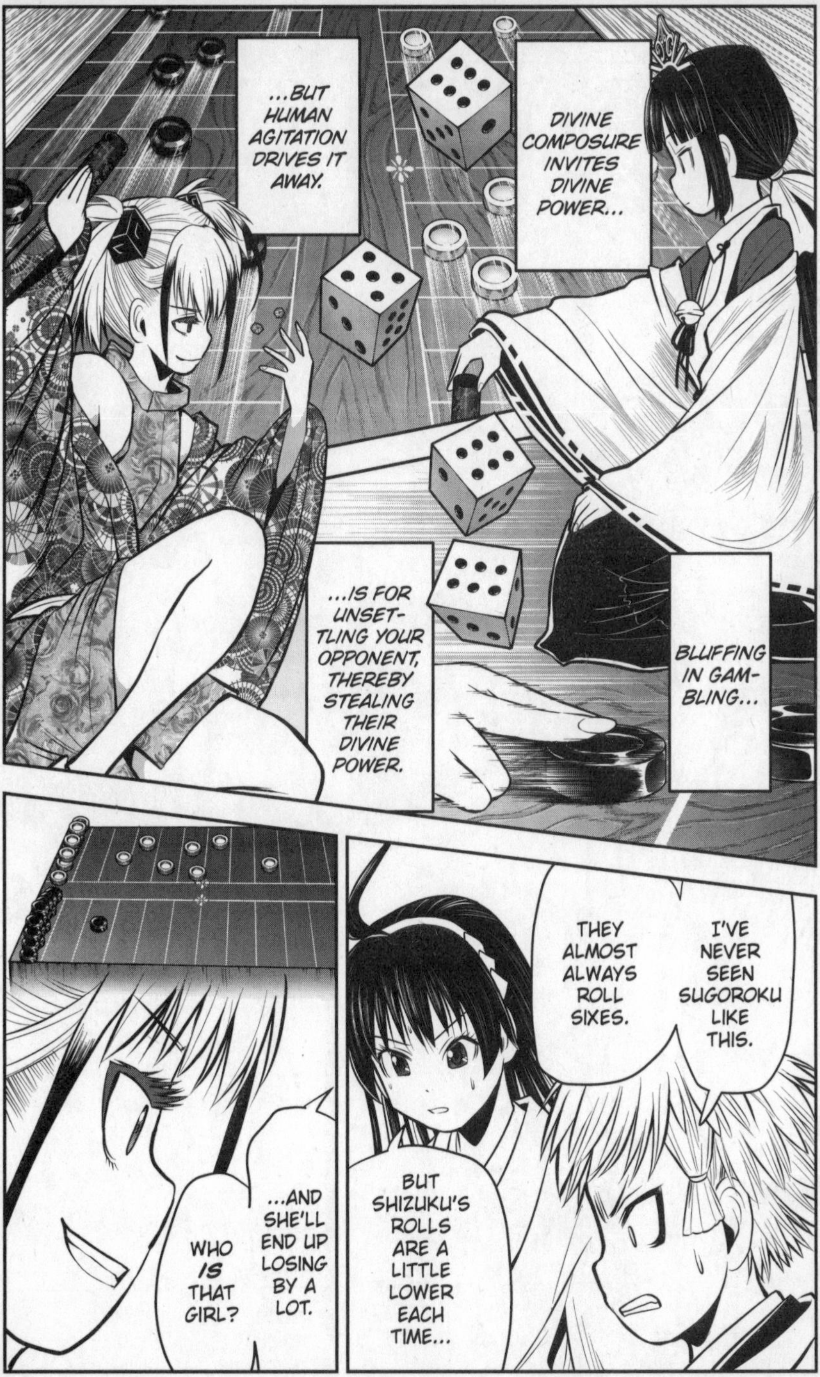
DIVINE COMPOSURE INVITES DIVINE POWER...
...BUT HUMAN AGITATION DRIVES IT AWAY.
BLUFFING IN GAMBLING...
...IS FOR UNSETTLING YOUR OPPONENT, THEREBY STEALING THEIR DIVINE POWER.
I'VE NEVER SEEN SUGOROKU LIKE THIS.
THEY ALMOST ALWAYS ROLL SIXES.
BUT SHIZUKU'S ROLLS ARE A LITTLE LOWER EACH TIME...
...AND SHE'LL END UP LOSING BY A LOT.
WHO *IS* THAT GIRL?

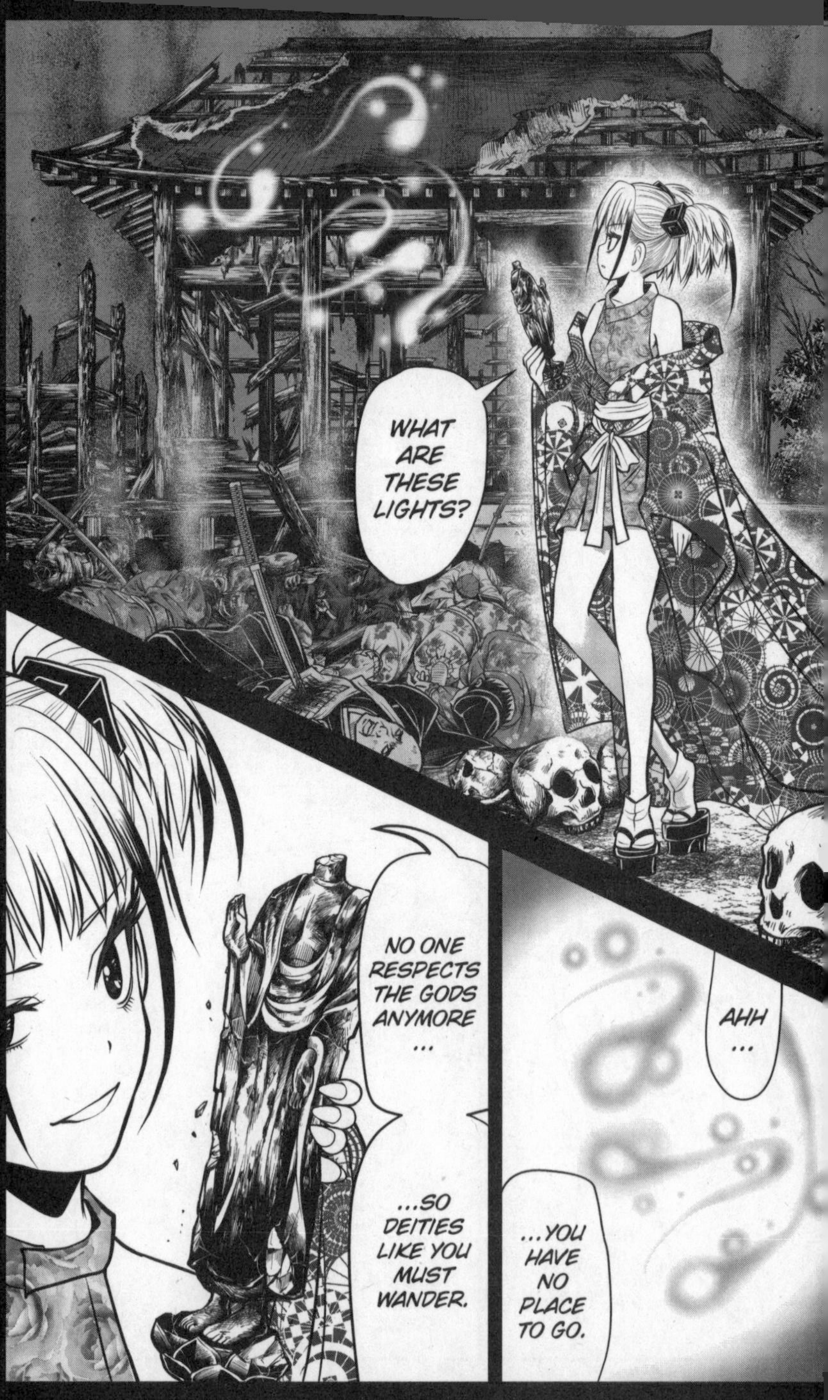
WHAT ARE THESE LIGHTS?
AHH ...
...YOU HAVE NO PLACE TO GO.
NO ONE RESPECTS THE GODS ANYMORE ...
...SO DEITIES LIKE YOU MUST WANDER.

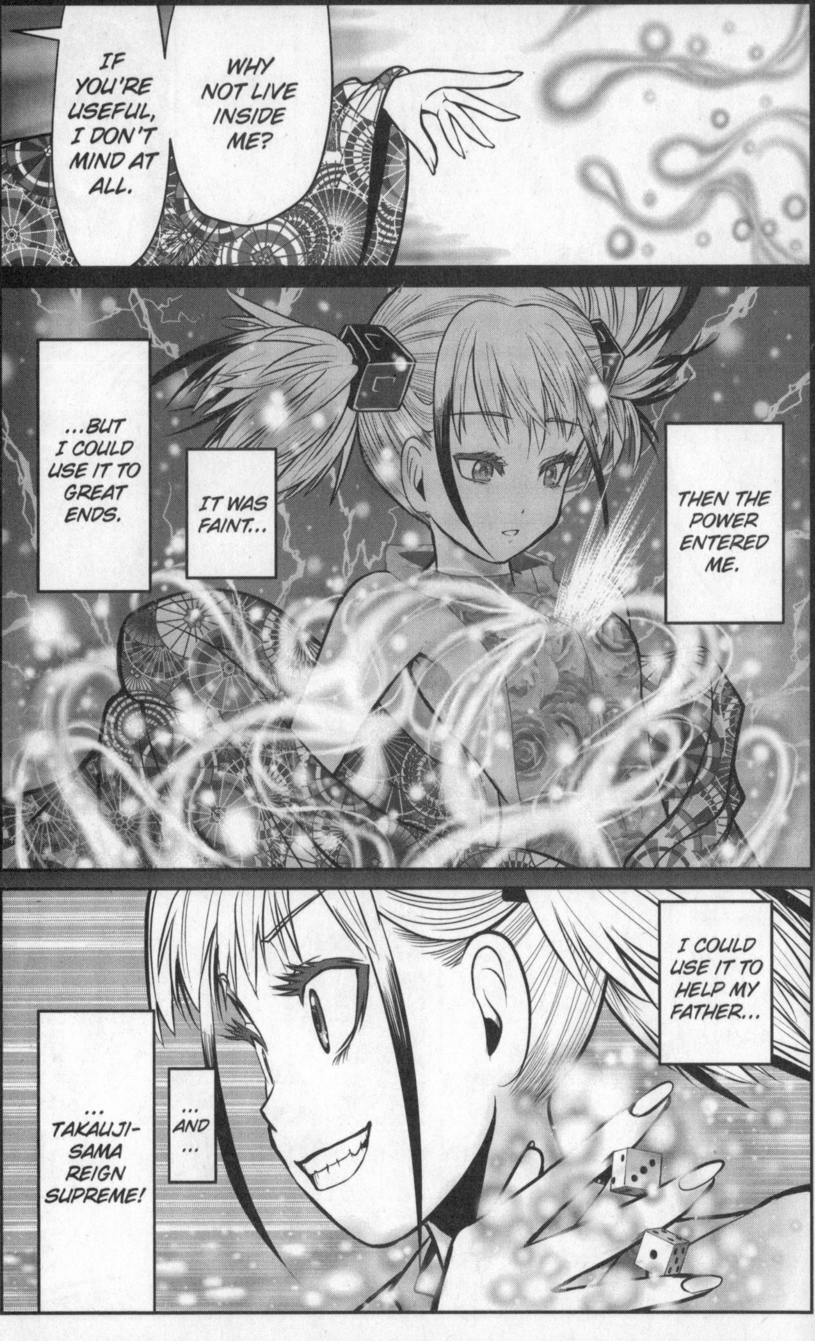
WHY NOT LIVE INSIDE ME?
IF YOU'RE USEFUL, I DON'T MIND AT ALL.
THEN THE POWER ENTERED ME.
IT WAS FAINT...
...BUT I COULD USE IT TO GREAT ENDS.
I COULD USE IT TO HELP MY FATHER...
... AND ...
... TAKAUJI-SAMA REIGN SUPREME!

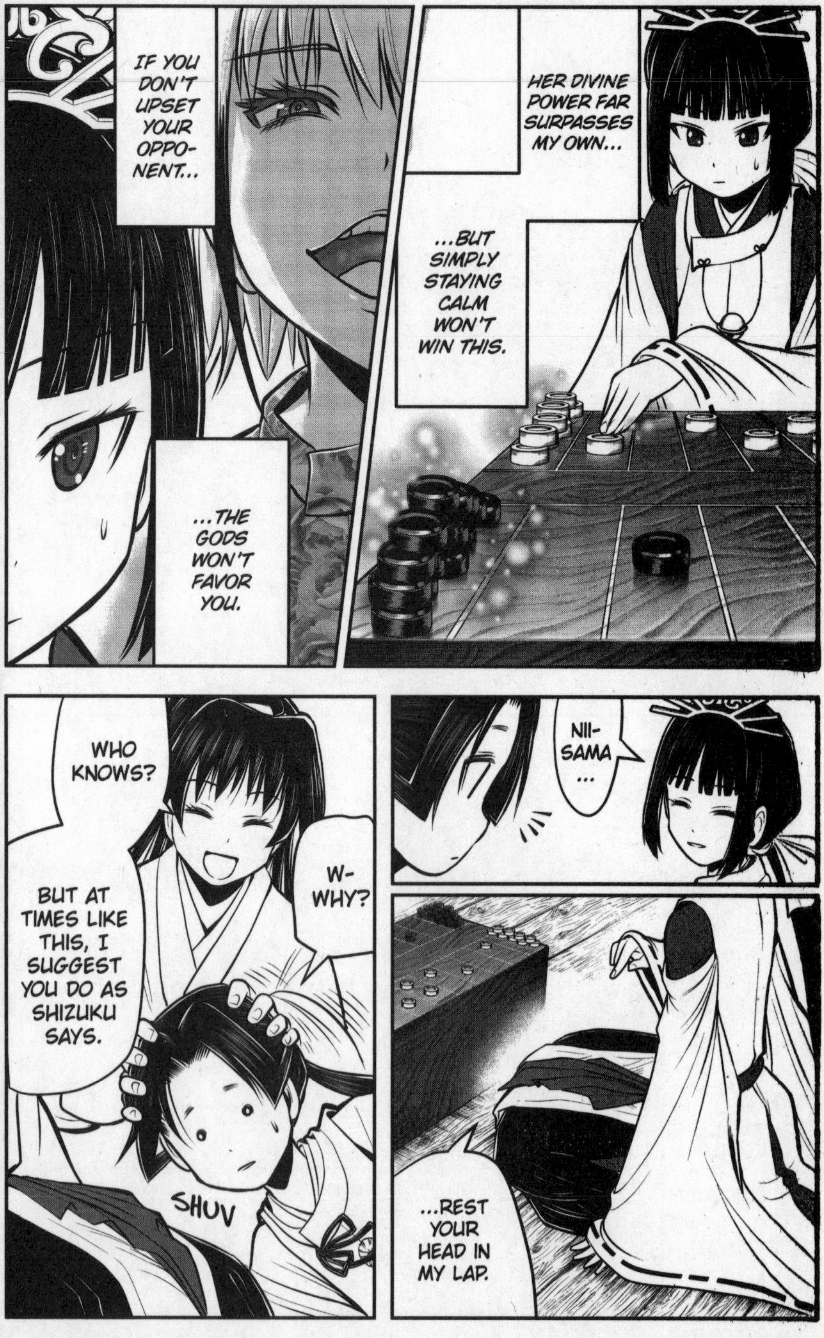
HER DIVINE POWER FAR SURPASSES MY OWN...
...BUT SIMPLY STAYING CALM WON'T WIN THIS.
IF YOU DON'T UPSET YOUR OPPO-NENT...
...THE GODS WON'T FAVOR YOU.
NII-SAMA ...
...REST YOUR HEAD IN MY LAP.
W-WHY?
WHO KNOWS?
BUT AT TIMES LIKE THIS, I SUGGEST YOU DO AS SHIZUKU SAYS.
SHUV

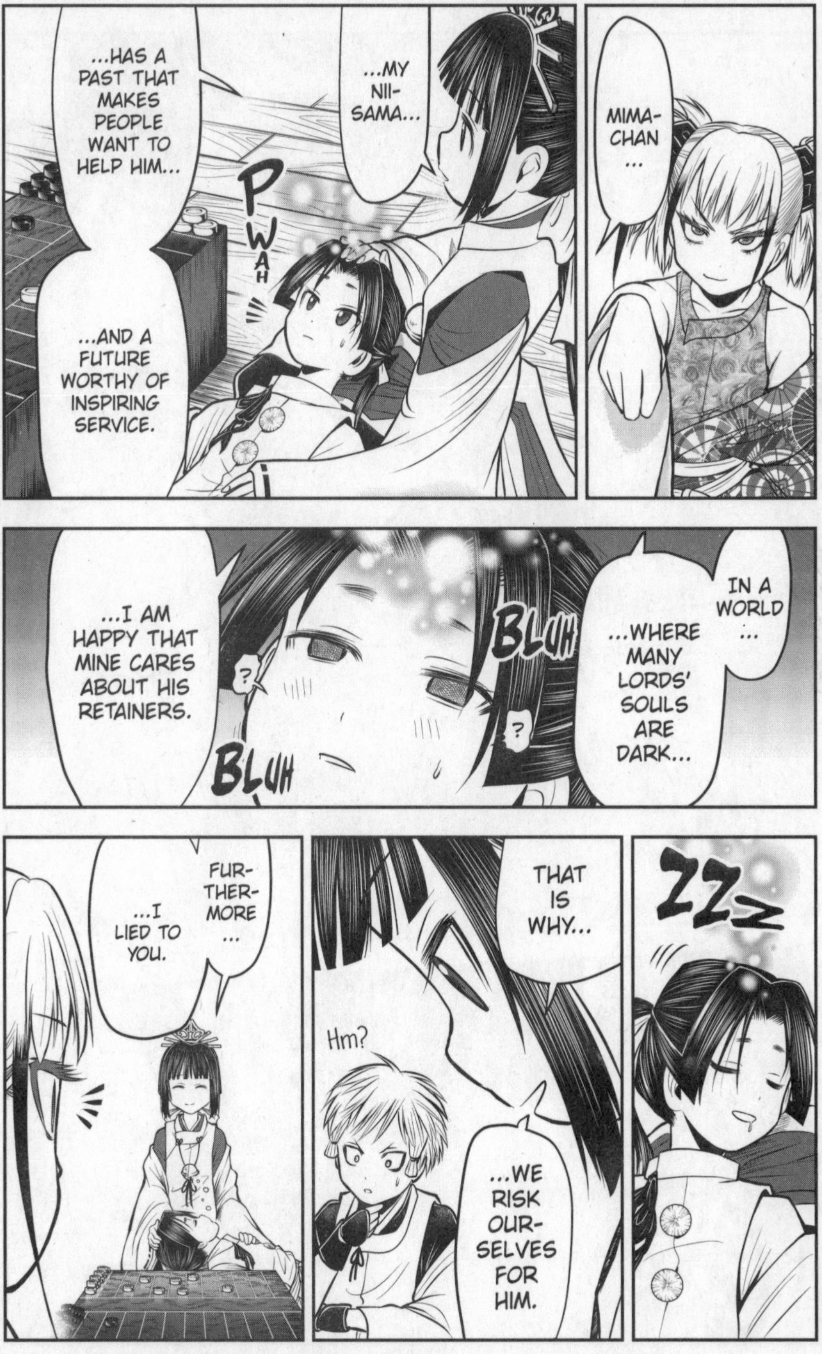
MIMA-CHAN ...
...MY NII-SAMA...
...HAS A PAST THAT MAKES PEOPLE WANT TO HELP HIM...
PWAH
...AND A FUTURE WORTHY OF INSPIRING SERVICE.
IN A WORLD ...
...WHERE MANY LORDS' SOULS ARE DARK...
BLUH
?
?
...I AM HAPPY THAT MINE CARES ABOUT HIS RETAINERS.
BLUH
ZZZ
THAT IS WHY...
Hm?
...WE RISK OURSELVES FOR HIM.
FURTHERMORE ...
...I LIED TO YOU.

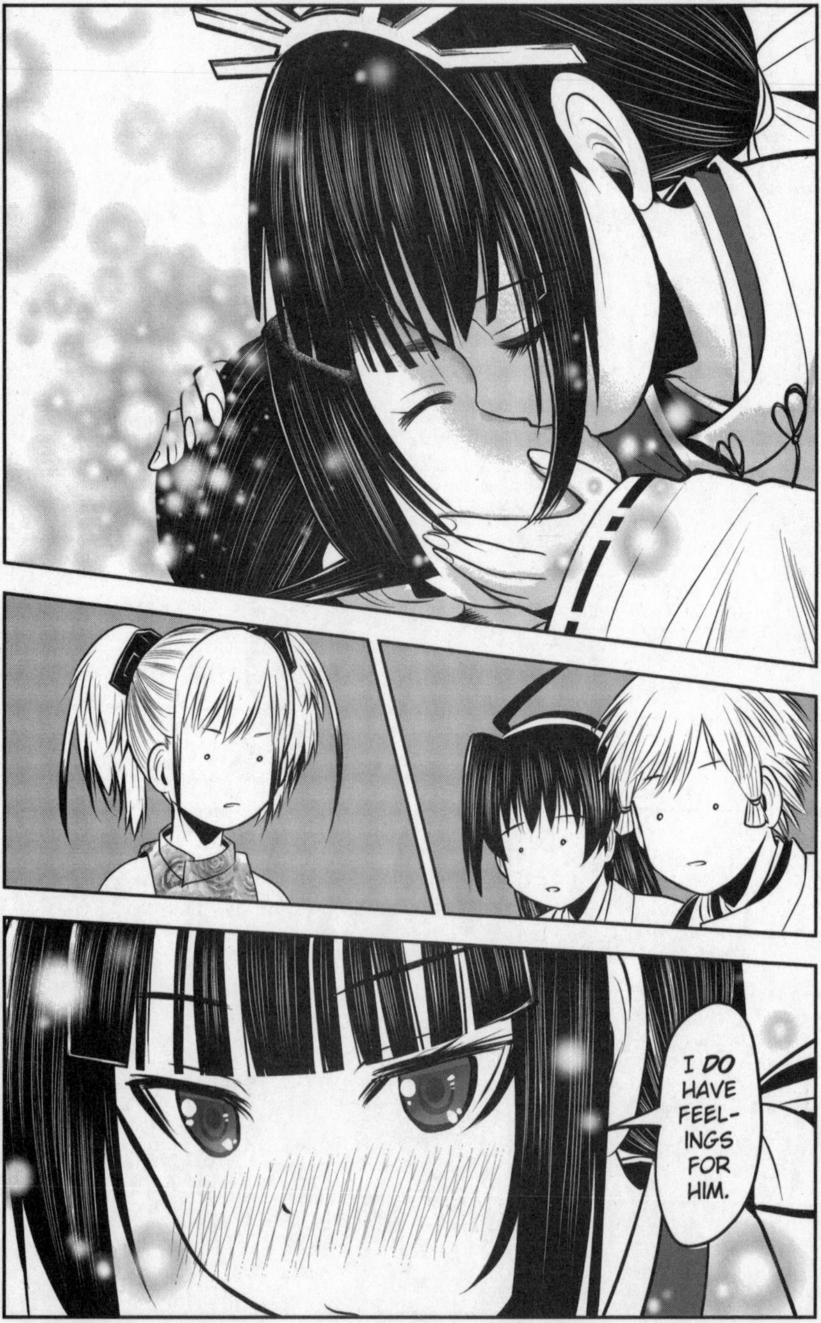
I *DO* HAVE FEEL-INGS FOR HIM.

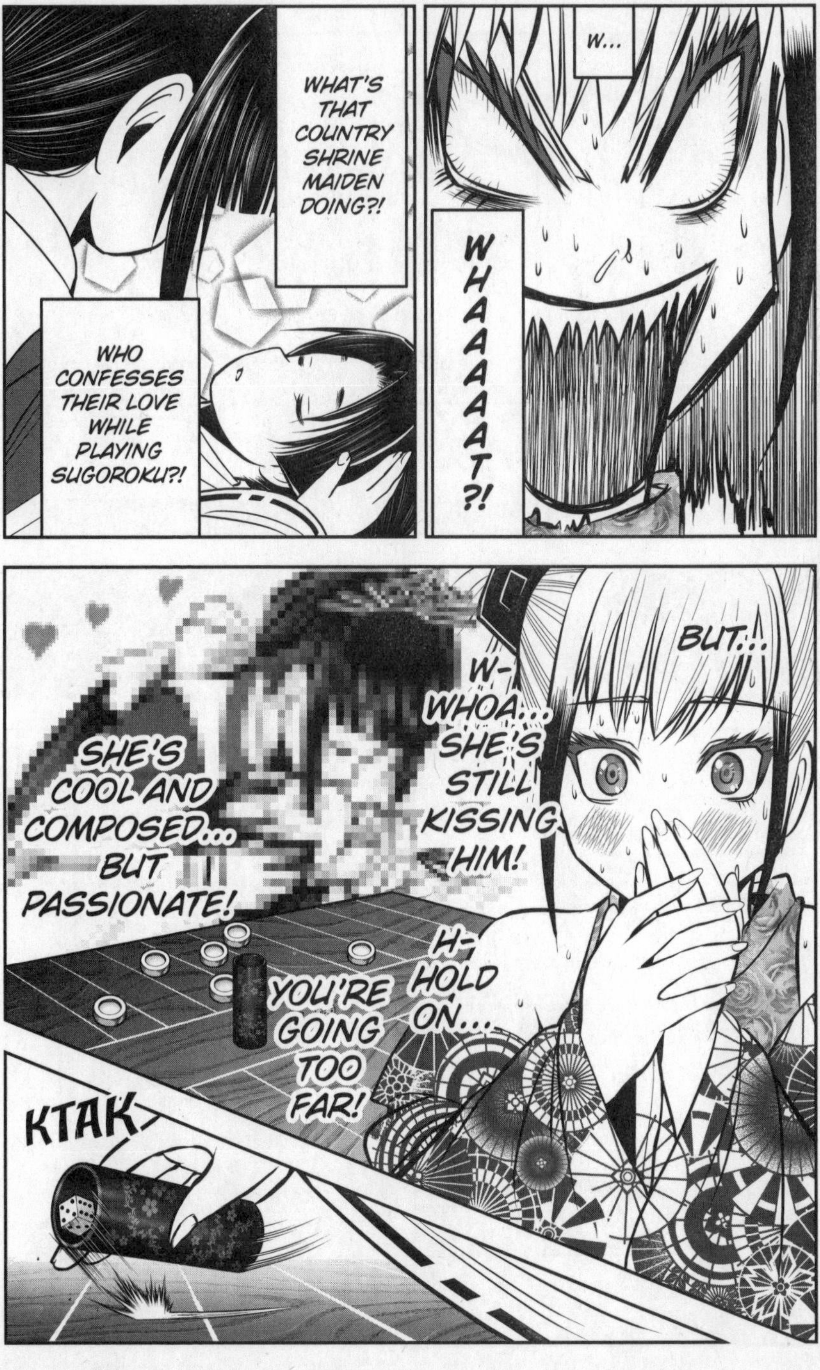

W...
WHAAAAAAT?!
WHAT'S THAT COUNTRY SHRINE MAIDEN DOING?!
WHO CONFESSES THEIR LOVE WHILE PLAYING SUGOROKU?!
BUT...
W-WHOA... SHE'S STILL KISSING HIM!
SHE'S COOL AND COMPOSED... BUT PASSIONATE!
H-HOLD ON...
YOU'RE GOING TOO FAR!
KTAK

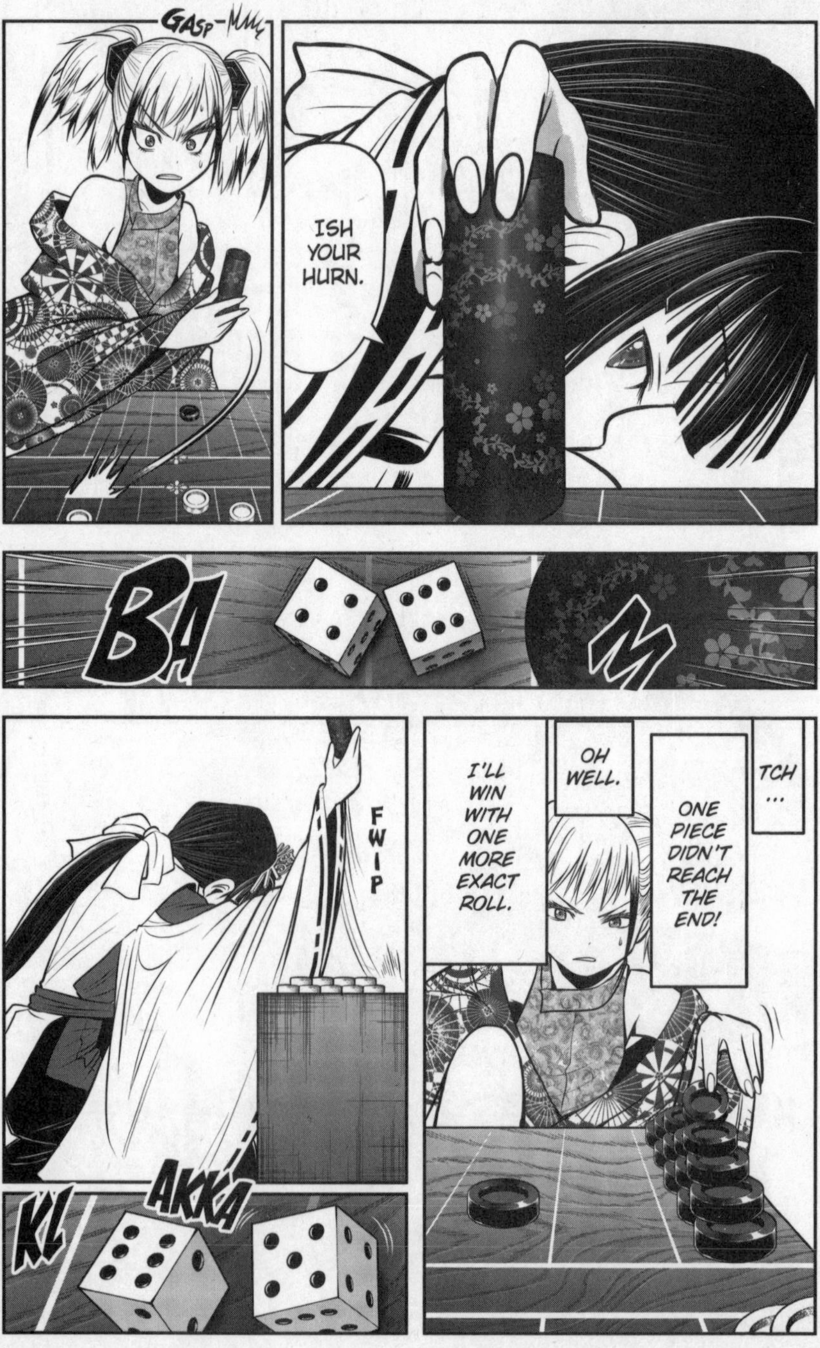
ISH YOUR HURN.
GASP-MMM
BAM
TCH ...
ONE PIECE DIDN'T REACH THE END!
OH WELL.
I'LL WIN WITH ONE MORE EXACT ROLL.
FWIP
KLAKKA

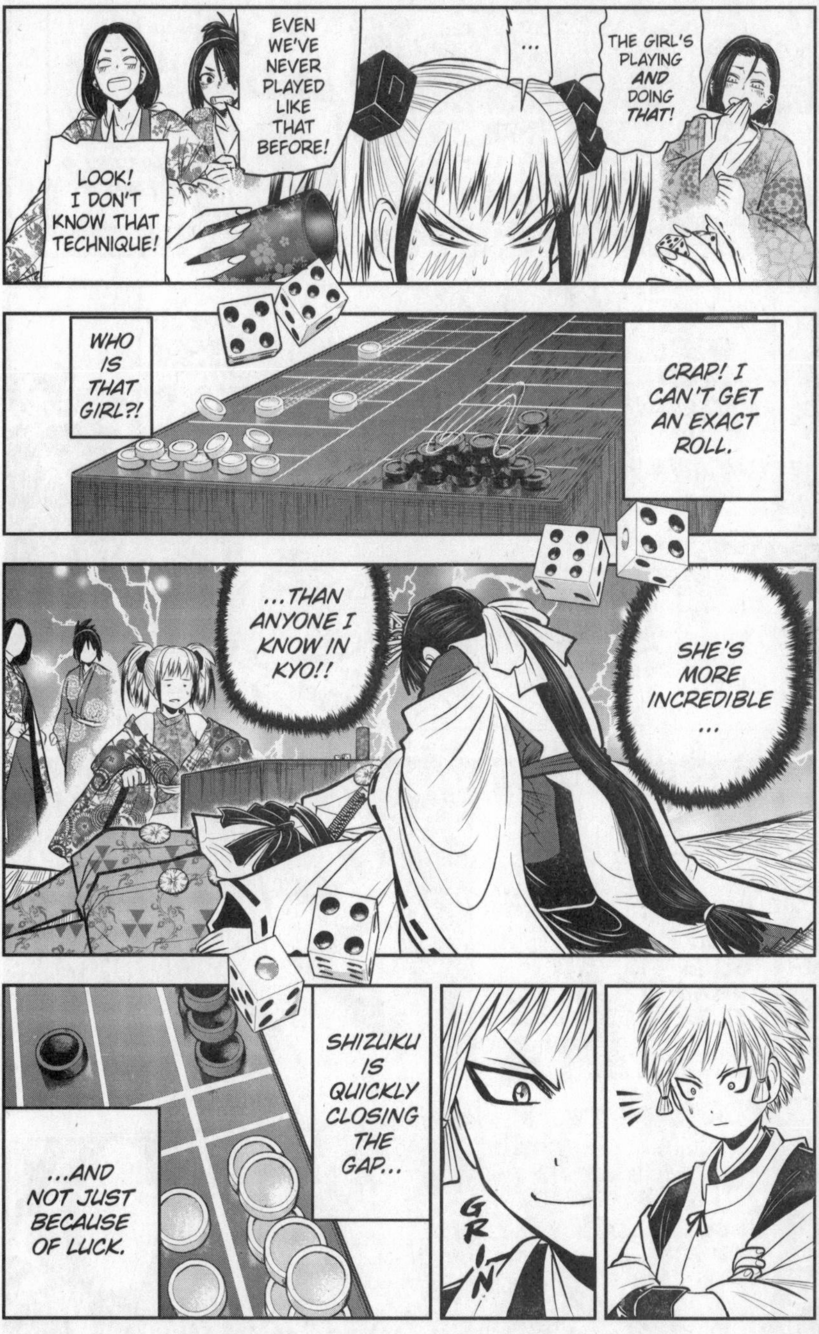
THE GIRL'S PLAYING AND DOING THAT!
...
EVEN WE'VE NEVER PLAYED LIKE THAT BEFORE!
LOOK! I DON'T KNOW THAT TECHNIQUE!
CRAP! I CAN'T GET AN EXACT ROLL.
WHO IS THAT GIRL?!
SHE'S MORE INCREDIBLE ...
...THAN ANYONE I KNOW IN KYO!!
GRIN
SHIZUKU IS QUICKLY CLOSING THE GAP...
...AND NOT JUST BECAUSE OF LUCK.

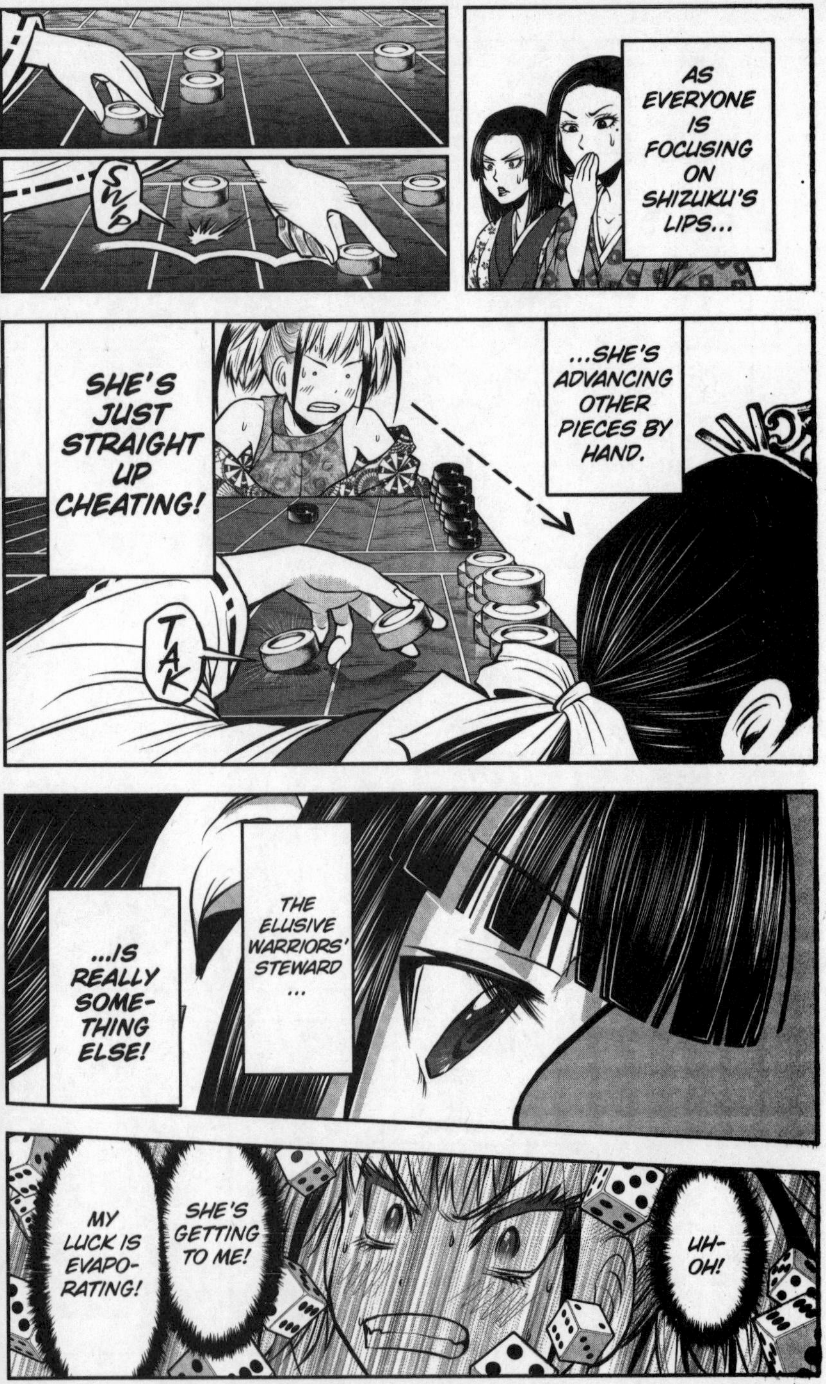
AS EVERYONE IS FOCUSING ON SHIZUKU'S LIPS...
SWIP
...SHE'S ADVANCING OTHER PIECES BY HAND.
SHE'S JUST STRAIGHT UP CHEATING!
TAK
THE ELUSIVE WARRIORS' STEWARD...
...IS REALLY SOME-THING ELSE!
UH-OH!
SHE'S GETTING TO ME!
MY LUCK IS EVAPO-RATING!

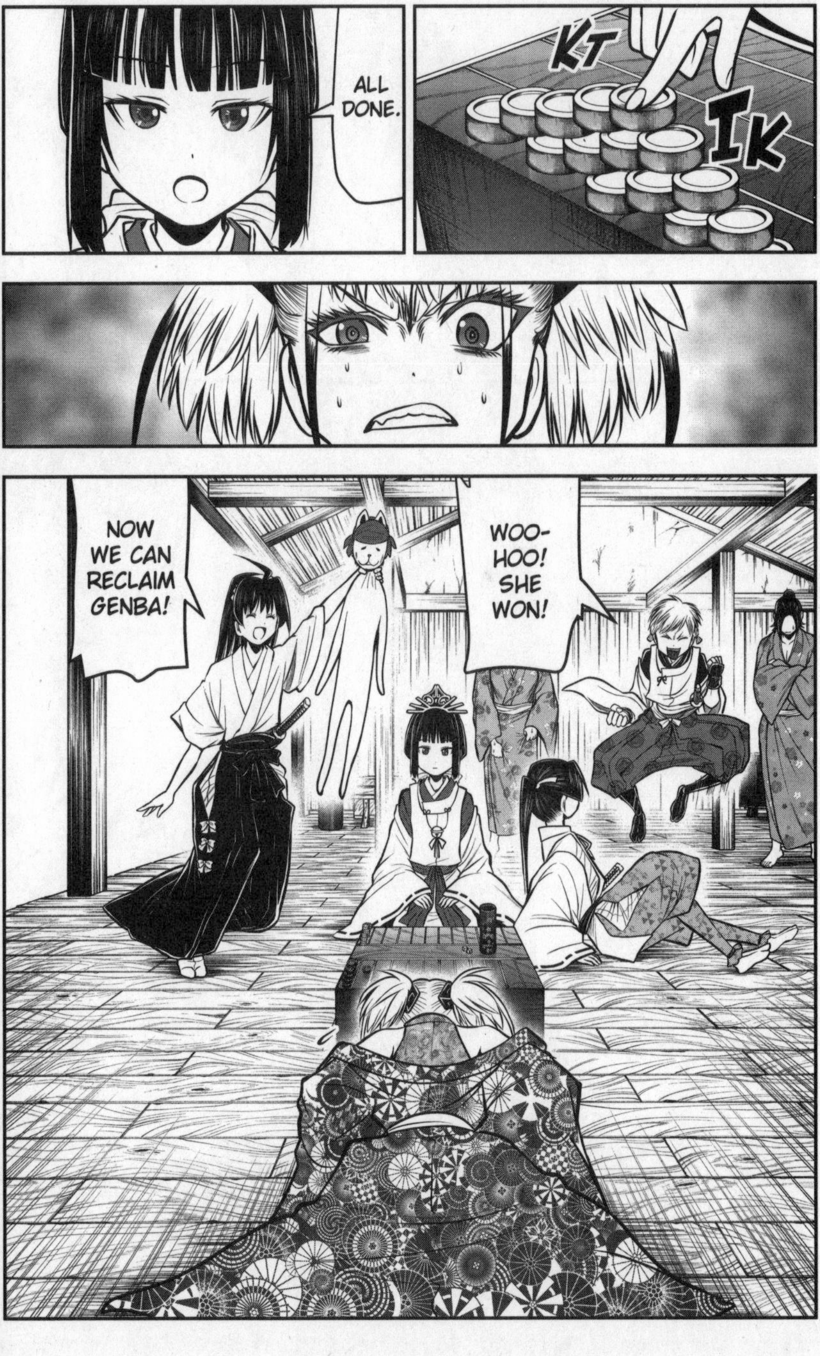
KT
IK
ALL DONE.
WOO-HOO! SHE WON!
NOW WE CAN RECLAIM GENBA!

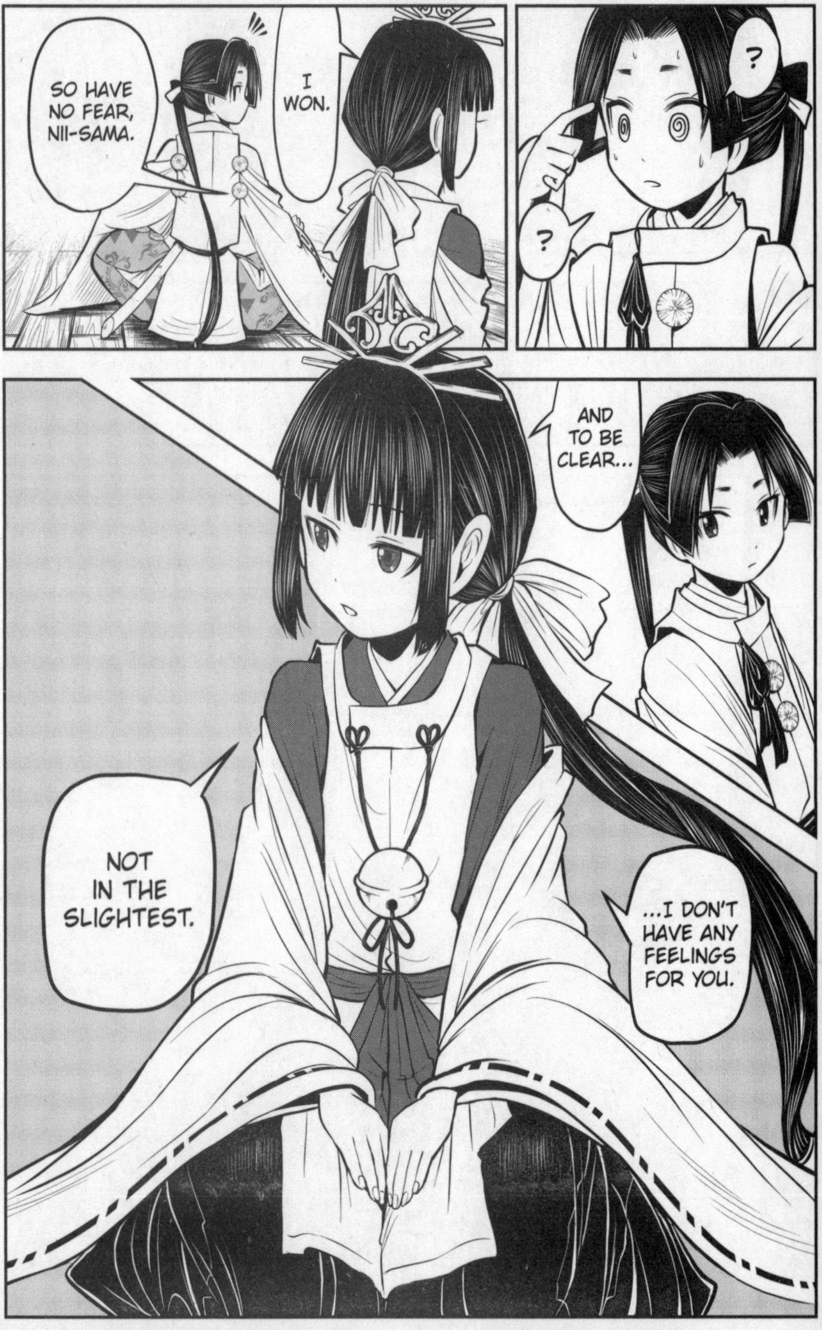
?
?
I WON.
SO HAVE NO FEAR, NII-SAMA.
AND TO BE CLEAR...
...I DON'T HAVE ANY FEELINGS FOR YOU.
NOT IN THE SLIGHTEST.

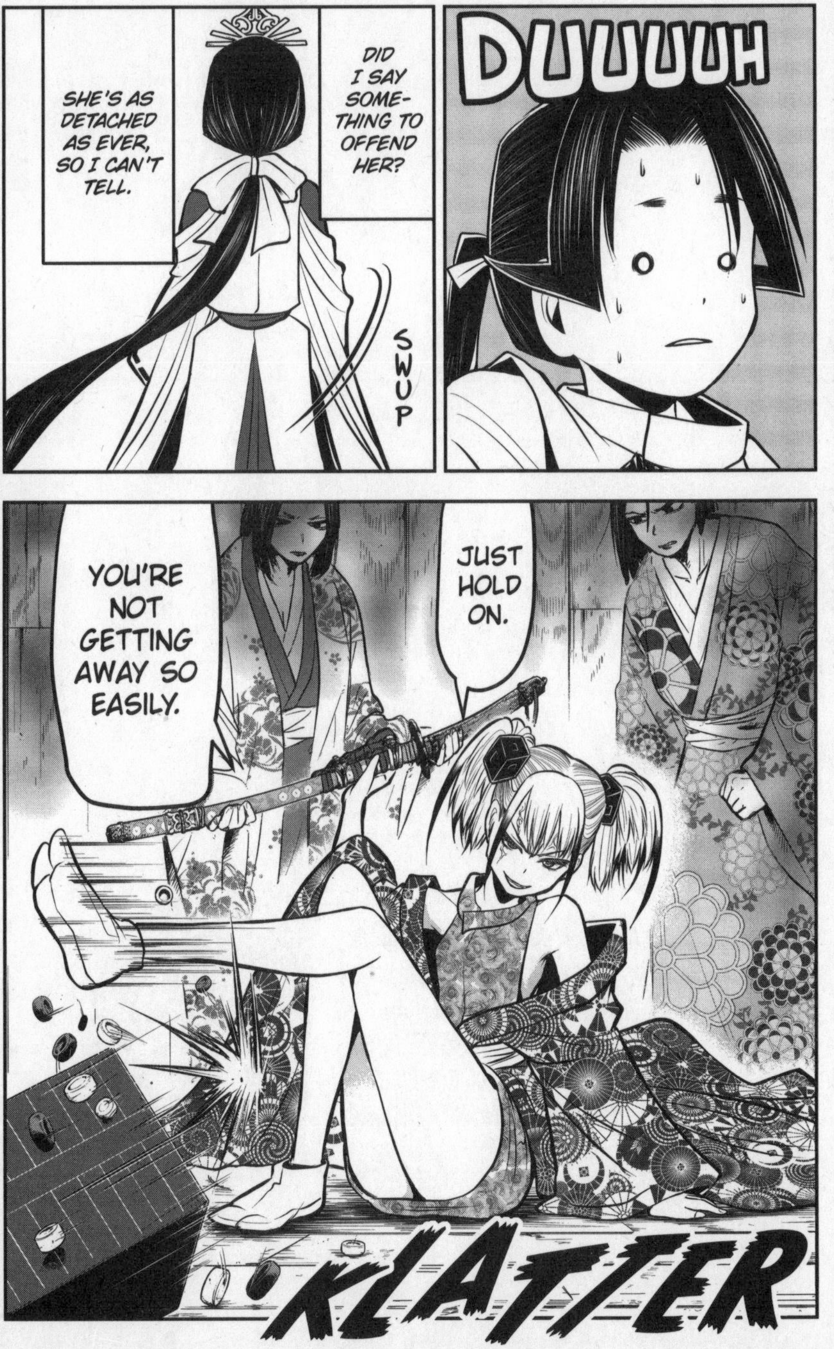
DUUUUH
DID I SAY SOME-THING TO OFFEND HER?
SHE'S AS DETACHED AS EVER, SO I CAN'T TELL.
SWUP
JUST HOLD ON.
YOU'RE NOT GETTING AWAY SO EASILY.
KLATTER

HIS CONCERN FOR HIS RETAINERS IS ADMIRABLE, AND HE LOOKS SO CUTE WHEN HE'S ASLEEP, AND HIS LIPS WERE REALLY SOFT...BUT AS A MAN, HE'S STILL COMPLETELY, UTTERLY, AND TOTALLY LACKING.

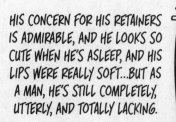

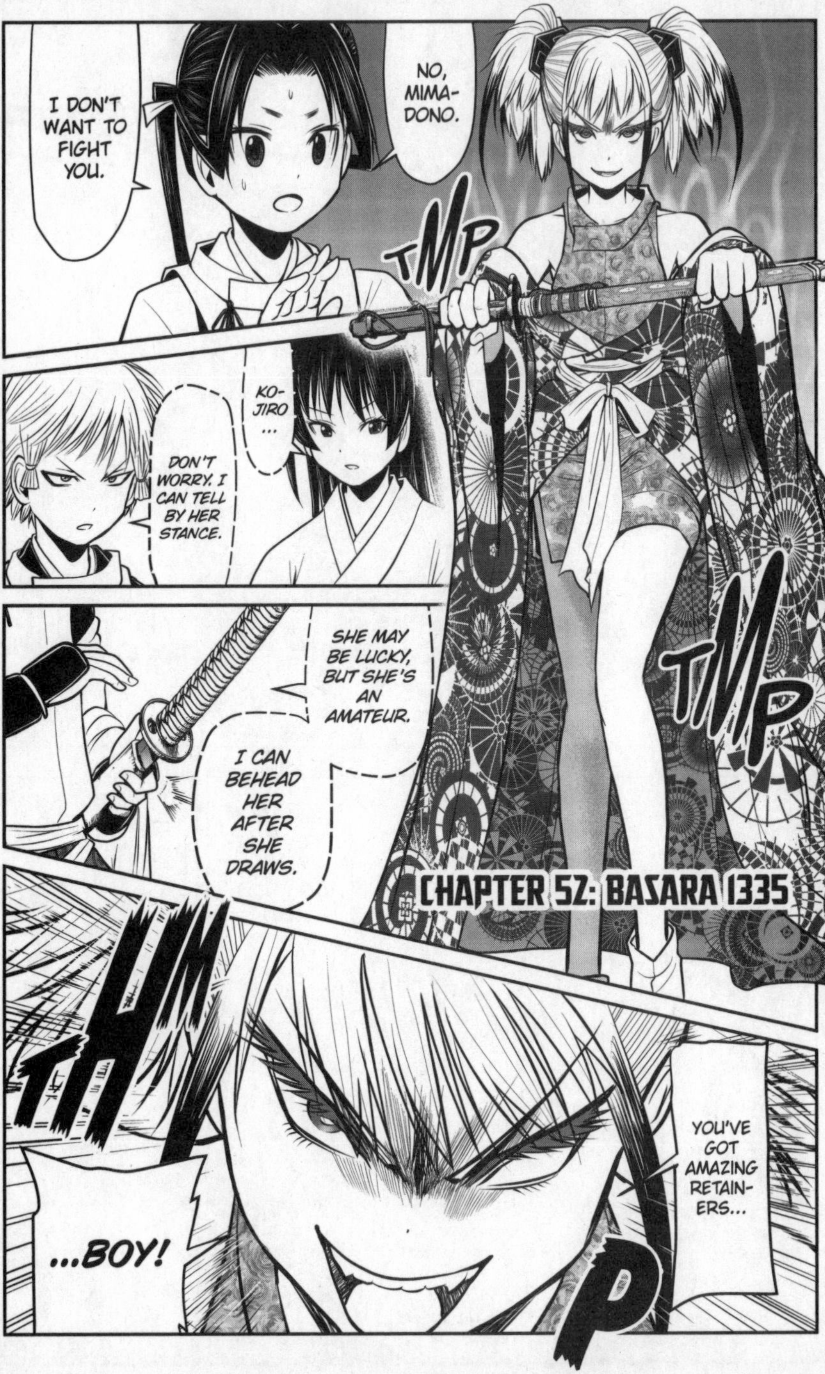
NO, MIMA-DONO.
I DON'T WANT TO FIGHT YOU.
TMP
TMP
CHAPTER 52: BASARA 1335
KOJIRO…
DON'T WORRY. I CAN TELL BY HER STANCE.
SHE MAY BE LUCKY, BUT SHE'S AN AMATEUR.
I CAN BEHEAD HER AFTER SHE DRAWS.
YOU'VE GOT AMAZING RETAINERS…
…BOY!
THMP

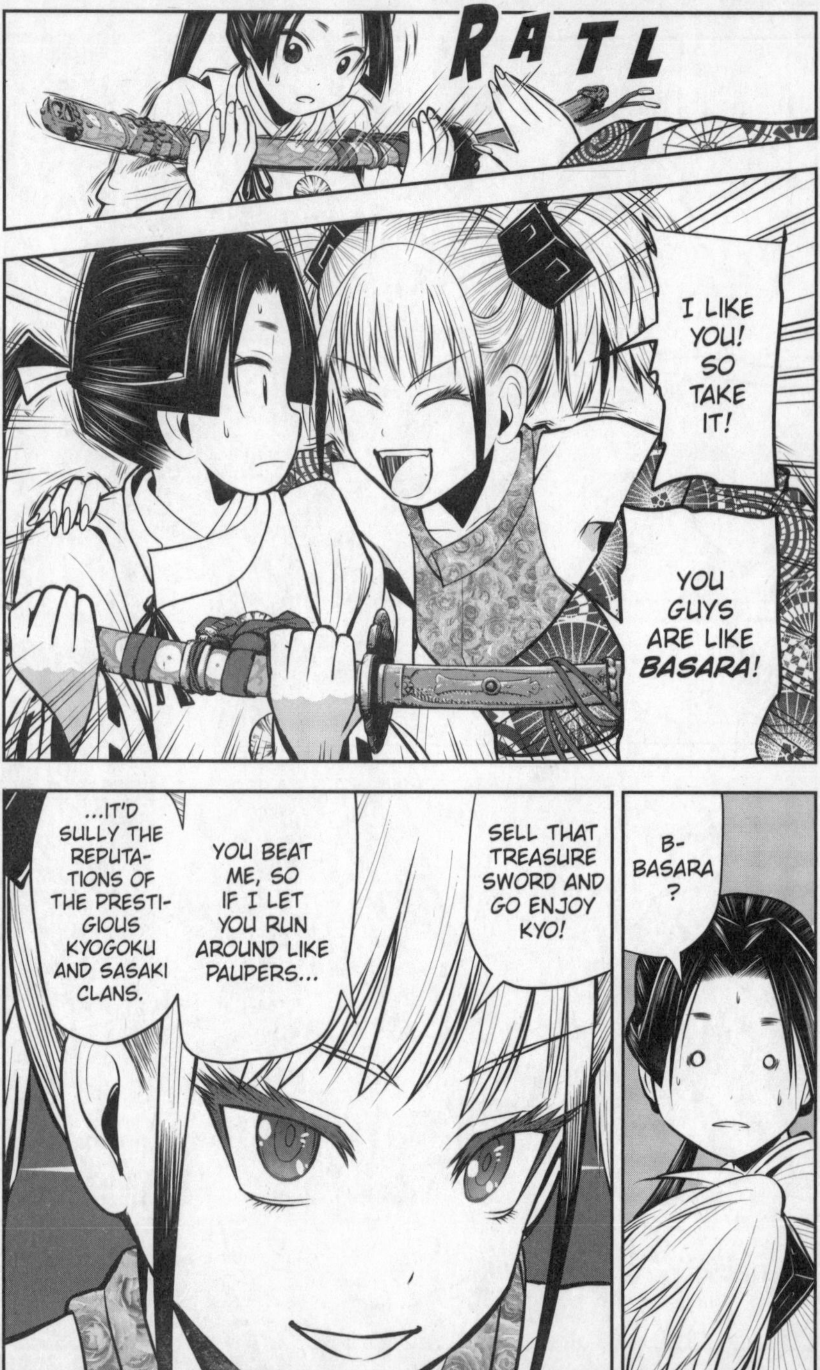
RATL
I LIKE YOU! SO TAKE IT!
YOU GUYS ARE LIKE BASARA!
B-BASARA?
SELL THAT TREASURE SWORD AND GO ENJOY KYO!
YOU BEAT ME, SO IF I LET YOU RUN AROUND LIKE PAUPERS...
...IT'D SULLY THE REPUTATIONS OF THE PRESTIGIOUS KYOGOKU AND SASAKI CLANS.

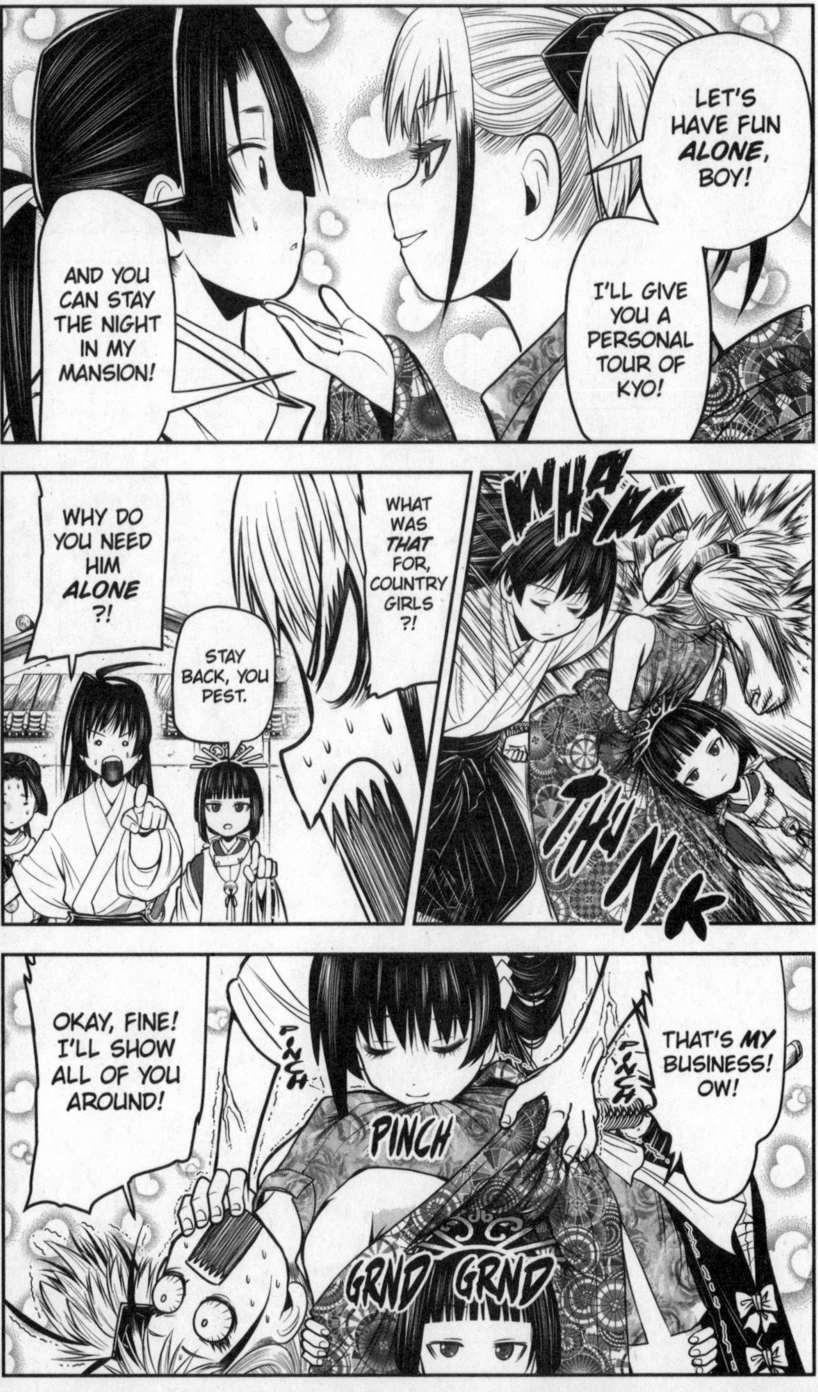
LET'S HAVE FUN ALONE, BOY!
I'LL GIVE YOU A PERSONAL TOUR OF KYO!
AND YOU CAN STAY THE NIGHT IN MY MANSION!
WHAM
THUNK
WHAT WAS THAT FOR, COUNTRY GIRLS?!
STAY BACK, YOU PEST.
WHY DO YOU NEED HIM ALONE?!
THAT'S MY BUSINESS! OW!
PINCH
PINCH
PINCH
GRND GRND
OKAY, FINE! I'LL SHOW ALL OF YOU AROUND!

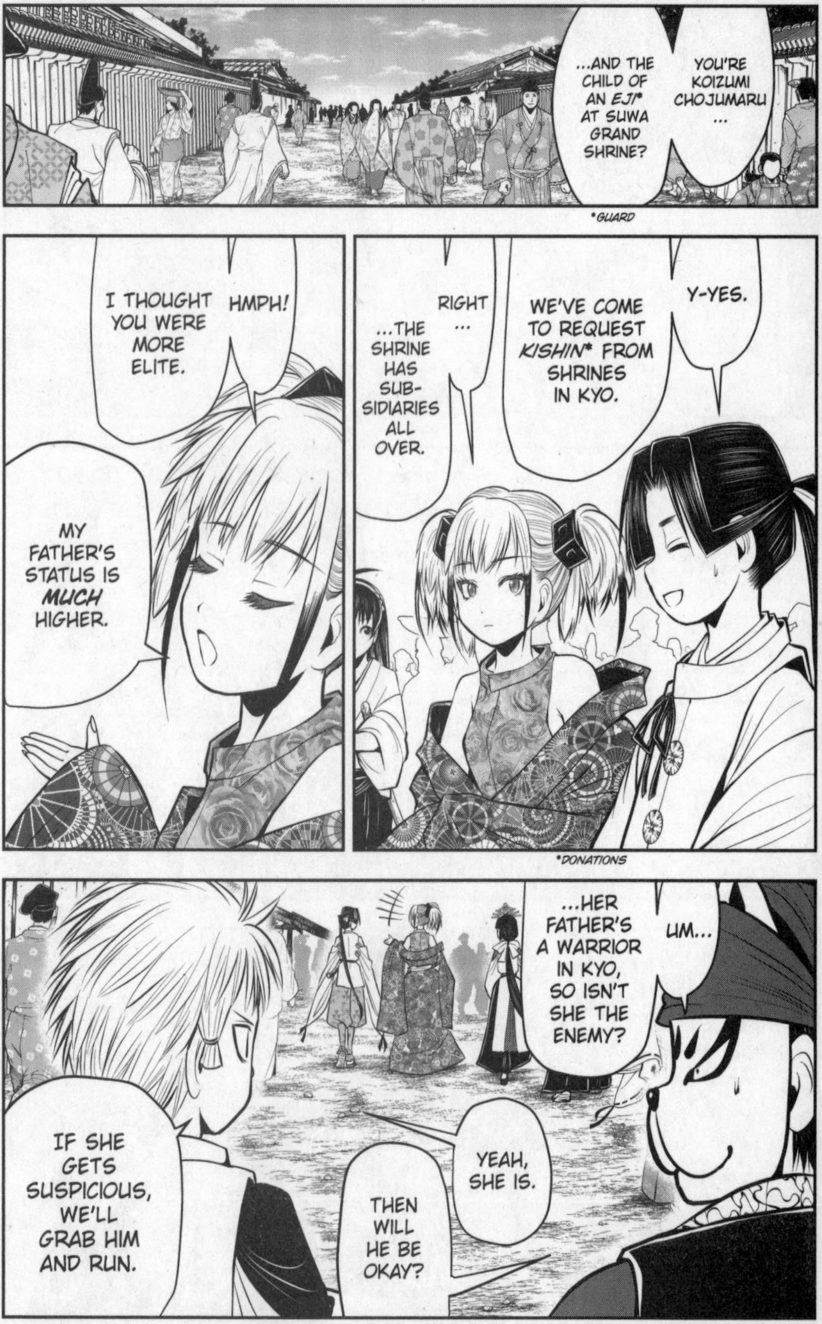
YOU'RE KOIZUMI CHOJUMARU ...
...AND THE CHILD OF AN *EJI** AT SUWA GRAND SHRINE?
Y-YES.
WE'VE COME TO REQUEST *KISHIN** FROM SHRINES IN KYO.
RIGHT ...
...THE SHRINE HAS SUBSIDIARIES ALL OVER.
HMPH!
I THOUGHT YOU WERE MORE ELITE.
MY FATHER'S STATUS IS *MUCH* HIGHER.
UM...
...HER FATHER'S A WARRIOR IN KYO, SO ISN'T SHE THE ENEMY?
YEAH, SHE IS.
THEN WILL HE BE OKAY?
IF SHE GETS SUSPICIOUS, WE'LL GRAB HIM AND RUN.

*GUARD

*DONATIONS

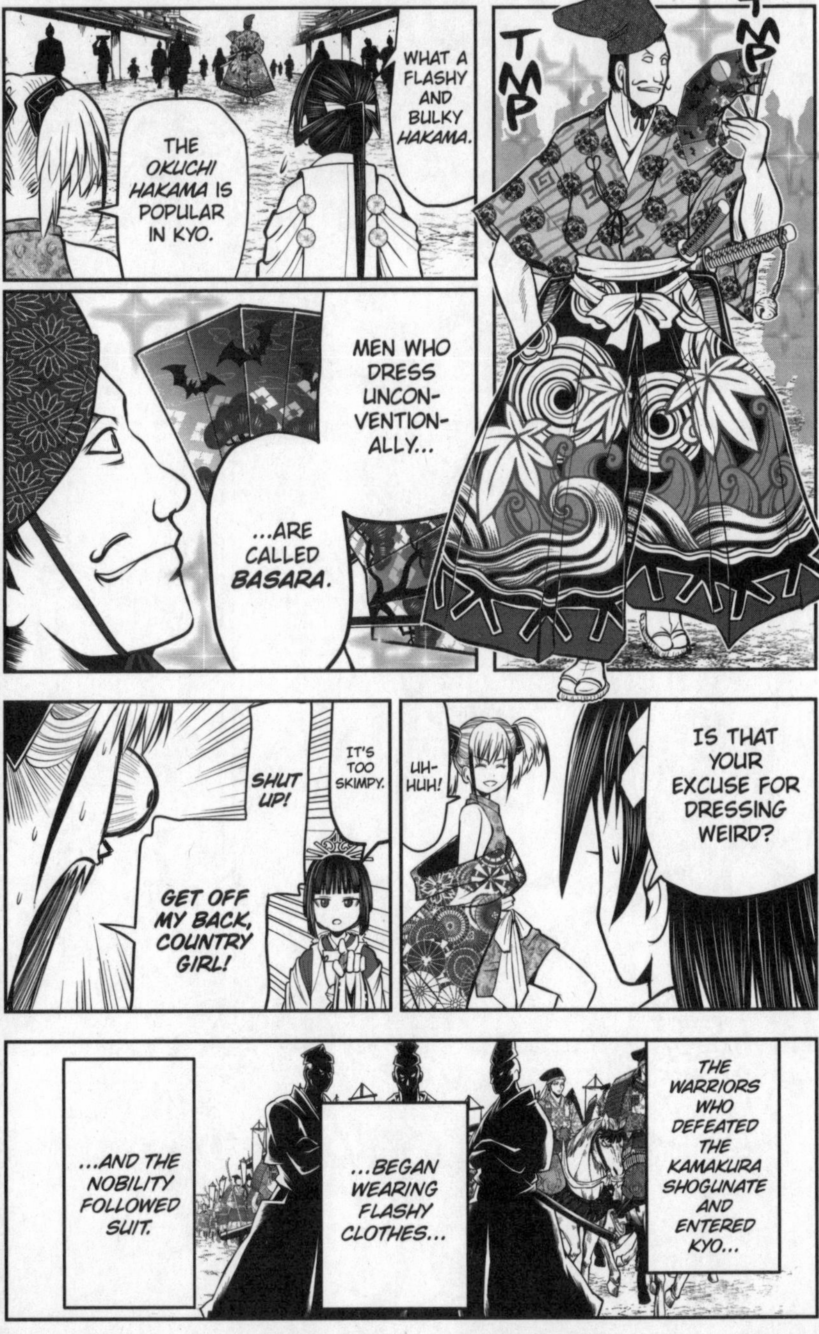
TMP
TMP
WHAT A FLASHY AND BULKY HAKAMA.
THE OKUCHI HAKAMA IS POPULAR IN KYO.
MEN WHO DRESS UNCONVENTIONALLY...
...ARE CALLED BASARA.
IS THAT YOUR EXCUSE FOR DRESSING WEIRD?
UH-HUH!
IT'S TOO SKIMPY.
SHUT UP!
GET OFF MY BACK, COUNTRY GIRL!
THE WARRIORS WHO DEFEATED THE KAMAKURA SHOGUNATE AND ENTERED KYO...
...BEGAN WEARING FLASHY CLOTHES...
...AND THE NOBILITY FOLLOWED SUIT.

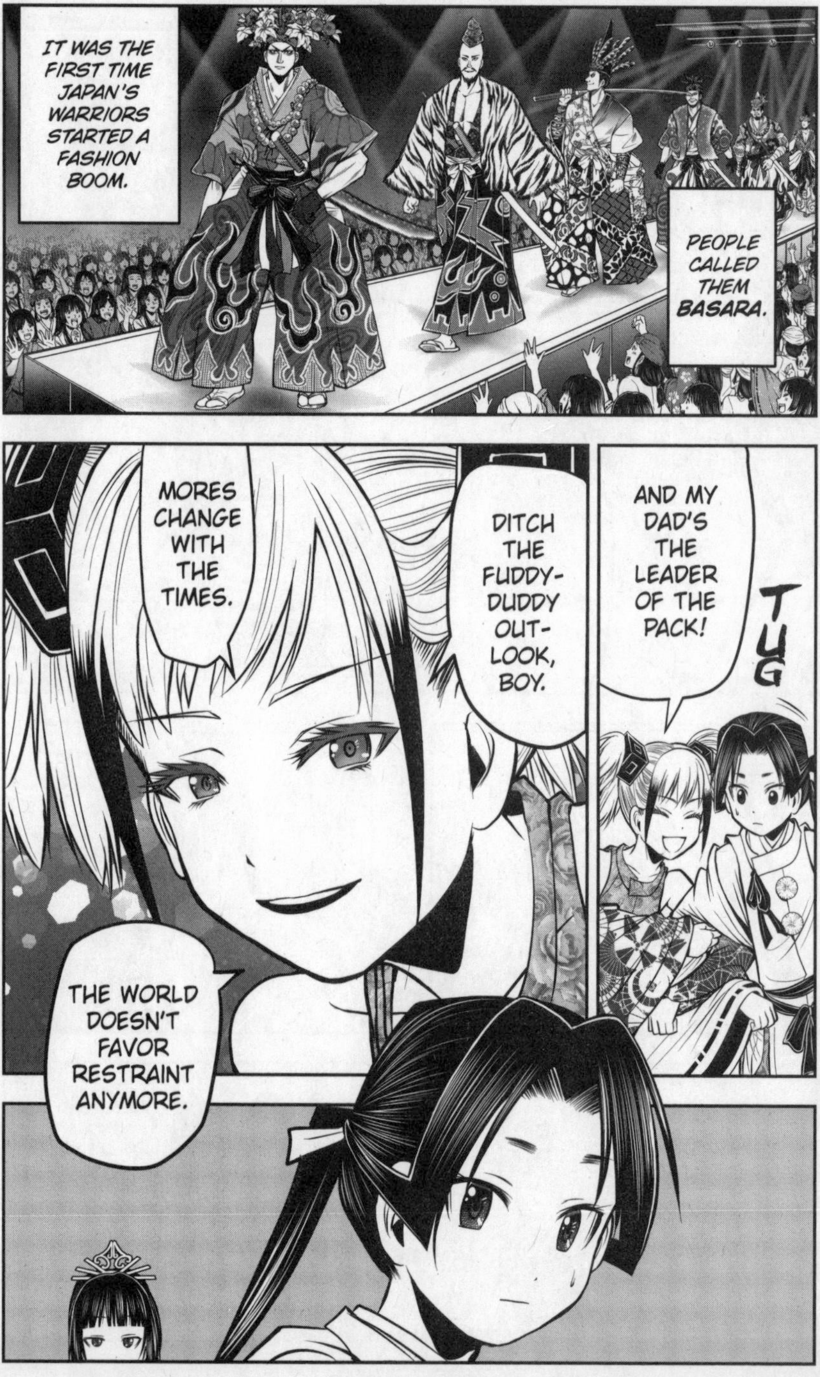
IT WAS THE FIRST TIME JAPAN'S WARRIORS STARTED A FASHION BOOM.
PEOPLE CALLED THEM BASARA.
AND MY DAD'S THE LEADER OF THE PACK!
TUG
DITCH THE FUDDY-DUDDY OUT-LOOK, BOY.
MORES CHANGE WITH THE TIMES.
THE WORLD DOESN'T FAVOR RESTRAINT ANYMORE.

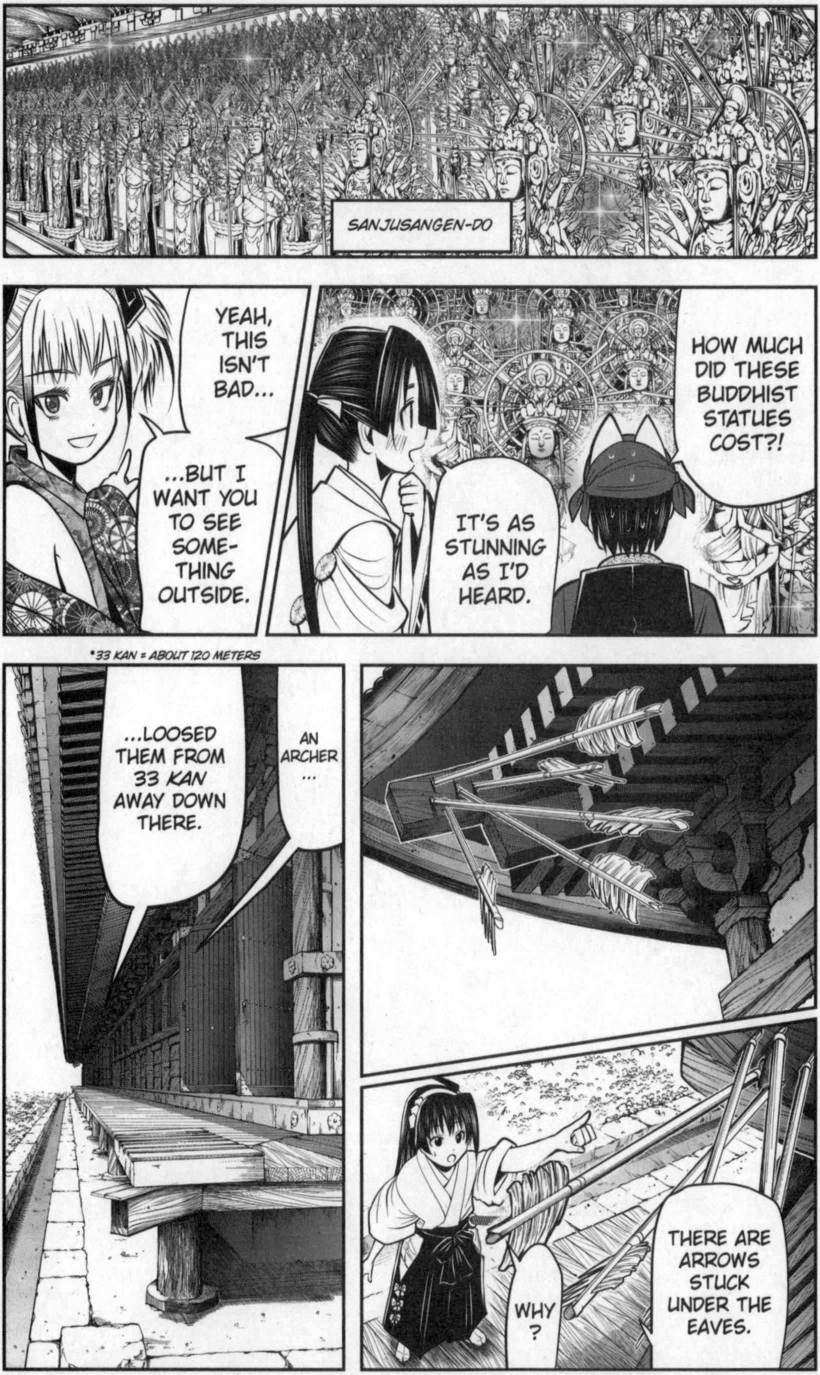
SANJUSANGEN-DO
HOW MUCH DID THESE BUDDHIST STATUES COST?!
IT'S AS STUNNING AS I'D HEARD.
YEAH, THIS ISN'T BAD...
...BUT I WANT YOU TO SEE SOMETHING OUTSIDE.
THERE ARE ARROWS STUCK UNDER THE EAVES.
WHY?
AN ARCHER...
...LOOSED THEM FROM 33 *KAN* AWAY DOWN THERE.
*33 KAN = ABOUT 120 METERS

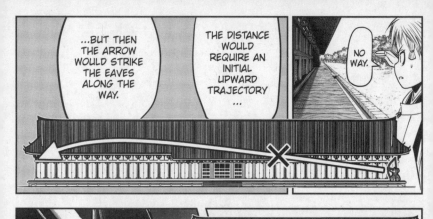

NO WAY.
THE DISTANCE WOULD REQUIRE AN INITIAL UPWARD TRAJECTORY...
...BUT THEN THE ARROW WOULD STRIKE THE EAVES ALONG THE WAY.
YES.
THE ARROW MUST FLY STRAIGHT...
...REQUIRING A STRONG BOW AND IMMENSE STRENGTH.
ALL THE WAR-RIORS WHO TRIED, FAILED.
BUT A COURT NOBLE NAMED *KITABATAKE AKIIE*...
...DID IT WITHOUT BREAKING A SWEAT.

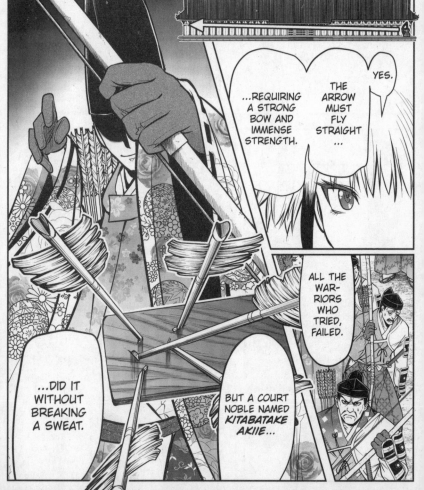

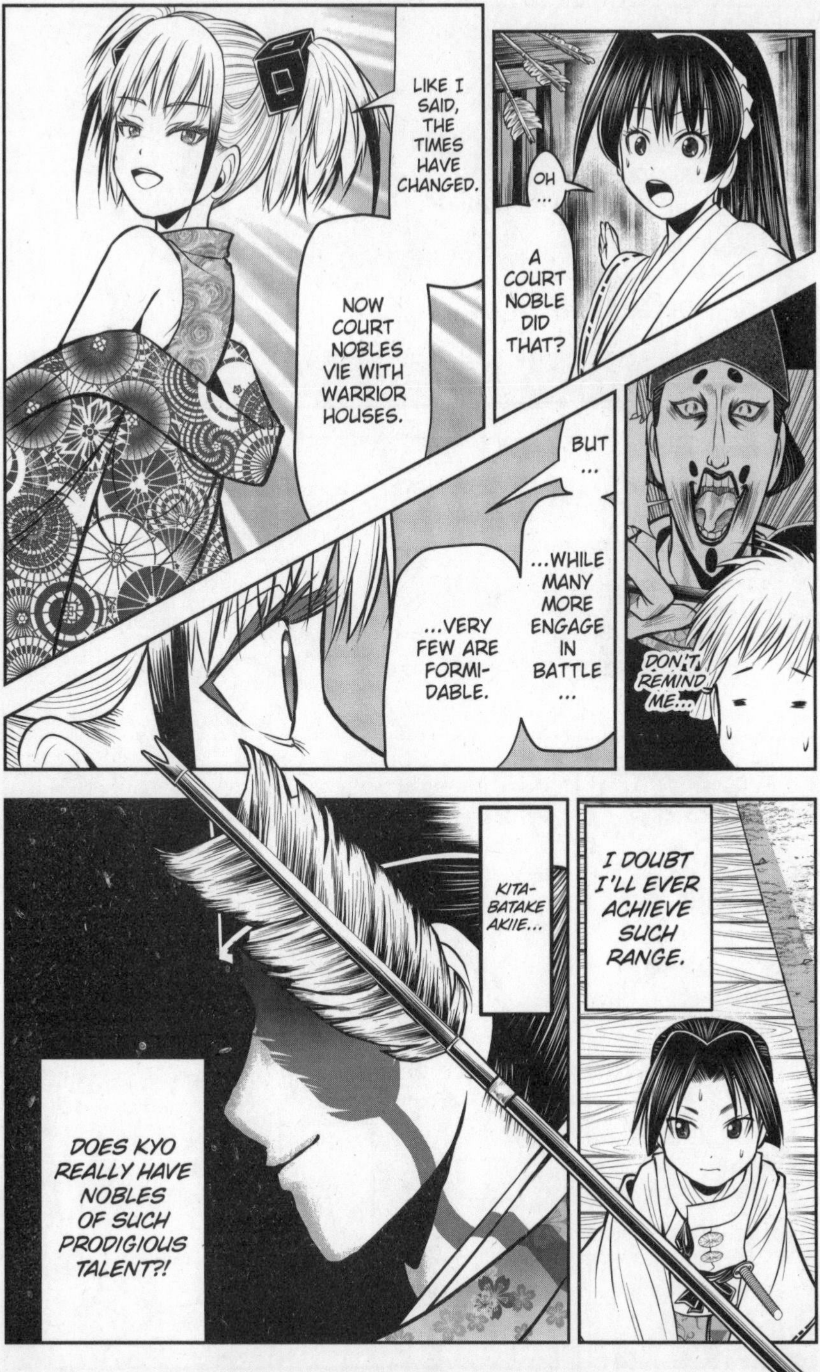
OH ...
A COURT NOBLE DID THAT?
LIKE I SAID, THE TIMES HAVE CHANGED.
NOW COURT NOBLES VIE WITH WARRIOR HOUSES.
DON'T REMIND ME...
BUT ...
...WHILE MANY MORE ENGAGE IN BATTLE ...
...VERY FEW ARE FORMIDABLE.
I DOUBT I'LL EVER ACHIEVE SUCH RANGE.
KITA-BATAKE AKIIE...
DOES KYO REALLY HAVE NOBLES OF SUCH PRODIGIOUS TALENT?!

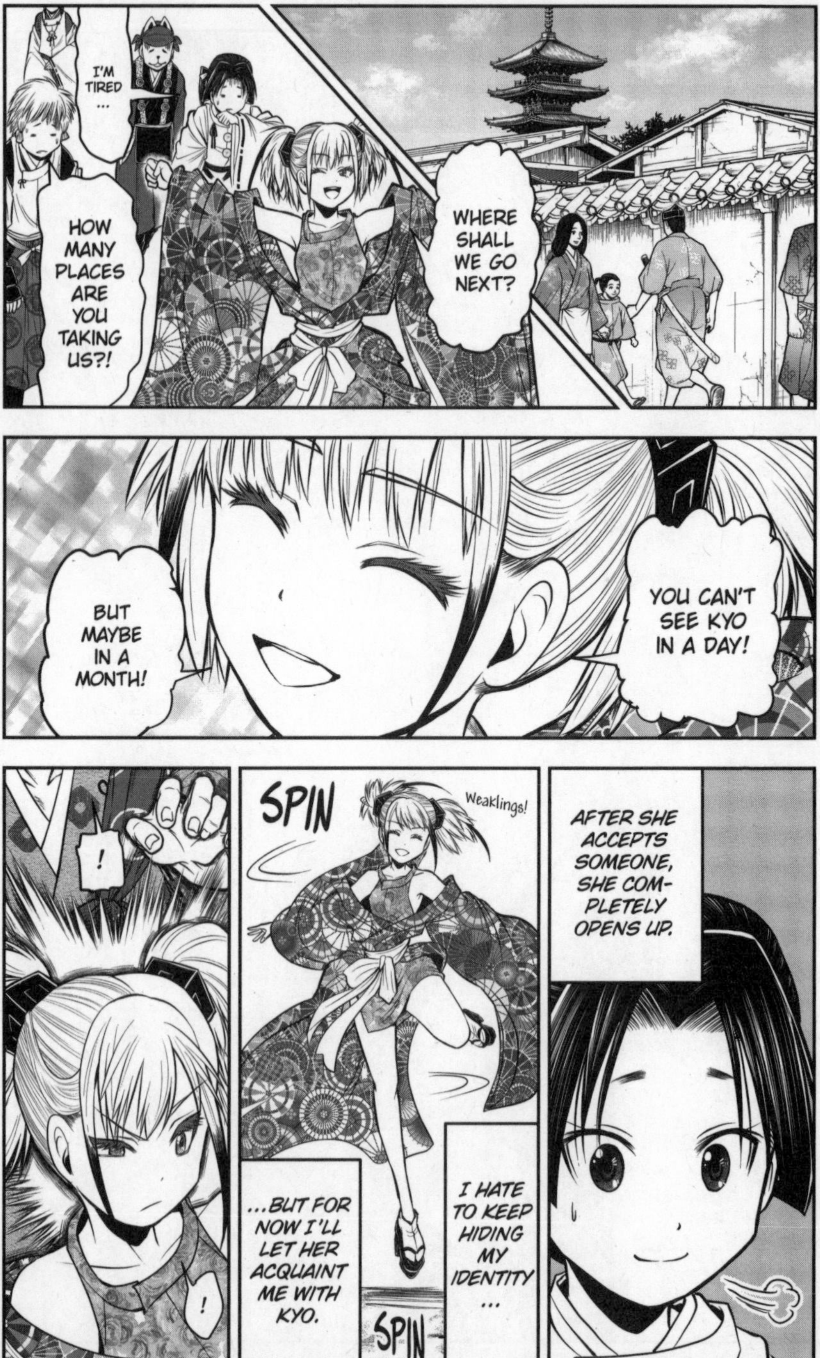
WHERE SHALL WE GO NEXT?
I'M TIRED ...
HOW MANY PLACES ARE YOU TAKING US?!
YOU CAN'T SEE KYO IN A DAY!
BUT MAYBE IN A MONTH!
AFTER SHE ACCEPTS SOMEONE, SHE COMPLETELY OPENS UP.
I HATE TO KEEP HIDING MY IDENTITY ...
...BUT FOR NOW I'LL LET HER ACQUAINT ME WITH KYO.
SPIN
Weaklings!
SPIN
!
!

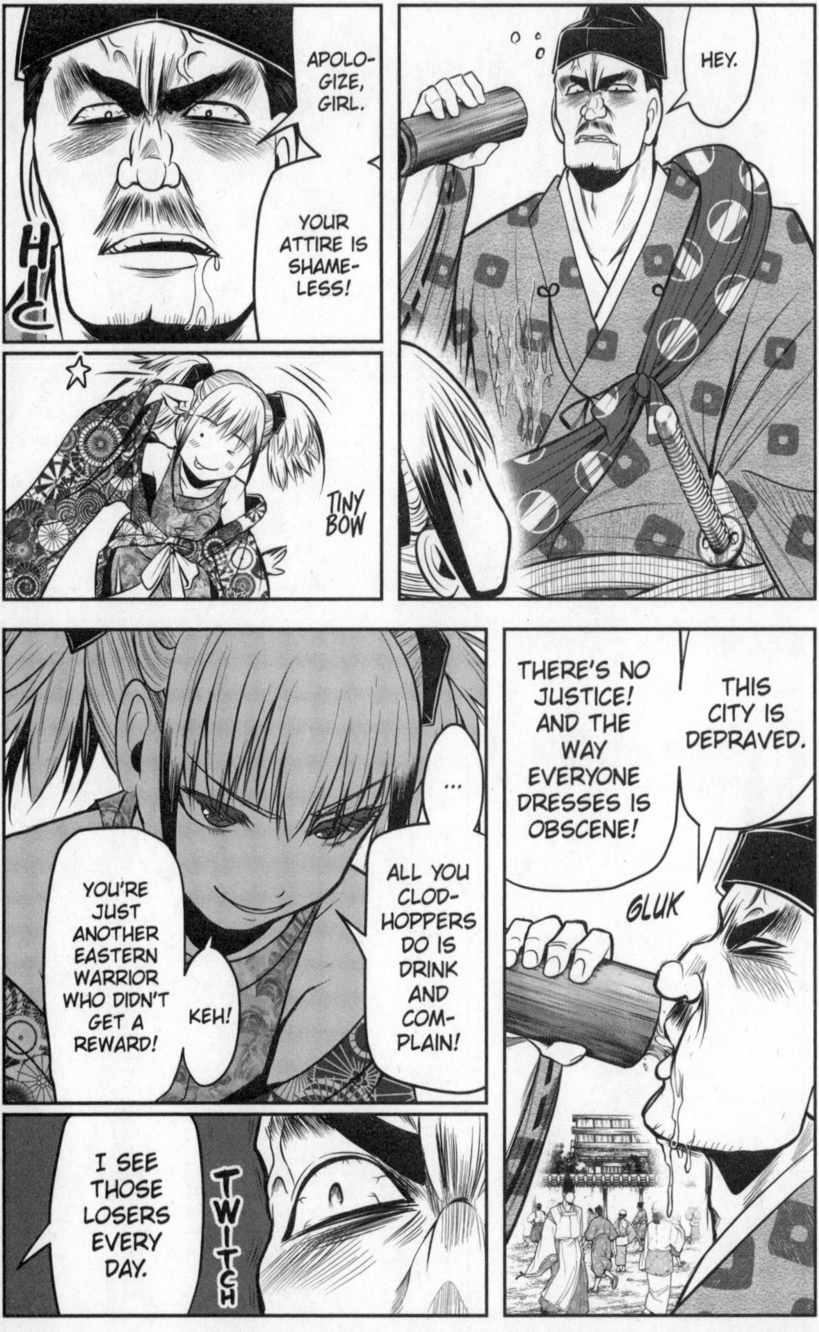
HEY.
APOLOGIZE, GIRL.
YOUR ATTIRE IS SHAMELESS!
HIC
TINY BOW
THIS CITY IS DEPRAVED.
THERE'S NO JUSTICE! AND THE WAY EVERYONE DRESSES IS OBSCENE!
GLUK
...
ALL YOU CLODHOPPERS DO IS DRINK AND COMPLAIN!
KEH!
YOU'RE JUST ANOTHER EASTERN WARRIOR WHO DIDN'T GET A REWARD!
TWITCH
I SEE THOSE LOSERS EVERY DAY.

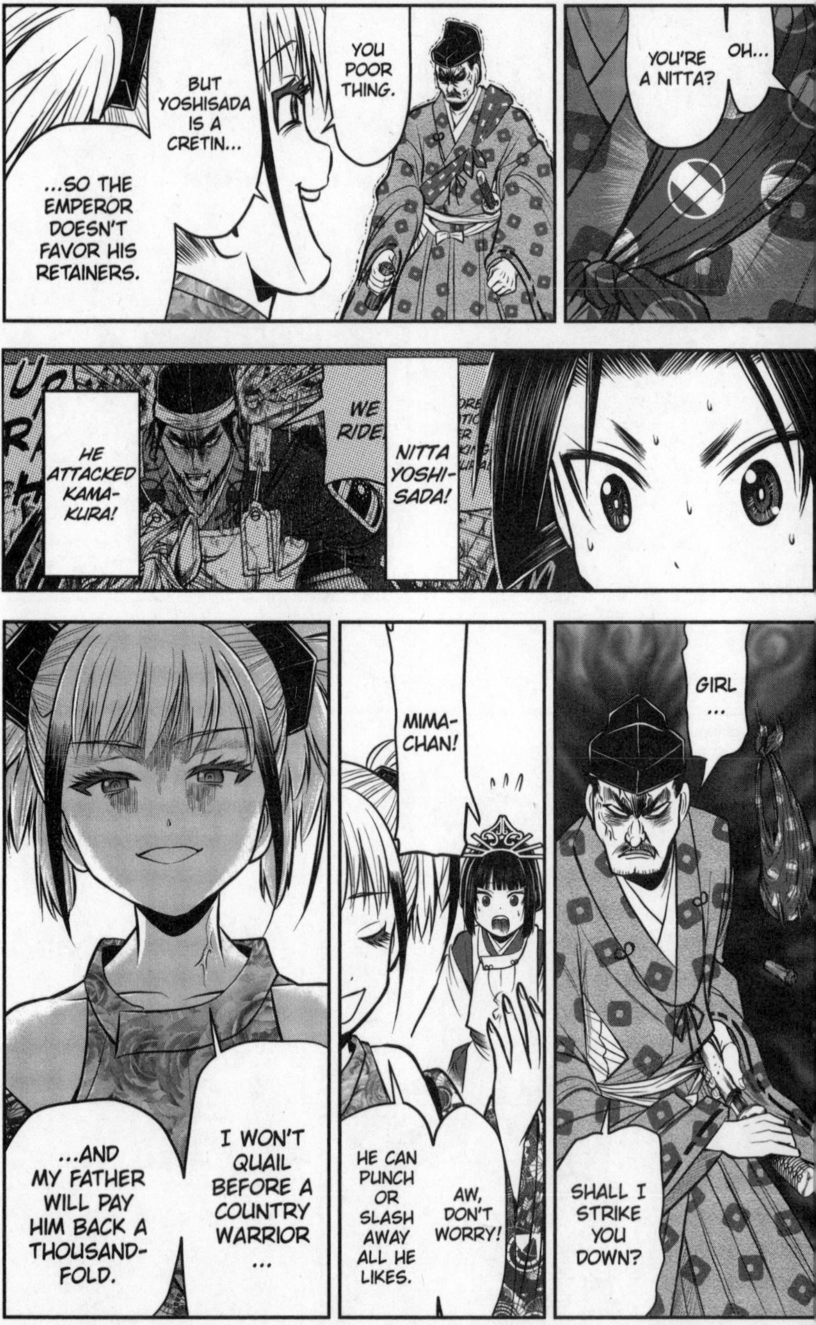
OH...
YOU'RE A NITTA?
YOU POOR THING.
BUT YOSHISADA IS A CRETIN...
...SO THE EMPEROR DOESN'T FAVOR HIS RETAINERS.
NITTA YOSHISADA!
WE RIDE
HE ATTACKED KAMAKURA!
GIRL ...
SHALL I STRIKE YOU DOWN?
MIMA-CHAN!
AW, DON'T WORRY!
HE CAN PUNCH OR SLASH AWAY ALL HE LIKES.
I WON'T QUAIL BEFORE A COUNTRY WARRIOR ...
...AND MY FATHER WILL PAY HIM BACK A THOUSAND-FOLD.

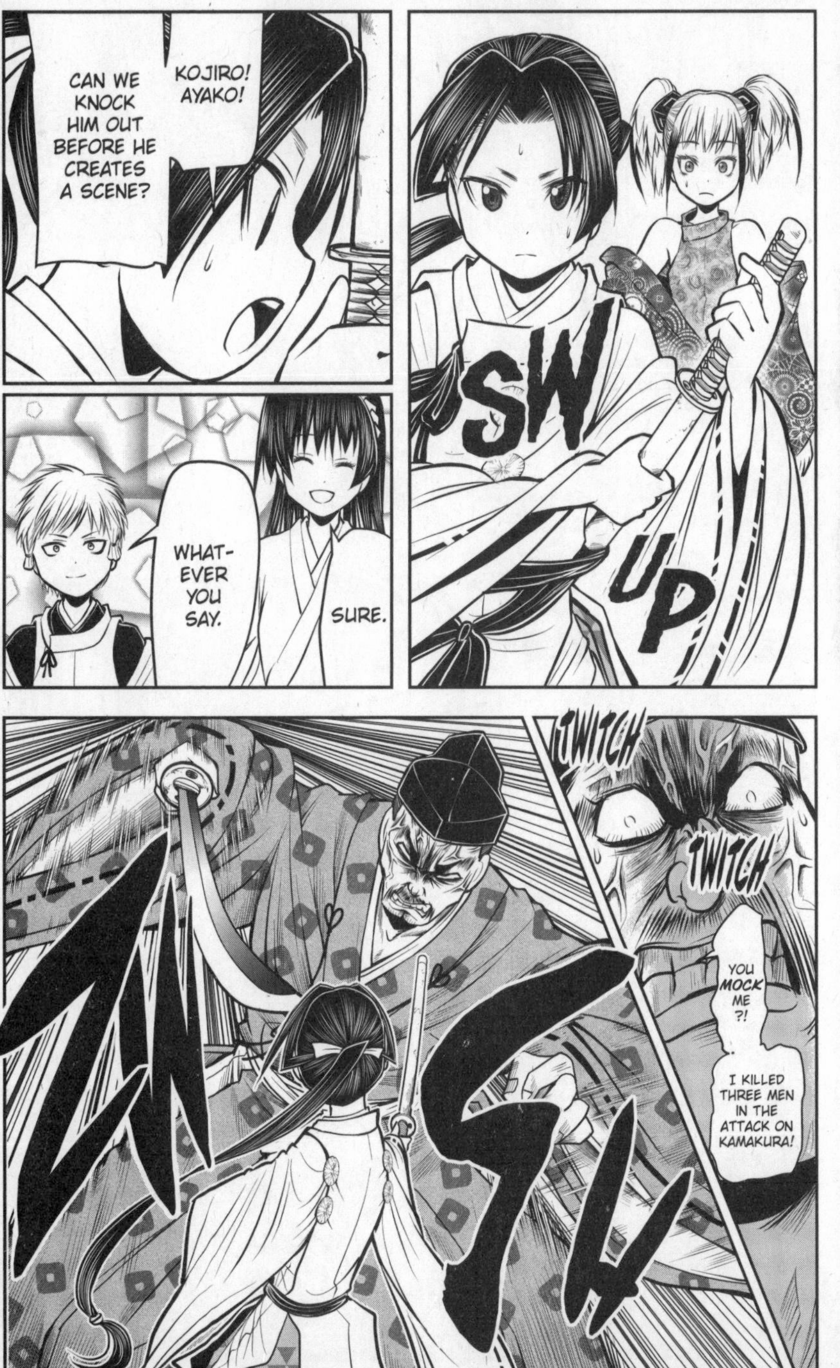

SW
UP
KOJIRO! AYAKO!
CAN WE KNOCK HIM OUT BEFORE HE CREATES A SCENE?
SURE.
WHAT-EVER YOU SAY.
TWITCH
TWITCH
YOU MOCK ME?!
I KILLED THREE MEN IN THE ATTACK ON KAMAKURA!

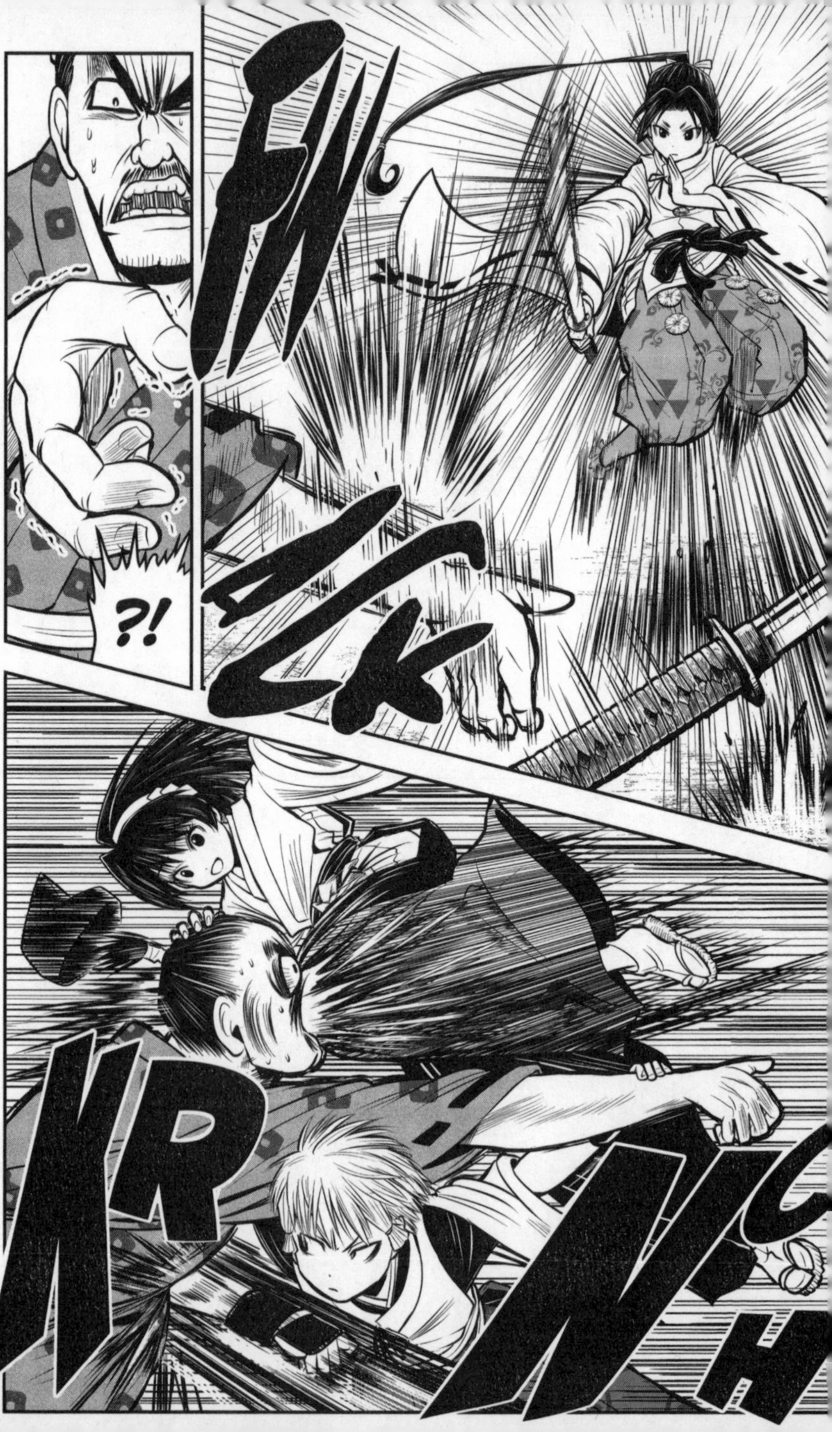
?!

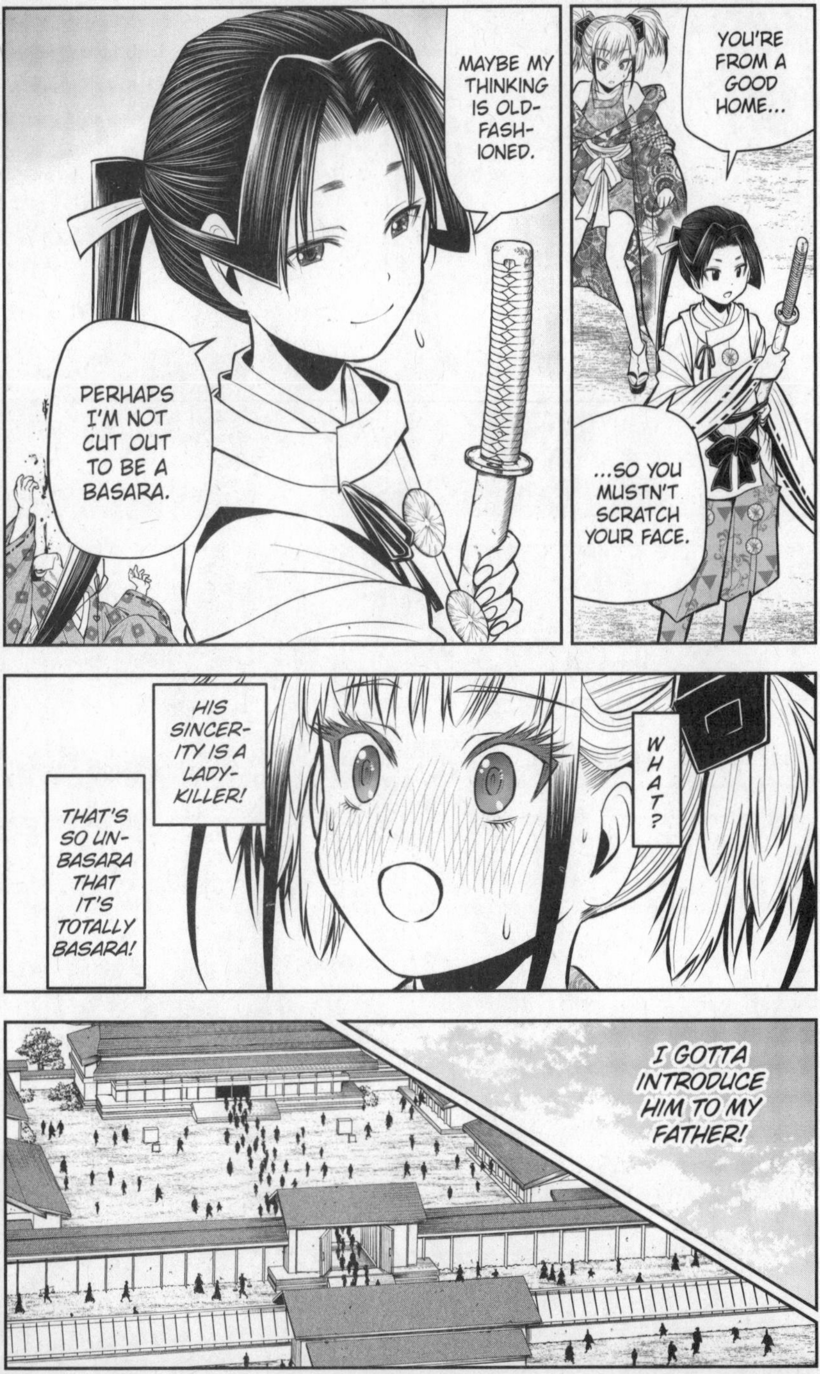
YOU'RE FROM A GOOD HOME...
...SO YOU MUSTN'T SCRATCH YOUR FACE.
MAYBE MY THINKING IS OLD-FASHIONED.
PERHAPS I'M NOT CUT OUT TO BE A BASARA.
WHAT?
HIS SINCERITY IS A LADY-KILLER!
THAT'S SO UN-BASARA THAT IT'S TOTALLY BASARA!
I GOTTA INTRODUCE HIM TO MY FATHER!

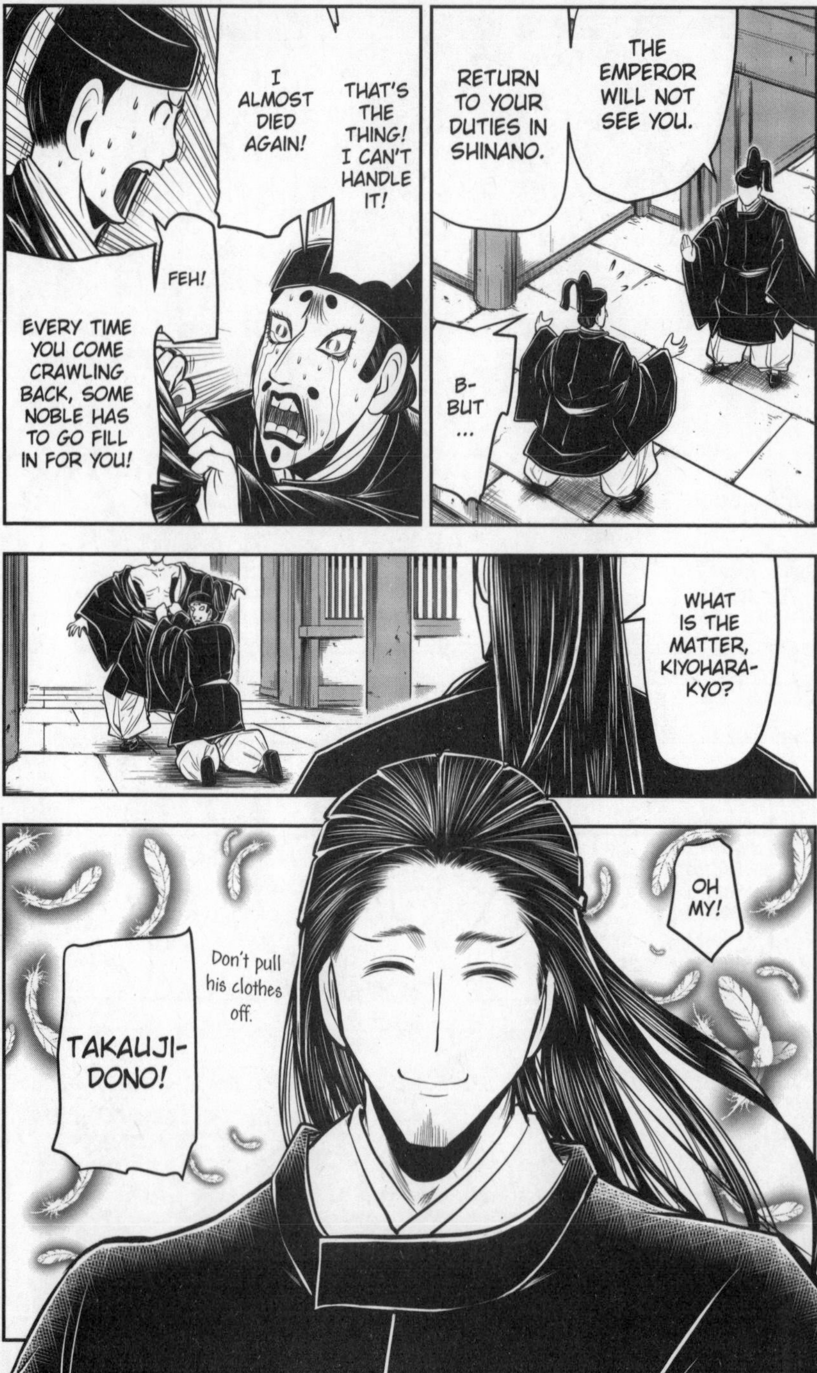
THE EMPEROR WILL NOT SEE YOU.
RETURN TO YOUR DUTIES IN SHINANO.
B-BUT...
THAT'S THE THING! I CAN'T HANDLE IT!
I ALMOST DIED AGAIN!
FEH!
EVERY TIME YOU COME CRAWLING BACK, SOME NOBLE HAS TO GO FILL IN FOR YOU!
WHAT IS THE MATTER, KIYOHARA-KYO?
OH MY!
Don't pull his clothes off.
TAKAUJI-DONO!

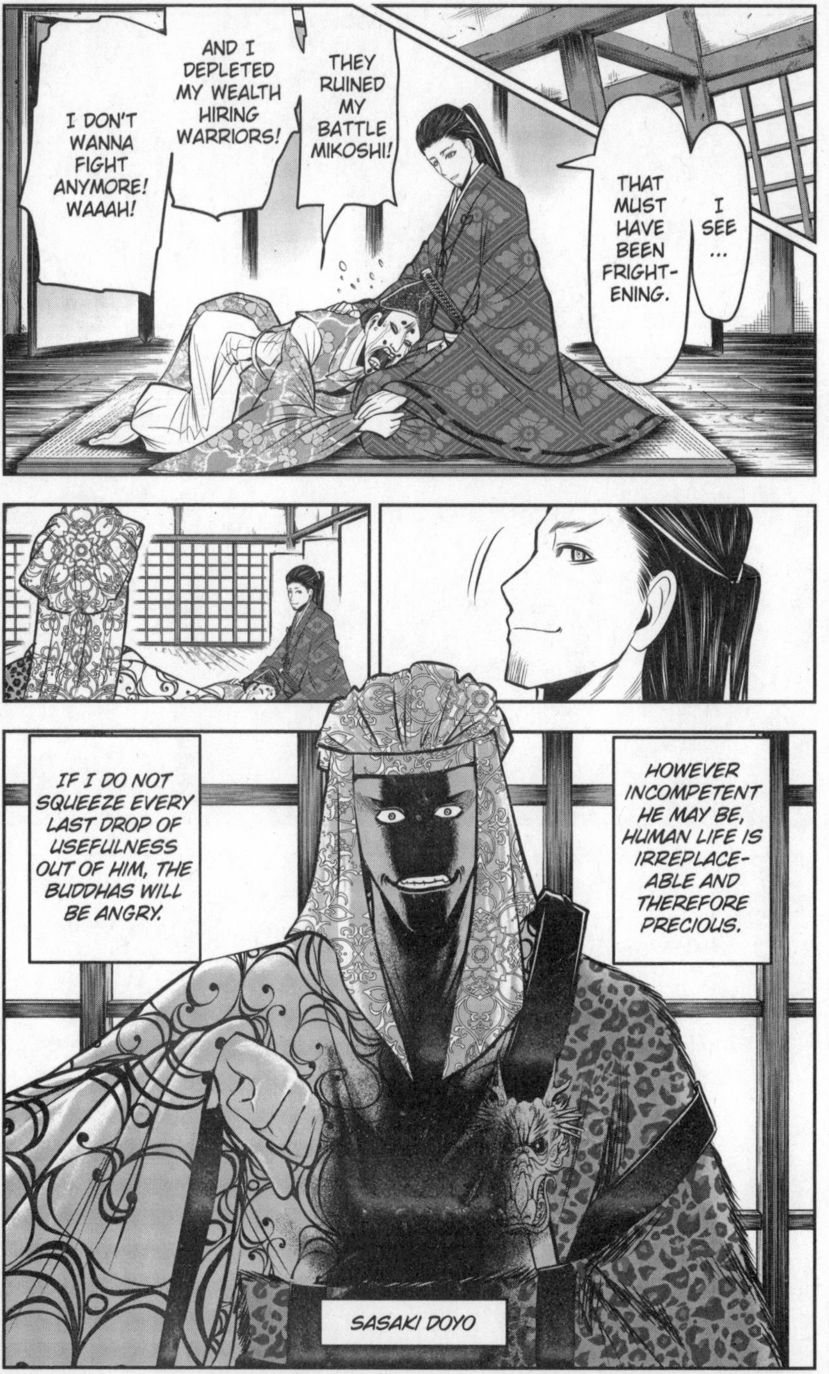
I SEE... THAT MUST HAVE BEEN FRIGHTENING.
THEY RUINED MY BATTLE MIKOSHI!
AND I DEPLETED MY WEALTH HIRING WARRIORS!
I DON'T WANNA FIGHT ANYMORE! WAAAH!
HOWEVER INCOMPETENT HE MAY BE, HUMAN LIFE IS IRREPLACEABLE AND THEREFORE PRECIOUS.
IF I DO NOT SQUEEZE EVERY LAST DROP OF USEFULNESS OUT OF HIM, THE BUDDHAS WILL BE ANGRY.
SASAKI DOYO

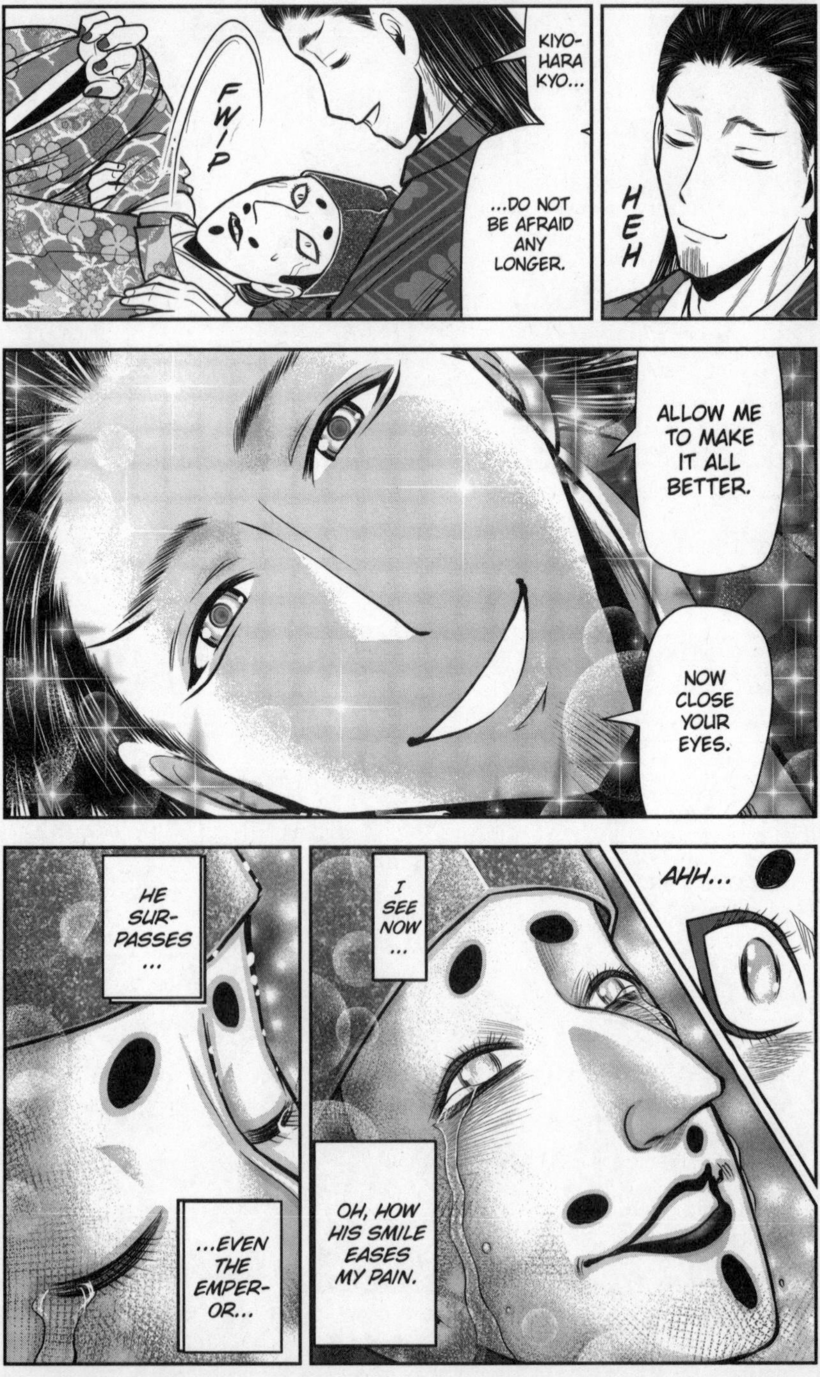
HEH
KIYO-HARA KYO...
FWIP
...DO NOT BE AFRAID ANY LONGER.
ALLOW ME TO MAKE IT ALL BETTER.
NOW CLOSE YOUR EYES.
AHH...
I SEE NOW...
OH, HOW HIS SMILE EASES MY PAIN.
HE SUR-PASSES...
...EVEN THE EMPER-OR...

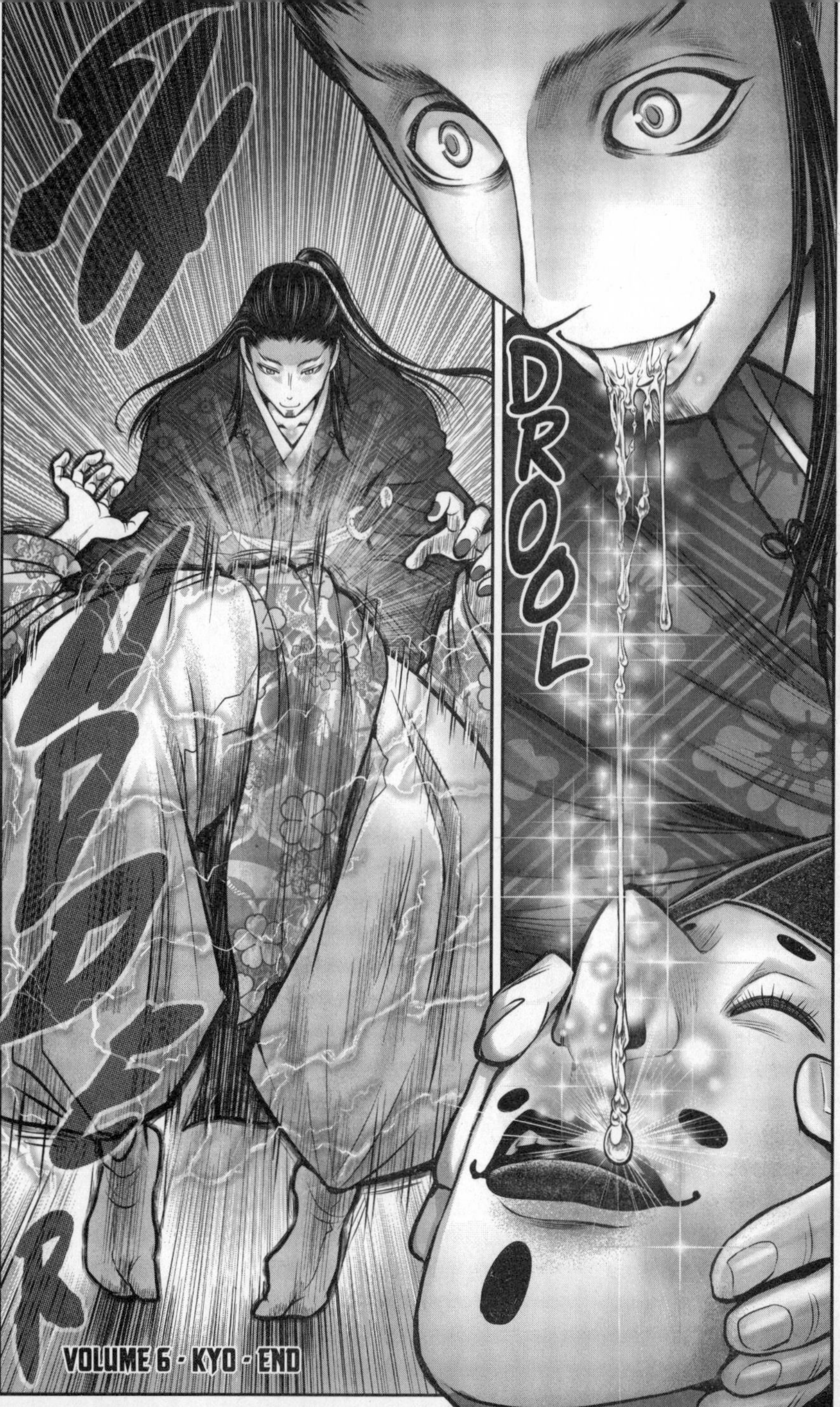
DROOL
VOLUME 6 - KYO - END

BONUS MANGA

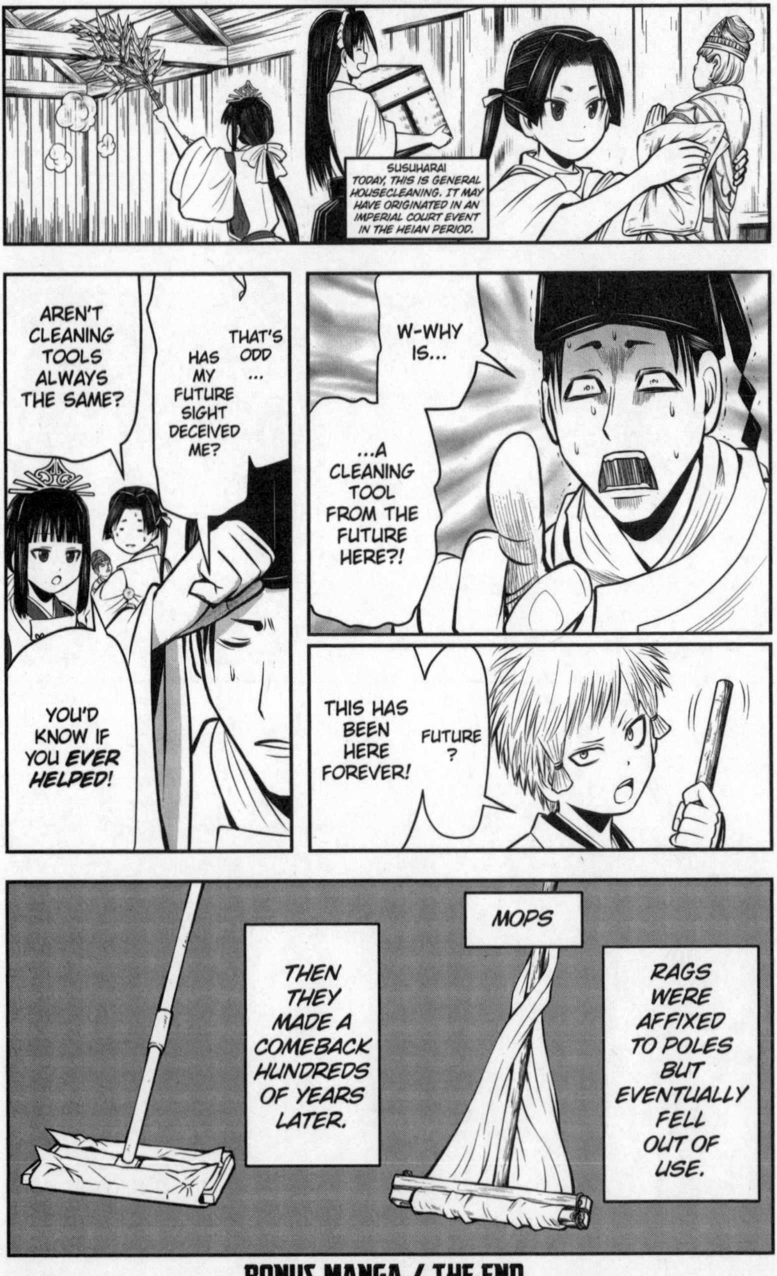
SUSUHARAI
TODAY, THIS IS GENERAL HOUSECLEANING. IT MAY HAVE ORIGINATED IN AN IMPERIAL COURT EVENT IN THE HEIAN PERIOD.
W-WHY IS...
...A CLEANING TOOL FROM THE FUTURE HERE?!
FUTURE ?
THIS HAS BEEN HERE FOREVER!
THAT'S ODD ...
HAS MY FUTURE SIGHT DECEIVED ME?
AREN'T CLEANING TOOLS ALWAYS THE SAME?
YOU'D KNOW IF YOU EVER HELPED!
MOPS
RAGS WERE AFFIXED TO POLES BUT EVENTUALLY FELL OUT OF USE.
THEN THEY MADE A COMEBACK HUNDREDS OF YEARS LATER.

BONUS MANGA / THE END

▶ DID *BUSHI* (WARRIORS) STUDY STRATEGY? ◀

Among the ancestors of Minamoto-no-Yoritomo, who founded the Kamakura shogunate, is a superstar named Hachimantaro Yoshiie (1039-1106), who fought in the Tohoku region. Hearing about this at the house of an important personage, the famous noble and scholar Oeno Masafusa commented that while Yoshiie-dono was a good warrior, he knew little about strategy. Upon hearing about this comment, Yoshiie visited Masafusa's mansion, asked to become his student, and learned Chinese military strategy.

Later, Yoshiie again left for battle in Tohoku. While on the battlefield, he saw some wild geese. They had been neatly lined up but then suddenly scattered. He guessed that this meant the enemy was nearby, so he closed in. Enemy soldiers were indeed in hiding, and Yoshiie won a magnificent victory. While studying under Masafusa, he had learned from *The Art of War* that birds taking flight indicate an ambush. He then told his subordinates that were it not for studying with Masafusa, they would have run into trouble. (This story is related in the *Kokon Chomonjū*.)

In the Kamakura period, wealthy and powerful warriors like Ashikaga Takauji and Ogasawara Sadamune had tutors when they were children, so they likely studied Chinese military texts like *The Art of War*, *Wuzi*, *Six Secret Teachings*, and *Three Strategies* in preparation for going to war. Yorishige must have drilled those texts into Tokiyuki in Suwa.

HAVE YOU HEARD?!

FAMOUS BOOKS OF STRATEGY

Seven representative works of Chinese strategy, including *The Art of War* and *Wuzi*, are known as the Seven Military Classics. They also include lessons useful for modern life.

THE ART OF WAR	Believed to be the work of Sun Tzu
WUZI	Believed to be the work of Wu Qi
WEI LIAOZI	Believed to be the work of Wei Liao
SIX SECRET TEACHINGS	Believed to be the work of Jiang Ziya
THREE STRATEGIES	
THE METHODS OF THE SIMA	Believed to be the work of Sima Qian
DIALOGUE BETWEEN EMPEROR TAIZON AND LI WEIGONG	A dialogue between Emperor Taizong and Li Jing

INCREASE YOUR ENJOYMENT OF THIS MANGA BY LEARNING THE REAL HISTORY BEHIND IT!!

ANALYSIS KAZUTO HONGO

WAS FALCONRY A SPECIAL SKILL?

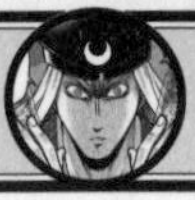

A falconer is someone who raises birds of prey and trains them for hunting. This line of work uses wild raptors, and taming them is no mean feat, requiring skills established over a long time. Teachers passed techniques on to pupils, and fathers to sons.

Takajō (falconers) were once called *takagai*. Despite their low rank, they were respected bureaucrats at the imperial court. They cooperated with dog keepers when hawking. According to old statutes, the *shuyōshi* (later the *hōyōshi*) was an office dedicated to the refined the art of falconry. The emperors back then enjoyed falconry. Emperor Saga of the early Heian period loved it so much that he even had a work written about it that is known as *Shinshūtakakyō*.

The Kamakura shogunate banned falconry out of fear that the bushi would become too preoccupied with it, but Suwa Grand Shrine received special treatment. A Shinto ritual had long existed in which devotees offered kills from hawking to the gods, so an exception was allowed. For that reason, the skills of the falconer in service to the priest at Suwa Grand Shrine (someone like Yorishige) spread around the land. Oda Nobunaga's falconers, Toyotomi Hideyoshi and Tokugawa Ieyasu, had training in the Suwa style.

FOR FIGHTING TOO?!

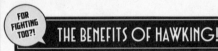

THE BENEFITS OF HAWKING!

Hawking was a way to learn important information for battle. While hunting prey, falconers learned the lay of the land and became knowledgeable about the territory and geography. It was also effective for improving military command since it provided an idea of how soldiers might move in war. Falconry also required a great deal of movement, so it was good exercise.

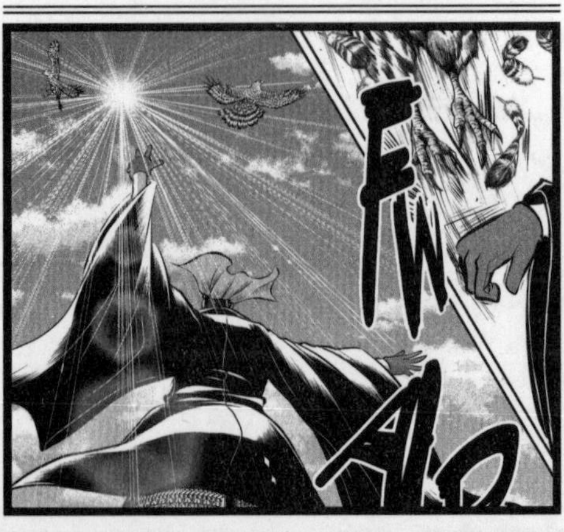

Misogi is applying water to remove sins or impurities. It's a kind of exorcism derived from Shinto for removing uncleanliness. You've probably seen people dumping water over themselves on a cold day. They shiver in what must be a sobering experience.

In Japanese mythology, Izanagi-no-Mikoto and Izanami-no-Miko created the Japanese archipelago. When Izanami passed away, her husband Izanagi went to the underworld to look for her. When he saw how she had changed there, he left in a hurry. Then he washed himself to remove the impurity of the underworld. That is said to have been the first instance of misogi. Furthermore, it created the goddess Amaterasu Ōkami.

Shinto disapproves of anything unclean or unhygienic. That's why shrines have so many people going around cleaning the grounds. And before praying to the gods, visitors first purify their hands with water or rinse out their mouths in a form of misogi.

In Japan, the gods demand cleanliness. That may be why Japanese people love baths so much. This emphasis on hygiene also helps prevent the spread of infectious diseases.

IZANAGI-NO-MIKOTO'S MISOGI CREATED MANY GODS

The three main gods of Japan were born from the body parts that Izanagi purified.

- ◉ **LEFT EYE**
- → **AMATERASU OKAMI**
  RULER OF TAKAMAGAHARA,
  THE HOME OF THE GODS

- ◉ **RIGHT EYE**
- → **TSUKUYOMI-NO-MIKOTO**
  RULER OF THE LAND OF NIGHT

- ◉ **NOSE**
- → **SUSANOO-NO-MIKOTO**
  RULER OF THE SEA

Gods were also born from the clothes he removed and the water he used for purification.

DID THE BUSHI KNOW HOW TO WRITE?

Notes dating to the mid-Kamakura period and written by a warrior known as Fujiwara Saneshige were found inside a Buddhist statue at Zenkyo Temple in Yokkaichi, Mie Prefecture. Fujiwara held the government post of *chikugo-no-kami*, which was a high position for a warrior. He wrote about the nature of his faith, such as what actions he performed for the buddhas.

The problem is how he wrote these notes. He used simple kanji characters like 大 (dai) and 田 (ta) and the rest was in awkward kana syllabary symbols.

In the Jōkyū War of 1221, a man named Hojo Yasutoki led 5,000 soldiers to Kyoto. At that time, the retired emperor Go-Toba issued a command known as an *inzen* against violent behavior. When a messenger delivered it to Yasutoki, the recipient asked for someone among his 5,000 men who could read, but only one person responded in the affirmative.

Considering that, I think it's likely that the bushi of the Kamakura period were not skilled at reading and writing.

JŌKYŪ WAR

This was a conflict between the imperial court and the shogunate during the Kamakura period. The shogun at the time, Minamoto-no-Sanetomo, whom the retired emperor Go-Toba favored, was assassinated, leading to unstable relations between the court and the shogunate.
Eventually, war began when Go-Toba issued an inzen for punishment of the shogunate's regent, Hojo Yoshitoki.

INZEN

Retired emperors were called *jōkō*. From the end of the Heian period to the early Kamakura period, they held governmental power. This form of government was called *insei*. A decree from a retired emperor was called an *inzen*, and it had immense influence over governmental policy.

WHAT KIND OF DIALECTS EXISTED?

I don't know. I really don't. At present, Japanese historical researchers proceed as if dialects just don't matter.

But a document exists that was written by the bushi Aokata, who operated out of the Goto Islands in Nagasaki Prefecture. In the document, kana accompany the kanji. The kana indicates pronunciation. The document contains a word designating a tax for Ise Grand Shrine: 役夫工米. The kana read *yakubutakumai*. We would naturally read that *yakubukumai*. Because of this document, researchers read it *yakubutakumai*, but that may have been Nagasaki dialect. Researchers just don't take that into account though.

In the latter half of the Kamakura period, some peasants began to write kana. Peasants of a manor in Wakayama Prefecture called Ategawa-no-sho, which appears in high school textbooks, drew up a complaint about their *jitō* (manor lord). In clumsy kana, they related how the lord threatened anyone who wouldn't sow grain, saying they would have their ears and noses cut off, be tied up, or be forced into nunhood. Given the state of the written language, it's no wonder we have little idea of the spoken language. Of course, there must have been dialects, but since we don't have documentation of them, we can only throw up our hands.

WHAT WERE MANORS LIKE?

Manors consisted of buildings possessed by nobility, the surrounding fields, and large temples. In the Kamakura period, the shogunate established manor lords to manage the land.

MANOR LAYOUT

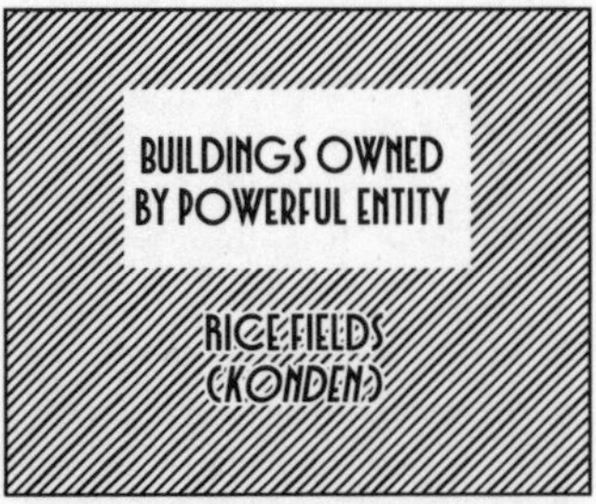

BUILDINGS OWNED BY POWERFUL ENTITY
RICE FIELDS (KONDEN)

↑ Manors were developed in the Heian period. Many were exempt from taxes.

WHAT DISEASES DID PEOPLE FEAR?

Three major health problems today are cancer, heart attack, and stroke. During the time period of this manga, the primary diseases were tuberculosis, beriberi, and diabetes. In modern times, we pursue an appropriate amount of exercise and a well-balanced diet, so the health problems that once took the lives of Japanese people are much less prevalent.

At present, the average life span in Japan for both men and women is over 80 years old. Research shows, however, that it has only passed 50 since World War II. In the Meiji period, many celebrated figures died young. Higuchi Ichiyo and Ishikawa Takuboku are famous examples, but Natsume Soseki died at the relatively young age of 49.

Right now, we're in the middle of the coronavirus pandemic, but what plagued Japanese people back then was smallpox and measles. We call measles both *mashin* and *hashika*. Weak children underwent great suffering and died from measles. People said that children belonged to the gods until age seven, and unfortunately many died before reaching that age.

THREE BIG DISEASES OF THE PAST

TUBERCULOSIS

The bacteria *Mycobacterium tuberculosis* cause this sickness. As an airborne disease, the bacteria proliferate in the lungs in what is called pulmonary TB, which causes coughing, phlegm, and difficulty breathing. Until development of a treatment, people considered it an incurable disease. Higuchi Ichiyo died at 24 and Ishikawa Takuboku died at 26 due to pulmonary TB.

BERIBERI

A vitamin B^1 deficiency causes this disease. Early symptoms are fatigue and lack of appetite, eventually leading to heart failure. Pork, brown rice, and beans contain large amounts of B^1. Polishing brown rice into white rice results in a decrease of B^1.

DIABETES

This is a lifestyle disease caused by overeating and lack of exercise. It can cause the hardening of blood vessels and other health complications. The best prevention is leading a healthy lifestyle and eating well-balanced meals. Natsume Soseki died from diabetes.

The most widespread disease these days is the common cold, but in medieval times, Japan wasn't hygienic. People weren't in the practice of washing their hands or gargling. They didn't bathe regularly either. The common folk didn't have enough to eat, so they lacked nutrition. Furthermore, modern medicine didn't exist. For that reason, people frequently caught colds and died. It really was true that people lived for around 50 years. Medical science has made great progress, but that's really only within the last 100 years. Life in the old days was harsh.

WAS MONEY IN CIRCULATION?

If asked what the first money in circulation in Japan was, what would you answer? There was *wadō kaichin*, and someone knowledgeable about history might say the *fuhonsen*. But what is money anyway? It's something you use to buy things. Were people really able to use *wadō kaichin* or *funhonsen*? If you think about it, people weren't really able to use *wadō kaichin* or the other 12 coinages in the subsequent years. In that case, you might say they weren't actually money. During the Heian period, Japan's economy was based on exchange of goods, so people used things like rice or silk.

Then when did people start using money? That was about the middle of the 13th century. A large amount of copper coins came from China, causing a monetary economy to spread across the Japanese archipelago from 1226 to 1250 and eventually stabilize. That really sped up commerce.

It's important to note that the Kamakura shogunate appears to have been unable to adapt sufficiently. Kamakura was still a remote locale to much of the country. It didn't have a sufficient distribution network, and the basis of the shogunate's economy was still agriculture. I believe the Kamakura shogunate collapsed because it couldn't keep up with rapidly expanding economic activity. That's why Ashikaga Takauji made Kyo the center of economic activity for the new shogunate. I think that's an easy way to describe it.

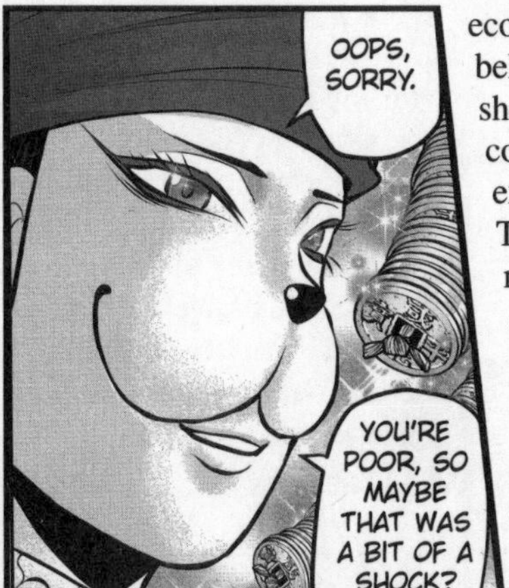
OOPS, SORRY.
YOU'RE POOR, SO MAYBE THAT WAS A BIT OF A SHOCK?

TELL ME ABOUT MAKEUP BACK THEN!

It is believed that women in Japan began to wear makeup in the pursuit of beauty in the latter half of the 6th century. That may have been due to the arrival of lip rouge and face powder from the continental mainland and Korean peninsula.

After the end of the Japanese missions to Tang Dynasty China in the Heian period, cosmetic styles began to change from Chinese to distinctly Japanese. During this time, upper-class women believed lustrous black hair was fundamental to beauty. To emphasize it, they painted their faces with *oshiroi* face powder, removing their eyebrows and drawing new ones high on their foreheads (called *maro* eyebrows), and dyeing their teeth black (*o-haguro*).

In the Kamakura and Nanboku-cho periods, the habits of these noble women began to spread to the warrior class. The women of the warrior houses used makeup in three colors. They used red lipstick, applied white face powder, and dyed their teeth black.

I just realized something. Children of upper-class families participated in a ceremony called the *yaguchi* festival for venerating local deities when becoming adults, and they munched on pounded rice colored red, white and black. Thus, while we see red, yellow, and blue as the primary colors in our time, for people in medieval Japan, they may have been red, white and black.

In the Muromachi period, forms of etiquette solidified for the warrior class, as did manners concerning makeup. Merchants specializing in cosmetics appeared and bushi began to adopt a common aesthetic.

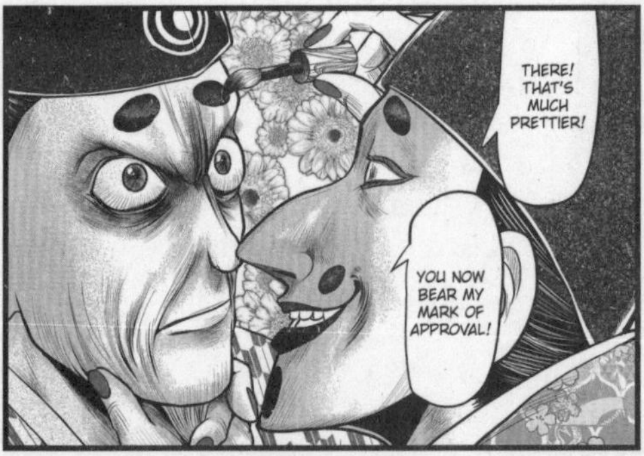
THERE! THAT'S MUCH PRETTIER!
YOU NOW BEAR MY MARK OF APPROVAL!

DID THE NOBILITY AND BUSHI GET ALONG?

The first point to make is that the nobility and bushi were on completely different standings in the Nanboku-cho period. The nobles were higher and the bushi were much lower. Even the status of the Hojo, the leader of the Kamakura bushi, was fixed at rank four (rank three and higher signified upper nobility). In ability, the bushi far outclassed the nobility, but they chose not to rise. Perhaps the Hojo were saying, "We bushi aren't like you nobles."

If the top Hojo were rank four, then of course their vassals were even lower. Basically, bushi were like bottom-ranking nobility. However, they were far more competent. Under such complicated circumstances, it must have been hard to get along. Nobles were like, "Hmf! You uncultured country bumpkins!" And the bushi were like, "Shut up, you weaklings!" It's easy to imagine that they detested each other. Nonetheless, some nobles did marry the daughters of bushi, and a woman in the Otomo household in Bungo (around Oita Prefecture today) even married the emperor and gave birth to a daughter. Such unions did occur, but they were rare.

Ashikaga Takauji skillfully used the antipathy of the bushi toward the nobility to unite them and bare his teeth at the imperial court. He rose to join the nobility, so many nobles came to serve the Ashikaga shogun in the Muromachi period. Furthermore, if they didn't cooperate with the bushi, nobles wouldn't have been able to collect taxes from territories in more remote areas. In that way, many nobles chose concrete gains over nominal status. Thus, the higher bushi and nobility joined to form a kind of celebrity class.

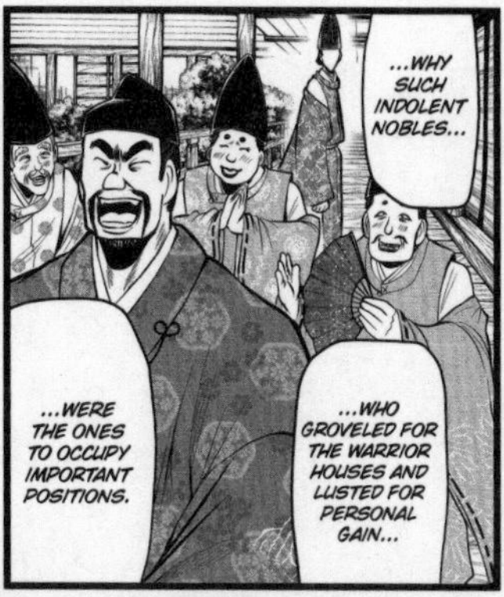
...WHY SUCH INDOLENT NOBLES...
...WHO GROVELED FOR THE WARRIOR HOUSES AND LUSTED FOR PERSONAL GAIN...
...WERE THE ONES TO OCCUPY IMPORTANT POSITIONS.

SPECIAL THANKS

I borrow a lot of people's talents for *The Elusive Samurai*.

PRODUCTION STAFF
DAISUKE ENOSHIMA
SAKUJU KOIZUMI
YUUKI IMADA
KEIJI INOUE
SHINJI WADA
ERI TSURUYOSHI
YUKI KAWAGUCHI

They're my Kamakura warriors who draw what I want, but they're
all so talented that I worry they'll get their own series and leave.

EDITOR
RIKI AZUMA

He's an editor for *Weekly Shonen Jump*. He's from a high-class upbringing,
so now he's got diabetes despite being so young.

GRAPHIC NOVEL EDITOR
SATOSHI WATANABE

He handles stuff related to the graphic novel, and he's got really thin legs.

DESIGNER
YUKI MATSUMOTO (BANANA GROVE STUDIO)

She's in charge of the logo and design for the graphic novel.
She's a licensed art curator.

JAPANESE-STYLE ARTIST
TAKAFUMI ASAKURA
I ask him to take care of the background and patterns for the graphic
novel covers. I hear he really cuts loose when out drinking.

CALLIGRAPHER
KAMARI MAEDA
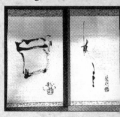
I ask him to do the calligraphy that appears when
introducing new demons. He takes requests for decorating
Japanese-style rooms, so I asked him to write two things I
love! On the right is "edamame," and on the left is "beer."

ADVISOR AND ARTICLE WRITER
KAZUTO HONGO
I call upon him to supervise the historical details and to write the pages of
historical analysis. Anything that departs from history is the author's own creation
or personal interpretation.

PERSONAL SYMBOL DESIGNER
MARIKA MATSUMOTO (& CAT)
She designs patterns for some of the characters' kimonos. She's very service
oriented, so she proposes numerous patterns.

3D CG MODELING
MELTA KABUSHIKI GAISHA
They do 3D modeling for things like armor, helmets, and swords that aren't for
sale commercially. The biggest element for this time period, about which there
aren't many manga, is armor. And that's a real pain, so I'm thankful to them and
their digital-age skills for solving that problem.

SUWA RESEARCH COOPERATION
MICHIHO ISHINO
She helps me with research about Suwa. She's had all kinds of experiences and has
a lot of curiosity, so she knows everything, not just about Suwa.

ILLUSTRATOR
SHIE NANAHANA
She creates colorful backgrounds. She's expanding her sphere of interest with a
focus on Japanese-style illustrations.

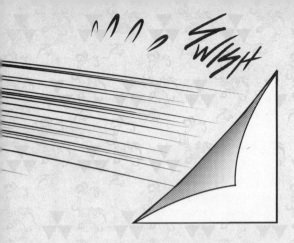

Yusei Matsui

How to fold a triangular milk pack, how to research threadworms, the commands for superspecial moves in early fighting games, the lyrics to songs no one sings anymore, how to draw manga the analog way...

I wish there was a way to uninstall knowledge I don't use anymore to open up memory space in my brain. As a middle-aged man, I seriously worry about losing memory retention.

Yusei Matsui was born on the last day of January in Saitama Prefecture, Japan. He has been drawing manga since elementary school. Some of his favorite manga series are *Bobobo-bo Bo-bobo*, *JoJo's Bizarre Adventure*, and *Ultimate Muscle*. Matsui learned his trade working as an assistant to manga artist Yoshio Sawai, creator of *Bobobo-bo Bo-bobo*. In 2005, Matsui debuted his original manga *Neuro: Supernatural Detective* in *Weekly Shonen Jump*. In 2007, *Neuro* was adapted into an anime. His next series, *Assassination Classroom*, captured imaginations worldwide and was adapted to anime, video games, and film. In 2021, *The Elusive Samurai* began serialization in *Weekly Shonen Jump*.

THE ELUSIVE SAMURAI
VOLUME 6
SHONEN JUMP Edition

Story and Art by
Yusei Matsui

Translation & English Adaptation John Werry
Touch-Up Art & Lettering John Hunt
Designer Jimmy Presler
Editor Mike Montesa

First published in Japan in 2021 by SHUEISHA Inc., Tokyo.
English translation rights arranged by SHUEISHA Inc.

Printed in the U.S.A.

Published by VIZ Media, LLC
P.O. Box 77010
San Francisco, CA 94107

10 9 8 7 6 5 4 3 2 1
First printing, May 2023

ratings.viz.com RATED T TEEN

PARENTAL ADVISORY
THE ELUSIVE SAMURAI is rated T for Teen and is recommended for ages 13 and up. This volume contains realistic and fantasy violence.

VIZ MEDIA
viz.com

SHONEN JUMP

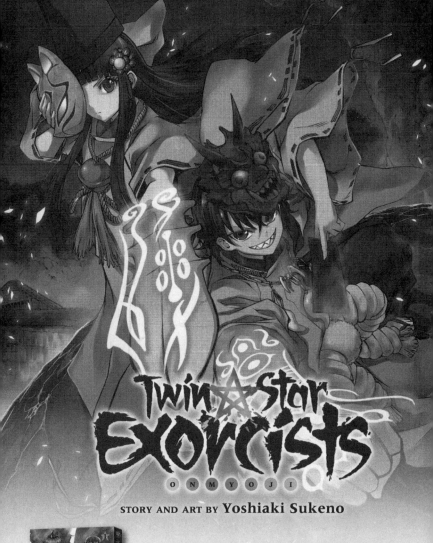

STORY AND ART BY **Yoshiaki Sukeno**

**The action-packed romantic comedy
from the creator of *Good Luck Girl!***

Rokuro dreams of becoming *anything* but an exorcist!
Then mysterious Benio turns up. The pair are dubbed the
"Twin Star Exorcists" and learn they are fated to marry...

Can Rokuro escape both fates?

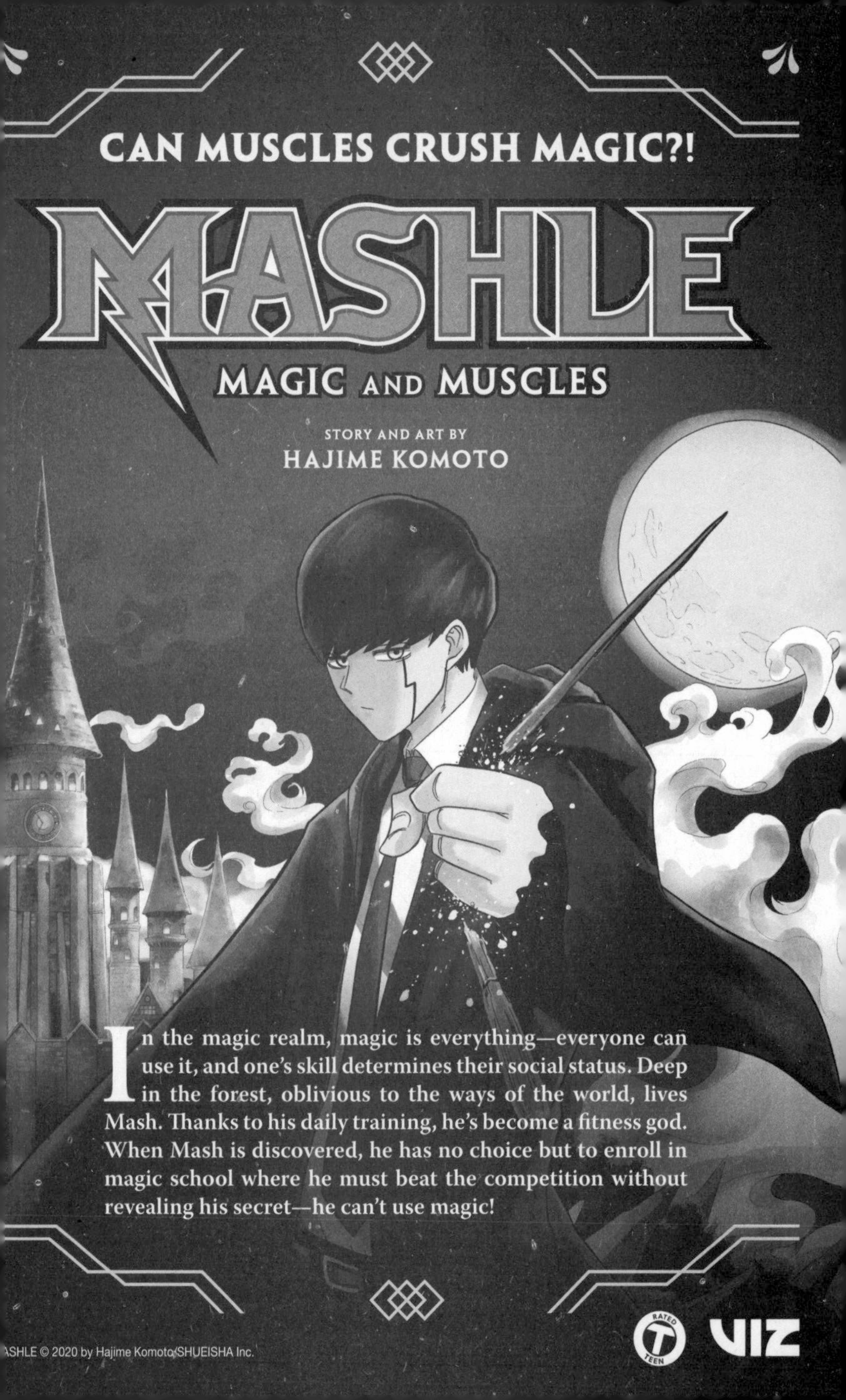
CAN MUSCLES CRUSH MAGIC?!
MASHLE
MAGIC AND MUSCLES
STORY AND ART BY
HAJIME KOMOTO
In the magic realm, magic is everything—everyone can use it, and one's skill determines their social status. Deep in the forest, oblivious to the ways of the world, lives Mash. Thanks to his daily training, he's become a fitness god. When Mash is discovered, he has no choice but to enroll in magic school where he must beat the competition without revealing his secret—he can't use magic!
RATED T TEEN
VIZ
ASHLE © 2020 by Hajime Komoto/SHUEISHA Inc.

DRAGON QUEST THE ADVENTURE OF DAI

©SQUARE ENIX

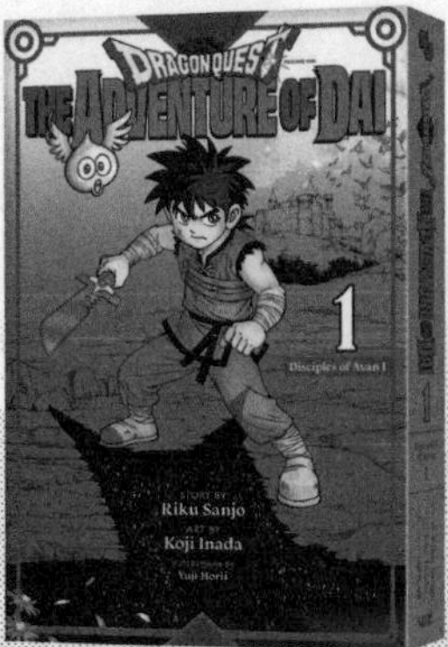

DRAGON QUEST
THE ADVENTURE OF DAI
1
Riku Sanjo
Koji Inada
Yuji Horii

Story by Riku Sanjo **Art by** Koji Inada
Supervision by Yuji Horii

Raised by monsters in a battle-scarred world, Dai has the heart of a hero! He sets off on a grand journey with brave friends, traveling the world to take down the Dark Lord's minions. Along the way, Dai must awaken the hero he was meant to be and master his dormant powers.

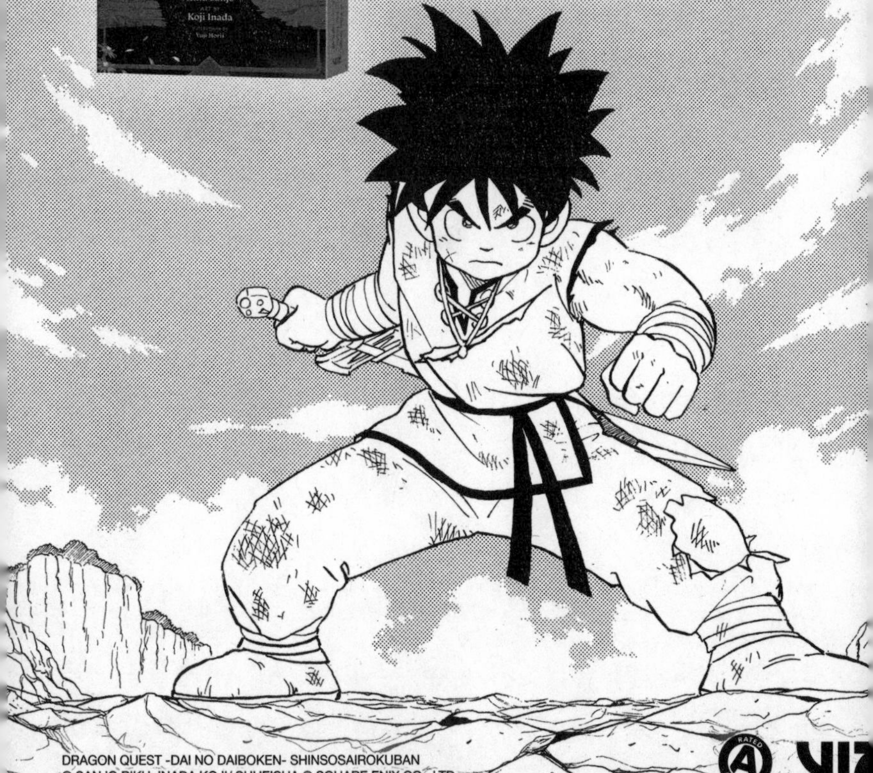

RATED A ALL AGES

VIZ

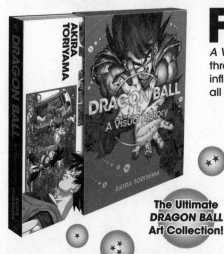

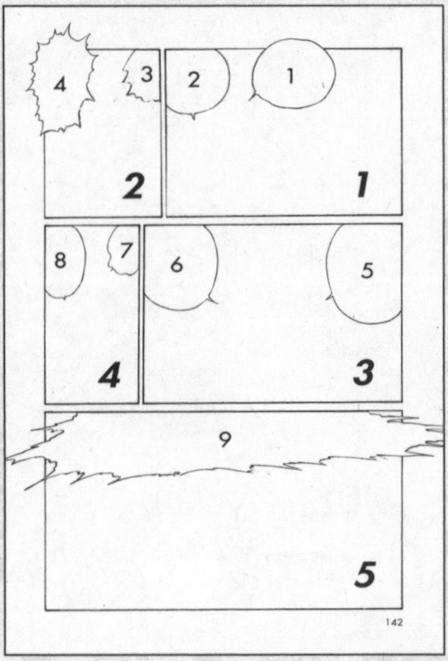
1
2
3
4
5
6
7
8
9
1
2
3
4
5
142

YOU'RE READING THE WRONG WAY!

THE ELUSIVE SAMURAI reads from right to left, starting in the upper-right corner. Japanese is read from right to left, meaning that action, sound effects, and word-balloon order are completely reversed from English order.

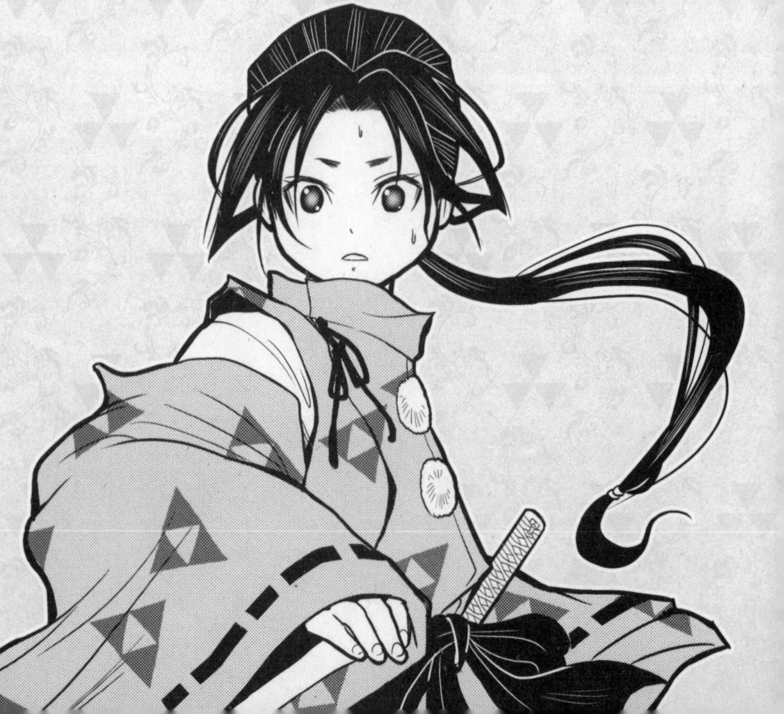